Logic, Argumentation & Reasoning

Interdisciplinary Perspectives from the Humanities and Social Sciences

Volume 19

Logic, Argumentation & Reasoning explores the links between Humanities and the Social Sciences, with theories including, decision and action theory as well as cognitive sciences, economy, sociology, law, logic, and philosophy of sciences. It's two main ambitions are to develop a theoretical framework that will encourage and enable interaction between disciplines as well as to federate the Humanities and Social Sciences around their main contributions to public life: using informed debate, lucid decision-making and action based on reflection.

The series welcomes research from the analytic and continental traditions, placing emphasis on four main focal areas:

- Argumentation models and studies
- Communication, language and techniques of argumentation
- Reception of arguments, persuasion and the impact of power
- Diachronic transformations of argumentative practices

The Series is developed in partnership with the Maison Européenne des Sciences de l'Homme et de la Société (MESHS) at Nord - Pas de Calais and the UMR-STL: 8163 (CNRS).

Proposals should include:

- A short synopsis of the work, or the introduction chapter
- The proposed Table of Contents
- The CV of the lead author(s)
- If available: one sample chapter

We aim to make a first decision within 1 month of submission. In case of a positive first decision, the work will be provisionally contracted—the final decision about publication will depend upon the result of an anonymous peer review of the complete manuscript. The complete work is usually peer-reviewed within 3 months of submission.

The series discourages the submission of manuscripts that contain reprints of previous published material and/or manuscripts that are below 150 pages / 85,000 words.

For inquiries and proposal submissions, authors may contact the editor-in-chief, Shahid Rahman at: shahid.rahman@univ-lille3.fr, or the managing editor, Juan Redmond, at: juan.redmond@uv.cl.

More information about this series at http://www.springer.com/series/11547

Shahid Rahman • Muhammad Iqbal • Youcef Soufi

Inferences by Parallel Reasoning in Islamic Jurisprudence

Al-Shīrāzī's Insights into the Dialectical Constitution of Meaning and Knowledge

Springer

Shahid Rahman
Department of Philosophy
Université de Lille
Lille, France

Muhammad Iqbal
Department of Philosophy
Université de Lille
Lille, France

Youcef Soufi
Department of Classical, Near Eastern, and Religious Studies
University of British Columbia
Vancouver, BC, Canada

ISSN 2214-9120 ISSN 2214-9139 (electronic)
Logic, Argumentation & Reasoning
ISBN 978-3-030-22384-7 ISBN 978-3-030-22382-3 (eBook)
https://doi.org/10.1007/978-3-030-22382-3

This Springer imprint is published by the registered company Springer Nature Switzerland AG.
The registered company address is: Gewerbestrasse 11, 6330 Cham, Switzerland

For
Cheryl, Laura Milena and Djamal-Alexander
Shahid Rahman

For
My late father Muhammad Noor and my mother Nuriah
Muhammad Iqbal

Preface

In his PhD dissertation *The Economy of Certainty* that set a landmark in the field and was written in 1984 but only published in 2013, Aron Zysow (2013, p. 159) proposed to study *uṣūl al-fiqh* (أصول الفقه), or Islamic legal theory, under an epistemological perspective, or more precisely as the *Islamic counterpart to* [contemporary] *philosophy of science*, motivated by the observation that *fiqh* (the Islamic legal system as interpreted from the *Qur'ān* and the *Sunna* by the jurists) constituted one if not the predominant science in classical Islam. Indeed, an epistemological perspective on *uṣūl al-fiqh* brings to the fore the fact that Islamic jurisprudence is deeply rooted in the task of pursuing rational knowledge and understanding.

Actually, the epistemological perspective is at the centre of the present study, and we hope that the development of such a stance will help to elucidate some of the fundamental concepts underlying the schemes for legal reasoning within *uṣūl al-fiqh*. The key point is that *uṣūl al-fiqh* is shaped by the epistemological task of making apparent the meaning of the norms for human conduct embodied in *fiqh*.

On the other hand, we should not lose sight of the point that *uṣūl al-fiqh* constitutes the body of knowledge and methods of reasoning that Islamic jurists deploy in order to provide solutions to *practical legal problems* linked to the dynamics of legal systems. Clearly, working out solutions to practical legal problems commits one to the practice of legal reasoning.

Furthermore, the general principle underlying legal reasoning is that law is largely a matter of practice and that one of the most suitable instruments for legal practice is argumentation (*jadal*). More precisely, since the ultimate purpose of such a kind of rational endeavour is to achieve decisions for new circumstances or cases not already established by the juridical sources, the diverse processes conceived within Islamic jurisprudence were aimed at providing both epistemological and practical tools able to deal with the evolution of the practice of *fiqh*. This dynamic feature animates Walter Edward Young's main thesis as developed in his book *The Dialectical Forge: Juridical Disputation and the Evolution of Islamic Law*.[1] In fact, the main claim underlying the work of Young is that the dynamic nature of *fiqh* is put into action by both the dialectical understanding and the dialectical practice of legal reasoning. These already set out the motivations for the development of a dialectical framework such as the one we are aiming at in the present study.[2]

The finest outcome of this approach to legal reasoning within *fiqh* is the notion of *qiyās* (قياس), known as *correlational inference*.[3] The aim of correlational inferences is to provide a rational ground for the application of a juridical ruling to a given case not yet considered by the original juridical sources. It proceeds by combining heuristic (and/or hermeneutic) moves with logical inferences. The simplest forms follow the following patterns:

- In order to establish if a given juridical ruling applies or not to a given case, called the *branch-case* (*al-far*ʿ (الفرع)), we look for a case we already know that falls under that ruling – the so-called root-case *(al-aṣl* (الأصل)). Then we search for the property or set of properties upon which the application of the ruling to the source case is grounded (the *ratio legis* or *legal cause* for that juridical decision).

  If that grounding property (or set of them) is known, we ponder if it can also be asserted of the new case under consideration. In the case of an affirmative answer, it is inferred that the new case also falls under the juridical ruling at stake, and so the range of its application is expanded. When the legal cause is explicitly known (by the sources) or made explicit by specifying a relevant set of properties, the reasoning schema at work is called *qiyās al-ʿilla* or correlational inference by the *occasioning factor*. Let us recall the classical example: date liquor intoxicates, just as (grape) wine does, so it is prohibited like wine. The canonical analysis identifies four elements in such an argument: the branch-case or case under consideration, date liquor; the root-case or case verified by the sources, wine; the character they have in common, their power to intoxicate; and their common, legal qualification, prohibition (inferred in the case of date liquor, verified by the sources in the case of wine). The crucial step that underlies this form of argumentation is the identification of the

---

[1]Young (2017, pp. 21–32) acknowledges and discusses his debt to the work of Hallaq in many sections of the book.

[2]Also relevant are the following lines of Hallaq (1997, pp. 136–137), quoted by Young (2017, p. 25): *In one sense, dialectic constituted the final stage in the process of legal reasoning, in which two conflicting opinions on a case of law were set against each other in the course of a disciplined session of argumentation with the purpose of establishing the truthfulness of one of them. The aim of this exercise, among other things, was to reduce disagreement (ikhtilāf) among legists by demonstrating that one opinion was more acceptable or more valid than another. Minimizing differences of opinion on a particular legal question was of the utmost importance, the implication being that truth is one, and for each case there exists only one true solution.*

[3]Cf. Young (2017, p. 10). The term quite often has a broader meaning which encompasses legal reasoning in general. However, Young's choice for its translation renders a narrower sense that stems from al-Shīrāzī's approach.

occasioning factor, the *'illa*, that lies behind its prohibition. The point here is that applying the general schema that *drinks that have the power to induce intoxication should be forbidden* to the case of date liquor *occasions* its interdiction.

When the grounds behind a given juridical ruling neither are explicit nor can they be made explicit, the reasoning schema at work is either *qiyās al-dalāla*, or correlational inferences by indication, or *qiyās al-shabah*, or correlational inferences by resemblance. Whereas the former are based on pinpointing specific relevant parallelisms between rulings (*qiyās al-dalāla*), the latter are based on resemblances between properties (*qiyās al-shabah*). Thus, *qiyās al-dalāla* and *qiyās al-shabah*, sometimes broadly referred to as arguments by analogy (or better by the Latin denomination arguments *a pari*), are put into action when there is an absence of knowledge of the occasioning factor grounding the application of a given ruling. The plausibility of a conclusion attained by parallelism between rulings (*qiyās al-dalāla*) is considered to be of a higher epistemic degree than the conclusion obtained by resemblance of the branch-case and the source case in relation to some set of (relevant) properties (*qiyās al-shabah*). The conclusions obtained by either *qiyās al-dalāla* or *qiyās al-shabah* have a lower degree of epistemic plausibility than the conclusions inferred by the deployment of *qiyās al-'illa*, where the occasioning factor can be identified.[4]

More generally, one interesting way to look at the contribution of the inception of the juridical notion of *qiyās* is to compare it with the emergence of European Civil Law. Indeed, European Civil Law emerged as a system of general norms or rules that were thought to generalize the repertory of cases recorded mainly by Roman Law. The emergence of *qiyās* can be seen as the inception of an instrument to identify or grasp the general meaning behind the cases recorded by the sources and the tradition. The dynamics triggered by implementing such an instrument "forges" the laws that structure Islamic Law.

Our study, focused on Abū Isḥāq al-Shīrāzī's (393H/1003 CE-476H/1083 CE) classification of *qiyās* as discussed in his *Mulakhkhaṣ fī al-Jadal* (*Epitome on Dialectical Disputation*), *Ma'ūna fī al-Jadal* (*Aid on Dialectical Disputation*) and *al-Luma' fī Uṣūl al-Fiqh* (*Refulgence of Islamic Legal Theory*), develops an examination based on a dialogical approach to Per Martin-Löf's (1984) *Constructive Type Theory* (CTT). According to our view, such an approach provides both a natural

[4]One striking example of the implementation of such a method is Arsyad al-Banjari's (1957, 1983) development of a dialectical model for integrating traditional Indonesian uses into Islamic Law. See Iqbal/Rahman (2019) and Iqbal (2019).

understanding and a fine-grained instrument to stress three of the hallmarks of this form of reasoning:[5]

(a) The interaction of hermeneutic, heuristic and epistemological processes with logical steps
(b) The dialectical dynamics underlying the meaning-explanation of the terms involved[6]
(c) The unfolding of parallel reasoning as similarity in action

What the dialogical framework adds to the standard natural deduction presentation of CTT is that this approach not only provides insights into the dynamics of meaning underlying the notion of *qiyās* but also leads to a conception of logic where logical rules too are understood as emerging from dialectical interaction. In other words, the dialogical reconstruction of the different forms of correlational inference is not to be conceived as the concatenation of a dialogical structure + logical rules + semantics + knowledge + jurisprudence but rather as a unifying system where all those levels are constituted, or *forged* at once by argumentative interaction; they are *immanent* to a dialogue that makes reason and knowledge happen. For a discussion on *immanent reasoning*, see the chapter IV.

Let us have a first glimpse at how this framework works out in the context of the traditional objections to *qiyās* discussed in Soufi Youcef's introduction to the present work.[7] The main objections can perhaps be summarized as follows:[8]

1. Within *fiqh*, one very rarely finds attempts to deduce a general rule from the specific rule for each legal act. What we actually find in the legal writings more often than not are specific rules.
2. Finding out the general rules by abduction or induction is not only pretentious, but it also leads to uncertainty. How do we ever know that we identified the most appropriate or *relevant* properties? This casts doubt on even *qiyās al-'illa*, purported to provide the most certain conclusion attained by legal reasoning.

[5]Miller (1984) is one of the first to mention the dialogical framework of Lorenzen/Lorenz (1978) as a suitable approach for the study of Islamic argumentation. The dialogical approach to CTT is called *immanent reasoning* (see Rahman/McConaughey/Klev/Clerbout (2018)). In fact, there is an ongoing work on deploying the dialogical setting in order to reconstruct logical traditions in ancient philosophy (see Castelnérac/Marion (2009), Marion/Rückert (2015), Crubellier/McConaughey/Marion/Rahman (2019)).

[6]The term *meaning-explanation* is due to Martin-Löf and has a natural dialogical reading (see Rahman/McConaughey/Klev/Clerbout (2018, Chapters II and III)); it amounts to setting the meaning of an expression by rules that establish how to challenge and defend it. Moreover, these rules also include formation prescriptions, that is, rules that prescribe the type of an expression: Is it an independent type like the set of natural numbers? Or is it a dependent type like a propositional function which renders a proposition from elements picked out from a relevant set, e.g. $French(x) : prop\ (x : Human)$ that can be glossed as "the proposition that x is French can be asserted from suitable candidates of the set of Humans"?

[7]As we will discuss in our conclusion to the present book, some contemporary philosophers, such as John Woods (2015, pp. 273-280), raised similar objections to the use of analogy in legal reasoning.

[8]For a thorough discussion on these points, see Zysow (2013, pp. 160-191).

3. The uncertainty of the results of applying *qiyās* stems from the fact that understanding the general norm behind a specific juridical ruling requires the deployment of an interpretative process rather than of a dubious epistemological argument.
4. Interpretation requires revelation.

According to our reconstruction of al-Shīrāzī's system of *qiyās*, the point on how to grasp the general meaning behind a specific law does not commit one to discover laws (legal laws are not discovered). Neither induction nor abduction is at work here. The process involved consists in the ability to grasp that the specific rule instantiates a general one, by making apparent the meaning constitution behind that specific rule.

Roughly, the generalization behind, which is very close to what Woods (2015, p. 278)[9] calls *generalization schema*, can be seen as a process of *exemplification*,[10] whereby one instance is grasped as exemplifying the whole (pars pro toto) – just as a sample of a carpet exemplifies the whole carpet. So the generalization schema exemplified by the case of wine can be formulated as follows:

The consumption of drink x is interdicted
Drink x has the property of inducing intoxication

This supports the assertion:

- The capability of drink x to induce intoxication leads to its interdiction.

More precisely, given some ruling $\mathcal{H}$ applied to some case b, i.e given the specific ruling $\mathcal{H}(b)$, when we delve into the *meaning-explanation*,[11] we might come to see that it is an instance of the following schema:

$\mathcal{H}(x)$ *true* $(x : \mathcal{P})$
"it is true that ruling $\mathcal{H}$ applies to x, provided x instantiates property $\mathcal{P}$",

which adds to the precedent schema the point not only that the inferential schema at stake has the form of a hypothetical judgement but also that the interdiction is an interdiction *specific to objects* (in our example, drinks) *instantiating the property* $\mathcal{P}$ (of inducing intoxication). Clearly, the interdiction of consuming some drink is different from the interdiction of, say, stealing. The legal consequences of the correspondent transgressions are certainly different.

Moreover, the *'illa* is the application of the schema to a particular specific instance. Technically speaking, in our framework, the causative feature of the occasioning factor amounts to shaping it as an application of the function that instantiates the schema. This allows us to distinguish the property relevant for

---

[9] As we will discuss in the conclusion of the present book, Woods' (2015, pp. 273-280) take on reasoning by the precedence in Common Law is strikingly close to al-Shīrāzī's system of *qiyās al-'illa*. The same applies to Brewer's (1996) *Exemplary Reasoning: Semantics, Pragmatics, and the Rational Force of Legal Argument by Analogy*.

[10] Here, we are using Goodman's notion of exemplification – see Goodman (1976, Chapter II).

[11] See above our footnote on the notion of *meaning-explantion*.

some specific juridical sanction from the actual procedure of triggering that sanction for some particular case instantiating the property. It is the triggering procedure that provides the notion of occasioning factor with its causal force.

Intuitively, given the schema $\mathcal{H}(x)$ *true* $(x : \mathcal{P})$,
if a instantiates $\mathcal{P}$,
then, there is a method (in the practice a juridical procedure), encoded by the function $b(x)$, that when applied to a renders the specific ruling $\mathcal{H}(a)$.

So far so good, but how do we know that this is the meaning behind $\mathcal{H}(a)$? How do we know that the chosen property is the relevant or the appropriate one? To come back to our canonical example, how do we know for certain that the property of inducing intoxication leads to the interdiction of consuming wine?

It is here that al-Shīrāzī's method of efficiency *taʾthīr* comes into action. In a nutshell, according to our analysis, al-Shīrāzī's notion of occasioning factor includes the following three main components:

1. *Waṣf*, the property $\mathcal{P}$ relevant for a juridical sanction $\mathcal{H}$, such that the latter is defined as being specific to the set of cases defined by $\mathcal{P}$ (e.g. those interdictions $\mathcal{H}(x)$ that apply to consume those drinks that instantiate the set $\mathcal{P}$ of drinks inducing intoxication).
2. The efficiency feature or *taʾthīr* that provides the means to test whether the property $\mathcal{P}$ purported to be relevant for the juridical sanction at stake is indeed so. The test declines into two complementary procedures: testing co-extensiveness or *ṭard* (if the property is present then the sanction too) and co-exclusiveness or *ʿaks* (if the property is absent then so is the juridical sanction – the consumption of vinegar is in principle not forbidden). While co-extensiveness examines whether sanction $\mathcal{H}$ follows from the verification of the presence of the property $\mathcal{P}$, co-exclusiveness examines whether exemption from the sanction $\mathcal{H}$ follows from the verification of the absence of $\mathcal{P}$.
3. The causal feature, i.e. the legal method encoded by the function $b(x)$, that when applied to some instance a of the relevan property $\mathcal{P}$ renders the ruling $\mathcal{H}(a)$ specific to that property. More precisely, when we focus on the causal feature of the occasioning factor, the function will be written as *ʿilla*(x). The function *ʿilla*(x) admits the substitution *ʿilla*(a) for some case a (that satisfies the *waṣf*), only after the efficiency of the property $\mathcal{P}$ has been verified by the test *taʾthīr*.

As pointed out by Zysow (2013, p. 215), the doctrine of efficiency represents an impressive attempt to answer the cardinal questions of those that opposed the deployment of *qiyās*. Notice that the method of efficiency not only tests the relevance but also responds to the point on the legal foundation of the general rules. The fact is that the general schema is both grounded and extracted from specific rulings found in the sources. Moreover, by means of *taʾthīr*, the occasioning factor is identified as the application that yields a ruling grounded in the sources.

Still, Abū Hāmid al-Ghazālī, who vehemently defended the deployment of *qiyās*, points out that co-extensiveness or co-presence and co-exclusiveness or co-absence do not always render the most appropriate or relevant (*munāsaba*) property for the ruling under consideration. His example involves the property of some particular smell, which is present when wine is present and absent when wine is absent, but these observations do not lead to the conclusion that particular smell of wine is the relevant property for its interdiction.[12]

What al-Ghazali observes is that though the tests of *ṭard* and *ʿaks* pave the way for grasping the intention behind the norms given by the Lawgiver, this might not be enough: grasping the meaning might require additional hermeneutical procedures.[13] Nevertheless, formulating explicitly a claim on the precise form of a general schema implicit in the use of a specific ruling brings this schema out into the open as liable to challenges and demands for justification.[14]

More generally, the idea is that the rational process invoked by the argumentative framework depends on the possibility of making explicit (in the form of claims) implicit commitments on the meaning-explanation of a ruling. In other words, the rational epistemological endeavour underlying *qiyās* consists in the possibility of publicly expressing claims concerning the general constitution of a ruling in order to subject them to ponderation and criticism.

Thus, on the one hand, our reconstruction might provide researchers on the Arabic tradition with some instruments for epistemological analysis, and on the other, we hope to motivate epistemologists and researchers in argumentation theory to explore the rich and thought-provoking texts produced by this tradition in order to also tackle issues concerning parallel reasoning in other legal or scientific contexts.

Altogether, we dare to say that at the centre of al-Shīrāzī's argumentative framework is the idea that rationality is featured by the task of bringing to the *space of games of giving and asking for reasons* those commitments and entitlements that structure the network of implicit beliefs and notions underlying legal practices.

Clearly, we indulge here (and before), in the anachronism, beside others, of deploying Robert Brandom's (1994) terminology in the context of a dialectical practice which is far in time and space from the background of his studies. Perhaps, this also suggests that the emergence of the dialectic stance on the rational assessment of notions and beliefs implicit in social practices has quite a long and rich history behind it. This is a general lesson of the Elders we should not ignore.

The book is structured as follows:

After an overview of the emergence of *qiyās* and of the work of al-Shīrāzī penned by Soufi Youcef, we start by discussing al-Shīrāzī's classification of correlational inferences of the occasioning factor (*qiyās al-ʿilla*) in the second part. The third part

[12] Al-Ghazālī (1324H, pp. 307-308). Cf. Hallaq (1987, pp. 61-62).

[13] Putting aside important differences, we might parallel al-Ghazālī's point with Frege's view that though concepts are ontological independent of the logical analysis that makes them explicity and publicly accessible to human understanding, this analysis clears the way to the grasping of those concepts. However, different to al-Ghazālī, Frege thinks that logical analysis is the *only way*.

[14] At this precise point, parallel reasoning in Common Law and *uṣūl al-fiqh* take different paths. Indeed, according to Woods (2015, p. 280), the generalization schema behind a parity argument is very rarely made explicit. We come back to this point in the conclusion.

of the volume discusses the system of correlational inferences by indication and resemblance (*qiyās al-dalāla, qiyās al-shabah*). The fourth part develops the main theoretical background of our work, namely, the dialogical approach to Constructive Type Theory. This we present in a general form and independently of adaptations deployed in Parts II and III. Part IV also includes an appendix on a brief overview of Martin-Löf's Constructive Type Theory written by Ansten Klev. We conclude the book with some brief remarks on contemporary approaches to analogy in law and also to parallel reasoning in general.

Lille, France — Shahid Rahman, Muhammad Iqbal

Vancouver, Canada — Youcef Soufi

References

Al-Banjarī, Muhammad Arsyad. (1957). *Sabīl al-muhtadīn.*Riyadh: King Saud University.

Al-Banjarī, Muhammad Arsyad. (1983). *Tuḥfat al-rāghibīn*. Banjarmasin: Toko Buku Murni.

Al-Ghazālī, Abū Hāmid. (1324 H). *Al-Mustaṣfā min 'ilm al-Uṣūl, 2* vols. Būlāq: al-Maṭba'a al-Amīrīyya.

Al-Shīrāzī, Abū Isḥāq. (1987). *Al-Maʿūna fī al-jadal*. ('Alī b. ʿAbd al-ʿAzīz al-ʿUmayrīnī. Al-Safāh, Ed.). Kuwait: Manshūrāt Markaz al-Makhṭūṭāt wa-al-Turāth.

Al-Shīrāzī, Abū Isḥāq. (2003). *Al-Lumaʿ fī uṣūl al-fiqh*. Beirut: Dār al-Kutub al-'Ilmiyah.

Al-Shīrāzī, Abū Isḥāq. (2016). *Mulakhkhaṣ fī al-jadal.* Retrieved February 1, 2016 from https://upload.wikimedia.org/wikisource/ar/e/ea/خ_الملخص_في_الجدل.pdf.

Brandom, R. (1994). *Making it explicit.* Cambridge: Harvard University Press.

Brewer, S. (1996, March). Exemplary reasoning: Semantics, pragmatics, and the rational force of legal argument by analogy. *Harvard Law Review*, 109(5), 923–1028.

Castelnérac, B., & Marion, M. (2009). Arguing for inconsistency: Dialectical games in the academy. In G. Primiero, & S. Rahman (Eds.), *Acts of knowledge: History, philosophy and logic* (pp. 37–76). London: College Publications.

Crubellier, M., McConaughey, Z., Marion, M., & Rahman, S. (2019). Dialectic, The dictum the omni and ecthesis. *History and philosophy of logic*. In print.

Goodman, N. (1976). *Languages of art*. Cambridge, MA: Hackett Publishing Co..

Hallaq, W. (1987b). The development of logical structure in Islamic legal Theory. *Der Islam*, 64/1, 42–67.

Hallaq, W. (1997). *A history of islamic legal theories: An introduction to Sunnī Uṣūl al-Fiqh*. Cambridge/New York: Cambridge University Press.

Iqbal, M. (2019). *Arsyad al-Banjari's approaches to rationality: Argumentation and Sharia*. PhD-University of Lille Press, Lille. (Forthcoming).

Iqbal, M., & Rahman, S. (2019). "Arsyad al-Banjari's dialectical model for integrating Indonesian traditional uses into Islamic law. Arguments on *Manyanggar*, *Membuang Pasilih* and *Lahang*". (Forthcoming).

Lorenzen, P., and Lorenz, K. (1978). *Dialogische Logik*. Damstadt: Wissenschaftliche Buchgesellschaft.

Marion, M. and Rückert, H. (2015). Aristotle on universal quantification: A study from the perspective of game semantics. *History and Philosophy of Logic, 37*(3), 201–209.

Martin-Löf, P. (1984). *Intuitionistic type theory. Notes by Giovanni Sambin of a series of lectures given in Padua, June 1980*. Naples: Bibliopolis.

Miller, L. B. (1984). *Islamic disputation theory: A study of the development of dialectic in Islam from the tenth through fourteenth centuries*. Princeton: Princeton University. (Unpublished dissertation).

Rahman, S., & Iqbal, M. (2018). Unfolding parallel reasoning in Islamic Jurisprudence. Epistemic and dialectical meaning within Abū Isḥāq al-Shīrāzī's system of correlational inferences of the occasioning factor. *Cambridge Journal for Arabic Sciences and Philosophy*, 28, 67–132.

Rahman, S., McConaughey, Z.; Klev, A., & Clerbout, N. (2018). *Immanent reasoning. A plaidoyer for the play level*. Dordrecht: Springer.

Woods, J. (2015). *Is legal reasoning irrational? An introduction to the epistemology of law*. London: College Publications.

Young, W. E. (2017). *The dialectical forge. Juridical disputation and the evolution of Islamic law*. Dordrecht: Springer.

Zysow, A. (2013). *The economy of certainty. An introduction to the typology of Islamic legal theory*. Atlanta: Lockwood Press.

Acknowledgments

Herewith, we would like to thank Prof. Roshdi Rashed (CNRS, SPHERE, Paris VII), chief editor of the Cambridge journal *Arabic Sciences and Philosophy*, who allowed us to deploy for the first part of our study the paper by S. Rahman and M. Iqbal (2018) "Unfolding Parallel Reasoning in Islamic Jurisprudence. Epistemic and Dialectical Meaning within Abū Isḥāq al-Shīrāzī's System of Correlational Inferences of the Occasioning Factor" (Cambridge journal *Arabic Sciences and Philosophy* 28 (2018), pp. 67-132). Many thanks too to Erwan Penchèvre (Paris VII) for his excellent editorial work on the paper mentioned above and also to Ahmad Hasnawi (CNRS, SPHERE, Paris VII), managing editor of the *ASP* (until June 2018), who contributed to the publication of the paper and who also contributed with many reflections during a seminar at the MESHS-Nord-Pas de Calais, where we presented some early versions of our proposal.

Special thanks to Walter E. Young (McGill University) who not only inspired the present study by his impressive work on juridical disputation and the evolution of Islamic Law but also assisted with fruitful relevant remarks. We are also grateful to Mawusse Kpakpo Akue Adotevi (Université de Lomé), Matthias Armgardt (Universität Konstanz), Cristina Barés Gómez (Universidad de Sevilla), Eduardo Barrio (Universidad de Buenos Aires), Charles Zacharie Bowao (Université M. Ngouabi, Brazzaville), Nicolas Clerbout (Universidad de Valparaíso), Marcelo Dascal (University of Tel Aviv), Souleymane Bachir Diagne (Columbia University), Mathieu Fontaine (CFCUL-Universidade de Lisboa), Johan Georg Granström (Zürich), Mlika Hamdi (Université de Kairouan), Karl-Heinz Hülser (Univeristät Konstanz), Ansten Klev (Academy of Sciences, Prague), Rodrigo López (Universidad de Valparaíso), Mathieu Marion (Université Montréal), Angel Nepomuceno Fernández (Universidad de Sevilla), Marcel Nguimbi (Université M. Ngouabi, Brazzaville), Gildas Nzokou (Université Omar Bongo, Libreville), Olga Pombo (CFCUL-Universidade de Lisboa), Moussa Abou Ramadan (Université Strasbourg), Juan Redmond (Universidad de Valparaíso), Zaynab Salloum (Université Beyrouth), Mohammad Shafiei (Shahid Beheshti University, Teheran), Göran Sundholm (Universiteit Leiden), Hassan Tahiri (CFCUL-Lisbon), Farid

Zidani (Université d'Alger II), John Woods (University of British Columbia), Joseph David (Yale University) and two anonymous reviewers for their rich and helpful comments on the earlier versions of the contents included in the volume.

The authors would like to thank the Laboratory STL, UMR-CNRS 8163, particularly so to Leone Gazziero (STL), Laurent Cesalli (Genève), leaders of the ANR Project *SEMAINO* (STL), and Claudio Majolino (STL), associated researcher to that project, for fostering the research leading to the present study. Let us point out that the reflections on which this book is based evolved under the influence of the responses of many audiences to which the different versions have been presented in recent years. We are profoundly grateful to all those members of the institutions mentioned above and the laboratory STL who contributed by thinking together about these issues, specially to Giuliano Bacigalupo, Simon Brunin, Christian Berner, Patrice Canivez, Pierre Cardascia, Michel Crubellier, Sandrine Chassagnard-Pinet, Bernadette Dango, Steephen Rossy Eckoubili, Hanna Karpenko, Clément Lion, Zoe McConaughey, Sébastien Magnier, Fosca Mariani, Raffaele Pisano, Louis Rose, Fachrur Rozie, Juliette Senechal, Juliele Sievers, Ruth Webb, and Sequoya Yiaueki. Muhammad Iqbal, the second author of the present book, thanks his home institution *Universitas Islam Negeri Antasari* Banjarmasin, Indonesia, and the funding of the *Indonesian Ministry of Religious Affairs* for a grant that made it possible to develop his research at the University of Lille and the Laboratory STL.

The first author would like to point out that his recent interest in Islamic philosophy, logic, and epistemology is an outcome of his collaboration with Dr. Hassan Tahiri (CFCUL-Lisbon), during the latter's PhD on philosophy of mathematics at the University of Lille and further research on the history of sciences. Rahman's interest in this field continued to grow steadily, thanks to the joint work with Dr. Zaynab Salloum (Lebanese University) on Ibn Sīnā, and with Muhammad Iqbal, the second author of the present book, on legal reasoning within Islamic jurisprudence and epistemology. As the Germans say, PhD students ensure the continuing education of their professors.

Contents

1 Introduction: The Life and *Qiyās* of Abū Isḥāq al-Shīrāzī (393H/1003 CE-476H/1083 CE) 1
- 1.1 From Firuzabad to the Niẓāmiyya: Al-Shīrāzī's Climb Within the Shāfi'ī School Hierarchy 2
- 1.2 The Background History to Al-Shīrāzī's *Qiyās*: The Contentiousness of Inference by Parallel Reasoning 6
- 1.3 The Evolution of *Qiyās* Argumentation: Al-Shīrāzī as Inheritor to the Surayjī-Shāfi'ī Line of Legal Theory 9
- 1.4 *Qiyās* in the Eleventh Century Debate Gathering 13
- 1.5 Concluding Remarks 15
- References 16

2 *Qiyās al-'Illa*: al-Shīrāzī's System of Correlational Inferences of the Occasioning Factor 19
- 2.1 Introduction 19
- 2.2 A Dialectical Genealogy of Abū Isḥāq al-Shīrāzī's System of *Qiyās* 24
- 2.3 Motivating the Deployment of CTT Within an Interactive Stance 29
  - 2.3.1 The Meaning-Explanation of Juridical Rulings in *Qiyās al-'Illa* 31
  - 2.3.2 Towards the Interactive Stance 40
- 2.4 A Dialogical Framework for Correlational Inferences of the Occasioning Factor 47
  - 2.4.1 Overall View of the Development of a Dialogue for *Qiyās al-'illa* 48
  - 2.4.2 Special Moves 52
  - 2.4.3 Examples of Dialogues 58

2.4.4 The Main Rules of the Dialogical Framework for *Qiyās al-ʿIlla* . . . 66
2.5 Conclusions . . . 89
References . . . 90

3 *Qiyās al-Dalāla* and *Qiyās al-Shabah*: al-Shīrāzī's System of Correlational Inferences by Indication and Resemblance . . . 95
3.1 Introduction: On al-Shīrāzī's Classification of *Qiyās al-Dalāla* and *Qiyās al-Shabah* . . . 95
3.2 *Qiyās al-Dalāla* . . . 98
3.2.1 *Khaṣīṣa, Shahādat al-Uṣūl* and the First Type of *Qiyās al-Dalāla* . . . 100
3.2.2 *Naẓīr, Shahādat al-Uṣūl* and the Second Type of *Qiyās al-Dalāla* . . . 108
3.3 *Qiyās al-Shabah* . . . 114
3.4 The Dialectical Structure of *Qiyās al-Dalāla* and *Qiyās al-Shabah* . . . 117
3.4.1 The Overall Development of a Dialogue for *Qiyās al-Dalāla* and *Qiyās al-Shabah* . . . 117
3.4.2 Some Examples of Dialogues for *Qiyās al-Dalāla* and *Qiyās al-Shabah* . . . 120
3.5 A Dialogical Framework for *Qiyās al-Dalāla* and *Qiyās al-Shabah* . . . 128
3.5.1 The Dialogical Approach to Logic . . . 128
3.6 Conclusions . . . 142
References . . . 143

4 Dialogues, Reasons and Endorsement . . . 145
4.1 Introduction . . . 145
4.2 Local Reasons . . . 148
4.2.1 Local Meaning and Local Reasons . . . 150
4.2.2 The Dialogical Roots of Equality: Dialogues for Immanent Reasoning . . . 160
4.2.3 Content and Material Dialogues . . . 171
4.3 Strategic Reasons in Dialogues for Immanent Reasoning . . . 181
4.3.1 Introducing Strategic Reasons . . . 182
4.3.2 Rules for the Synthesis of P-Strategic Reasons . . . 186
4.3.3 Rules for the Analysis of P-Strategic Reasons . . . 188
4.4 A Plaidoyer for the Play-Level . . . 190
4.4.1 Dialogue-Definiteness and Propositions . . . 190
4.4.2 The Built-in Opponent and the Neglect of the Play Level . . . 194
4.4.3 Pathological Cases and the Neglect of the Play Level . . . 197
4.4.4 Conclusion: The Meaning of Expressions Comes from the Play Level . . . 201

4.5 Normativity and the Dialogical Framework 202
4.5.1 A New Venue for the Interface Pragmatics-Semantics . . . 202
4.5.2 The Semantic and Communicative Interface in Dialogical Setting 208
4.6 Final Remarks 210
References 212

Appendix: Some Basic Notions of Constructive Type Theory 215

Final Remarks and the Work Ahead 237

Glossary of Some Relevant Technical Terms from Islamic Jurisprudence 249

Bibliography 251

Name Index 261

Subject Index 265

Chapter 1
Introduction: The Life and *Qiyās* of Abū Isḥāq al-Shīrāzī (393H/1003 CE-476H/1083 CE)

In the chapters that follow, Shahid Rahman and Muhammad Iqbal provide us with a comprehensive logical analysis of Abū Isḥāq al-Shīrāzī's two forms of *qiyās*-based argumentation, which they aptly translate as inference by parallel reasoning. Their painstaking labour is bound to interest both the Islamic studies historian and the contemporary logician. For the former, among whom I include myself, their methodological approach of embedding *qiyās* argumentation within its proper historical dialectical context sheds new light on Islamic legal argumentation. Building upon Walter Young's thesis that Islamic legal rules and argumentative principles were "forged" through debate itself,[1] Rahman and Iqbal demonstrate the series of steps al-Shīrāzī deemed necessary to secure a successful deployment of *qiyās* while in a debate gathering. In marked contrast to typical scholarly treatment of *qiyās* which (implicitly) assumes a solitary jurist whose monological comparison of like-cases goes unquestioned, they show how the successful deployment of *qiyās* often depended upon a jurist offering a deeper defense of his background assumptions about two cases. The juristic use of *qiyās* therefore necessitated a wider exploration of the legal system. For the logician, Rahman and Iqbal suggest that the Islamic tradition can enter into conversation with the modern study of dialectical argumentation. Like Amira Mittermaier, whose study of contemporary dreams in Egypt, argues that Ibn ʻArabī and al-Ghazālī are just as valuable as Freud or Sartre to our understanding of dreams and the imagination, Rahman and Iqbal show that al-Shīrāzī and the Islamic legal tradition are worthy interlocutors of Wittgenstein and other contemporary logicians.[2] In particular, they show that meaning and knowledge are immanent or internal to dialogical exchanges insofar as the reasons justifying claims depend on a set of propositions embraced by both participants.

This introduction aims at placing al-Shīrāzī within social and intellectual historical context. The man whose intellectual contributions to *qiyās* is the object of the

[1] Young (2017, p. 1).

[2] Mittermaier (2010).

S. Rahman et al., *Inferences by Parallel Reasoning in Islamic Jurisprudence*, Logic, Argumentation & Reasoning 19, https://doi.org/10.1007/978-3-030-22382-3_1

present study was born in the small Persian town of Firuzabad in 393H/1003 CE. Abū Isḥāq al-Shīrāzī, known throughout Shāfiʿī history as the one and only Shaykh Abū Isḥāq, would go on to become the first law professor of the illustrious Niẓāmiyya College of Baghdad in 459H/1067 CE.[3] His legal texts in the areas of dialectic (*jadal*), substantive law (*furū ʿal-fiqh*), and legal theory (*uṣūl al-fiqh*) would continue to be reference points for his Shāfiʿī school up until the present.[4] In what follows, I trace al-Shīrāzī's gradual and arduous rise to fame and the scholarly lineages that influenced his theorizations of *qiyās*-based argumentation. By demonstrating that al-Shīrāzī's *qiyās* theory is part of an understudied branch of Baghdad Shāfiʿī theoretical thought, I hope to place in greater relief the original contribution of Rahman and Iqbal's analysis.

1.1 From Firuzabad to the Niẓāmiyya: Al-Shīrāzī's Climb Within the Shāfiʿī School Hierarchy

The story of Shirazi's journey to scholarly fame tells us much about the intellectual community to which he would attach himself. Al-Shīrāzī's intellectual journey to the summit of Shāfiʿī scholarship was by no means an easy one. Biographers say nothing of his family background, which gestures towards his poor socio-economic position.[5] In fact, poverty would follow al-Shīrāzī his entire life: Muslim historians even convey that he could not undertake the Meccan pilgrimage for lack of means to purchase a suitable travelling mount.[6] The rise of an economically poor member of society to intellectual fame was not anomalous among the eleventh century Muslim jurists. Abū ʿAbd Allāh al-Dāmaghānī, for instance, was a Ḥanafī jurist of poor economic origins who would eventually become chief judge (*qāḍī*) of Baghdad.[7] However, poverty did make al-Shīrāzī's rise a more arduous one than those who came from more established juristic families and goes some ways towards explaining his pedagogical path.

What al-Shīrāzī lacked in financial means, he made up in scholarly determination. As a young man, al-Shīrāzī travelled to Shiraz, the largest city of the central Persian province of Fars, to study under the Shāfiʿī jurist Abū ʿAbd Allāh al-Bayḍāwī

[3]Peacock (2015); Talas (1939).

[4]See for instance Brinkley Messick's study of modern-day Yemeni legal scholars (Messick 1996).

[5]The most comprehensive biography of al-Shīrāzī is found in al-Subkī (1964, p. 4:215–256). See also Ibn Khallikān (1978, pp. 1:29–31), Ibn-Qāḍī Shuhba (1987, pp. 1:238–240), Ibn al-Ṣalāḥ al-Shahrazūrī, al-Nawawī, and al-Mizzī (1992, pp. 1:302–10), Ibn Kathīr (2002, pp. 430–442) and Hītū (1980).

[6]Al-Subkī (1964, p. 4:227).

[7]Ephrat (2000, p. 51).

(d. 424H/1033 CE).[8] His native Firuzabad would have been too small for al-Shīrāzī to satisfactorily pursue his educational aspirations. The ancient Persian town was blessed with fertile lands and temperate climate but was dwarfed in size by Shiraz. More importantly, Shiraz had emerged as an intellectual hub boasting jurists and philosophers that would make their mark on Islamic history. In fact, it was from his brief sojourn in Shiraz that he would obtain the title al-Shīrāzī—the one from Shiraz—which gestures towards the relative provinciality of Firuzabad.

Al-Shīrāzī's teacher, al-Bayḍāwī, had been a disciple (*ṣāḥib*) of Abū al-Qāsim al-Dārakī who was the leader of the Shāfi'īs of Baghdad at the time of his death in 375H/985 CE.[9] Baghdad Shāfi'īs dominated the discursive landscape of Shāfi'ism in the eleventh century. Their interpretative efforts in developing Shāfi'ī thought had gained pre-eminence with the learning circle of Ibn Surayj.[10] Ibn Surayj and his towering disciples such as al-Qaffāl al-Shāshī, Abū Bakr al-Ṣayrafī, Ibn al-Qāṣṣ, Abū 'Alī al-Ṭabarī, and Abū Isḥāq al-Marwazī elaborated upon and determined the doctrinal evolution of al-Shāfi'ī thought. They assessed the sometimes divergent statements of their school master, Muḥammad ibn Idrīs al-Shāfi'ī, weighed and determined the best proofs bearing on contentious legal questions, and extended al-Shāfi'ī's methodological reasoning to new cases. Known for their systematic tackling of legal questions, they made Baghdad the pre-eminent centre of Shāfi'ī learning. Al-Shīrāzī would write that Ibn Surayj's opinions "spread throughout the land" and that Shāfi'īs generally followed his opinions.[11] Aspiring jurists came from near and far to gain knowledge from the Baghdad luminaries, and al-Bayḍāwī continued this trend when he went to study under al-Dārakī before becoming a top Shāfi'ī scholar of Shiraz.

Al-Bayḍāwī initiated al-Shīrāzī to the substantive legal corpus (*furū'al-fiqh*) of the Shāfi'ī school. Al-Shīrāzī's training consisted of learning the vast array of contentious legal issues (*masā'il al-khilāf*) that divided Muslim jurists and the responses his school colleagues provided to them.[12] He was to learn centuries of accrued proofs that Shāfi'īs posited in favour of their doctrinal positions. This was a long and painstaking task, only complicated by the fact that different Shāfi'ī jurists knew and championed different evidences supporting their positions. It was for this reason that the great Imām al-Ḥaramayn, Abū al-Ma'ālī al-Juwaynī, a Shāfi'ī contemporary of al-Shīrāzī, had amassed the divergent legal opinions of Shāfi'īs throughout his significant travels all over the Muslim East in producing his opus of

---

[8] All biographical entries agree that al-Shīrāzī's study period with al-Bayḍāwī was in Shiraz. I follow them within this biographical sketch. However, the critical historian should know that this might actually be mistaken as al-Shīrāzī himself notes that al-Bayḍāwī lived in Baghdad and biographical sources on al-Bayḍāwī do not place him in Shiraz, see for instance Ibn Qāḍī Shuhba (1987, p. 1:177).

[9] For more on al-Dārakī, see al-Shīrāzī (1970, p. 117).

[10] Al-Subkī (1964, p. 3:22).

[11] Al-Shīrāzī (1970, p. 109).

[12] Al-Shīrāzī often speaks of jurists' preserving school opinions (*ḥāfizan li'l-madhhab*), al-Shīrāzī (1970, pp. 130–131).

substantive law, *Nihāyat al-Maṭlab*.[13] Shāfi'īs of the eleventh century often trained with several jurists and moved from one town to another in order to obtain a greater sense of the complex debates existing within their legal school. It was only a matter of time until al-Shīrāzī exhausted the knowledge he could gain from Shiraz and moved on to the city of Basra in Iraq. There, he studied under another of al-Dārakī's former students, the jurist Ibn Rāmīn.[14]

We cannot fully understand al-Shīrāzī's academic context or challenges without taking note of his origins as a non-native Arabic speaker. Basra marked a transition for al-Shīrāzī from a Persian context to an Arab one. Al-Shīrāzī's initiation would have been eased by the cosmopolitan background of his fellow students. Many, including his future teachers, would be of Persian stock, although the *lingua franca* of learning was Arabic and they all gained great proficiency in it. The community of jurists were known as *ṭulāb al-'ilm* (seekers of knowledge) and deemed the search for God's law (*ijtihād*) to be a devotional act that aims to please God. In fact, the eleventh century jurist, al-Khaṭīb al-Baghdādī, would contend that seeking knowledge was the most meritorious of pious acts because it was a precondition to the correct performance of all other devotional acts. The juristic labours of the eleventh century provided crucial guidance to lay-Muslims who were unable to seek out religious learning themselves. These lay-Muslims were busy raising families and seeking a livelihood. They needed juristic guidance to guarantee their proper religious observance. The vocation of a jurist, then, was imbued with a sense of selfless nobility.

Al-Shīrāzī soon made his way to the Caliphal capital of the 'Abbasid dynasty and the intellectual hub of the Shāfi'ī school. He entered Baghdad in 1024 CE at a mere 22 years of age. Baghdad Shāfi'ism was dominated at the time by a pre-eminent scholar named Abū Ḥāmid al- Isfarāyinī. Students rushed to al-Isfarāyinī's lectures. He attracted hundreds of eager students—some accounts say seven hundred—hoping to hear his intricate exposition and commentary of Shāfi'ī law.[15] Some contemporary jurists even judged al-Isfarāyinī superior to al-Shāfi'ī himself. Al-Shīrāzī had occasion to listen and learn from al-Isfarāyinī, but the towering jurist passed away a few years later. The intellectual leadership of the Shāfi'īs then passed on to an elder jurist by the name of Abū Ṭayyib al-Ṭabarī, who would train the successive generations of Baghdad Shāfi'ī leaders. Al-Shīrāzī would stay at al-Ṭabarī's side for decades, in time becoming his most devoted disciple; Al-Ṭabarī would eventually hire al-Shīrāzī to be his class repetitor (*mu'īd*) before bestowing on him the distinction of teaching his own learning circle within al-Ṭabarī's mosque.

[13]Al-Juwaynī (2007), Al-Subkī (1964, pp. 5:165–172).

[14]According to biographers, al-Shīrāzī studied with Ibn Rāmīn in Shiraz. This appears improbable since Shīrāzī himself tells us that Ibn Rāmīn was a Basran jurist, al-Shīrāzī (1970 p. 125). Al-Shīrāzī apparently also studied under a jurist named al-Kharazī but al-Shīrāzī does not mention him in his own biographical dictionary (1970).

[15]Al-Subkī (1964, p. 3:62).

During his training with al-Ṭabarī, al-Shīrāzī began distinguishing himself in the science of *khilāf* which dealt with contentious issues between legal schools. In particular, al-Shīrāzī focused on the legal opinions dividing the Shāfi'īs from the juristic opinions of the Ḥanafī school. He authored a book titled *al-Nukat fī Masā'il al-Khilāf bayna al-Shāfi'iyya wa-al-Ḥanafiyya* detailing the divergent proofs each school offered on legal cases.[16] Al-Subkī tells us that "no one equalled al-Shīrāzī" in matters of *khilāf*. The Ḥanafī/Shāfi'ī rivalry was often occasion for debate gatherings between the two schools. Debate gatherings were occasions for jurists of each school to defend their doctrines against their rival detractors. Al-Shīrāzī took a keen interest in also theorizing dialectical argumentation (*jadal*) which he might use in critiquing debate opponents. He authored two extant books of *jadal, Al-Mulakhkhas fī al-Jadal* and the shorter *Al-Ma'ūna fī al-Jadal*. His dialectical proficiency began to attract students across legal schools seeking to learn debating skills. Among his most distinguished students in *jadal* were the Ḥanbalī jurist Abū al-Wafā' Ibn 'Aqīl and the Mālikī jurist, Abū al-Walīd al-Bājī, both of whom authored their own dialectical manuals that resembled and built upon al-Shīrāzī's thought.

After al-Ṭabarī's death in 450H/1058 CE, al-Shīrāzī continued to labour humbly at the juristic craft. Al-Ṭabarī's students included formidable minds. Al-Shīrāzī gradually distinguished himself from most of his colleagues and gained a reputation as one of the two leading Baghdad Shāfi'īs of his time, alongside his rival Abū Naṣr ibn al-Ṣabbāgh. Students in Baghdad began referencing either al-Shīrāzī's *Al-Tanbīh* or Ibn al-Ṣabbāgh's *Al-Shāmil* in their attempts to learn al-Shāfi'ī doctrine.[17] Al-Shīrāzī's legacy within Shāfi'ī thought was cemented by his appointment to the most prestigious professorial chair in the Muslim world. In 1065 CE, the powerful wazir of the new ruling Seljuq Empire, Niẓām al-Mulk, decided to erect a college of unprecedented splendour that would furnish funding for aspiring Shāfi'ī students. He built the college intending that al-Shīrāzī would lead it. However, 2 years later, al-Shīrāzī was nowhere to be found on the College's inaugurating day in 1067 CE. Al-Shīrāzī had misgivings about taking up his new appointment; rumours were swirling across Baghdad that Niẓām al-Mulk had unlawfully expropriated lands on which the College was erected.[18] Al-Shīrāzī had until then lived as a humble ascetic and exemplified the honest and pious living for which his fellow natives of Firuzabad were known. For several weeks, he thus refused to assume the professorial chair until he felt compelled by the strong insistence of his students. Al-Shīrāzī's appointment to the Niẓāmiyya permitted him to more widely disseminate his ideas in the last two decades of his life. During the year prior to his death, al-Shīrāzī travelled on a political mission to Khurāsān.[19] He found that

[16]The *Nukat* is among the few texts al-Shīrāzī authored which is still only available in manuscript form, currently in the Princeton collection. It is available online at http://pudl.princeton.edu/objects/sb397b864 (accessed October 16, 2018).

[17]See Turkī's introduction in the *Sharḥ al-Luma'* (1987, p. 44).

[18]Ibn Athīr (2012, p. 8: 212).

[19]Ibn Athīr (2012, pp. 8:283–284); al-Subkī (1967, p. 4:219); Ibn al-Jawzī (1992, p. 16:227).

every city he passed boasted jurists that had studied under his scholarly guidance and now worked as judges, law professors, and jurisconsults.[20]

1.2 The Background History to Al-Shīrāzī's *Qiyās*: The Contentiousness of Inference by Parallel Reasoning

Al-Shīrāzī's life-vocation was to master the legal tradition by delving into and weighing the substantive legal proofs of his Shāfi'ī school. *Qiyās* played a paramount role in this process, by taking the known ruling (*ḥukm*) of an original or root-case (*al-aṣl*) and extending it to an undetermined derivative or branch-case (*far'*).[21] It is instructive to note that every one of al-Shīrāzī's recorded debate transcripts begins with a *qiyās* argument.[22] *Qiyās* itself had a lengthy history. Reviewing this history up until the time of al-Shīrāzī allows us to better comprehend *qiyās*' place within the development of classical Islamic law.

Qiyās appears to have emerged—or at the very least, become prominent—within the fertile legal environment of eighth century Iraq.[23] The method was by no means uncontroversial. Iraqi pietists associated with the *ahl al-ḥadīth* movement resisted the deployment of rational faculties in legal reasoning and favoured diligently following transmitted statements from the Prophet and the early Muslims even when their historical authenticity was dubious.[24] Al-Shāfi'ī is typically credited with redeeming *qiyās* as a legitimate source of law among the hard textualists of the *ahl al-ḥadīth*.[25] Al-Shāfi'ī tried to show that rational interpretation was a necessary means of fulfilling God's commands by positing an example which might compel jurists across the ninth century legal spectrum. He imagined a Muslim worshipper too distant to see the Meccan temple to which the faithful must face to correctly perform their prayer.[26] How might such an individual fulfil the ordained ritual prayer without the empirical certainty of his sight? Al-Shāfi'ī's answer was that he needed to examine the natural signs surrounding him: the sun, the moon, stars, the direction of the wind, etc. were interpretable signs that might help him orient himself towards the right direction. The natural signs leading to the prayer direction mirrored the textual signs that God had provided through scripture (the Qur'an and *ḥadīth*). These textual signs also sometimes needed interpretation so that the worshipper

[20]Al-Subkī (1964, p. 216).

[21]Al-Shīrāzī (1988, p.788).

[22]See debate transcripts in al-Subkī (1967, pp. 4:237–256).

[23]J. Schacht (1959) effectuated the early research on *qiyās*, see chap. 9.

[24]For instance, Aḥmad ibn Ḥanbal had no compunction about including dubiously transmitted *ḥadīth* within his collection *Al-Musnad*. For more on the *ahl al-ḥadīth* methodology, see Lucas (2010) and Spectorsky (1982).

[25]El Shamsy (2007).

[26]Shāfi'ī (2005 p. 24); for secondary literature on the topic, see Lowry (2007).

might fulfil his religious obligations. Both were a process of *ijtihād*, meaning a rational interpretative effort, in seeking to fulfil divine law.[27] *Qiyās* was the foremost interpretive method that al-Shāfi'ī championed because it was grounded in authentic signs God provided through scripture.

In the next centuries, *qiyās* gained wide assent among the juristic community.[28] Still, Shāfi'ī jurists continued to argue against its detractors. Al-Shīrāzī identified two historical groups of opponents to *qiyās*. The first were those who denied the rational plausibility of *qiyās* as a legal proof. They decried *qiyās* by invoking its incompatibility with the rational apprehension of God's divine nature. Among this camp were some of the Baghdad Mu'tazila.[29] The Baghdad Mu'tazila argued that God was compelled to command laws that ensured humans' individual and social benefit. They worried that the subjective dimension at play in finding similarities between cases would inevitably lead to injunctions at odds with human benefit. The Shāfi'ī response reflected a trust in humans' ability to judiciously analogize differing cases. Al-Shīrāzī noted that human benefit was not in jeopardy because the same benefit discernible in the first case would be extended to the second.[30] We might better grasp al-Shīrāzī's argument if we think of the classic example of *qiyās*, namely the analogy of *khamr* (wine) to *nabīdh* (an alcoholic beverage made of dates, barley, honey, or spelt). Whilst the Qur'an affirms the prohibition of wine, it leaves unmentioned other alcoholic beverages. A pure textualist would therefore be compelled to accept *nabīdh* as a lawful beverage. Shafi'īs, however, extended the ruling of wine to *nabīdh* by arguing that the true legal cause prohibiting wine-drinking was intoxication (literally, euphoric intensity, "*shidda muṭriba*"). The analogy here guaranteed human benefit by preserving clear-headedness of one's rational faculties.

Al-Shīrāzī posited another argument of this camp associated with the eighth century Baghdad thinker al-Naẓẓām which revealed much about al-Shīrāzī's own thinking about legitimate *qiyās* use. Al-Naẓẓām cast doubt on the whole enterprise of comparing cases by pointing out examples of counterintuitive rulings in the existing Islamic legal system. He contended that the jurists often accepted different rulings for similar cases and the same ruling for widely divergent cases. For instance, Muslim law prohibited a woman from revealing herself with the exception of her face and hands. The same ruling for both the face and the hands appeared odd to al-Naẓẓām who pointed out that the face was incomparably more beautiful than hands.[31] Another example was the obligation of a menstruating woman to make up her fasts but not her prayers. Al-Naẓẓām saw the two cases as analogous because it was menstruation that hindered their ritual performance. And yet, the rulings applicable to one case diverged from those applicable to the other. The Shāfi'īs had

---

[27] El Shamsy has shown the prayer direction to be an enduring metaphor for *ijtihād* within Shāfi'ī juristic thought (2008). See also Soufi (2017).

[28] For instance, al-Jaṣṣāṣ (2000), al-Bāqillānī (2012), Qāḍī Abū Ya'lā (1990), al-Juwaynī (1997).

[29] Al-Shīrāzī also mentions some Shi'ī groups, al-Shīrāzī (1988, p. 760) and (1980, p. 419).

[30] Al-Shīrāzī (1988, pp. 762–763).

[31] Al-Shīrāzī (1988, p. 767).

developed rebuttals to al-Naẓẓām's objections, just as they had done to the case of the first objection. Al-Shīrāzī believed that all legal distinctions were explainable. The face and the hands were exceptions to female modesty out of practical necessity: their exposure helped women in their daily interactions. Likewise, obliging women to make up prayers missed during menstruation imposed an undue burden upon them because it is difficult to keep track of an accruing number of missed prayers. In contrast, counting missed days of fasting during the month of Ramadan was a more manageable task.[32] A staple of Al-Shīrāzī's thought was that any analogical argumentation needed to countenance the potential lack of parity between cases.

The second camp of *qiyās*-deniers was represented by the Ẓāhirī legal school.[33] In contrast to the first camp, the Ẓāhirīs saw no rational reason that could prevent God from imposing *qiyās* as a valid proof in the Islamic legal system. Nonetheless, the Ẓāhirīs insisted that God, through the Qur'an, had explicitly condemned the use of *qiyās* in juristic thought. Their evidences were copious. God had insisted in his holy book "Do not follow blindly what you do not know to be true" [Quran 17: 36] and "assumptions can be of no value at all against the Truth [Quran 10: 36]."[34] Another verse warned not to "say things about God that you do not really know." [Quran 2: 169]. The Ẓāhirīs claimed that all these verses imposed upon Muslims the duty to rely upon proofs guaranteeing them the highest level of epistemological certainty. Ẓāhirīs argued that such epistemological certainty could not be guaranteed by *qiyās*. Inference by parallel reasoning was fundamentally guess-work, and jurists across the Muslim schools agreed that it could only produce a presumptive belief on the ruling in question. Still another verse stated, "We have not omitted anything from the book" [Quran 6:38], giving the impression that only direct textual sources were valid proofs of legal derivation.

The Ẓāhirī objection was a harder one for the Shāfi'īs to reject because their school agreed on the presumptive nature of *qiyās*.[35] They nonetheless found a clever rebuttal by stating that scripture itself allowed them to accept epistemologically uncertain legal proofs. One evidence was the *ḥadīth* of Mu'ādh ibn Jabal.[36] The *ḥadīth* sees the Prophet questioning Mu'ādh before sending him as his emissary to rule over newly conquered Yemeni lands. Mu'ādh asserts that he will base his decision-making upon the Qur'an and the Prophetic example. When asked what he will do if he cannot find the answer in these sources, Mu'ādh asserts that he will "strive to find the answer using my rational opinion" (*ajtahid ra'yī*) and receives Prophetic blessings and prayers for his commendable answer.[37] This argument had its limitations, however, since the report itself was part of that category of *ḥadīth*

[32]Al-Shīrāzī (p. 768).

[33]For more on the Ẓāhirīs, see Osman (2014).

[34]Al-Shīrāzī (p. 779). The translation of Qur'anic verses is taken from Abdel Haleem (Oxford: Oxford World Classics).

[35]See e.g., (1997, p. 8).

[36]Al-Shīrāzī (1988, p.869) and (1980, p. 425).

[37]Al-Shīrāzī (1988, p.869).

whose chain of transmission was epistemologically uncertain. Moreover, the Ẓāhirīs invoked a variant narration where Mu'ādh and the Prophet affirm they will correspond with each other through letter writing to ensure Mu'ādh's correct judgement. Another Shāfi'ī argument against the Ẓāhirīs invoked the consensual practice of Muḥammad's companions. Invoking the agreement or consensus of Muḥammad's companions allowed the Shāfi'īs to stand on more solid ground, as consensus was widely considered within the juristic community to produce epistemological certainty. In turn, al-Shīrāzī listed copious reports of Muḥammad's companions engaging in analogical reasoning to support the Shāfi'ī claim. This normative precedent was a weighty argument for Shāfi'īs against their Ẓāhirī detractors.

By Al-Shīrāzī's time, the Shāfi'īs, alongside jurists of the Ḥanafī, Ḥanbalī, and Mālikī schools, had all but won the debate in favour of *qiyās*.[38] The great Mu'tazila legal scholars of the time accepted analogy as rationally defensible.[39] As for the Ẓāhirīs, they had receded from the Baghdad landscape, and Ibn Hazm's emergence in the Western lands of the Muslim world would mark the school's last notable contributor to Muslim legal history. Practically speaking, the Eastern Muslim juristic world depended upon *qiyās* argumentation as a staple tool of their legal practice. Wael Hallaq has contended that the Ẓāhirīs died out specifically because of their refusal to embrace analogical reasoning.[40] Certainly, as we shall see, it is difficult to imagine a jurist participating in the thriving eleventh century culture of debate in the Muslim East who rejected rather than heavily drew on *qiyās*.

1.3 The Evolution of *Qiyās* Argumentation: Al-Shīrāzī as Inheritor to the Surayjī-Shāfi'ī Line of Legal Theory

The progression of *qiyās* was first and foremost "forged", as Young would say, through practical legal debates.[41] It was through the testing out of arguments on contentious legal topics of substantive law that jurists developed an understanding and appreciation of the potential uses of *qiyās* to their legal system.[42] The practical deployment of *qiyās* in legal cases eventually gave rise to theoretical debates about *qiyās*. In particular, jurists started to ask themselves "What is *qiyās* exactly?" "Are there different types of *qiyās*? And which ones are valid?" Two bodies of theoretical literature delved into these questions in great detail; both emerged around the same time in the tenth century. The first were *jadal* (dialectic) books which were produced with the intent of refining the jurists' argumentative strategies in their disputations

[38] Al-Bājī (2004), Al-Jaṣṣāṣ (2000), Ibn al-Farrā' (1990).

[39] E.g. Al-Baṣrī (1995, p. 2:215).

[40] Hallaq (1997, p. 127).

[41] Young (2017, pp. 491–492).

[42] As al-Shīrāzī would explain, a jurist learnt the craft of legal argumentation through his exposure to legal debates (1988, 161–162).

(*munāẓara*).[43] The second were books of *uṣūl al-fiqh* (legal theory) which enumerated and explicated the valid categories of proofs in Islamic law.[44] Most jurists considered *qiyās* to be one of those categories and dedicated a substantial section of their theoretical books to its attention. Texts of *uṣūl al-fiqh* resembled texts of *jadal* to a great extent, but tended to offer a more detailed explication of each legal proof and the arguments justifying its inclusion within the legal system. *Jadal* manuals had a particularly practical orientation, as is evident in their characteristically pithy definition of a proof-type, followed by illustrative examples of its use and possible rebuttals for a disputation. Five of Al-Shīrāzī's texts of *jadal* and *uṣūl al-fiqh* are extant and provide us a window into the way he understood *qiyās* arguments and differed from his juristic colleagues.

Young's study and the logical analysis developed by Rahman and Iqbal are invaluable to our historical understanding of *qiyās* precisely because they shed light on the unique aspects of Al-Shīrāzī's theorizations traceable to his pedagogical lineage. Al-Shīrāzī was a representative of the *jadal* and *uṣūl al-fiqh* produced among the Baghdad Shāfi'īs.[45] This pedagogical line harkened back to Ibn Surayj and his learning circle. Ibn Surayj, his disciples, and the later leading Baghdad Shāfi'īs like Abū Bakr ibn al-Daqqāq are referenced copiously throughout Al-Shīrāzī's legal theory texts.[46] A deep sense of indebtedness and belonging to this scholarly cohort is evident in al-Shīrāzī's continual reference to them as "our colleagues" (*aṣḥābunā*).[47]

The Surayjī line of legal theory did not rule supreme among all eleventh century Shāfi'īs. In particular, the Shāfi'īs of the North-Eastern Persian lands of Khurāsān had developed *uṣūl al-fiqh* texts that showed greater influence and allegiance to the theorizations of the theologian Abū al-Ḥasan al-Ash'arī and his disciples than to Ibn Surayj's party.[48] In particular, they copiously referenced the *uṣūl al-fiqh* texts of the Ash'arī theologian Abū Bakr al-Bāqillānī. Al-Bāqillānī's *Al-Taqrīb wa'l-Irshād* was a detailed exposition of legal theory from Ash'arī epistemological and theological positions.[49] Two Baghdad Shāfi'īs belonging to the Ash'arī school, Ibn Fūrak and Abū Isḥāq al-Isfarāyinī, developed their own hybrid legal theory positions that incorporated some of al-Baqillānī's positions alongside those of Ibn Surayj and the

[43]Al-Subkī attributes to Ibn Surayj the honour of having been the first to teach the Shāfi'īs the "way of [doing] *jadal*", Al-Subkī, (1964, p. 22); Al-Shīrāzī tells us his student al-Qaffāl al-Shāshī was the first to write a book of "good *jadal*" (*al-jadal al-ḥasan*) (1970, p. 112).

[44]Muslims have historically seen al-Shāfi'ī as the founder of the Islamic legal tradition, but contemporary historians have increasingly seen his seminal text *Al-Risāla* as belonging to a different genre than later mature *uṣūl al-fiqh* texts (Hallaq 1993, 1997; Lowry 2007; Stewart 2016). For more on the subject, see Soufi (2018).

[45]Another representative text, albeit of the tenth rather than the eleventh century, is Ibn al-Qaṣṣ's *al-Talkhīs* (1999).

[46]E.g. al-Shīrāzī (1995, p. 44).

[47]Al-Shīrāzī (1988, p. 813).

[48]Some of al-Ash'arī's *uṣūl al-fiqh* positions are relayed by Ibn Fūrak's *Mujarrad Maqalāt* (1987).

[49]Al-Juwaynī (2003) and al-Bāqillānī (2012).

Shāfi'īs. Both Ibn Fūrak and al-Isfarāyinī settled down and taught in the Khurāsān region. Al-Shīrāzī himself would state that the people of the Khurāsānian capital of Nishapur took their *uṣūl al-fiqh* from al-Isfarāyinī.[50] The result was the type of eleventh century *uṣūl al-fiqh* text that Abū al-Ma'ālī al-Juwaynī and his student Abū Ḥāmid al-Ghazālī produced in their respective *Al-Burhān* and *Al-Mustaṣfā*.[51]

Al-Shīrāzī's *uṣūl al-fiqh* texts reflect modest influences from Ash'arī thought. More precisely, al-Shīrāzī adopts some of the epistemological positions that al-Bāqillānī had posited. This influence is traceable to his training under al-Ṭabarī. Al-Ṭabarī had studied under Abū Isḥāq al-Isfarāyinī in Isfarāyīn before making his way to Baghdad.[52] Al-Shīrāzī sometimes references al-Ṭabarī as an authoritative source in relaying Ash'arī thought. Nonetheless, as George Makdisi and Eric Chaumont have argued, the Baghdad Shāfi'īs of al-Shīrāzī's time overwhelmingly opposed the theoretical positions of the Ash'arī camp of *uṣūl al-fiqh*.[53] Al-Shīrāzī's *qiyās* theorizations therefore provide us with a glimpse into the Surayjī line of legal theory in the early second half of the fifth/eleventh century.

The Surayjī line theorized *qiyās* based on al-Shāfi'ī's initial treatment of the subject. However, al-Shāfi'ī's followers were not always in agreement over the correctness of their school master's theoretical views on *qiyās*'s conceptual underpinnings and relationship to other legal notions. For instance, many disagreed with al-Shāfi'ī's view that *qiyās* and *ijtihād* were synonymous terms.[54] Al-Shīrāzī himself rejected this view because it ignored the many other instances of legal interpretation that the jurist must effectuate, including, for instance, textual hermeneutics.[55] The later Shāfi'īs therefore elaborated upon and slightly modified their school master's *qiyās* theory. They developed categories of *qiyās* based on al-Shāfi'ī's initial division between *qiyās al-ma'nā* or *'illa* (*qiyās* by cause) and *qiyās al-shabah* (*qiyās* by resemblance).[56] Al-Shāfi'ī considered *qiyās al-'illa* to depend upon the juristic identification of an underlying cause or reason for a case's ruling. The analogy mentioned above, comparing *khamr* to *nabīdh*, is a concrete example of this type of *qiyās*. As al-Ghazālī notes, this type of *qiyās* became uncontroversial and widely accepted among later jurists (with the exception of those who denied *qiyās* any

[50]He adds that he also taught them theology (*al-kalām*), al-Shīrāzī (1970, pp. 126–127).

[51]Al-Ghazālī (1993).

[52]Al-Shīrāzī (1970, p. 126)

[53]Chaumont (1991), Makdisi (1984a, pp. 26–27)

[54]Al-Shāfi'ī (2005, p. 477).

[55]Al-Shīrāzī (1988, p.755). Although al-Shīrāzī clearly departs from al-Shāfi'ī at times, he never explicitly says that he is rejecting his school master. Instead, he tends to present his departures as interpretations, see the *Sharḥ* (1988, p. 814). In fact he ascribes a ruling by mere resemblance *mujarrad al-shabah* to the Ḥanafī jurists within the *Tabṣira* rather than his Shāfi'ī colleagues, (1980 pp. 458–459).

[56]Al-Shāfi'ī (2005, p. 479). We might also add the *a fortiori* argument among the list of types of *qiyās* al-Shāfi'ī recognized, see p. 513; see also Lowry's discussion (2007, p.158) and al-Ghazālī (1970, p. 334). Al-Shīrāzī rejected the *a fortiori* as a type of *qiyās*, seeing it instead as a linguistic argument (1988, p. 428).

validity such as the Ẓāhirīs).[57] Where jurists differed on this type of *qiyās* was in relation to a relatively small matter, namely, the manner in which the *'illa* was to be identified. Al-Shīrāzī lists a lengthy number of means of ascertaining the *'illa* and affirms that some yield greater probability than others. In contrast, *qiyās al-shabah* was subject to greater discrepancy and division among later Shāfi'īs. Al-Shāfi'ī defined the *qiyās al-shabah* as an analogy established on the basis of similarity between two cases. For instance, a jurist might see a resemblance between a slave and a freeman in that both were subject to legal commandments and to divine punishment or reward. The jurist in this case might therefore extend the rulings of a freeman to those of a slave.[58] Al-Shāfi'ī believed that such a *qiyās* was more amenable to juristic disagreements. Another jurist might, for instance, analogize the slave to an animal since both were property forms. Some Shāfi'īs considered *qiyās al-shabah* unfounded because it failed to establish that an occasioning cause existed linking the two cases together. Al-Shīrāzī had learnt from his master, al-Ṭabarī, that this form of *qiyās* was highly suspect.[59] Following al-Ṭabarī, he believed that *qiyās* was only valid if there existed a common occasioning cause between the cases.

In the place of *qiyās al-shabah*, al-Shīrāzī developed an alternate category of *qiyās* called *qiyās al-dalāla* (*qiyās* by indication).[60] *Qiyās al-dalāla* referred to all cases of inference by parallel reasoning made without explicitly referencing the occasioning cause. *Qiyās al-shabah al-mujarrad* (*qiyās* by mere resemblance) was only one form of *qiyās al-dalāla*.[61] Al-Shīrāzī's rejection of *qiyās al-shabah al-mujarrad* was the product of his doubt about the relevance of the resemblance in producing a shared ruling. Nearly everything resembles something in some way, so why should this particular resemblance matter? Al-Shīrāzī did believe that valid forms of *qiyās al-dalāla* existed.[62] These valid forms ascertained the existence of an occasioning cause without making it explicit. Thus, for instance, the smell of alcohol was not the reason for a *nabīdh*'s prohibition but it did allow a jurist to infer the

[57]Al-Ghazālī (1970, p. 334).

[58]Lowry (2007, p. 334).

[59]Al-Shīrāzī (1988, p. 813). For English and French language sources on al-Shīrāzī's *qiyās*, refer to Young (2017), especially section 4.1, and to Chaumont's translation and detailed commentary of al-Shīrāzī's *Kitāb al-Luma'*(1999).

[60]In fact, al-Juwaynī saw the *qiyās al-dalāla* as a form of *qiyās al-shabah* (1997, p. 2: 39). It is difficult to determine whether al-Shīrāzī was the first to posit the concept of *al-qiyās al-dalāla*. It could certainly have been other Baghdad contemporaries such as his teacher al-Ṭabarī, who, like al-Shīrāzī, rejected *qiyās al-shabah al-mujarrad,* or Abū Ḥāmid al-Isfarāyinī, who is known to have had a wide influence among Shāfi'ī Baghdad juristic thought. However, we can say with some certainty that the concept did not exist, or at least, it did not have wide currency, before al-Shīrāzī's generation and that later Shāfi'īs would single out al-Shīrāzī when introducing the concept, see al-Zarkashī (1992, p. 5:40).

[61]Al-Shīrāzī (1988, p. 812). In the *Ma'ūna fī al-Jadal*, al-Shīrāzī explains this *qiyās* by stating that the jurist proceeds by "inferring [his ruling] based on some common point of resemblance" between cases (*an yastadill bi-ḍarb min al-shabah*) (1987, p. 38).

[62]Al-Shīrāzī (1988, pp. 809–10), where he says that there are three types of *qiyās al-dalāla*. See also al-Shīrāzī (1987, pp. 37–38).

existence of the occasioning cause for its prohibition, namely intoxication. As Rahman and Iqbal explain, al-Shīrāzī spent considerable time explaining the *qiyās al-dalāla* types he considered founded. The transformation of *qiyās al-shabah* into *qiyās al-dalāla* is an essential part of the historical evolution of Baghdad Shāfi'ī thought and al-Juwaynī makes clear that al-Shīrāzī was not the only Baghdad jurist to promote it. Nonetheless, centuries later, the great encyclopaedist of Shāfi'ī *uṣūl al-fiqh*, Badr al-Dīn al-Zarkashī (d.1392) explicitly named and singled out al-Shīrāzī when speaking of proponents of *qiyās al-dalāla*.[63] Al-Zarkashī evidently saw in al-Shīrāzī's *qiyās al-dalāla* an important milestone in the evolution of *qiyās* theory.[64]

1.4 *Qiyās* in the Eleventh Century Debate Gathering

I will finish by emphasizing the importance of *qiyās* for al-Shīrāzī and his eleventh century colleagues' legal thought. Al-Shāfi'ī had considered *qiyās* a necessary method to determine the law when lacking scriptural sources. He considered *qiyās* a methodological compromise between the excessive rationalism of the Ḥanafī jurists and the extreme anti-rationalistic bent of the *ahl al-ḥadīth*.[65] But its use had dramatically changed by the eleventh century. *Qiyās* was no longer a proof of last resort; rather, it had become the foremost tool in defending legal doctrine, even when textual evidences were available. Textual evidences were useful in justifying the unmediated scriptural support for a position, but they always ran up against the problem of divergent interpretations. What a Shāfi'ī interpreted one way, a Ḥanafī might interpret otherwise. The legal schools could rely upon very few texts whose context and wording were sufficiently clear for them all to agree upon its meaning. Thus for instance, if a Shāfi'ī argued that a male bridal guardian was necessary on the basis of the Prophetic *ḥadīth* that states "there is no marriage without a guardian", a Ḥanafī jurist might easily respond that this *ḥadīth* refers only to cases of minors who are too young for independent decision-making.[66] The strength of *qiyās* was its ability to find common ground with an opposing school. If a Shāfi'ī analogized from a base case supported by Ḥanafī doctrine, the Ḥanafī was now placed in the defensive position of explaining why the analogy was invalid. For instance, Shāfi'īs diverged from Ḥanafīs on a father's right to marry his virgin daughter without her consent. The Shāfi'īs often analogized the adult virgin to the virgin of minority age

---

[63] Al-Zarkashī (1992, p. 5:40). Post-Shīrāzī scholars who accepted the *qiyās al-dalāla* were found in the Mālikī and Ḥanbalī schools (e.g. Ibn Qudāma, 2002, p. 2:246).

[64] Part of what supports the possibility that al-Shīrāzī was the first to posit the term, or at least give it great prominence, is its complete absence from al-Shīrāzī's earlier work of *uṣūl al-fiqh*, *Al-Tabṣira* (1980).

[65] Hallaq (1997), Schacht (1959).

[66] Al-Shīrāzī (1992, p. 119).

since the Ḥanafīs accepted that her father represent her in her marriage contract without receiving her explicit consent.[67] The analogy forced the Ḥanafīs to explain why they made a distinction between a minor and an adult woman.

Qiyās played another essential role. It permitted jurists to probe the foundations of their legal system. By analogizing between cases, jurists were better able to see the intended legislative object of scripture. By analogizing *nabīdh* to *khamr*, they could see that wine-drinking was only a surface prohibition and that the true object of legislation was the effects upon mental clarity. This process was particularly important in smoothing out inconsistencies within the Islamic legal system. Eleventh century jurists could see whether or not their school predecessors had successfully pushed their legal reasoning to their logical conclusions. For instance, al-Shāfiʿī had expressed different opinions as to whether a person who knew with certainty that he had prayed in the wrong direction after trying his best to face Mecca needed to repeat his prayer. Some of his followers used the case of mistakenly fasting on the wrong day to argue that prayer repetition was unnecessary.[68] This kind of cross-referencing between cases served to ensure logical consistency in their body of law.

Qiyās was invoked frequently by al-Shīrāzī and his Shāfiʿī colleagues particularly in the context of debate. Debate gatherings were a solemn and sacred practice among the eleventh century juristic communities of Iraq and Persia. Disputations were held in homes, mosques, colleges, and rulers' courts.[69] They sometimes took place before a large literate public on special occasions like professorial appointments or periods of post-funerary mourning. But they were also more mundane affairs that took place relatively privately among friends.[70] Each school had the collective responsibility to defend its doctrinal commitments against potential detractors. Doctrinal legitimacy depended upon continuing to prove its viability in the face of critique. Al-Shīrāzī was known among his peers as an incomparable debating virtuoso.[71] The dialogical exchange of the debate gathering is thus the proper context to think about eleventh century *qiyās*. Al-Shīrāzī never thought of *qiyās* as a rational operation that could be employed divorced from critical exchange.

Al-Shīrāzī's substantive legal texts show his widespread reliance upon *qiyās al-ʿilla* and *qiyās al-dalāla*. The *qiyās al-ʿilla* is used far more greatly. This is unsurprising because *qiyās al-ʿilla* succeeded in going to the heart of a legal matter. It answered the question of what the object of the law really was. In contrast, *qiyās al-dalāla* left the law unarticulated. The jurist knew that the ruling of another case applied, but did not know what quality they had in common that made it applicable. It was nonetheless an essential part of al-Shīrāzī's thinking. Underlying his use of *qiyās al-dalāla* is al-Shīrāzī's insistence that patterns are discernible within Islamic

[67]Al-Marghīnānī (2000, pp. 476–477).

[68]Al-Marghīnānī (2000, p. 2:81).

[69]Makdisi (1984b, p. 134).

[70]Al-Subkī (1964, pp. 3:23–24) where al-Subkī presents Ibn Surayj and Ibn Dāwud al-Ẓāhirī debating in the home of a judge.

[71]He was called "a lion (*ghaḍanfar*)" in debate, al-Subkī (1964, p. 4:222).

law. Prayer ritual, initiation of divorce, and marriage contracts are examples of cases in which al-Shīrāzī uses existing patterns to assume that a ruling can be extended without explicitly identifying the occasioning cause of the case.[72]

1.5 Concluding Remarks

Al-Shīrāzī's *qiyās*-theory was largely the product of its practical deployment within legal reasoning. As al-Shīrāzī climbed the ladder of the Shāfiʿī school, he took a keen interest in the Shāfiʿī/Ḥanafī rivalry that marked eleventh century Baghdad. Al-Shīrāzī therefore sought to refine his argumentative skills while often representing the Shāfiʿī school in large debate gatherings before the juristic community. Like other jurists of the time, al-Shīrāzī's own theorizations of *qiyās* found their way into his debate practice.[73] The foremost tools within al-Shīrāzī's legal arsenal were *qiyās al-ʿilla* and *qiyās al-dalāla*, and he deployed them in attempting to outdo his debate opponents. Both *qiyās*-forms served to reinforce school doctrine lacking support from unambiguous scriptural sources. They also served to ensure consistency across legal cases by identifying the occasioning causes serving as the legal basis of divergent cases.

In texts of *uṣūl al-fiqh* and *jadal*, al-Shīrāzī was able to produce a sober and thorough analysis of *qiyās* as one among only a few categories of valid legal proofs. He dealt with the divergent definitions of *qiyās,* engaged with and argued against its historical detractors, and identified the valid types of *qiyās* arguments. Through example, texts of *jadal* shed light on the diverse ways al-Shīrāzī and his colleagues deployed *qiyās* and the types of debate challenges they faced from their opponents.

The historical and intellectual value of the following pages' in-depth study of al-Shīrāzī's mode of *qiyās* cannot be overestimated. Indebted to his pedagogical lineage, al-Shirazi's *qiyās* was passed on from his master al-Ṭabarī – it was he who had taught him the *uṣūl al-fiqh* and *jadal* positions developed by the Baghdad Shāfiʿīs since Ibn Surayj. This genealogical line of scholarship has been greatly overshadowed by the copious scholarly attention to other branches of *uṣūl al-fiqh.*[74] The examination of al-Shīrāzī's *qiyās* therefore opens up a largely unexplored lens onto the early development of *qiyās* theory among Baghdad Shāfiʿīs. It permits us to better comprehend the ways Baghdad Shāfiʿīs both appropriated but also slightly modified the *qiyās* theory they had inherited from al-Shāfiʿī. Of course, al-Shīrāzī was not a mere representative of this Surayjī line; he was also one of its most

[72]See al-Shīrāzī (1988, pp. 806–814).

[73]Other jurists deployed their own theorizations of *qiyās* in the debate arena. See for instance, al-Juwaynī's differing manner of identifying the *ʿilla* of a *qiyās* in his debate with al-Shīrāzī, al-Subkī (1964, pp. 5:214–218).

[74]Bernard Weiss (2010) provides a brilliant overview of one of the most important texts of the Shāfiʿī-Ashʿarī line of *uṣūl al-fiqh*; and Zysow (2013) is likewise an essential reference for anyone interested in the Ḥanafī line of *uṣūl al-fiqh.*

illustrious theorists. While his thought might be greatly indebted to his teachers, he was also an original thinker who diverged from some of his Baghdad colleagues. As Rumee Ahmed has taught us, we must look closely to the leading jurists of the Muslim tradition to see the unique ways that they engage with their complex tradition.[75] Rahman and Iqbal's study issues a clarion call for us to study legal argumentation within its historical dialogical context and promises to push the field of classical Islamic law in a new direction. By now, we see how *qiyās* ought not to be understood as the product of a singular mind working in an ivory tower, but as the product of an ongoing dialogue between jurists.

References

Ahmed, R. (2012). *Narratives of Islamic legal theory*. Oxford: Oxford University Press.

Al-Bājī, Abū al-Walīd. (2004). *Al-Minhāj fī tartīb al-ḥijāj*. Riyadh: Maktabat al-Rushd.

Al-Bāqillānī, Abū Bakr. (2012). *Al-Taqrīb wa'l-irshād fī uṣūl al-fiqh*. Beirut: Dār al-Kutub al-'Ilmiyya.

Al-Baṣrī, Abū al-Husayn. (1995). *Al-Mu'tamad fī uṣūl al-fiqh*. Beirut: *Dār al-Kutub al-'Ilmiyya.*

Al-Ghazālī, Abū Ḥāmid. (1970). *Al-Mankhūl min ta'līqāt al-uṣūl*. ('Abd al-Malik Ibn 'Abd Allāh, Ed.). Damascus.

Al-Ghazālī, Abū Ḥāmid. (1993). *Al-Mustaṣfā fī 'ilm al-uṣūl*. (Ḥamzah ibn Zuhayr Ḥāfiẓ, Ed.). Medina: Ḥamzah ibn Zuhayr Ḥāfiẓ.

Al-Jaṣṣāṣ, Abū Bakr. (2000). *Uṣūl al-Jaṣṣāṣ al-musammā al-fuṣūl fī al-uṣūl*. Beirut: Manshūrāt Muḥammad 'Alī Bayḍūn.

Al-Juwaynī, 'Abd al-Malik ibn 'Abd Allāh. (1997). *Al-Burhān fī uṣūl al-fiqh*. (Ṣalāh ibn Muḥammad ibn 'Awīḍa, Ed.). Beirut: Dār al-Kutub al-'Ilmiyya.

Al-Juwaynī, 'Abd al-Malik ibn 'Abd Allāh. (2003). *Al-Talkhīs fī uṣūl al-fiqh*. (Muḥammad Ḥasan Ismā'īl Shāfi'ī, Ed.). Beirut: Dār al-Kutub al-'Ilmīyya.

Al-Juwaynī, 'Abd al-Malik ibn 'Abd Allāh. (2007). *Nihāyat al-maṭlab fī dirāyat al-madhhab*. Jeddah: Dār al-Minhāj.

Al-Marghīnānī, 'Alī ibn Abī Bakr. (2000). *Al-Hidāya : Sharḥ bidāyat al-mubtadī*. Cairo: Dār al-Salām lil-Ṭiba'a wa'l-Nashr.

Al-Shīrāzī, Abū Isḥāq. (1970). *Ṭabaqāt al-fuqahā*. Beirut: Dār al-Rā'id al-'Arabī.

Al-Shīrāzī, Abū Isḥāq. (1980). *Al-Tabṣira fī usūl al-fiqh*. (Muḥammad Ḥasan Hītū, Ed.). Damascus: Dār al-Fikr.

Al-Shīrāzī, Abū Isḥāq. (1987). *Al-Ma'ūna fī al-jadal*. ('Alī ibn 'Abd al-'Azīz al-'Umayrīnī, Ed.). Kuwait City: Manshūrāt Markaz al-Makhṭūṭāt wa-al-Turāth, 1987.

Al-Shīrāzī, Abū Isḥāq. (1988). *Sharḥ al-luma' fī uṣūl al-fiqh*. ('Abd al-Majīd Turkī, Ed.). Beirut: Dār al-Gharb al-Islāmī.

Al-Shīrāzī, Abū Isḥāq. (1992). *Al-Muhadhdhab fī fiqh al-Imām al-Shāfi'ī*. (Muḥammad al-Zuhaylī, Ed.). Damascus: Dār al-Qalam.

Al-Shīrāzī, Abū Isḥāq. (1995). *Al-Luma' fī uṣūl al-fiqh*. Beirut: Dār Ibn Kathīr.

Al-Shīrāzī, Abū Isḥāq (1999) *Kitāb al-luma' fī uṣūl al-fiqh; Le livre des rais illuminant les fondements de la compréhension de la loi: traité de théorie légale musulmane*. (E. Chaumont Trans. & Ed.). Berkeley: Robbin.

Al-Subkī, Tāj al-Dīn. (1964). *Ṭabaqāt al-shāfi'iyya al-kubrā*. (Maḥmūd Muḥammad Ṭanāḥī & 'Abd al-Fattāḥ Muḥammad al-Ḥulū eds.). Cairo: 'Isā al-Babīb al-Halabī.

[75] Ahmed (2012).

Al-Zarkashī, Badr al-Dīn (1992). *Al-Baḥr al-muḥīt fī uṣūl al-fiqh.* ('Abd al-Qādir Al- 'Ānī, Ed.). Kuwait: Wizārat al-Awqāf wa'l-Shu'ūn al-Islāmiyya.

Chaumont, E. (1991). Encore au sujet de l'Ashʿarisme d'Abū Isḥāq al-Shīrāzī. *Studia Islamica*, (74), 167–177.

El Shamsy, A. (2007). The first Shāfi'ī: The traditionalist legal thought of Abū Ya'qūb al-Buwaytī (d. 231/846). *Islamic Law and Society, 14*(3), 301–341.

Ephrat, D. (2000). *A learned society in a period of transition : The Sunni 'Ulama' of Eleventh-Century Baghdad.* Albany: State University of New York Press.

Hallaq, W. B. (1993). Was al-Shāfi'ī the master architect of Islamic jurisprudence? *International Journal of Middle East Studies, 25*(4), 587–605.

Hallaq, W. B. (1997). *A history of Islamic legal theories : An introduction to Sunnī Uṣūl al-Fiqh.* New York: Cambridge University Press.

Hītū, Muḥammad Ḥasan. (1980). *Al-Imām al-Shīrāzī : Ḥayātuhu wa-arā'uhu al-uṣūliyya.* Damascus: Dār al-Fikr.

Ibn al-Farrā', Abū Ya'lā. (1990). *Al-'Udda fī uṣūl al-fiqh.* Riyadh: Sayr al-Mubārakī.

Ibn al-Jawzī, Abū al-Faraj. (1992). *Al-Muntaẓam fī tārīkh al-mulūk wa'l-umam.* (Muḥammad 'Abd al-Qādir 'Aṭā & Muṣṭafā 'Abd al-Qādir 'Aṭā, eds.). Beirut: Dār al-Kutub al-'Ilmiyya.

Ibn al-Ṣalāḥ, al-Nawawī, and al-Mizzī. (1992). *Ṭabaqāt al-fuqahā' al-shāfi'iyya.* (Muḥyī al-Dīn 'Alī Najīb, Ed.). Beirut: Dār al-Bashā'ir al-Islāmiyya.

Ibn al-Qāṣṣ. (1999). *Al-Talkhīṣ.* ('Ādil Aḥmad 'Abd al-Mawjūd & 'Alī Muḥammad Mu'awwaḍ, eds.). Mecca: Maktabat Nizār Muṣṭafā al-Bāz.

Ibn Fūrak, Abū Bakr. (1987). *Mujarrad maqālāt al-Shaykh Abī al-Ḥasan al-Ash'arī : Min imlā' al-Shaykh al-Imām Abī Bakr Muḥammad ibn al-Ḥasan ibn Fūrak (t. 406/1015).* Beirut: Al-Tawzī' al-Maktaba al-Sharqiyya.

Ibn Kathīr, Ismaīl ibn 'Umar. (2002). *Ṭabaqāt al-shāfi'iyya.* ('Abd al-Ḥafīz Manṣūr, Ed.). Beirut: Dār al-Madār al-Islāmī.

Ibn Khallikān, Abū al-'Abbās. (1978). *Wafayāt al-a'yān.* (Iḥsān 'Abbās, Ed.). Beirut: Dār al-Ṣādir.

Ibn Qāḍī Shuhba. (1987). *Ṭabaqāt al-shāfi'iyya.* ('Abd al-'Alīm Khān & 'Abdallāh Anīs al-Ṭabbā', eds.). Beirut: 'Ālam al-Kutub.

Ibn Qudāma, Muwaffaq al-Dīn. (2002). *Rawḍāt al-nāẓir wa-jannat al-munāẓir.* Beirut: Mu'assasa al-Rayyān.

Lowry, J. E. (2007). *Early Islamic legal theory : The Risāla of Muḥammad ibn Idrīs al-Shāfi'ī.* Leiden; Boston: Brill.

Lucas, S. (2010). Principles of traditionist jurisprudence reconsidered. *The Muslim World, 100*(1), 145–156.

Makdisi, G. (1984a). The juridical theology of Shāfi'ī: Origins and significance of Uṣūl al-Fiqh. *Studia Islamica*, (59), 5–47.

Makdisi, G. (1984b). *The rise of colleges: Institutions of learning in Islam and the west.* Edinburgh: Edinburgh University Press.

Messick, B. (1996). *The calligraphic state: Textual domination and history in a Muslim society.* University of California Press.

Mittermaier, A. (2010). *Dreams that matter: Egyptian landscapes of the imagination.* Berkeley: University of California Press.

Osman, A. (2014). *The Ẓāhirī Madhhab (3rd/9th–10th/16th Century): A textualist theory of Islamic law.* Leiden: Brill.

Peacock, A. C. S. (2015). *Great Seljuk Empire.* Edinburgh: Edinburgh University Press.

Schacht, J. (1959). *The origins of Muhammadan jurisprudence.* Oxford: Clarendon Press.

Soufi, Y. (2017). *Pious critique: Abū Isḥāq al-Shīrāzī and the 11th century practice of juristic disputation (Munāẓara).* Toronto: University of Toronto. (Unpublished dissertation).

Soufi, Y. (2018). The historiography of Uṣūl al-Fiqh. In A. Emon & R. Ahmed (Eds.), *The Oxford handbook of Islamic law* (pp. 249–267). Oxford: Oxford University Press.

Spectorsky, S. A. (1982). Aḥmad Ibn Ḥanbal's Fiqh. *Journal of the American Oriental Society, 102*(3), 461–465.

Stewart, D. (2016). Muḥammad B. Dā'ūd al-Ẓāhirī's manual of jurisprudence, al-Wuṣūl ilā Ma'rifat al-Uṣūl. In W. B. Hallaq (Ed.), *The formation of Islamic law* (pp. 277–315). New York and London: Routledge.

Talas, A. (1939). *L'enseignement chez les Arabes: La madrasa Niẓāmiyya et son histoire*. Paris: P. Geuthner.

Weiss, B. (2010). *The search for God's law: Islamic jurisprudence in the writings of Sayf al-Dīn al-Āmidī (revised edition)*. Salt Lake City: University of Utah Press.

Young, W. E. (2017). *The dialectical forge: Juridical disputation and the evolution of Islamic law*. Dordrecht: Springer.

Zysow, A. (2013). *The economy of certainty: An introduction to the typology of Islamic legal theory*. Atlanta: Lockwood Press.

Chapter 2
Qiyās al-ʿIlla: al-Shīrāzī's System of Correlational Inferences of the Occasioning Factor

One of the epistemological results emerging from the present study is that the different forms of *correlational inference*, known in the Islamic jurisprudence as *qiyās*, represent an innovative and sophisticated form of reasoning that not only provides new epistemological insights into legal reasoning in general but also furnishes a fine-grained pattern for *parallel reasoning* which can be deployed in a wide range of problem-solving contexts and does not seem to reduce to the standard forms of analogical argumentation studied in contemporary philosophy of science.

In the present chapter, after a general introduction that provides an overview on the general classification of *qiyās* by al-Shīrāzī, we will discuss the case of what is known as the *correlational inferences of the occasioning factor*.

2.1 Introduction[1]

Uṣūl al-fiqh (أصول الفقه), that is, Islamic Legal Theory, is deeply rooted in the notion of rational knowledge and understanding. Indeed, *uṣūl al-fiqh* constitutes the body of knowledge and methods of reasoning that Islamic jurists deploy in order to provide

[1]Herewith we would like to thank Prof. Roshdi Rashed (CNRS, SPHERE, Paris VII), chief-editor of the *Cambridge Journal of Arabic Sciences and Philosophy* who allowed us to deploy for the present part of our study important parts of the the paper S. Rahman and M. Iqbal (2018) "Unfolding Parallel Reasoning in Islamic Jurisprudence . Epistemic and Dialectical Meaning within Abū Isḥāq al-Shīrāzī's System of Correlational Inferences of the Occasioning Factor." *Cambridge Journal of Arabic Sciences and Philosophy* 28 (2018), pp. 67–132. Many thanks too to Erwan Penchèvre (Paris VII) for his excellent editorial work on the paper mentioned above. However, the present study contains some significative technical and conceptual modifications of the paper published in the ASP. Indeed, what is new in the presentation that follows is that we articulate by means of an explicit formulation the distinction between (a) the property relevant for a juridical decision, (b) the devices for testing if the purported property has the required efficiency to cause the juridical decision, and (c) the causal process that applies the property to a given case triggering

S. Rahman et al., *Inferences by Parallel Reasoning in Islamic Jurisprudence*, Logic, Argumentation & Reasoning 19, https://doi.org/10.1007/978-3-030-22382-3_2

solutions to legal problems based on the juridical understanding of the sources – led by the aim of delving into God's intended norms for human conduct. According to *uṣūl al-fiqh*, legal knowledge is achieved by rational endeavour, the intellectual effort of human being: this is what is meant when the term *ijtihād* (اجتهاد), endeavour of the intellect, is attached to *fiqh*. Let us quote the beautiful paragraph on *ijtihād* by Wael B. Hallaq in his landmark work *A History of Islamic Legal Theories*:

> *In his Mustaṣfā Ghazali depicts the science of legal theory in terms of a tree cultivated by man. The fruits of the tree represent the legal rules that constitute the purpose behind planting the tree; the stem and the branches are the textual materials that enable the tree to bear the fruits and to sustain them. But in order for the tree to be cultivated, and to bring it to bear fruits, human agency must play a role.* [...]. *We shall now turn to the "cultivator," the human agent whose creative legal reasoning is directed toward producing the fruit, the legal norm. The jurist (faqīh) or jurisconsult (muftī) who is capable of practising such legal reasoning is known as the mujtahid, he who exercises his utmost effort in extracting a rule from the subject matter of revelation while following the principles and procedures established in legal theory. The process of this reasoning is known as ijtihād, the effort itself.*[2]

One of the most remarkable features of the practice of *ijtihād* is that it presupposes that *fiqh* is dynamic in nature. Indeed, since the ultimate purpose of such a kind of rational endeavour is to achieve decisions for new circumstances or cases not already established by the juridical sources, the diverse processes conceived within Islamic jurisprudence were aimed at providing tools able to deal with the evolution of the practice of *fiqh*. This dynamic feature animates Walter Edward Young's main thesis as developed in his book *The Dialectical Forge*.[3] In fact the main claim underlying the work of Young is that the dynamic nature of *fiqh* is put into action by both the dialectical understanding and the dialectical practice of legal reasoning. The following lines of Young set out the motivations for the development of a dialectical framework such as the one we are aiming at in the present study.[4]

> *The primary title of this monograph is "The Dialectical Forge," and its individual terms provide a suitable launching point for discussing the current project as a whole. As for the first, the most common Arabic terms for "dialectic" are jadal and munāẓara, both denoting formal disputation between scholars in a given domain, with regard to a specific thesis. When one encounters the term "dialectical" in the present work, one should think foremost*

---

sowith the relevant juridical decision. Introducing the distinctions just mentioned required a formal analysis quite different to that developed in Rahman/Iqbal (2018).

[2]Hallaq (1997, p.117).

[3]Young (2017, pp. 21–32) acknowledges and discusses his debt to the work of Hallaq in many sections of the book.

[4]Also relevant are the following lines of Hallaq (1997, pp. 136–7), quoted by Young (2017, p. 25): "In one sense, dialectic constituted the final stage in the process of legal reasoning, in which two conflicting opinions on a case of law were set against each other in the course of a disciplined session of argumentation with the purpose of establishing the truthfulness of one of them. The aim of this exercise, among other things, was to reduce disagreement (*ikhtilāf*) among legists by demonstrating that one opinion was more acceptable or more valid than another. Minimizing differences of opinion on a particular legal question was of the utmost importance, the implication being that truth is one, and for each case there exists only one true solution."

> *of procedure-guided debate and the logic inherent to this species of discourse. A dialectical confrontation occurs between two scholars, in question and answer format, with the ultimate aims of either proving a thesis, or destroying it and supplanting it with another. A proponent-respondent introduces and attempts to defend a thesis; a questioner-objector seeks (destructively) to test and undermine that thesis, and (constructively) to supplant it with a counter-thesis. Through progressive rounds of question and response the questioner endeavours to gain concession to premises which invalidate the proponent's thesis, justify its dismantling, and provide the logical basis from which a counter-thesis necessarily flows.*
>
> *Ultimately, and most importantly, a truly dialectical exchange – though drawing energy from a sober spirit of competition – must nevertheless be guided by a cooperative ethic wherein truth is paramount and forever trumps the emotional motivations of disputants to "win" the debate. This truth-seeking code demands sincere avoidance of fallacies; it views with abhorrence contrariness and self-contradiction. This alone distinguishes dialectic from sophistical or eristic argument, and, in conjunction with its dialogical format, from persuasive argument and rhetoric. And to repeat: dialectic is formal – it is an ordered enterprise, with norms and rules, and with a mutually-committed aim of advancing knowledge.*[5]

According to this perspective, the practice of *ijtihād* takes the form of an interrogative enquiry where the intertwining of giving and asking for reasons features the notion of meaning that grounds legal rationality.[6] More precisely, the conception of legal reasoning developed by Islamic jurisprudence is that it is a combination of deductive moves with hermeneutic and heuristic ones deployed in an epistemic frame. Let us once more quote Hallaq:

> *Armed with the knowledge of hermeneutical principles, legal epistemology and the governing rules of consensus, the mujtahid is ready to undertake the task of inferring rules. Inferring rules presupposes expert knowledge in hermeneutics because the language of the texts requires what may be called verification; namely, establishing, to the best of one's ability, the meaning of a particular text as well as its relationship to other texts that bear upon a particular case in the law. For this relationship, as we have seen, may be one of particularization, corroboration or abrogation. Before embarking on inferential reasoning, the mujtahid must thus verify the meaning of the text he employs, and must ascertain that it was not abrogated by another text. Knowledge of the principles of consensus as well as of cases subject to the sanctioning authority of this instrument is required to ensure that the mujtahid's reasoning does not lead him to results contrary to the established consensus in his school. This knowledge is also required in order to ensure that no case that has already been sanctioned by consensus is reopened for an alternative rule.*[7]

In fact, the dissatisfaction with the efficiency of the standard post-Aristotelian notion of syllogism in jurisprudence led to an ambitious dialectical frame for argumentation by parallelisms (including exemplification, symmetry and analogy) which should offer a new unifying approach to epistemology and logic for the

---

[5]Young (2017, p. 1).

[6]See too Hallaq (1987a, b, 2004, 2009a, b). Another early study that stressed this point is Larry Miller's (1984) PhD thesis of 1984 on the development of dialectic in Islam. Hassan Tahiri (2008, pp. 183–225) discusses the crucial role of dialectical reasoning for astronomy and for the development of sciences in general. See also Tahiri (2014, 2015, 2018).

[7]Hallaq (1997, p. 82).

practice of *ijtihād*.[8] The finest outcome of this approach to legal reasoning within *fiqh* is the notion of *qiyās* (قياس), known as *correlational inference*.[9]

The aim of correlational inferences is to provide a rational ground for the application of a juridical ruling to a given case not yet considered by the original juridical sources. It proceeds by combining heuristic (and/or hermeneutic) moves with logical inferences. The simplest form follows the following pattern:

- In order to establish if a given juridical ruling applies or not to a given case, we look for a case we already know that falls under that ruling – the so-called source-case. Then we search for the property or set of properties upon which the application of the ruling to the source-case is grounded. If that grounding property (or set of them) is known, we ponder if it can also be asserted of the new case under consideration. In the case of an affirmative answer, it is inferred that the new case also falls under the juridical ruling at stake, and so the range of its application is extended.

Complications arrive when the grounds behind a given juridical ruling are not explicitly known or even not known at all. In such a case, other devices are put into action. The latter situation, as discussed in the next sections, yields a system of different forms of *qiyās* that are hierarchically organized in relation to their epistemic strength.

More generally, one interesting way to look at the contribution of the inception of the juridical notion of *qiyās* is to compare it with the emergence of European Civil Law. Indeed, European Civil Law emerged as a system of general norms or rules that were thought to generalize the repertory of cases recorded mainly by Roman-Law. The idea of *qiyās* can be seen as providing an epistemological instrument to establish those general norms behind the cases recorded by the sources and by tradition. The dynamics triggered by implementing such an instrument "forges" the general norms that structure Islamic Law.

According to our view, the dialogical conception of Per Martin-Löf's *Constructive Type Theory* provides both a natural understanding and a precise instrument to stress three of the hallmarks of this form of reasoning[10]:

(a) the interaction of heuristic and epistemological processes with logical steps,

[8]Cf. *Ibn Taymiyya against the Greek Logicians*, edited and translated by Hallaq (1993).

[9]Cf. Young (2017, p. 10). The term has quite often a broader meaning encompassing legal reasoning in general. However, Young's choice for its translation renders a narrower sense that stems from al-Shīrāzī's approach.

[10]In fact there is ongoing work on deploying the dialogical setting in order to reconstruct logical traditions in ancient philosophy (see Castelnérac/Marion (2009), Marion/Rückert (2015) and medieval logical theories (C. Dutilh Novaes (2007), Popek (2012).

(b) the dialectical dynamics underlying the meaning-explanation of the terms involved,[11]
(c) the unfolding of parallel reasoning as similarity in action.

Our study is focused on Abū Isḥāq al-Shīrāzī's classification of *qiyās* as discussed in his *Mulakhkhaṣ fī al-Jadal* (*Epitome on Dialectical Disputation*), *Maʿūna fī al-Jadal* (*Aid on Dialectical Disputation*) and *al-Lumaʿ fī Uṣūl al-Fiqh* (*Refulgence of Islamic Legal Theory*).[12] Let us point out that, though our work is grounded on confrontation with the original textual sources, we deploy the thorough studies of these texts (and others) by Hallaq and Young.[13]

Furthermore, we are not claiming (yet) that the framework we propose in the present study is either a literal description or a complete formalization of the *jadal* disputation form in which the *qiyās* is carried out. Our study provides a *dialectical meaning-explanation* of the main notion of correlational inference relevant for the development of al-Shīrāzī's system of *qiyās*.[14] In other words, what we are aiming at is to set out a kind of interactive language game that makes apparent the dialectical meaning of the main notions involved in these forms of reasoning.

Actually, since all of the steps prescribed by our dialogical framework are based on moves involved in al-Shīrāzī's dialectical conception of *qiyās al-ʿilla*, we think that our proposal can be further developed into a system for actual juridical disputation that provides a full reconstruction of *jadal* (جدل) as deployed in *uṣūl al-fiqh*.[15]

Thus, on the one hand our reconstruction might provide researchers on the Arabic tradition with some instruments for epistemological analysis, and on the other, we hope to motivate epistemologists and researchers in argumentation theory to explore the rich and thought-provoking texts produced by this tradition. Indeed, one of the main epistemological results emerging from this initial study is that the different forms of *qiyās* as developed in the context of *fiqh* represent an innovative approach that not only provides new epistemological insights into legal reasoning in general,

---

[11]The term *meaning-explanation* stems from Martin-Löf's CTT (see Sect. 4.2). It refers to a way of providing meaning to an expression by setting out rules that determine what needs to be known in order to make an assertion involving that expression.

[12]Actually, al-Shīrāzī, who was a follower of the *Shāfiʿī* school of jurisprudence, endorsed the mistrust of the *Shāfiʿī-s* in relation to what they considered *subjective features* of *istiḥsān* and *maṣlaḥa*. Indeed, although he accepted that the extension of the scope of a juridical ruling is necessary, he was convinced that extensions should result from a rational process such as the one deployed by a *qiyās*.

[13]See above, nos. 71 and 74 in Chap. 1.

[14]The notion of *dialectical meaning-explanation* is the dialogical counterpart of Martin-Löf's (inferential) *meaning-explanation* mentioned above. The dialectical meaning-explanation of an expression amounts to setting rules that establish how to challenge and defend that expression. These rules also indicate how to produce a local reason for a claim and how to analize such a reason – see Sect. 4.4 in the present part of the book.

[15]It is also worth mentioning that, to the best of our knowledge, there is no systematic study yet comparing the theory of juridical argumentation as developed within the Islamic tradition with the dialectical form of medieval disputations known as *Obligationes*. Such a study, that will fill up some flagrant gaps in the history of the development of rational argumentation, is certainly due.

but also furnishes a fine-grained pattern for *parallel reasoning*[16] that can be deployed in a wide range of problem-solving contexts where degrees of evidence and inferences by drawing parallelisms are relevant.

2.2 A Dialectical Genealogy of Abū Isḥāq al-Shīrāzī's System of *Qiyās*

In the classical studies on juridical argumentation or *jadal* by Abū al-Ḥusayn al-Baṣrī (436H/1044 CE) in his *Kitāb al-Qiyās al-Sharʿī* (*Book of Correlational Inference Consonant to God's Law*, edited 1964) and by Abū Isḥāq al-Shīrāzī in his *Mulakhkhaṣ fī al-Jadal* (*Epitome on Dialectical Disputation*), recorded, commented and worked out by Young,[17] we can find the following description of the *qiyās*:

> the aim of a *qiyās*, in its more general form, is to provide a rational ground to the ascription of some *juridical ruling* or *ḥukm* (حكم) such as (forbidden, allowed, obligatory) to a given case not yet considered by the sources acknowledged by *uṣūl al-fiqh* (for short, *juridical sources*).[18]

In fact, in this context, a *qiyās* involves bringing forward a case to which, according to the claim of the thesis, a particular *ḥukm* applies. The point is to ground this claim by relating it to an already juristically acknowledged application of such a ruling. Accordingly, the grounding is carried out in two main steps (involving two alternative developments):

1. It starts by bringing forward a case, known as *al-aṣl* or *the root-case* (الأصل), which the juridical sources have already established falls under the scope of the same juridical ruling as the one claimed to apply to the new case, called *al-farʿ* (الفرع), *the branch-case*.[19]
2. 2.1 (First alternative). It proceeds by the assumptions that the property (*waṣf*) determining the *ground* or *occasioning factor* (*ʿilla*) for the ruling of the root-case can be found,[20] and that this property also applies to the branch-case.

---

[16]We have borrowed the term "*parallel reasoning*" from Bartha (2010).

[17]Young (2017, chapter 4.3).

[18]In general the term *ḥukm* refers to norm or ruling. In the context of the *qiyās* it indicates the ruling of the *aṣl* which the proponent seeks to transfer to the *farʿ*. See Young (2017, p. 610).

[19]The Arabic terminology makes use of the botanic metaphor of, respectively, *root* and *branch* in order to express the relation between the case established by the juridical sources, *al-aṣl*, and the case under consideration, *al-farʿ*. The idea is not that the *farʿ* is a subcase of the *aṣl*, but that the ruling claimed to apply to the *farʿ* is rooted on that of the *aṣl*.

[20]According to a personal email to S. Rahman, Young indicated that his translation of the term *ʿilla* – namely, *occasioning factor* – is based on the one by Bernard Weiss (1992, 1998). The term is also translated as *effective cause, operative cause, ratio legis and ratio decidenci.* Some of these translations do not seem to bear the causal significance of the term. The term *ʿilla* is derived from ancient Syriac, where it means a "fault" or "blame" constituting the cause for returning articles or

Moreover, the proceeding assumes that the relevant property is to be found either by inspecting the sources or by epistemological considerations.

2.2 (Second alternative). It proceeds by finding some way to relate the branch-case to the root-case *in absence of knowledge of the occasioning factor* by developing a parallel reasoning based on some kind of similarity and it includes three cases:

2.2.1 both the root-case and the branch-case share some other juridical ruling,

2.2.2 in the absence of the similarities between the root-case and the branch-case, it can nevertheless be established that there is some parallelism between a pair of source-cases and a pair of branch-cases such that if some particular juridical ruling applies to the pair of source-cases, it also applies to the pair of branch-cases,

2.2.3 both the root-case and the branch-case share some properties.

The second of the alternatives to step two is called *qiyās al-dalāla* (قياس الدلالة) or *correlational inference of indication*, also known as *qiyās al-shabah* (قياس الشبه), and also as *correlational inference of resemblance* – though it might be perhaps useful to restrict the term *qiyās al-shabah* for the last form of *qiyās al-dalāla*.[21] *Qiyās al-dalāla* based on the resemblance of the branch-case to the root-case in relation to a *set of properties* is considered to be the weakest, epistemically speaking, and is very close to what is known in other traditions as analogical argumentation by similarity or agreement. By contrast, the *qiyās* based on the resemblance of the branch-case to the root-case in relation to a *set of juridical rulings* is considered to be epistemically the strongest form of inference of the type *al-dalāla*. The form of inference-form of *qiyās al-dalāla* based on double parallelisms constitutes a generalization and a deeply innovative approach to what is known as *proportionality-*

---

property. The term penetrated from Syriac into the lexicon of rational thought even before Aristotelianism penetrated Arabic culture (we owe the remark on the etymology of the term *ʿilla* to David Joseph (2010; 2014)). In a general context, a distinction is drawn between providing a *ground* (*ʿilla*) and providing a *factual cause* or *reason* (*sabab*): while grounding is a rational endeavour, providing a *sabab* might be limited to an empirical task. It seems to be related to St. Thomas' (*Summa Theologiae* 2.2c:) distinction between *propter quid* and *quia* that stems from Aristotle's distinction in *Posterior Analytics* 13 (for a discussion in the context of CTT see J. Granström (2011, p. 157). In the context of the *qiyās* the notion of *sabab* seems to allude to the justification underlying the choice of one specific occasioning factor. This use is witnessed by al-Shīrāzī's denomination of the second subtype of *qiyās al-ʿilla* as *qiyās plainly evident by reported reason* (*al-wāḍiḥ bi-al-sabab*). That is, those *qiyās* where the *ʿilla* is not found in the *naṣṣ* but specified on the basis of some reason stemming from a specific historical background of *naṣṣ* reported by the Companion of the Prophet. In fact we should also mention the notion *ḥikma* that stands for the underlying higher purpose of the *ʿilla*. Moreover, the notion of *ḥikma* underlies the *doctrine of rational juridical preference* or *istiḥsān*, and *the theory of public welfare* or *maṣlaḥa* mentioned before. However, this notion does not seem to play a role in the inferential processes deployed by the use of a *qiyās*.

[21] See al-Shīrāzī (2016), *Mulakhkhaṣ, fī al-jadal*, fol. 5a.

based analogical reasoning.[22] In relation to its epistemic strength it is placed between the former two.

وأما قياس الدلالة فهو أن يحمل الفرع على الأصل بضرب من الشبه غير العلة التي علق الحكم عليها في الشرع. وهذا ضرب من القياس لا تعرف صحته إلا بالاستدلال بالأصول وهو على ثلاثة أضرب.[23]

> As for *Qiyās al-Dalāla*, it is that one that links the branch-case with the source-case by way of a type of resemblance other than the occasioning factor upon which the ruling is made contingent in God's Law. The validity of this type of correlational inference is not known except by way of drawing indication from the authoritative source-cases; and it is [also] of three types.[24]

Al-Shīrāzī calls the first alternative to the second step *qiyās al-ʿilla* (*correlational inference of the occasioning factor*) – that provides the subject of the present chapter – and distinguishes three main cases classified by the strength of the evidence for the *ʿilla*:

(i) the evidence for the identification of the *ʿilla* stems from unambiguous and explicit passages in the texts (*naṣṣ*) of the Qurʾān and of the prophetic tradition (*al-jalī bi-al-naṣṣ*), or from a consensus of the jurists (*al-jalī bi-al-ijmāʿ*)
(ii) the identification of the *ʿilla* stems from some hermeneutical process of the texts (*al-wāḍiḥ bi-al-nuṭq*) or it is based upon some historical background reported by the Companion of the Prophet (*al-wāḍiḥ bi-al-sabab*)
(iii) the *ʿilla* is identified by positing some suitable hypothesis (*al-khafī*) about the general law occasioning the ruling of the root-case.[25] The latter has some relation to Aristotle's *argument from example* (*paradeigma*) described in the *Rhetoric* (1402b15) and the *Prior Analytics* (*Pr. An.* 69a1).

فأما قياس العلة فهو أن يحمل الفرع على الأصل بالعلة التي علق الحكم عليها في الشرع وذلك على ثلاثة أضرب جلي وواضح وخفي.[26]

> As for *Qiyās al-ʿIlla*, it is that one that links the branch-case with the source-case by way of the occasioning factor upon which the ruling is made contingent in God's Law; and that is according to three types: *al-jalī* (clearly-disclosed), *al-wāḍiḥ* (plainly-evident), and *al-khafī* (latent).[27]

---

[22]Cf. C. Cellucci (2013, pp. 340–41). Moreover, it seems to be very close to Bartha's (2010) own model.

[23]See al-Shīrāzī, *Mulakhkhaṣ fī al-jadal*, fol. 5a.

[24]Cf. Young (2017, p. 115).

[25]See al-Shīrāzī, *Mulakhkhaṣ fī al-jadal*, fol. 5a, cf. Young (2017, pp. 113–14). Al-Baṣrī distinguishes a positive inferential process (*Qiyās al-ṭard, correlational inference of co-presence*), covered by the description above, from a negative one (*Qiyās al-ʿaks, correlational inference of the opposite*). The result of the negative one is to deny that some designated juridical ruling that applies to the root-case also applies to the branch-case, on the grounds that the occasioning factor does not apply to the branch-case – see Abū al-Ḥusayn al-Baṣrī (1964, pp. 697–9) and *K. al-qiyās al-sharʿī* (pp. 1031–3) (trans. of the latter in Hallaq (1987a)); quoted by Young (2017, p. 109).

[26]See al-Shīrāzī, *Mulakhkhaṣ fī al-jadal*, fol. 5a.

[27]Cf. Young (2017, p. 109).

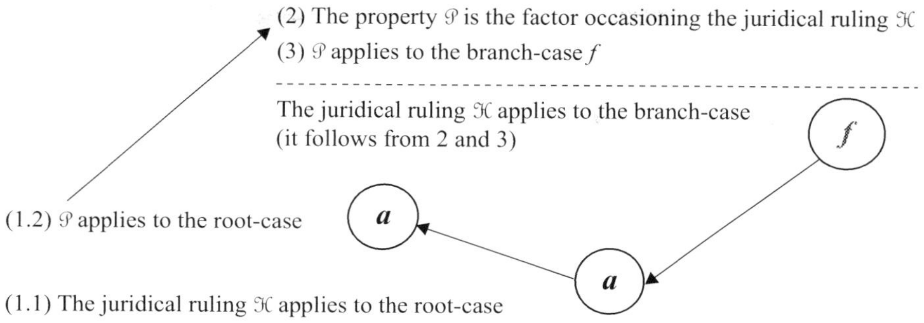

Example:
Branch-case ***f***: *Reading someone else's correspondence without permission.*
Root-case ***a***: *Entering someone else's house without permission*
Property $\mathcal{P}$: *Violation of Privacy*
Juridical decision $\mathcal{H}$: *Forbidden*

Schema 2.1 *Qiyās al-ʿIlla.* (The diagram has been adapted from Bartha's (2010, p. 36) figure for Aristotle's reasoning by *paradeigma*)

Remarks:

1. One way to express the rationale behind Al-Shīrāzī's typology (not shared by all of the other authors) is that he conceives *qiyās* as a system of parallel reasoning that deploys arguments by
   (a) exemplification (of a general law): *qiyās al-ʿilla.*
   (b) symmetry between structures (established by either chains of rulings or pairs of parallel rulings) (the two first forms of *qiyās al-dalāla*).
   (c) resemblance between the root-case and the branch-case (*qiyās al-shabah*).
2. Some paragraphs of al-Shīrāzī's *al-Lumaʿ fī Uṣūl al-Fiqh* seem to support a three-fold rather than a two-fold classification – the three-fold classification comes close to the triad a, b, c.[28] However, the *Mulakhkhaṣ* and the *Maʾūna* provide solid textual evidence of a two-fold classification, where b and c are both included in a general category of *qiyās* where the occasioning factor is not present.[29]
3. *Qiyās* constitutes a system of juridical reasoning that is in the middle of two other (sometimes contested) forms of rational juridical change deployed in *fiqh* called, respectively, *the doctrine of rational juridical preference* or *istiḥsān* (استحسان), that might produce the withdrawal of a conclusion achieved by a *qiyās*-procedure, and *the theory of public welfare* or *maṣlaḥa* (مصلحة), that can trigger the production of a new juridical ruling. Indeed, while the use of a *qiyās* might extend the scope of application of a particular juridical ruling, it does not actually refute the ruling or the occasioning factor that the juridical source explicitly

[28]See al-Shīrāzī (2003, pp. 99–101; 1995, pp. 204–10).
[29]See al-Shīrāzī (1987, pp. 36–8).

declares as the ground for that ruling. The changes made possible by the use of *qiyās* are, in some sense, of a more logical and semantic nature.

Before delving into the logical structure of *qiyās al-ʿilla*, let us motivate the underlying dialectical processes with the help of an informal diagram. The diagram presents the most general form of the *qiyās al-ʿilla*, without (for the moment) drawing a distinction between subdivisions inside each type of correlational inference (Schema 2.1).

Simplified Argumentation-Schema
Main Claim:

Proponent: The branch-case *Reading someone else's correspondence without permission is forbidden*.

Development

Opponent:	Why?
Proponent:	Consider the root-case *Entering someone else's house without permission.* There is evidence in the Sources that these kinds of actions are *forbidden.*
Opponent:	I agree; this can be found in the Sources.
Proponent:	*Entering someone else's house without permission* is forbidden **because** it constitutes a case of *Violation of Privacy.*
Opponent:	This too can be found in the Sources. In fact, more precisely it says that entering without permission would allow that person to see something the owner would not like to be public.
Proponent:	So do you agree that any case of violation of privacy, in the sense you just specified, should be forbidden?
Opponent:	This is indeed the norm grounding the interdiction to enter someone else's house without permission.
Proponent:	The branch-case *Reading someone else's correspondence without permission* also constitutes a case of *Violation of Privacy,* in the sense that it would allow the reader to see something the author of the correspondence would not like to be public.
Opponent:	Clearly so.
Proponent:	Therefore, *Reading someone else's correspondence without permission* is *forbidden* too.
Opponent:	I concede.

Thus, the point of the *al-ʿilla*-form of correlational inference is to find a general law and a property, shared by both the branch and the source-case, which allows the inference of the ruling we are looking to ground. It is not really a case of analogy by resemblance, but a kind of what is nowadays called *deductive parallel reasoning*, since it combines some kind of *symmetric* reasoning with inferential moves. Notice that in the diagram neither of the assertions gathered in the steps 1.1. and step 1.2 are premises for the last inferential step. Indeed, steps 1.1 and 1.2 have the heuristic role of obtaining assertions that should lead to the required general rule. In order to extract from the diagram the underlying *jadal*-structure, we need to read the arrows as dialectical actions or argumentative moves, whereby the first action (the arrow on the right of the diagram) amounts to the heuristic move of finding a suitable root-case, then the short arrow from 1.1 to 1.2 indicates the result of finding out the property that provides the occasioning factor specific to the ruling of the root-case, and the last arrow stresses the core of the process, namely: *to learn from the ruling of the root-case that it instantiates a general juridical norm.* Once this has been achieved, a simple logical mechanism leads us to the conclusion sought.

In the next section we motivate the use of a notation inspired by Constructive Type Theory. In fact, we only deploy very basic features of the CTT-framework; a deep and thorough development is still due.

2.3 Motivating the Deployment of CTT Within an Interactive Stance[30]

The expressive power of Per Martin Löf's Constructive Type Theory[31] allows the following features underlying the *qiyās* to be expressed at the object language level:

1. The stress on assertions (or judgements) rather than on propositional sentences. The dialectical process underlyping correlational inferences is triggered by both an assertion concerning the identification of the factor occasioning the relevant ruling and the process of the justification of such an assertion. In the specialized literature these assertions are called *ta'līl* (affirmation of the relevance of a particular property for the determination of the *'illa*), or more generally *ithbāt* (affirmation).
2. The intensional rather than extensional understanding of the sets underlying the semantics of the *qiyās*.
3. The deployment of hypothetical judgements. This dovetails with the *qiyās*-notion of dependence of a given juridical ruling on a particular occasioning factor.
4. The restrictive form of the substitution rules.

The last point will be discussed in the chapter III since it relates to correlational inferences by indication.

What the dialogical framework adds to the standard natural-deduction presentation of CTT is that this approach not only provides insights into the dynamics of meaning underlying the notion of *qiyās*, but also leads to a conception of logic where logical rules too are understood as emerging from dialectical interaction. In other

[30] We owe the expression "*Interactive Stance*" to the title of Ginzurg (2012).

[31] See the appendix. For a systematic presentation of CTT see Martin-Löf (1984, 1996), Nordström/Petersson/Smith (1990; 2000), Ranta (1994), Granström (2011). For philosophical and historical insights into CTT see Ranta (1988), Primiero (2008), Sundholm (2009, 2012).

words, the dialogical reconstruction of the different forms of correlational inference is not to be conceived as the concatenation of a dialogical structure + logical rules + semantics + knowledge + jurisprudence, but rather as a unifying system where all those levels are constituted, or *forged,* at the same time by argumentative interaction, they are *immanent* to a dialogue that makes reason and knowledge happen. For a discussion on *immanent reasoning* see the chapter IV, where we provide the main notions recently developed in Rahman/McConaughey/Klev/Clerbout (2018).

Certainly, other formal reconstructions are possible, and in particular, we might not need an intensional framework in order to deal with changing extensions. However,

1. the deployment of intensional frameworks seems to be a natural approach in historical contexts,[32]
2. CTT provides a solid theory for the deployment of intensionally grounded **sets**,[33]
3. CTT seems to match well with dialectical approaches to meaning and normative approaches to logic, such as the dialogical one. This is particularly so in a CTT-framework where non-mathematical propositions are understood as language-games, as suggested for the first time by Ranta.[34]

The main idea to be developed in the following two sections is that our framework allows to isolate within the general notion of occasioning factor its causal feature. Indeed, according to our approach, implementing the causal feature of the occasioning factor is reconstructed as the application of a method (function) that triggers a particular juridical decision $\mathcal{H}(x)$, whenever a given action qualifies as being a case of $\mathcal{P}$.

- For example, the factor that **occasions or causes** the interdiction $\mathcal{H}(x)$ of entering someone else's house without permission is the application of a method or process that triggers the interdiction of those acts that qualify as cases of *Violation of Privacy* (i.e. to those acts that are elements of the **set** $\mathcal{P}$ of cases of *Violation of Privacy*) and exempts of that interdiction those cases that do not constitute a case of *Violation of Privacy*.

Thus, our reconstruction renders the implementation of the causal feature of the occasioning factor as having a purely dynamic nature, namely that of an act that causes some juridical sanction based on a qualification identified as relevant for that sanction.

This allows us to distinguish the property relevant for some specific juridical sanction, from the actual procedure of triggering that sanction for some particular case. It is the triggering procedure that provides the notion of occasioning factor with its causal force.

---

[32]See for example, Marion/Rückert (2015) and Martin-Löf (2012).

[33]From now on we write "**set**" (boldface) instead of "set" in order to indicate that we deploy intensional sets as developed within CTT (see the appendix).

[34]Ranta (1994, pp. 55–7).

In fact, as mentioned in the preface, the notion of occasioning factor as deployed in Islamic jurisprudence includes the following three main components:

1. *Waṣf,* the property $\mathcal{P}$ relevant for a juridical sanction $\mathcal{H}$, such that the latter is defined as being specific to the set of cases defined by $\mathcal{P}$ (e.g. those interdictions $\mathcal{H}(x)$ that apply to consuming those drinks that instantiate the set $\mathcal{P}$ of drinks inducing intoxication).
2. The efficiency feature or *ta'thīr*, that provides the means to test whether the property $\mathcal{P}$ purported to be relevant for the juridical sanction at stake is indeed so. The test declines into two complementary procedures: testing *ṭard*, co-extensiveness or co-presence (if the property is present then the sanction too) and testing *ʿaks*, co-exclusiveness or co-absence (if the property is absent, then so is the juridical sanction – the consumption of vinegar is in principle not forbidden). While co-extensiveness examines whether sanction $\mathcal{H}$ follows from the verification of the presence of the property $\mathcal{P}$, co-exclusiveness examines whether exemption from the sanction $\mathcal{H}$ follows from the verification of the absence of $\mathcal{P}$.
3. The causal feature, i.e., the legal method encoded by the function $b(x)$, that when applied to some instance a of the relevan property $\mathcal{P}$ renders the ruling $\mathcal{H}(a)$ specific to that property. More precisely, when we focus on the causal feature of the occasioning factor, the function will be written as *ʿilla*(x). The function *ʿilla*(x) admits the substitution *ʿilla*(a) for some case a (that satisfies the *waṣf*), only after the efficiency of the property $\mathcal{P}$ has been verified by the test *ta'thīr*.

Let us now work out these notions.

2.3.1 *The Meaning-Explanation of Juridical Rulings in* Qiyās al-ʿIlla

We first furnish the main formal elements of Martin-Löf's theory which are relevant for our logical analysis (for more details see the appendix).

2.3.1.1 Elements of CTT in the Context of *Qiyās al-ʿIlla*: The Specificity of *waṣf*

Per Martin-Löf's (1984) Constructive Type Theory (CTT) provides a thorough formal framework whereby categorical and hypothetical judgements can be explicitly distinguished at the object-language level without conflating judgements with the propositions that constitute them.[35]

- **On Categorical Judgements.** In the CTT framework it is possible to express at the object-language level

  A true,

  which, when asserted by some individual **g**, conveys the information that this individual is in possession of some proof-object for *A*. Moreover, it can be rendered explicit by means of the **categorical judgement**

  d: *A*,

  which reads: *there is a proof-object d of A* – or the individual **g** can bring forward the proof-object *d* in support of his claim that *A* is *true*.

  More generally, within CTT a proposition is interpreted as a **set** the elements of which represent the proofs of the proposition, the solution to a problem, and the fulfilments of an expectation. Accordingly,

d: A	*A true*
can be read as	
d is an element of the **set** *A*	*A* has an element
d is a proof of the proposition *A*	*A* is *true*
d is a solution to the problem *A*	*A* has a solution
d fulfils the expectation *A*	*A* is fulfilled

  Ranta (1994, p. 54) combines CTT with Davidson's (1980, essays 6–10) idea that an action makes an action-proposition *true*. Accordingly the proposition

  (that) Al-Fārābī read Aristotle's *Analytica Posteriora*

  is made *true* by individual readings of Al-Fārābī performing actions of that type. This interpretation is not far from the interpretation mentioned above of expectations as propositions and fulfilments as proof-objects. We will here follow Ranta's suggestion and assume that we have action-propositions that are made *true* by some evidence that some action of the type expressed by those propositions has been performed.
- **On Hypothetical Judgements.** One of the characteristic features of CTT is that it also allows, at the object-language level, the expression of a hypothetical judgements as a form of statement distinguishable from the assertion of the truth of an implicational proposition. Hypothetical judgements give rise to dependency structures in CTT, such as

  B true (*x: A*)

---

[35]For a brief overview of CTT see Sect. 4.2. More details can be found in the short introductory survey by Ansten Klev in Rahman/McConaughey/Klev/Clerbout (2018, chapter II) – the appendix to the chapter IV of our present book is composed of relevant extracts of Klev's survey.

or, in its explicit form:

$b(x)$: B (x: A),

which reads: $b(x)$ is a (dependent) proof-object of B, provided x is a proof-object of the **set** A.

Or: the function b takes elements from the **set** A, and yields proof-objects for B.[36]

In other words, in this frame the dependence of the truth of B upon the truth of A amounts to the dependence of the proof-object of B upon the proof-object of A. And the dependence of the proof-object of B upon the proof-object of A is expressed by means of the function $b(x)$ (from A to B), where x is a proof-object of A and where the function $b(x)$ itself constitutes the dependent proof-object of B.

In our context, we have the **set** of (evidences of) performances of actions qualified by a property $\mathcal{P}$ (such, as say, *acts of Violation of Privacy*) and the **set** $\mathcal{H}$ of juridical decisions **specific** to that property (***forbidding*** *Violation of Privacy*).

Thus, given the assertion $b(x)$: $\mathcal{H}(x)$ (x: $\mathcal{P}$), and the assertion that there is a performance a that qualifies as $\mathcal{P}$, then we can infer that performing action a (such as entering the house of someone else without permission), is forbidden.

In plain words, from the premises

1. Performances x of an action of the type *of Violation of Privacy* $\mathcal{P}$ trigger the juridical process $b(x)$ by means of which those performances are sanctioned as forbidden ($b(x)$: $\mathcal{H}(x)$ (x: $\mathcal{P}$));
2. a is such a performance (a: $\mathcal{P}$);
   we can infer that

Performance a is forbidden ($b(a)$: $\mathcal{H}(a)$).

For short:

$$\frac{a: \mathcal{P} \qquad b(x): \mathcal{H}(x)\ (x: \mathcal{P})}{b(a): \mathcal{H}(a)}$$

According to this analysis, the juridical meaning of a given ruling is rendered by the rules that establish its **dependence** upon a property identified as being relevant for that ruling. The identified property, as mentioned above, is called *waṣf* (in our

[36] For example, intuitively, if A is the **set** of natural numbers and B is the **set** of whole numbers, then the function takes one natural number and yields an element of the **set** of whole numbers B, e.g. $b(x) = 2x$.

example the **set** $\mathcal{P}$) and determines the occasioning factor (the causal link) relevant to that ruling.[37] Thus, assertions such as *Entering someone else's house without permission is forbidden* obtain their juridical meaning from those rules that establish how to justify this interdiction. The required form of justification is rooted in the **causal link** (implemented by the function $b(x)$) between the interdiction and the relevant property, in our case qualifying as an act of *Violation of Privacy*.

In fact, as mentioned above, in order to isolate the causal agent, we will call the function $b(x)$ the *ʿilla*–function. This yields

$$\frac{a: \mathcal{P} \qquad \text{ʿ}illa(x): \mathcal{H}(x)\ (x: \mathcal{P})}{\text{ʿ}illa(a): \mathcal{H}(a)}$$

Actually, the property occasioning the juridical rule is more naturally conceived as a predicate defined over a **set** rather than an independent **set**. For example, the property of *constituting an act of Violation of Privacy*, is naturally formulated as a subset of some ***set*** $\mathcal{D}$ *of performances of acts, "separated" by the the property* $\mathcal{P}$ (i.e. we separate within $\mathcal{D}$ the **subset** of those acts that qualify as acts of privacy-violation– a construction extensively discussed by the commentators of Aristotle).[38] In CTT this alternative form of characterizing the relevant property yields the following:

Forbidden(x): *prop* $(\{x: Act \mid Violation\ of\ Privacy(x)\})$
(subset-separation: the **set** of those elements of the **set** of acts that constitute violations of privacy)

The general abstract notation for arbitrary **set**, and arbitrary property $\mathcal{P}(x)$ qualifying elements of $\mathcal{D}$ is:

$\mathcal{H}(x)$: *prop* $(\{x: \mathcal{D} \mid \mathcal{P}(x)\})$

In order to avoid a too heavy notation we will use the following formal notation:

Abstract Abbreviated Notation

$\mathcal{H}(x)$: *prop* $(\{x: \mathcal{P}_{\mathcal{D}}\})$

Abbreviated Notation with Explicit Content

Forbidden(x): *prop* $(x: Violation\ of\ Privacy_{acts})$.

According to the proposed abbreviation the specificity of the juridical decision $\mathcal{H}(x)$ to those elements of the **set** $\mathcal{D}$ qualified as being $\mathcal{P}(x)$ will carry the notation

ʿ*illa*(x): $\mathcal{H}(x)$ $(x: \mathcal{P}_{\mathcal{D}})$

---

[37]Hallaq (1985, pp. 88–91; 1987b, pp-50-58). See also Young (2017, p. 162).

[38]Alexander of Aphrodisias called such a form of construction *prosleptic proposition* – see L. Gili (2015).

where *ʿilla*(x) is a legal procedure that yields some juridical decision $\mathcal{H}(x)$ (such as *Forbidden*(x)) concerning elements of the **set** $\mathcal{P}_{\mathcal{D}}$ (in our example, acts that qualify as constituting cases of *Violation of Privacy,* such as inspecting the bags of someone else without permission, reading the correspondence of someone else without permission, ...).

This displays the relations of content linking ruling and property: the **relevance** of the property for the ruling. What we need now is to make it apparent that *Privacy-Violation* has the efficiency required to occasion the relevant juridical ruling. As mentioned above, Islamic jurisprudents identified three general conditions to be met by the *waṣf* occasioning a ruling:

1. Efficiency (*ta'thīr*).
2. Co-extensiveness or co-presence (*ṭard*) – the presence of the property when the judgement is present.
3. Co-exclusiveness or co-absence (*ʿaks*) – the absence of the property when the judgement is absent.

Arguments for endorsing some proposed property as efficient are based on showing both that when the property is present (*wujūd*) the ruling at stake is present, and that when the property is absent (*salb*) so is the property. It is quite often the case that an argument for endorsing a property as constitutive of the occasioning factor ends with the formulation:

Therefore, the presence of the ḥukm is due to the presence of the property, and the absence of the ḥukm is due to its absence.

Thus, a property is efficient (*ta'thīr*) in relation to a given ruling **if the ruling is defined in terms of this property** (relevance has been established) and the property satisfies both co-extensiveness (*ṭard*) and co-exclusiveness (*ʿaks*).

Let us then analyze

Privacy-Violation occasions the juridical ruling sanctioning its proscription – given the efficiency of Privacy-Violation in relation to that proscription.

as the construction

Cases of Privacy-Violation ($\mathcal{P}_{\mathcal{D}}$) *occasion the interdiction* $\mathcal{H}(x)$ *– given the efficiency of* $\mathcal{P}(x)$ *in relation to* $\mathcal{H}(x)$.

Furthermore, if the property $\mathcal{P}(x)$ is efficient in relation to the ruling $\mathcal{H}(x)$, then there is a method that provides the justification of applying the ruling to every case qualified as $\mathcal{P}_{\mathcal{D}}(x)$ – and dually, it provides the justification of applying $\neg\mathcal{H}(x)$, given instances of $\neg\mathcal{P}_{\mathcal{D}}(x)$.

In the argumentative practice, the efficiency of a proposed property is tested by *choosing an* arbitrary element a_i of the same **set**, and showing that

If a_i has the tested property, then the juridical sanction follows.
If a_i is an element of $\mathcal{D}$ but does not have the tested property $\mathcal{P}_{\mathcal{D}}(x)$, then the juridical sanction $\mathcal{H}(x)$ does not follow

The efficiency is said to have been established if it can be shown that this holds *for any arbitrary choice* of elements of $\mathcal{P}_{\mathcal{D}}(x)$.

Example

Entering someone else's house without permission (a_1)
Entering someone else's house with the permission of the owner (a_2)
The first case, which constitutes a case of privacy-violation $((a_1))$, is forbidden: $\mathcal{H}(a_1)$
The second case, which does not constitute a case of privacy-violation $(\neg(a_1))$, is not forbidden: $\neg\mathcal{H}(a_2)$.
Therefore, acts of privacy-violation are forbidden because of the property $\mathcal{P}_{\mathcal{D}}(x)$.

- In such a context the factor occasioning the application of the ruling $\mathcal{H}(x)$ to some case a is conceived as procedure of substitution *ʿilla*(x/a): $\mathcal{H}(x/a)$, given a: $\mathcal{P}_{\mathcal{D}}$.

More generally, each particular instance of *Privacy-Violation* occasions the proscription of that instance. *E.g. entering the house of someone else without permission*, an instance of *Privacy-Violation*, provides the *ʿilla* occasioning the proscription of such an action. In other words, the occasioning factor in relation to a juridical ruling $\mathcal{H}(x)$ defined over the **set** $\mathcal{P}_{\mathcal{D}}$ is the function *ʿilla*(x) that for any instance of $\mathcal{P}_{\mathcal{D}}$ it produces an instance of the ruling $\mathcal{H}(x)$. However, this assumes that *ṭard* and co-exclusiveness (*ʿaks*) have been verified before.

Thus, establishing that a given ruling applies to the branch-case of the thesis involves two main steps:

1. Recognizing that the ruling $\mathcal{H}(x)$ at stake is defined in terms of a property $\mathcal{P}_{\mathcal{D}}$ and that there is a root-case exemplifying how a given normative method (specific to that ruling and property) occasions that every case that satisfies the property falls under the ruling (and dually, for the absence of that property). In other words, the root-case exemplifies the application of the function that verifies the universal norm *Every x that is a* $\mathcal{P}_{\mathcal{D}}$ *falls under the ruling* $\mathcal{H}(x)$ (and its dual),
2. Recognizing that this general norm also applies to the branch-case.

The point is that the construction underlying the meaning of application of the ruling to the root-case is, to put it in Bartha's terms, *precursor to a generalization.*[39] However, the idea is quite different from what is nowadays called *one-step induction.*[40]

Indeed, identifying the occasioning factor for the root-case under consideration amounts to grasping it as exemplifying (the application of) a general law: this is what the notion of causality in *uṣūl al-fiqh* comes down to.

[39]Bartha (2010, p. 109).

[40]See *e.g.* Bartha (2010, pp. 36–40).

The generality of the norm results from a typical dialogical understanding of universal quantification, namely, that the challenger can choose an arbitrary element of the **set** at stake in order to test the efficiency of the property for triggering the legal sanction under scrutiny. If the efficiency claim resists the test of any arbitrary choice of the challenger, then the generality of the norm has been justified – for the dialogical interpretation of universal quantifiers see the chapter IV of the present book.

Let us now have a closer look at the logical structure of the notion of efficiency.

2.3.1.2 More Elements of CTT in the Context of *Qiyās al-ʿIlla*: On *Taʾthīr, Ṭard* and *ʿAks*

In the context of *jadal* and dialectical frameworks, there are moves aimed at testing if the selected property is actually the one occasioning the juridical ruling. Let us take this time the widely discussed example of the *prohibition of consuming wine*. Let us further assume that the property selected as relevant was *being red*. The refusal to accept *being a red drink* as the factor occasioning the relevant ruling is not only a refusal to endorse the generalization *Every red drink is to be forbidden*. The refusal lies deeper in the structure. It is about denying that *being a red drink is* legally relevant to the *prohibition of consuming wine*.[41] This is what our formulation *ʿilla*(x): $\mathcal{H}(x)$ (x: $\mathcal{P}_{\mathcal{D}}$) in the precedent section brings to the fore.

Accordingly, the logical form of the method *taʾthīr*$^{\mathcal{P}}$ that establishes the efficiency of the property $\mathcal{P}_{\mathcal{D}}$ in relation to the ruling $\mathcal{H}(x)$ is structured as follows:

taʾthīr$^{\mathcal{P}}$ {

- *ṭard*: If x is a drink where toxicity is present (*wujūd*), then its consumption is forbidden.[42] Thus, "*tard*" is the function that when applied to a drink inducing intoxication, yields a legal sanction forbidding its consumption.
- *ʿaks*: if x is a drink where toxicity is absent (*salb*), then its consumption is not forbidden. Thus, "*aks*" is the function that when applied to a drink that does not induce intoxication, yields a legal sanction allowing its consumption.

- While *ṭard* triggers the sanction if the relevant property is present, *ʿaks* assures that the case under consideration *does not build an exception*.

In fact, the fully explicit formulation is the following:

Given the disjunction $\mathcal{P}_{\mathcal{D}} \vee \neg\mathcal{P}_{\mathcal{D}}$, of toxic drinks ($\mathcal{P}_{\mathcal{D}}$) and non-toxic ones ($\neg\mathcal{P}_{\mathcal{D}}$); and given that interdiction and non-interdiction for consumption have been defined in terms of this disjunction interdiction and non-interdiction distributes as follows:

[41]We borrowed the example from Hallaq (1985, pp. 88–9).

[42]Let us call *toxic drink*, or drink where *toxicity is present*; those drinks inducing *intoxication*.

All those drinks inducing toxicity, if identical to the ones identified as the wujūd, are ***forbidden for consumption*** *– i.e., they are forbidden if they are identical to the drinks instantiating the* ***left*** *side of the disjunction* $\mathcal{P}_{\mathcal{D}} \vee \neg \mathcal{P}_{\mathcal{D}}$*).* Furthermore,

All those drinks not inducing toxicity, if identical to the ones identified as the salb, are ***allowed for consumption*** *– i.e., they are allowed if they are identical to the drinks instantiating the* ***right*** *side of the disjunction* $\mathcal{P}_{\mathcal{D}} \vee \neg \mathcal{P}_{\mathcal{D}}$*).*

Technically speaking, "*wujūd*" and "*salb*" stand for functions (injections) that render the disjunction $\mathcal{P}_{\mathcal{D}} \vee \neg \mathcal{P}_{\mathcal{D}}$ *true*.[43] Recall that in constructive logic, the truth of a disjunction requires not only some proof-object for the disjunction, but also an indication signalizing which side of the disjunction is made *true* by that proof-object. Accordingly, while *wujūd* stands for the injective function from the **set** $\mathcal{P}_{\mathcal{D}}$ to the **set** $\mathcal{P}_{\mathcal{D}} \vee \neg \mathcal{P}_{\mathcal{D}}$, *salb* stands for the injective function from the **set** $\neg \mathcal{P}_{\mathcal{D}}$ to the **set** $\mathcal{P}_{\mathcal{D}} \vee \neg \mathcal{P}_{\mathcal{D}}$.

Thus, *wujūd* indicates that the disjunction $\mathcal{P}_{\mathcal{D}} \vee \neg \mathcal{P}_{\mathcal{D}}$ is *true* since its **left** side is made *true* by some element of $\mathcal{P}_{\mathcal{D}}$; and *salb* indicates that the disjunction $\mathcal{P}_{\mathcal{D}} \vee \neg \mathcal{P}_{\mathcal{D}}$ is *true* since its **right** side is made *true*; and *taʾthīr*$^{\mathcal{P}}(x)$ is the function:

$$ta'th\bar{\imath}r^{\mathcal{P}}(x) : \{\ [\ (\forall y : \mathcal{P}_{\mathcal{D}})\ wuj\bar{u}d^{\vee}(y) =_{\{\mathcal{P}\mathcal{D} \vee \neg \mathcal{P}\mathcal{D}\}} x \supset \mathcal{H}(y)\ ] \wedge [\ (\forall z : \neg \mathcal{P}_{\mathcal{D}})\ salb^{\vee}(z) =_{\{\mathcal{P}\mathcal{D} \vee \neg \mathcal{P}\mathcal{D}\}} x \supset \neg \mathcal{H}(z)\ ]\ \}\ (x : \mathcal{P}_{\mathcal{D}} \vee \neg \mathcal{P}_{\mathcal{D}})$$

In other words, the function *taʾthīr*$^{\mathcal{P}}(x)$ provides the proof-object of the following hypothetical:

$$\{\ [\ (\forall y : \mathcal{P}_{\mathcal{D}})\ wuj\bar{u}d^{\vee}(y) =_{\{\mathcal{P}\mathcal{D} \vee \neg \mathcal{P}\mathcal{D}\}} x \supset \mathcal{H}(y)\ ] \wedge [\ (\forall z : \neg \mathcal{P}_{\mathcal{D}})\ salb^{\vee}(z) =_{\{\mathcal{P}\mathcal{D} \vee \neg \mathcal{P}\mathcal{D}\}} x \supset \neg \mathcal{H}(z)\ ]\ \}\ true\ (x : \mathcal{P}_{\mathcal{D}} \vee \neg \mathcal{P}_{\mathcal{D}})$$

If we pull all this together and write it as a universal expression we obtain the following formalization, where the lambda-abstract of the function *taʾthīr*$^{\mathcal{P}}(x)$ constitutes the proof-object of the universal.[44] In a dialectical framework the lambda-abstract $\lambda x.$*taʾthīr*$^{\mathcal{P}}(x)$ corresponds to those reasons that, at the strategic level, justify the universal assertion that co-extensiveness and co-exclusiveness are being satisfied – in a nutshell: they stand for those objects that instruct the proponent of the universal to sanction the ruling $\mathcal{H}(x)$ for any element (chosen by the antagonist) that enjoys the relevant properyt $\mathcal{P}_{\mathcal{D}}$, and to sanction the non-application of the ruling if

[43]In the notation of CTT *wujūd* and *salb* stand for special cases of the injections $\mathbf{i}(x)$ and $\mathbf{j}(x)$ – see Sect. 4.2.

[44]As explained in the appendix the proof-object of a universal such as $(\forall x: A)\ B$ *true* is $\lambda x.\ b: (\forall x: A)\ B$. Since in our case the function $b(x): B\ (x: A)$ is actually *taʾthīr*$^{\mathcal{P}}(x)$: $[(\forall y: \mathcal{P}_{\mathcal{D}})\ wuj\bar{u}d^{\vee}(y) =_{\{\mathcal{P} \vee \neg \mathcal{P}\}} x \supset \mathcal{H}(y)] \wedge [(\forall z: \neg \mathcal{P}_{\mathcal{D}})\ salb^{\vee}(z) =_{\{\mathcal{P} \vee \neg \mathcal{P}\}} x \supset \neg \mathcal{H}(z)]\ (x: \mathcal{P}_{\mathcal{D}} \vee \neg \mathcal{P}_{\mathcal{D}})$, the proof-object of the universal is $\lambda x.$ *taʾthīr*$^{\mathcal{P}}$. Note that $\lambda x.$ *taʾthīr*$^{\mathcal{P}}(x)$ and *taʾthīr*$^{\mathcal{P}}(x)$ are entities of different types: while the latter is a function (i.e. a dependent object); we may conceive $\lambda x.$ *taʾthīr*$^{\mathcal{P}}(x)$ as an (independent) individual that codes this function (see the appendix).

the chosen element does not enjoy that property (see Sect. 2.4 below, the sections on strategic reasons in the chapter IV, and the section on CTT in the chapter IV).

$$\lambda x.ta\text{'}th\bar{\imath}r^{\mathcal{P}} : (\forall x : \mathcal{P}_{\mathcal{D}} \vee \neg\mathcal{P}_{\mathcal{D}}) \left\{ \left[(\forall y : \mathcal{P}_{\mathcal{D}})\ wuj\bar{u}d^{\vee}(y) \right.\right.$$
$$\left.\left. = _{\{\mathcal{PD}\vee\neg\mathcal{PD}\}}\ x \supset \mathcal{H}(y) \right] \wedge \left[(\forall z : \neg\mathcal{P}_{\mathcal{D}})\ salb^{\vee}(z) = _{\{\mathcal{PD}\vee\neg\mathcal{PD}\}}\ x \supset \neg\mathcal{H}(z) \right] \right\}$$

In the dialectical framework to be developed in the next sections, one of the players, the Proponent **P**, claims that since the property $\mathcal{P}$ satisfies efficiency in relation to sanction $\mathcal{H}$, he can show that applying the branch-case to this property **causes** the juridical sanction $\mathcal{H}$. This claim engages him to force **O** to endorse first the assertion

$$ta\text{'}th\bar{\imath}r^{\mathcal{P}\mathbf{X}}p_{\mathrm{i}}^{\mathbf{Y}} : (\forall x : \mathcal{P}_{\mathcal{D}} \vee \neg\mathcal{P}_{\mathcal{D}}) \left\{ \left[(\forall y : \mathcal{P}_{\mathcal{D}})\ wuj\bar{u}d^{\vee}(y) \right.\right.$$
$$\left.\left. = _{\{\mathcal{PD}\vee\neg\mathcal{PD}\}}\ x \supset \mathcal{H}(y) \right] \wedge \left[(\forall z : \neg\mathcal{P}_{\mathcal{D}})\ salb^{\vee}(z) = _{\{\mathcal{PD}\vee\neg\mathcal{PD}\}}\ x \supset \neg\mathcal{H}(z) \right] \right\}$$

Generally speaking, the player **X** (**P** or **O**), who endorses such an assertion, claims that he has a *reason* for justifying the universal and that this *reason*, called *strategic reason*, has the form $ta\text{'}th\bar{\imath}r^{\mathcal{P}}{}_{\mathrm{j}}{}^{\mathbf{X}}[\![p_{\mathrm{i}}{}^{\mathbf{Y}}]\!]$. The notation of the strategic reason stands for the following:

- $p_{\mathrm{i}}{}^{\mathbf{Y}}$ is the value (object or performance of an action) chosen by the challenger to test the universal quantifier ($\forall x\text{: } \mathcal{P}_{\mathcal{D}} \vee \neg\mathcal{P}_{\mathcal{D}}$) – i.e., the challenger asks the defender to show that some arbitrary case p_{i} at stake p_{i} satisfies co-presence and co-absence. In the context of the debates under study the cases chosen by both of the players are precisely the branch-case and the root-case.
- $ta\text{'}th\bar{\imath}r^{\mathcal{P}\mathbf{X}}$ is the process launched by **X** in order to test the efficiency of the property $\mathcal{P}$ in relation to sanction $\mathcal{H}$, with the help of the case p_{k} (chosen by the challenger). In the terminology of the dialogical framework (see Sect. 2.4 below) $ta\text{'}th\bar{\imath}r^{\mathcal{P}\mathbf{X}}$ stands for the *instruction* to bring forward a *local reason* for the proposition (the conjunction) under the scope of the quantifier, given the antagonist's choice of p_{k}.[45]
- $ta\text{'}th\bar{\imath}r^{\mathcal{P}\mathbf{X}}[\![p_{\mathrm{i}}{}^{\mathbf{Y}}]\!]$ encodes the process $ta\text{'}th\bar{\imath}r^{\mathcal{P}}$ for ***any*** p_{i} chosen by the challenger **Y**. In other words, it conveys the relevant moves by the means of which **X** succeeds in showing that any case p_{i} chosen by **Y** satisfies co-presence and co-absence.[46]

Accordingly, when we apply the process $ta\text{'}th\bar{\imath}r^{\mathcal{P}}$ to a concrete case *a* we verify if the property under consideration is or not relevant for the juridical sanction recorded by the sources. Coming back to our example, if *wine* (*grape-juice* in a state that

[45]Within the language of CTT $ta\text{'}th\bar{\imath}r^{\mathcal{P}}$ stands for the **function** $ta\text{'}th\bar{\imath}r^{\mathcal{P}}(x)$: $\{[(\forall y\text{: } \mathcal{P}_{\mathcal{D}})\ wuj\bar{u}d^{\vee}(y) = _{\{\mathcal{PD}\vee\neg\mathcal{PD}\}}\ x \supset \mathcal{H}(y)] \wedge [(\forall z\text{: } \neg\mathcal{P}_{\mathcal{D}})\ salb^{\vee}(z) = _{\{\mathcal{PD}\vee\neg\mathcal{PD}\}}\ x \supset \neg\mathcal{H}(z)]\}\ (x\text{: } \mathcal{P}_{\mathcal{D}}\vee\neg\mathcal{P}_{\mathcal{D}})$.

[46]While in the framework of CTT *encoding of a process* is a way to understand the role of a lambda operator on a function (see the appendix), in the dialogical framework the encoding is understood as a *recapitulation* or *reprise* of the moves constituting plays won by **P** (see *strategic reason* in the chapter IV of the present book).

induces intoxication) is chosen as the element that makes the disjunction *true*, and it is identified as one of those elements of the set of toxic drinks $\mathscr{P}_{\mathscr{D}}$, (that is, if *wine*: $\mathscr{P}_{\mathscr{D}}$) then, the sanction $\mathscr{H}$ interdicting its consumption follows. We can then say that the consumption of wine is forbidden **because** it induces intoxication.[47]

Technically speaking, the choice of wine triggers an **application** of the proof-object of the universal to wine which yields its interdiction for consumption – that is, the value of the function *ta'thīr*(*wine*): $\mathscr{P}_{\mathscr{D}}$ makes the proposition $\mathscr{Interdiction}$ (*wine*) true.[48] In short, the application of *ta'thīr*$^{\mathscr{P}}$(*x*) to wine constitutes the ***verification of the efficiency of property*** $\mathscr{P}$ for causing the proscription of wine-consumption. This leads us to deploy the following expression in order to indicate that the consumption of grape-juice, in the state of wine, is forbidden:

ap(λ*x*.*ta'thīr*$^{\mathscr{P}}$, *wine*): $\mathscr{H}$(*wine*)

The point is that **applying** λ*x*.*ta'thīr*$^{\mathscr{P}}$ to the case of *wine* amounts to the assertion that the function *ta'thīr*(*wine*) provides the **verification** that the property $\mathscr{P}$ causes its interdiction:

ap(λ*x*.*ta'thīr*$^{\mathscr{P}}$, *wine*) = *ta'thīr*$^{\mathscr{P}}$(*wine*): $\mathscr{H}$(*wine*)

The dialogical formulation of the strategic reason (i.e. the object that instructs how to develop a winning strategy for **P**) when **O** asserted the universal is the following:

ap(*wine*.*ta'thīr*$^{\mathscr{P}}$): $\mathscr{H}$(*wine*)

This indicates that the strategic reason brought forward by **P** in order to justify the interdiction of wine amounts to launching the process of verification *ta'thīr*$^{\mathscr{P}}$ for the case of wine (asserted to be one of the substances prone inducing intoxication).

Let us now develop the first steps towards the interactive stance.

2.3.2 Towards the Interactive Stance

In order to provide meaning-explantions to the basic notions of al-Shīrāzī's System of *qiyās* we deployed CTT which is rooted on natural deduction, whereas al-Shīrāzī's approach is a dialectical framework. Thus, we need now to motivate the interface of CTT with a dialectical framework. We will develop this motivation in two main steps, namely

[47]Dually, if grape-juice in a state that does not induce intoxication is the element that makes the (right side of the) disjunction *true*, then this substance is exempted from the interdiction.

[48]More generally, if *c*: (∀*x*: $\mathscr{P}$)$\mathscr{H}$(*x*), *b*(*x*): $\mathscr{H}$(*x*) (*x*:$\mathscr{P}$) and *a*: $\mathscr{P}$; the application **ap** of *c* to *a* (i.e. **ap** (*c*,*a*), amounts to applying the lambda abstract of the function *b*(*x*) to *a* (recall that the proof-object of a universal involving the function *b*(*x*) is (or must be equal to) the lambda-abstract of that function); that is, **ap**(*c*,*a*) is equal to the value of *b*(*a*) – see the appendix.

1. by a (brief) discussion of the interface *epistemic-assumption*, *formal rule* and the notion of *epistemic strength*
2. by the distinction of play and strategic level and the notion of winning and losing within the dialectical framework underlying the system of *qiyās al-ʿilla*

2.3.2.1 Epistemic-Assumptions, the Formal Rule and Epistemic Strength

In recent lectures in Paris, Per Martin-Löf (2015) advanced some important motivations for linking CTT with a dialectical conception of logic. They mainly involve the normative approaches to logic in general and to CTT in particular. The main proposal of Martin-Löf involves the deployment of the so-called *formal rule* of dialogical logic in order to provide a normative understanding of Göran Sundholm's[49] notion of *epistemic assumption*.[50] Indeed, one of the main features of the dialogical framework is the so-called *formal rule*, nowadays more aptly named the *Socratic Rule*, by Marion/Rückert (2015), by the means of which:

- the Proponent is entitled to use the Opponent's moves in order to develop the defence of his own thesis.

Morever, when the Proponent challenges some statement of the Opponent, such as a universal quantified one, he might ask the Opponent to concede that the selected individual falls under the kind of individuals about which the predicate is said to universally apply. This, as pointed out by Marion/Rückert (2015), is at the roots of Aristotle's meaning-explanation of the universal quantifier in the *Prior Analytics* (A 24b28–29) as discussed in the *Topics* (Θ 157a34–37 and 160b1–6)[51], and has evident roots in Plato's dialogues (Cooper, Trans. & Ed. (1997)). The general point is that the Socratic Rule induces the players to bring explicitly all the premises to the fore in order to integrate them as part of the debate at stake:

> *It is also worth emphasizing that the Socratic Rule is not merely projected on Plato's text: it has clear motivation within his dialogues, since it explains both Socrates' 'avowals of ignorance', as well as the 'doxastic' or 'say what you believe' constraint on Answerer's answers, for example, at* ***Protagoras*** *331c–d or* ***Charmides*** *166d–e.63. Indeed, it is of the utmost importance for Socrates qua Questioner that he does not introduce a premise of his own in Answerer's scoreboard, if he is convincingly to infer a contradiction from Answerer's beliefs. Otherwise, one would simply counter the charge of inconsistency by pointing out*

[49]Sundholm (2013, p. 17).

[50]"*The solution [. . .], it seems to me now, comes naturally out of this* ***dialogical analysis*** *(not in bold in the original text). [. . .] the premisses here should not be assumed to be known in the qualified sense, that is, to be demonstrated, but we should simply assume that they have been asserted, which is to say that others have taken responsibility for them, and then the question for me is whether I can take responsibility for the conclusion. So, the assumption is merely that they have been asserted, not that they have been demonstrated. That seems to me to be the appropriate definition of epistemic assumption in Sundholm's sense.*" Transcription by Ansten Klev of Martin-Löf's talk in May 2015.

[51]Aristotle (Barnes, Trans. & Ed. (1984)).

that one had not agreed to this or that premise. It is therefore important that the premises are put in Answerer's scoreboard only once Answerer has granted them—this is the 'say what you believe' constraint—but also that Socrates insists on his having no view on any given matter during the exchange—this being the 'avowal of ignorance', for example, in the middle of the game in ***Lesser Hippias*** *372b–e. As it turns out, Socrates very often introduces premises, but he always requests assent from the respondent. For that reason, readers often complain that Answerer is merely a sort of 'yes-man' to Socrates or whoever else is playing Questioner, for example, Parmenides in the second half of Parmenides, but this complaint misses the need for Answerer to be explicitly committed to all premises in his scoreboard.*

As we will see below, the Socratic Rule is crucial for the dialectical reconstruction of the logic underlying the *qiyās*. However, in such a context, the Socratic Rule needs to be refined and levelled: it must be extended to a context where content is at the basis of any concession of the Opponent.[52] In fact, the epistemological aims of the dialectical structure of the *qiyās* require the claims to be backed either by the sources or by some arguments. Only after this has been achieved will he (the Opponent) be prepared to provide a concession upon which the logical argument will rely.

Within the framework of the *qiyās* the Socratic Rule is given an additional new role, namely to structure the level of epistemic strength attained by its deployment, in relation to the ways the claim requested to be conceded is grounded:

Epistemic Strength and Degree of Commitment

1. If a player backs his claim with a reference to the sources, it has the maximal authoritative force and it must be conceded.
2. If the Proponent backs his claim by appealing to the Opponent's own concessions during the dialectical process, then it has a logical force. *Logical force* underlies the logical fragments of a *qiyās*-process. However, Opponent's concessions (leaving aside the sources) might be the result of a cooperative move by the means of which the Opponent brings forward some kind of justification for the selection of a particular property, based on its efficiency in relation to the relevant ruling. More generally, Opponent's concessions, when not rooted in the sources, usually assume some underlying (often empirical) process leading to those concessions, particularly in the case of the branch-case (see below).
3. The deployment of concessions based on similarities and/or resemblances, has less authoritative and epistemic force than all the previous ones. This form of justification involves the deployment of *qiyās al-dalāla* (see the chapter III of the book).

Conceding *farʿ* as Instantiating *waṣf*

One crucial step for the successful ending of the play by the Proponent is to force the Opponent to concede that the branch-case under consideration instantiates the proposed property $\mathcal{P}$ as being the ***waṣf*** relevant for occasioning the sanction $\mathcal{H}$. Before responding, the Opponent might ask for some kind of justification that this is the case. Take the example of acknowledging that the branch-case *date-wine* is a *toxic drink* – in a sense that causes its interdiction. The Proponent might need to

[52]Such kinds of dialogue are related to what is referred to as *material dialogues*. See E. C. Krabbe (2006), Keiff (2009).

bring some factual evidence of the presence of toxicity. There are several forms to implement this, for example assuming some sort of subargument, by the means of which the players acknowledge the deployment of some kind of measurement or empirical test that provides the required evidence.[53]

In fact, if we examine closely al-Baṣrī's and al-Shīrāzī's own examples of debates, it is clear that their dialectical procedure assumes that, when this point of the debate has been achieved, the issue has been settled positively – that is, the empirical test has been carried out and the result is that the branch-case indeed satisfies property $\mathcal{P}$. Following their practice we will keep only those plays where it is assumed that there is evidence that the branch-case instantiates the relevant property. In other words, we will assume that, once the general law expressing the occasioning factor has been identified and acknowledged by the Opponent, he will respond positively to the further request to acknowledge that the branch-case is an instance of the relevant property. In short, such kinds of assertions will be given the status *of epistemological assumptions*.

We will proceed in a similar way with requests concerning the acknowledgement that the root-case is an instance of the proposed property. However, notice that this move *does not* amount to recognizing the property as relevant for the determination of the occasioning factor: the Opponent can concede that the root-case satisfies some property (eg. being a red drink) and at the same time refuse that this property is relevant for the juridical sanction under consideration (forbidden for consumption).

The point of such a way of proceeding is that if the Opponent rejects such kind of requests, there is something fundamentally wrong in the way the Proponent is developing his argumentation: if the property does not apply at all to either the root-case or the branch-case it is not really relevant for carrying out a *qiyās*- process (e.g. take the case where the Proponent asks the Opponent to acknowledge that *wine* is an animal product). If the proposed property does not apply, then the dialogues should start from scratch. Al-Baṣrī's and al-Shīrāzī's strategy has the desirable effect that the whole dialectical process focuses on the central point of *qiyās al-ʿilla*, namely identifying the occasioning factor and deciding if it does or not apply to the branch-case: victory and defeat will be determined by the achievement or not of these main tasks.

This is a consequence of inserting the deployment of the Socratic Rule to the branch-case within the sequence of moves that define a dialogical play for *qiyās al-ʿilla*. It is interesting to note that Aristotle's dialectic games have a similar way of dealing with challenges on universals, by the means of which the challenger brings forward one individual in order to test the generality of the universal. The defender of the universal must accept that the individual instantiates the antecedent of a universal unless he can produce some evidence that this is not the case. This point is being worked out by Zoe McConaughey in her PhD thesis and has been implemented in Crubellier/McConaughey/Marion/Rahman (2019).

[53]See our section on material dialogues in part II.

2.3.2.2 The Choice of the Dialogical Framework

Inqiṭāʿ*, *Ifḥām*, *Ilzām* and the Aims of *Qiyās al-ʿIlla

As mentioned above, it is not our intention to develop a complete formalization of the *jadal*-structure underlying the *qiyās al-ʿilla* but to provide the dialectical meaning-explanations of the main notions involved in this form of reasoning. This does not mean that we are not aiming at a formalization of the *jadal* theory at all. It is rather the case that in the present study we are engaged with the more modest target of setting the basic conceptual elements for such a development.

Today there are numerous dialectical frameworks to choose from for our task. Our choice is the dialogical framework of Paul Lorenzen and Kuno Lorenz[54] which seems natural given that we made the choice to deploy the formal language of CTT, and as argued in the preceding sections there are some good motivations for linking the epistemic perspectives of CTT with the dialogical approach to logic in general.

We should now explain our choice of the dialogical conception of logic as our instrument for the study of dialectical structure underlying the theory of *qiyās* – leaving aside the important fact that Miller's work, that sets a landmark in the understanding of *jadal*, deploys for his reconstruction notions stemming precisely from the dialogical framework of Lorenzen and Lorenz.

In this context, let us recall that the very idea of developing a general system of *qiyās* was to achieve knowledge in an interactive setting that engaged hermeneutical, heuristical and logical moves.[55] One important feature of the objectives of deploying *qiyās* is that attaining victory by the use of linguistic traps or fallacies is absolutely excluded.

In other words, what distinguishes the dialectical framework of the *jadal* from Sophistical dialectics is its ambition of pursuing truth. This feature of the *qiyās* dovetails nicely with the main normative tenets of the dialogical approach to logic. Indeed, the dialogical approach was developed in order to implement an epistemic and pragmatist conception of logic where meaning and knowledge are constituted by interaction, not in order to describe the logic of a dialogue. This is the main idea behind the Socratic Rule mentioned above: epistemological assumptions and textual data are internalized within a dialectical frame in such a way that all notions are cast into what Young calls the *dialectical forge*.

Furthermore, most (but not necessarily all) of the developments within the dialogical framework define plays as being finite and ending with the victory or defeat of one of the players. This feature of Lorenzen-Lorenz's dialogical framework, which as discussed in the chapter IV of our book provides the notion of proposition, makes good sense in the context of *jadal* since it is crucial that juridical debate ends, given that the final aim is to come to a juridical decision. In fact, the

---

[54]P. Lorenzen and K. Lorenz (1978).

[55]See Miller (1984, pp. 9–49), Hallaq (1997, pp. 136–7), and Young (2017, p. 1).

theory of *jadal* has three main notions that capture these last two points, namely *ilzām*, *ifḥām*, *inqiṭāʿ*.

While *ilzām* refers to *conceding inexorable defeat*, and *ifḥām* refers to *bringing the antagonist to silence*, *inqiṭāʿ* or *termination* amounts to a description of all cases where a debate terminates and leads to the defeat of one of the contenders – because of self-contradiction or some other form of mistake, or because of evidence of a counterexample.[56]

So it is assumed that some end of the debate must be reached and that when reached one of the players concedes defeat (or is brought to silence). There has been some evolution in relation to the meaning of these terms: in the early times it looks as if *ilzām* described the general situation of the defeat of one of the contenders, whereas later on it was attached to the Questioner's (Opponent's) concession of defeat. While developing our own dialogical reconstruction we adopted the following usage:

1. We describe the end of a debate where the Proponent has been brought to silence with the term *ifḥām*.
2. We describe the end of a debate where the Opponent concedes defeat with the term *ilzām*.

Be that as it may, Young convincingly argues that both of them describe the end-situation of a debate rather than a special form of objection deployed during such a debate, as sometimes suggested by Miller.[57] In fact, Miller, while translating al-Samarqandī's *Qusṭās*, translates these terms precisely in the sense defended by Young[58]:

> *The debate continues until R is silenced (ifḥām) or Q is forced to accept his argument (ilzām).*[59]

Miller then explains al-Samarqandī's argument for the finite termination, *inqiṭāʿ*, of a debate:

> [...] *al-Samarqandī explains why a debate is necessarily finite. He argues in the following way. If P and Q each make use of the techniques at their disposal, Q making objections and P countering them with further evidence in support of his thesis, then there must necessarily come a point in the debate where P is unable to answer Q's objections or Q must accept P's thesis, whether it be true or false. In the first case Q wins, in the second, P wins. If an opponent should deny the second alternative, al- Samarqandī argues that either P would be forced to bring an infinite number of proofs or he would be unable to respond (ʿajz). But the first possibility is excluded because it would entail an infinite chain of reasonings from a single beginning (mabdaʾ) or cause (ʿilla). This is because al- Samarqandī understands the relation of the "proof" (dalīl) to the "proven" (madlūl) as that of the cause to its effect. An*

[56]Cf. Miller (1984, p. 211); Young (2017, pp. 183–8).

[57]Young (2017, p. 183); Miller (1984, p. 134).

[58]Young (2017, p. 183).

[59]Miller (1984, p. 211).

infinite chain of reasonings is absurd, and, therefore, it follows that P has been refuted since he cannot establish an infinite number of things.[60]

In the context of *qiyās al-ʿilla*, the finiteness of the debates is assured by the fact that challenges to the efficiency of a proposed property amount to finding a counterexample within the sources (including the consensus of the experts). Certainly, a new debate might start later on; but then data and assumptions will have changed and we will be in the presence of a new cycle of the dialectical forge.

Still, it might look as if the terminology *winning* and *losing* a play and the resulting notion of *winning strategy*, an important feature of standard games within this dialogical framework, works against the *jadal* conception of a *cooperative endeavour* towards the pursuit of truth – recall our quote of Young[61] in the introduction to the present chapter.

In our view, one of the epistemological results gathered by the examination of *jadal* is that it suggests a novel perspective on how to integrate cooperative and revision moves in a dialectical framework: a winning strategy is to be thought of as a kind of *recapitulation* of the different attempts to attain truth. According to our reconstruction, the existence of a winning strategy in this context includes the following steps:

1. *internal cooperation*: keeping only the successful moves (including sub-arguments) of the actual plays developed;
2. *external or metalogical cooperation*: including moves and plays that have not actually been played but that due to the background of existing factual and logical knowledge should have been considered.

The second step assumes the perspective of an expert in the field that prescribes how the debate should have proceeded.

What is at stake here is a particular form of what Kuno Lorenz calls *dialogische Geltung*,[62] or legitimacy, instead of logical validity. More precisely it is *material legitimacy*. In the context of *qiyās al-ʿilla* legitimacy amounts to establishing whether there is or not enough evidence to decide about the application of a juridical ruling to the case at stake, given the epistemological circumstances involving the thesis and the logical features of the framework.

So the real target is to achieve a conclusion in relation to some particular legitimacy claim (*Geltungsanspruch*). Legitimacy claims are not to be thought of as bounded by the particular identity of a player: it is an intersubjective notion. If a claim is legitimate it is independent of the particular skills of the player who sustains it. Moreover, the existence of a winning strategy does not amount to the victory of any particular player. However, it is not about claims of logical universality either, but about content-based truth. A winning strategy within a debate structured by a system of *qiyās* displays the collective effort towards pursuing truth.

[60] Miller (1984, pp. 219–20).

[61] Young (2017, p. 15).

[62] K. Lorenz (2000, pp. 87–106).

As we will illustrate below, the development of a debate includes cooperative moves, called *muʿāraḍa*, by means of which a player might collaborate, with the task of grounding the main claim. As just explained, at the strategy level (the level at which the result of the whole dialectical procedure is evaluated), only the outcome of the collaboration will be displayed.

This indicates that the normativity of the dialectical process underlying the *qiyās* admits the following stages:

1. conceptual normativity: the dialectical framework provides the notions by means of which the reasoning involving the legitimacy of the claims underlying a debate is to be developed;
2. heuristic normativity: the inclusion of cooperative moves allows correction and revision during a play in order to obtain the optimal moves for selecting the relevant property;
3. strategic normativity: the optimal moves in order to test the legitimacy of the main claim.

Summing up, while the first level involves the core of what normativity is, by providing us with what Jaroslav Peregrin calls the *material for reasoning*, the second and the third level correspond to normativity in the sense of *tactics*, or on *how to move*.[63] Al-Shīrāzī's dialectical framework leaves the precise description of the optimal moves open, since the inclusion of means for cooperation intends to provide a contextually dependent instrument for heuristic normativity. We will illustrate this point with some examples below.

Notice that revision takes place at the play level. If it is the main claim that must be revised by adding some fresh information, then strictly speaking there is no revision but rather a new start – because the original claim was thought to be knowledge but has been shown to be ungrounded. Thus, the dynamics underlying al-Shīrāzī's dialectical system of *qiyās* seems to be closer to what we nowadays call epistemic approaches rather than to non-monotonic reasoning.

2.4 A Dialogical Framework for Correlational Inferences of the Occasioning Factor

One distinctive feature of Dialogues for ***Qiyās*** is that, though they involve the development of **plays**, the main aim of the Proponent is to provide a **winning strategy** for the thesis. More precisely, the main aim is to develop an argument in such a way that it forces the Opponent to concede that there is a winning strategy for the claim that the branch-case falls under the scope of the juridical sanction $\mathcal{H}$. In other words, by running one or more relevant plays **P** will try to force **O** to concede

[63]J. Peregrin (2014, pp. 228–9).

that there is a strategic reason justifying his claim $\mathcal{H}$(*farʿ*), and more precisely that the justification of the assertion takes the form

ʿilla(*farʿ*): $\mathcal{H}$(*farʿ*),
given O's endorsement of *farʿ*: $\mathcal{P}$
and of
ap(*farʿ*. *taʾthīr*$^{\mathcal{P}}$): $\mathcal{H}$(*farʿ*);
i.e. **O**'s endorsement that the efficiency of the property $\mathcal{P}$ has been verified

Actually, the main claim is to be grounded by **running the plays** relevant for constituting a winning strategy. Furthermore, in real-life situations the running of a play might not provide the moves suitable for building a winning strategy. The winning strategy has to be understood as a kind of recapitulation of the relevant moves, including revisions (of weak moves) taking place at the play level (see introduction to 2.4.4.2 below). Accordingly, the prescriptions for the development of a dialogue for ***qiyās*** leave room for a move that it is not optimal and for its possible correction by the cooperative criticism of the Opponent.

So at the start of a dialogue, the strategic reason for the thesis is left tacit until the relevant plays have been run and the sequence of moves constituting the winning strategy has been described (see our remark on the strategic reason for such an assertion in Sect. 2.4.4.2.2).

The overall view of the next section will be later integrated into the structural rules for the dialogues in Sect. 2.4.4. However, despite the fact that the reader will find this once more further on in our text, we will nevertheless present it here already in order to facilitate the reading of the examples that follow.

2.4.1 *Overall View of the Development of a Dialogue for* Qiyās al-ʿilla

1. A dialogical play for *qiyās al-ʿilla* starts with the Proponent claiming that some specific legal ruling applies to a certain branch-case.

   P!$\mathcal{H}$(*farʿ*)

2. After agreement on the finiteness of the argument to be developed, the Opponent will launch a challenge to the assertion by asking for justification.

   O Why?

   The Proponent's aim is to develop an argument in such a way that it forces the Opponent to concede the justification of the challenged assertion (see step 13). In other words **P** will try to force **O** to concede

$\text{ʿ}illa(far\text{ʿ})$: $\mathcal{H}(far\text{ʿ})$,
given **O**'s endorsement of *farʿ*: $\mathcal{P}$
and of
ap$(far\text{ʿ}.\ ta\text{'}th\bar{\imath}r^{\mathcal{P}})$: $\mathcal{H}(far\text{ʿ})$;

3. In order to develop his argument, the Proponent will start by choosing (to the best of his juridical knowledge) a suitable root-case from the sources to which the ruling at stake has been applied. The move consists in the Proponent forcing the Opponent to acknowledge this fact.
4. Since the evidence comes from the sources the Opponent is forced to concede it.

   Steps 3 and 4 yield:

$$\mathbf{P}\ \mathcal{H}(a\d{s}l)?$$

$$!\mathcal{H}(a\d{s}l)$$

   The "S" in "$\mathcal{H}$" indicates that there is evidence from the *sources* that the ruling $\mathcal{H}$ applies to the root-case.
5. Once conceded, the Proponent will start by choosing (to the best of his juridical and epistemological knowledge) a suitable property (that should lead to the relevant occasioning factor). The move consists in the Proponent forcing the Opponent to acknowledge that the root-case instantiates that property. Recall (Sect. 2.3.2.1) that we adopt here al-Baṣrī's and al-Shīrāzī's practice of keeping only those plays where the Opponent responds positively to this form of request.

$$\mathbf{P}\ a\d{s}l : \mathcal{P}?$$

$$\mathbf{O}\ a\d{s}l : \mathcal{P}$$

6. Once the Opponent concedes that both the ruling and the selected property apply to the root-case, the Proponent will ask the Opponent to concede that the property just selected is the one that constitutes the relevant occasioning factor.[64] The request can indicate the sources or not.

$$\mathbf{P}\ \text{ʿ}illa(a\d{s}l) : \mathcal{H}(a\d{s}l)?$$

   If the *ʿilla* has been determined by the sources the Opponent must accept by endorsing the efficiency of the property. This endorsement commits the Opponent to asserting the universal **O**! $(\forall x: \mathcal{P}_{\mathcal{D}} \vee \neg \mathcal{P}_{\mathcal{D}})$ { [$(\forall y: \mathcal{P}_{\mathcal{D}})$ $wuj\bar{u}d^{\vee}(y) =_{\{\mathcal{P}\mathcal{D} \vee \neg \mathcal{P}\mathcal{D}\}}$

[64]In the context of *jadal* this move is called "*ta'līl*" by the means of which the Proponent asserts that a given property determines the factor occasioning the relevant ruling. See Young (2017, pp. 24–25, p. 568, p. 624).

$x \supset \mathcal{H}(y)] \wedge [\ (\forall z{:}\ \neg\mathcal{P}_{\mathcal{D}})\ salb^{\vee}(z) =_{\{\mathcal{P}\mathcal{D}\vee\neg\mathcal{P}\mathcal{D}\}} x \supset \neg\mathcal{H}(z)]\}$.[65] If there is no explicit backing from the sources the Opponent can either ask for justification (*muṭālaba*), cooperate in such a justification or *strongly* reject it.

7. If the Opponent asks for a justification, the Proponent will switch to the development of a dialogue of the form *qiyās al-ʿilla al-khafī* and will develop an argument towards establishing its efficiency. In other words, the Proponent must be able to bring forward arguments showing that the property satisfies *ṭard* and *ʿaks*. These duties commit the Proponent to assert **P**! $(\forall y{:}\ \mathcal{P}_{\mathcal{D}})\mathcal{H}(y))$ and **P**! $(\forall z{:}\ \neg\mathcal{P}_{\mathcal{D}})\ \neg\mathcal{H}(z)$. Both assertions lead to the further assertion **O**! $(\forall x{:}\ \mathcal{P}_{\mathcal{D}}\vee\neg\mathcal{P}_{\mathcal{D}})\ \{\ [\ (\forall y{:}\ \mathcal{P}_{\mathcal{D}})\ wuj\bar{u}d^{\vee}(y) =_{\{\mathcal{P}\mathcal{D}\vee\neg\mathcal{P}\mathcal{D}\}} x \supset \mathcal{H}(y)] \wedge [\ (\forall z{:}\ \neg\mathcal{P}_{\mathcal{D}})\ salb^{\vee}(z) =_{\{\mathcal{P}\mathcal{D}\vee\neg\mathcal{P}\mathcal{D}\}} x \supset \neg\mathcal{H}(z)]\}$, that establishes *taʾthīr* (the efficiency of the property $\mathcal{P}$ for causing the juridical decision $\mathcal{H}$, for any concrete case satisfying $\mathcal{P}$).
8. If **P** does not succeed, the play stops unless the Opponent decides to cooperate as described in the next step.
9. The Opponent might react by deciding to cooperate by first proposing a more precise formulation of the property advanced or by proposing a new property for the constitution of the occasioning factor.[66] This will trigger a sub-play where the Opponent will defend the choice of an alternative property following the procedure prescribed for a *muʿāraḍa*-move or constructive criticism. Once the sub-play has ended, the play proceeds to step 12. A *muʿāraḍa*-move assumes (1) that the choice of the root-case and the choice of the ruling are relevant for the thesis, even if the Proponent chooses the wrong property for determining the occasioning factor, and (2) that the branch-case instantiates the "right" (newly proposed) property.

   The launching of a constructive criticism by **O** will be indicated with the following notation:

$$\mathbf{O}!\mathbb{V}\,{}^{\text{ʿ}}illa(a\d{s}l) : \mathcal{H}^{\mathcal{P}*}\ (a\d{s}l)$$

   where the "$\mathbb{V}$" indicates that **O** proposes to develop an argument for establishing $\mathcal{P}^*$ rather than $\mathcal{P}$ as the relevant property.
10. The Opponent might also react by *strongly* rejecting the Proponent's proposal. We distinguish two cases that we call (1) *Destruction of the thesis*. The main target of this form of objection is the thesis rather than only objecting to the Proponent proposal for determining the *ʿilla*. In such a case it is he, the Opponent, who has to bring forward a counterexample from the sources. This will trigger a sub-play where the Opponent develops his counter argumentation, following the prescriptions for one of the forms of destructive criticism, namely:

---

[65]Recall our remark in Sect. 2.3.1.1 concerning the fact that identifying an occasioning factor amounts to characterizing it as a general law.

[66]This counterattack of the Opponent is a *muʿāraḍa* move, extensively discussed by Miller (1984, pp. 33–39) and by Young (2017, p. 151), who calls it *constructive criticism*. It is opposed to the *destructive criticism* or *naqḍ* displayed in the following step.

qalb (reversal), *naqḍ* (*inconsistency*), or *kasr* (*breaking apart*). (2) *Destruction of the ʿilla.* The counter-argument involves bringing forward objections to the proposed *waṣf* as determining the *ʿilla*, following the prescriptions for attacks of the forms *fasād al-waḍʿ* (invalidity of occasioned status) or *ʿadam al-taʾthīr* (lack of efficiency). If the Opponent succeeds, the play stops.

11. If, after the justification, the Opponent concedes that the property determines the occasioning factor for the ruling of the root-case, then the same moves as step 7 follow. In other words, the Opponent commits himself to asserting the universal

$$\mathbf{O}!(\forall x : \mathcal{P}_{\mathcal{D}} \vee \neg\mathcal{P}_{\mathcal{D}}) \left\{ \left[(\forall y : \mathcal{P}_{\mathcal{D}})\ wuj\bar{u}d^{\vee}(y) = {}_{\{\mathcal{P}\mathcal{D}\vee\neg\mathcal{P}\mathcal{D}\}}\ x \supset \mathcal{H}(y) \right] \wedge \left[(\forall z : \neg\mathcal{P}_{\mathcal{D}})\ salb^{\vee}(z) = {}_{\{\mathcal{P}\mathcal{D}\vee\neg\mathcal{P}\mathcal{D}\}}\ x \supset \neg\mathcal{H}(z) \right] \right\}.$$

12. After the Opponent's assertion of the universal stated in the previous step, the Proponent will ask the Opponent to acknowledge that the property also applies to the branch-case – recall (Sect. 2.3.2.1) that we adopt here al-Baṣrī's and al-Shīrāzī's practice of keeping only those plays where the Opponent responds positively to this form of request. The point of this assumption is that, if the property does not apply, even though it determines the occasioning factor, then it is the main thesis that should be rejected. In other words, if the Opponent refuses to concede that the branch-case instantiates the relevant property, a kind of strong rejection results. Request and answer will be expressed by means of the following notation:

$$\mathbf{P}\ far^{\text{ʿ}} : \mathcal{P}?\ (\text{or } \mathcal{P}^*)$$

$$\mathbf{O}\ far^{\text{ʿ}} : \mathcal{P}\ (\text{or } \mathcal{P}^*)$$

13. After the Opponent concedes that the property does apply to the branch-case, and since the Opponent also concedes that the property is the one that characterizes the relevant occasioning factor, the Proponent will ask the Opponent to acknowledge that the branch-case falls under the ruling at stake. This move forces the Opponent to concede the challenged thesis. A play ends if there are no other moves allowed. If the Proponent's defence is successful, the play will end by a move where he indicates that the Opponent has finished by endorsing the thesis under scrutiny.

P *farʿ*: $\mathcal{P}$ (challenging the universal that expresses the *ṭard*-condition)[67]

$$\mathbf{O}\ \boldsymbol{ap}[far^{\text{ʿ}}.ta\text{ʾ}th\bar{\imath}r^{\mathcal{P}}] : \mathcal{H}(far^{\text{ʿ}})$$

P *ʿilla*(*farʿ*): $\mathcal{H}$(*farʿ*) (answer to the request for justification of the thesis that can be glossed as: you just stated the justification of the thesis you asked for)

---

67 Or **P** *farʿ*: $\mathcal{P}^*$

Let us condense the development of such a play with the following diagram:

Development of a play for *qiyās al-ʿilla*

P ! The ruling $\mathcal{H}$ applies to the branch-case
O ! Why?
P Don't the Sources record that the ruling $\mathcal{H}$ applies to the root-case?
O ! Yes they do
P Doesn't the root-case instantiate the property $\mathcal{P}$?
O ! Yes it does

P Given your previous assertions, and the *evidence from the sources*, you must concede that the property $\mathcal{P}$ has the efficiency to determine the occasioning factor for the ruling $\mathcal{H}$. Don't you?

O ! Indeed, every case that instantiates the property $\mathcal{P}$ falls under the ruling $\mathcal{H}$.

P Doesn't the branch-case instantiate the property $\mathcal{P}$? ($\mathcal{P}$*)
O ! Yes it does
P ! Accordingly the ruling also applies to the branch case. Doesn't it?
O ! Yes it does
P ! ***This answer justifies the thesis***

P Given your previous assertions, you must concede that the property $\mathcal{P}$ has the efficiency to determine the occasioning factor for the ruling $\mathcal{H}$. Don't you?

O ! Why should I ? Justify !

P ! the presence of the ruling is due to the presence of the occasioning factor and the absence of the ruling is due to its absence (*taʾthīr*)

O Constructive criticism

O Destructive criticisms

O ! Am convinced now. Every case that instantiates the property occasions the ruling on that case

P Doesn't the branch-case instantiate the property $\mathcal{P}$? ($\mathcal{P}$*)
O ! Yes it does
P ! Accordingly the ruling also applies to the branch case. Doesn't it?
O ! Yes it does
P ! ***This answer justifies the thesis***

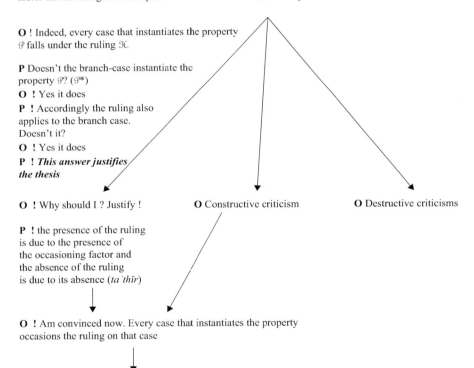

2.4.2 *Special Moves*

2.4.2.1 Requiring Justification: *muṭālaba*

The conditions of co-extensiveness and co-exclusiveness determine the way to challenge and defend the assertion that links property and ruling. A counterexample to the condition of *efficiency* amounts to bringing up a case where the purported property is present but does not provide the material for the occasioning factor (for example vinegar, as counterexample to identifying *red liquid* as the factor leading to the interdiction of consuming wine).

In the context of a debate structured by the *qiyās*, if there is no evidence from the sources of a property $\mathscr{P}_{\mathscr{D}}$ being the relevant one for the ruling $\mathscr{H}(aṣl)$ of the root-case, then $\mathscr{P}_{\mathscr{D}}$ is only assumed to constitute the *ʿilla* of the *aṣl*. So we indicate this fact by

ʿilla(*aṣl*): $\mathscr{H}^{\mathscr{P}}$(*aṣl*)

instead of

ʿilla(*aṣl*): $\mathscr{H}_{\mathbb{S}}{}^{\mathscr{P}}$(*aṣl*),

which indicates evidence from the sources.

Sometimes, we use the abbreviated forms

ʿilla(*a*): $\mathscr{H}^{\mathscr{P}}(a)$
ʿilla(*a*): $\mathscr{H}_{\mathbb{S}}{}^{\mathscr{P}}(a)$

- If the context makes it clear that the ruling has been defined to be specific for the property $\mathscr{P}$, we may leave it tacit. This yields the notations:

ʿilla(*a*): $\mathscr{H}(a)$, and
ʿilla(*a*): $\mathscr{H}^{\mathbb{S}}(a)$

- For the sake of notational simplicity, when occurring within a formula we write $\mathscr{P}$ instead of $\mathscr{P}_{\mathscr{D}}$

In the case where *ʿilla*(*a*): $\mathscr{H}^{\mathscr{P}}(a)$ has been asserted rather than *ʿilla*(*a*): $\mathscr{H}_{\mathbb{S}}{}^{\mathscr{P}}(a)$, a justification for selecting the property $\mathscr{P}_{\mathscr{D}}$ can be required: the request is called *muṭālaba*. The justification process involves showing that the proposed property satisfies co-extensiveness and co-exclusiveness. This suggests the following dialectical structure:

(a) the original claim on the applicability of a ruling to a case not recorded by the sources presupposes singling out a particular property;
(b) a *qiyās al-ʿilla* process contemplates the possibility of making explicit the reasons that led to select one property rather than a different one: this is what *muṭālaba* is about.

2.4.2.2 Constructive Criticism: *Muʿāraḍa*

Assume that the Proponent backed his choice of the property $\mathscr{P}$ as constituting the occasioning factor for the juridical ruling $\mathscr{H}$. Let us further assume that the

Opponent is not convinced, but is willing to collaborate with the task of searching for the suitable property. The Opponent now becomes the defender in a sub-play where he is committed to bringing forward a new argument that either makes the formulation of the proposed property more precise or proposes a new property. In practice, the Opponent launches such a form of cooperative move when he thinks that the claim of the thesis is correct but he also thinks that the Proponent made wrong choices during his argumentation in support for it. The sub-play proceeds in the following way:

1. The Opponent starts by asserting that the relevant factor for the root-case at stake is the property $\mathcal{P}_{\mathcal{D}}{}^{*}$ rather than $\mathcal{P}_{\mathcal{D}}$.
2. If the assertion of the Opponent is rooted in the sources, the Proponent must accept it and the play will continue from step 5. If it is not based on the sources, the Proponent responds by challenging the Opponent to open a *sub-play* where the latter must defend his thesis.
3. In the sub-play, before providing the required justification, the Opponent might first choose to force the Proponent to accept that there is a root-case that contradicts the Proponent's choice of $\mathcal{P}_{\mathcal{D}}$ as relevant for the juridical ruling at stake.
4. The Opponent will then proceed by showing that the new property $\mathcal{P}_{\mathcal{D}}{}^{*}$ satisfies the conditions *ta'thīr*, *ṭard* and *ʿaks* in relation to $\mathcal{H}$.
5. Once the new property $\mathcal{P}_{\mathcal{D}}{}^{*}$ has been accepted by both contenders as the relevant one for $\mathcal{H}$, the sub-play ends and the dialogue continues with the Proponent endorsing that $\mathcal{P}_{\mathcal{D}}{}^{*}$ applies to the branch-case involved in the thesis. Then he will proceed to show that this leads to justifying the thesis.
6. The tree displaying the winning strategy will delete the unsuccessful attempts and also the justification of the sub-play.

This challenge is a *muʿāraḍa*-move, profusely discussed in the *jadal*-literature. Young calls it *constructive criticism.*[68] It is opposed to *destructive criticism.*

The launching of a constructive criticism will be indicated with the following notation:

$$\mathbf{O}!\mathbb{V}^{\text{`}}illa(a) : \mathcal{H}_{\mathbb{S}}{}^{\mathcal{P}*}(a)$$

In bringing forward such a move, the Opponent is committed to running a sub-play where he advances the thesis that the relevant property is $\mathcal{P}^{*}$ rather than the proposed $\mathcal{P}$.

2.4.2.3 Forms of Destructive Criticism

The Opponent might also react by *strongly* rejecting the Proponent's proposal. We distinguish two cases that we call

[68]Young (2017, p. 151).

1. *Destruction of the thesis*;
2. *Destruction of the ʿilla*.

The main target of the form of objection we call *destruction of the thesis* is the thesis rather than only objecting to the Proponent's proposal for determining the *ʿilla*. In such a case it is he, the Opponent, who has to bring forward a counterexample from the sources. This will trigger a sub-play where the Opponent develops his counter argumentation. In practice, the Opponent launches such a form of destructive criticism when he thinks that the claim of the thesis is incorrect and that the only way to correct it is to start from scratch.

This form of criticism declines into different kinds of objections distinguished by the type of counterexample brought forward. We will restrict ourselves to only three main forms of non-cooperative criticism. Let us point out that we decided to include the third one as implementing the destruction of the thesis, because of the examples found in the texts, but in principle it does not need to be classified in that way. Thus, according to our classification destruction of the thesis amounts to:

1. Bringing forward a root-case of which it is recorded that exactly the opposite of the claimed ruling applies, despite the fact that the property itself applies.[69] It is called *qalb* (reversal). The counterexample undermines the *ṭard*-condition of the purported property – the property applies but the opposite of the ruling is the case.
2. Bringing forward a root-case of which it is recorded that a ruling different from the claimed ruling applies and that it has been acknowledged that both rulings are incompatible, despite the fact that the property itself applies. It is called, *naqḍ* (*inconsistency*). The counterexample can also be seen as undermining the *ṭard*-condition (provided both rulings are incompatible).
3. Bringing forward a root-case of which it is recorded that a ruling different to the claimed ruling applies despite the fact that the property, in fact a compound of properties, itself is present but with some qualifications. The point is that some component of the the proposed compound property does not lead to the expected ruling, and this suggests that one of the components is not efficient and the other(s) do not induce the expected ruling. It is called *kasr* (*breaking apart*). The counterexample can also be understood as a particular form of *naqḍ*.

One crucial feature of destructive criticisms of the thesis is that the counterexample must involve a root-case that is closely related to the branch-case proposed. In

[69]Our formulation is slightly more general than that of Young (2017, p. 166), since according to our setting the root-case that triggers the counterargument does not need to be the same as that chosen by the Proponent. The point is that if we follow Young's restriction to only one root-case, then it all comes down to accepting or not that the ruling of the thesis applies to that root-case. This assumes that the Proponent either misinterprets the sources or misses some relevant evidence that can be found in those sources. Our formulation might be closer to a specific form of reversal called *reversal and oppositeness* (*al-qalb wa-al-ʿaks*) – see Young (2017, pp. 166–167).

fact quite often, the counterexamples brought forward by a destructive criticism involve a root-case that is some subset of the branch-case. Thus, the criticism will proceed by forcing the Proponent to concede that the counterexample shows that the ruling to be applied contradicts the one claimed to hold for the branch-case.

The second form of objection, *destruction of the ʿilla,* will trigger a sub-play where the Opponent brings forward objections to the efficiency of the proposed *waṣf.* Destruction of the *ʿilla is* implemented by one of the following two criticisms:

1. Bringing forward a root-case of which it is recorded in the sources that a property assumed to apply to the branch-case occasions, in fact, the opposite ruling to the one proposed by the Proponent in the thesis. It is called *fasād al-waḍʿ* (invalidity of occasioned status) and unlike the next criticism it amounts to producing evidence for a new *ʿilla.*[70]
2. Bringing forward a root-case of which it is recorded that the claimed ruling applies despite the absence of the property claimed to specify the occasioning factor. It is called *ʿadam al-taʾthīr* (lack of efficiency). The counterexample undermines the *taʾthīr* condition of the purported property because the occasioning factor for the ruling is not specified by the proposed property (is not dependent upon the property). This also undermines the other two conditions.[71]

In the following section we will develop some examples displaying different forms of criticism, but let us illustrate first the different forms of objection in a succinct manner and introduce a suitable formal notation. The assertion "**O**! $\mathbb{F}\varphi$ "indicates that the Opponent is committed to a sub-play where he will bring up a counterexample to the Proponent's assertion φ when applied to destructive criticism which yields:

1. ***Qalb***: **O**!$\mathbb{F}$ $(\forall y: \mathcal{P}_{\mathcal{D}})\mathcal{H}(y)$. The Opponent is committed to a sub-play where he brings forward a root-case of which it is recorded that an opposite ruling to the claimed ruling applies, even if $\mathcal{P}$ applies to this new root-case. Hence the root-case is presented as a counterexample to the Proponent's claim that every $\mathcal{P}$ falls under the ruling $\mathcal{H}$ and in particular to the claim that this ruling applies to the branch-case.

   Thesis: Saliva of beasts of prey (*farʿ*) is impure ($\mathcal{H}$). *Claim*: "Having canine teeth" determines the *ʿilla*. *Counterexample*: The saliva of cats, which are beasts of prey with canine teeth, is not impure.[72]
2. ***Naqḍ***: **O**! $\mathbb{F}$ $(\forall y: \mathcal{P}_{\mathcal{D}})\mathcal{H}(y)$, given $aṣl^{*}: \mathcal{P}_{\mathcal{D}}$, $\mathcal{H}^{S*}(aṣl^{*})$, and $\neg(\mathcal{H}(aṣl^{*}) \wedge \mathcal{H}^{*}(aṣl^{*}))$. The Opponent is committed to a sub-play where he brings forward a root-case of which it is recorded that a different ruling to the claimed ruling applies and both rulings are incompatible. Hence the root-case is presented as a counterexample to the Proponent's assertion that every $\mathcal{P}$ falls under the ruling $\mathcal{H}$

[70] Young (2017, pp. 158–9).

[71] Young (2017, pp. 150–64).

[72] Young (2017, p. 159, p. 166).

and in particular to the claim that this ruling applies to the branch-case. *Thesis*: Killing (*farʿ*) should be punished with jail ($\mathcal{H}$). *Claim*: "Having commited homicide" determines the *ʿilla*. *Counterexample*: Some forms of homicide neither lead to jail nor to being set free but to the obligation of carrying out certain specific social services.[73]

3. ***Kasr***: **O**! $\mathbb{F}(\forall y\text{: } \{ y\text{: } \mathcal{P}_{\mathcal{D}} | \ \mathcal{P}^*(y)\})\mathcal{H}(y)$, given **P**'s claim that the relevant property is in fact the compound $\{ y\text{: } \mathcal{P}_{\mathcal{D}} | \ \mathcal{P}^*(y)\}$ (it could be also composed by more than two properties), then the Opponent is committed to a sub-play where he brings forward a root-case that enjoys one of the components $\mathcal{P}_{\mathcal{D}}$ but is recorded falling under the scope $\mathcal{H}^*$, rather than the claimed $\mathcal{H}$, and it is the case that the remaining property (or cluster of properties) cannot induce $\mathcal{H}$. This rule involved many discussions, and rightly so, since it looks as it comes close to committing the fallacy of compound and divided sense. The defender might reject the objection by insisting that his claim is about the *compound* taken as unity; not that each property taken separatedly, is efficient by their own to induce the judgment.[74] *Thesis*: Interdiction ($\mathcal{H}$) of transaction of goods where the buyer did not see those goods before the contract was closed (*farʿ*). *Claim*: "Establishing a contract with someone for the transaction of goods in such a way that the benefactor has no access to the object of the contract" determines the *ʿilla*. *Counterexample*: Contract-Marriages closed before the members of the couple have acquaintance with each other are not forbidden. Clearly, in this case, the defender might respond pointing out that his claim involved the compound transaction-contracts with no access to the good specified by the contract. It is about having no access in the context of transaction-contracts like purchasing or renting (*bayʿ*), not about having no access in general to the good specified by some contract.[75]

---

[73]Young (2017, p. 170).

[74]In fact expressions such as { y: $\mathcal{P}_{\mathcal{D}}| \ \mathcal{P}^*(y)$, that can ge glossed as *Those y instantiating* $\mathcal{P}_{\mathcal{D}}$*, are such that they enjoy* $\mathcal{P}^*$(y) (e.g. those transaction-contracts, where the beneficiary has no access to the goods specified by those contracts), have either *a compound* understanding or a divided understanding. The compound understanding, requires that if we isolate one of the components it always carries information about the second component – technically speaking the way to isolate one component is to use the function *left-* and *right-projection*. In the divided understanding one can isolate one component that does not carry information about the other – technically speaking it amounts to the use of *injections*. One of the difficulties of *kasr* is that the Opponent seems to understand the construction in its divided sense, but the Proponent might insist that his claim assumes a compound sense.

[75]Young (2017, p. 174). Young pointed out in a personal email to the authors tht al-Juwaynī in the *Kāfiya* (1979, p. 211-213), pays special attention to arguments against the validity of kasr. The contemporary author'Abd al-Karīm b. 'Ālī b. Muḥammad al-Namla provided in his work *al-Muhadhdhab fī 'Ilm Uṣūl al-Fiqh al-Muqārin* (1999, pp 2287-2288) the following reconstruction of kasr. The Opponent starts by presenting a counterexample to the claim that the compound property at stake is inefficient for the relevant juridical ruling. The Proponent defends his claim by breaking the component and claim that the other part is the efficient one. If he succeds he justified the main claim if not it is the antagonist's objection the one that is justified.

4. ***Fasād al-waḍʿ***: **O**! $\mathbb{F}(\forall y: \mathcal{P}_{\mathcal{D}})\mathcal{H}(y)$. The Opponent is committed to a sub-play where he shows that, according to the sources, some specific property that applies to the branch-case is the one that is relevant for the occasioning of the juridical decision. Moreover this property occasions the opposite ruling to that proposed by the Proponent. In short, the Opponent brings forward an *ʿilla* that invalidates the one deployed by the Proponent and leads to the destruction of the thesis. *Thesis*: Saliva of beasts of prey (*farʿ*) is impure ($\mathcal{H}$). *Claim*: "Having canine teeth" determines the *ʿilla*. *Counterexample*: *Being beast of prey* determines the *ʿilla*. This *ʿilla* occasions the ruling *Saliva of beasts of prey is **not** impure*.[76]
5. ***ʿAdam al-taʾthīr***: **O**! $\mathbb{F}(\forall y: \mathcal{P}_{\mathcal{D}})\mathcal{H}(y) \land (\forall z: \neg\mathcal{P}_{\mathcal{D}})\ \neg\mathcal{H}(z)$. The Opponent is committed to a sub-play where he brings forward a root-case which constitutes a counterexample to the efficiency of the proposed property asserted by the Proponent. The counterexample refutes at least one of the constituents of the conjunction. *Thesis*: The consumption of cherry red wine (*farʿ*) is forbidden. *Claim*: "Presence of euphoric intensity and having red colour" determines the *ʿilla*. *Counterexample*: Grape white wine is forbidden, despite the fact that it is not red.[77]

2.4.3 Examples of Dialogues

Most of the examples discussed in the present section are based on textual sources, with the exception of the branch-case of our first example (on reading the emails of someone else). The point of the anachronism is to illustrate how to apply an ancient juridical rule to a new branch-case. However, the root-case and the identification of the property determining the relevant occasioning factor are based on textual sources to which we refer.

We will only display the tree of the resulting winning strategy for the last example, since the other examples follow basically the same pattern. Let us first provide the general schema that determines the development of our examples.

Notational Conventions

We slightly changed the usual notation of the dialogical framework and added some further indications specific to the *qiyās*. More precisely:

1. Proponent's moves are numbered with even numbers starting from **0**. Those moves are recorded at the outmost right column.
2. Opponent's moves are numbered with odd numbers starting from **1**. Those moves are recorded at the outmost left column.
3. The inner columns record the form (challenge or defence) of response and the line to which the move responds. So, while "? 0" indicates that the corresponding move is a challenge (by the Opponent) to line 0 of the Proponent; "! 3" indicates

[76] Young (2017, pp. 158–159).

[77] Hallaq (1985, pp. 88–89).

that the corresponding move is a defence of a challenge launched by the Opponent in move 3.

4. Formal expressions with a preceding **exclamation mark** such as ! *'$\mathcal{H}^{\mathcal{S}}$(aṣl)* indicate the assertion that there is some (not yet specified) evidence in the sources for the fact that the ruling $\mathcal{H}$ applies to the root-case. Similarly expressions such as ! $\mathcal{H}$(*farʿ*) indicate the assertion that there is some (not yet specified) evidence for the fact that the ruling $\mathcal{H}$ applies to the branch-case.
5. Formal expressions **without** a **preceding exclamation mark** such as *ʿilla*(*farʿ*): $\mathcal{H}$(*farʿ*) asserted by the Proponent indicate that the justification for the application of the ruling to the branch-case follows from applying that branch-case to the universal

$$(\forall x : \mathcal{P}_{\mathcal{D}} \vee \neg\mathcal{P}_{\mathcal{D}}) \left\{ \left[(\forall y : \mathcal{P}_{\mathcal{D}})\ wuj\bar{u}d^{\vee}(y) = {}_{\{\mathcal{P}\mathcal{D}\vee\neg\mathcal{P}\mathcal{D}\}}\ x \supset \mathcal{H}(y) \right] \wedge \left[(\forall z : \neg\mathcal{P}_{\mathcal{D}})\ salb^{\vee}(z) = {}_{\{\mathcal{P}\mathcal{D}\vee\neg\mathcal{P}\mathcal{D}\}}\ x \supset \neg\mathcal{H}(z) \right] \right\}$$

which is precisely the universal the Proponent tries to force the Opponent to endorse.
6. For the sake of notational simplicity we did not include the moves related to the repetition rank (for the notion of *repetition rank* see Sect. 4.1)

More Notational Conventions

- The dialectical framework for *qiyās al-ʿilla* deploys not only the usual challenges and defences but also requests. With a request a player brings forward an assertion and asks the contender to endorse it.
- The notation deployed for a request has the form "¿*n*, ¿! *m*", where "*n*" and "*m*" stand for natural numbers (that reads: the Proponent responds to move *n* of the Opponent by requesting him to endorse the assertion brought forward in move *m*.).
- Sometimes a request formulated in move *k* responds to move *n* of the antagonist **X**, given a previous move *m* of **X**. This request will be indicated with the notation "¿*n*(*m*),! *k*".
- Before endorsing the requested assertion brought forward with move *m* the requested contender might himself ask for justification of the assertion requested to be endorsed. This response will be indicated with the notation "?*m*¿".
- We will also deploy

$$(\forall x : \mathcal{P} \vee \neg\mathcal{P})[(\forall y : \mathcal{P})w^{\vee}(y) = {}_{\{\mathcal{P}\vee\neg\mathcal{P}\}}x \supset \mathcal{H}(y)] \wedge \left[(\forall z : \neg\mathcal{P})s^{\vee}(z) = {}_{\{\mathcal{P}\vee\neg\mathcal{P}\}}x \supset \neg\mathcal{H}(z)\right]\}$$

instead of

$$(\forall x : \mathcal{P}_{\mathcal{D}} \vee \neg\mathcal{P}_{\mathcal{D}}) \left\{ \left[(\forall y : \mathcal{P}_{\mathcal{D}})\ wuj\bar{u}d^{\vee}(y) = {}_{\{\mathcal{P}\mathcal{D}\vee\neg\mathcal{P}\mathcal{D}\}}\ x \supset \mathcal{H}(y) \right] \wedge [(\forall z : \neg\mathcal{P}_{\mathcal{D}})\ salb^{\vee}(z) = {}_{\{\mathcal{P}\mathcal{D}\vee\neg\mathcal{P}\mathcal{D}\}}\ x \supset \neg\mathcal{H}(z)]\right\}$$

- We will not write explicitly the strategic reason *ta'thīr*$^{\mathcal{P}\mathbf{X}}[\![p_i{}^{\mathbf{Y}}]\!]$ justifying the main assertion of the efficiency-verification, but deploy the implicit form

$$\mathbf{X}!(\forall x : \mathcal{P} \vee \neg\mathcal{P})\{[(\forall y : \mathcal{P})w^{\vee}(y) = {}_{\{\mathcal{P}\vee\neg\mathcal{P}\}}x \supset \mathcal{H}(y)] \wedge [(\forall z, : \neg\mathcal{P})s^{\vee}(z) = {}_{\{\mathcal{P}\vee\neg\mathcal{P}\}}x \supset \neg\mathcal{H}(z)]\}$$

(for a justification of this convention see our discussion introducing Sect. 2.4 above and the remark on strategic reason in Sect. 2.4.4.2.2).

However, the defence is written in its explicit though abbreviated form:

$$\mathbf{X}!\boldsymbol{ap}[p_i.t^{\mathcal{P}}] : \mathcal{H}(p_i) - \text{given } \mathbf{Y}\; p_i : \mathcal{P}.$$

The defence is a short-cut of the following moves: (1) replacing x with p_i, and (2) defending the left side of the conjunction.

2.4.3.1 Example of *a Qiyās al-ʿIlla (al-Jalī bi-al-Naṣṣ)*

See Table 2.1. The importance of this form of *qiyās al-ʿilla*, despite its simplicity, is that it has a canonical form. Moreover, it is related to Aristotle's *reasoning by exemplification* or *paradigmatic inference*,[78] though, as pointed out before it is not to be understood as involving one-step induction – it might be even argued that Aristotle's notion does not involve one-step induction either.

2.4.3.2 Examples o*f Qiyās al-ʿIlla al-Khafī*

The following example, in Table 2.2, is a reconstruction that constitutes a variant of al-Shīrāzī's[79] refutation of Ḥanafī's analysis of the argument on the *purity status of beasts of prey*. As pointed out by Young,[80] al-Shīrāzī himself thought that the argument should be developed following a *fasād al-waḍʿ* (invalidity of the occasioned status) –move.[81] Indeed, al-Shīrāzī sees the argument as indicating that the main thesis is fundamentally false since it assumes that beasts of prey are impure, but there is direct evidence from the sources contradicting this. Thus, according to al-Shīrāzī we do not need to be involved in a discussion about the suitability or not of the property chosen by the Proponent. Our take on the example corresponds

[78] Cf. Aristotle, *Pr. An.* 69a1; Bartha (2010, pp. 36–40).

[79] Shīrāzī (1987, p. 112).

[80] Young (2017, p. 159).

[81] Different to Young's (2017, p. 159) analysis, Miller (1984, p. 119) concludes that al-Shīrāzī's presentation suggests that the two forms of destructive criticism, namely *qalb* and *fasād al-waḍʿ*, are indistinguishable.

rather to Miller's presentation of *qalb* or *destructive criticism by reversal.*[82] Moreover, it corresponds to a particular form of *qalb* called *reversal* and *oppositeness* (*al-qalb wa-al-ʿaks*).[83] Notice that in the sub-play the opponent is changing the roles and defending the claim that he has a winning strategy in order to reject $\mathcal{P}$ as the determining occasioning factor. This move, *a switch of roles,* was pointed out by scholars such as Hallaq ("The logic of legal reasoning") and Young (*The Dialectical Forge*).

The second example, the *wine example* in Table 2.3, is one that has received very much attention in the specialized literature.

Finally Table 2.4 develops a variant of the wine example. This variant deploys a *muʿāraḍa*-move. As already mentioned, *muʿāraḍa*-moves assume a cooperative attitude of the challenger. Here we assume that the original argument in favour of choosing the property of being a drink made of pressed fruit-juice as relevant for determining the relevant property, misses one of those conditions, namely co-presence (the counterexample is vinegar).:

Table 2.1 Reading the mail of someone else is forbidden

O			P		
		Responses	**Responses**	**Main thesis**	0
				Reading (without permission) letters of someone else is forbidden	
				! $\mathcal{H}$(*farʿ*)	
1	Why?	? 0 (challenges move 0)	¿1, ¿! 2 (responds to 1 with the request of endorsing 2)	Entering (without permission) into a house of someone else is forbidden by the Quran (sources $\mathcal{S}$), isn't it?[a]	2
				$\mathcal{H}^{\mathcal{S}}$(*aṣl*)?	
3	Yes	! 2 (responds to the request of move 2 with an endorsement)	¿3, ¿! 4	Entering (without permission) into a house of someone else violates privacy. Don't you agree?	4
	! $\mathcal{H}^{\mathcal{S}}$(*aṣl*)			*aṣl*: $\mathcal{P}$?	

(continued)

[82]Miller (1984, p. 119).

[83]See Young (2017, pp. 166–7).

Table 2.1 (continued)

5	I do.	! 4	¿5(3), ¿! 6	Given your own moves 3 and 5, and the evidence from the sources, you must concede that violation of privacy has the efficiency to determine the *ʿilla* of that *ḥukm*. Do you?	6
	aṣl: $\mathcal{P}$			*ʿilla*(*aṣl*): $\mathcal{H}_S^{\mathcal{P}}(aṣl)$?	
7	Indeed I endorse it since it comes from the sources of the assertion	! 6	¿7, ¿! 8	Does reading (without permission) personal letters of someone else violate the privacy of that person?	8
	$! (\forall x: \mathcal{P} \vee \neg\mathcal{P}) \{[(\forall y: \mathcal{P})\ w^{\vee}(y) =_{\{\mathcal{P}\vee\neg\mathcal{P}\}} x \supset \mathcal{H}(y)] \wedge (\forall z: \neg\mathcal{P}_{\mathcal{D}})\ s^{\vee}(z) =_{\{\mathcal{P}\vee\neg\mathcal{P}\}} x \supset \neg\mathcal{H}(z)]\}$			*farʿ*: $\mathcal{P}$?	
9	Yes, it does	! 8	? 7	So, since reading (without permission) personal letters of someone else violates the privacy of that person, it instantiates the antecedent of the *ṭard* -component of your assertion linking privacy-violation and interdiction. You should now assert the consequent. Right?	10
	farʿ: $\mathcal{P}$			*farʿ*: $\mathcal{P}$	
11	Indeed, I endorse this interdiction to the branch-case too	! 10	! 1	So, this provides the justification for the thesis you were asking for with your first move: The branch-case falls under the ruling because it instantiates the property you just endorsed as relevant for determining the occasioning factor.	12
	ʿap(*farʿ*.$t_S^{\mathcal{P}}$): $\mathcal{H}$(*farʿ*)			*ʿilla*(*farʿ*): $\mathcal{H}_S^{\mathcal{P}}(aṣl)$	
	ilzām				

[a]In fact this interdiction is explicitly sanctioned in the Quran as follows:
يَاأَيُّهَا الَّذِينَ ءَامَنُوا لَاتَدْخُلُوا بُيُوتًا غَيْرَ بُيُوتِكُمْ حَتَّى تَسْتَأْنِسُوا وَتُسَلِّمُوا عَلَى أَهْلِهَا
(O believers! Do not enter houses other than your own until you have sought permission and said greetings of peace to the occupants) [Q.S. 24: 27].

Table 2.2 On beasts of prey, impure saliva and the deployment of *qalb*

O			P		
		Responses	**Responses**	**Main thesis**	0
				The saliva of the beast of prey qualifies as impure (*najāsa*) ! $\mathcal{H}$(*far*‘)	
1	Why?	? 0	¿1, ¿! 2	Does the saliva of pigs qualify as impure (*najāsa*)? $\mathcal{H}^{S}$ (*aṣl*)?	2
3	Yes it does ! $\mathcal{H}^{S}$ (*aṣl*)	! 2	¿3, ¿! 2	Does the saliva of pigs come from an animal that has canine teeth (*dhū nābin*)? *aṣl*: $\mathcal{P}$?[a]	4
5	Yes it does *aṣl*: $\mathcal{P}$	! 4	¿5(3), ¿! 6	Given 3 and 5 it seems plausible to conclude that the saliva of animals with canines has the required efficiency for determining the relevant *‘illa* for its impurity. Don't you agree? *‘illa*(*aṣl*): $\mathcal{H}^{\mathcal{P}}$(*aṣl*)?	6
7	*qalb*‘! Do not agree! I have a counterexample to the assertion that impurity applies to the saliva of any animal possessing canines	? 6			8
	! $\mathbb{F}(\forall x: \mathcal{P})\mathcal{H}(x)$		?7		
	START OF THE SUB-PLAY --------------------------------			START OF THE SUB-PLAY -------------------------------- Still I stick to the following assertion: Impurity applies to the saliva of any animal possessing canines ! $(\forall x: \mathcal{P})\mathcal{H}(x)$	
9	Cats possess canine teeth. Thus, according to your characterization of $\mathcal{P}$ (*saliva of animals possessing canines*), their saliva is impure. ! *cat-saliva*: $\mathcal{P}$	?8	! 9	Indeed, I have to concede this **!** $\mathcal{H}$(*cat-saliva*)	10
11	We know (from the sources) that the saliva of cats is not impure. Do you agree? $\neg\mathcal{H}$(*cat-saliva*)?.	¿10, ¿! 11	! 11	I must agree. It comes from the sources ! $\neg\mathcal{H}$(*cat-saliva*)	12
13	! *tanāquḍ* 10–12. You asserted before that according to your view on the relevant property, it follows that the saliva of cats is impure. You contradict yourself![b]	? 12		I concede.	14

(continued)

Table 2.2 (continued)

	Therefore possessing canine teeth is not the relevant property for determining saliva's impurity.				
15	Moreover, cats are beasts of prey. So, their saliva is the saliva of a beast of prey. Furthermore, the saliva of a beast of prey is a case of the saliva of animals with canines. Right? [c]	¿14, ¿! 15	! 15	Yes, it is	16
	*far*ʿ: $\mathcal{P}$?			*far*ʿ: $\mathcal{P}$	
17	So you must also concede that their saliva is not impure either?	¿16, ¿! 17	! 17	Indeed.	18
	$\neg\mathcal{H}$(*far*ʿ)?			$\neg\mathcal{H}^{S}$(*far*ʿ)	
19	! *tanāquḍ* 0–18	?18		I give up	
	This contradicts your main thesis.			*ifḥām*.	

[a]For the sake of simplicity we do not reflect in our formalization the mereological relation between animals and their saliva

[b]The player that brings up the expression *tanāquḍ*, accuses the antagonist of self-contradiction – for a thorough discussion on this notion see Young (2017, pp. 537–43)

[c]In order to focus on the main argumentation thread we did not include (formally) the moves that lead from *saliva of animals of prey* to *saliva of the cats*

Table 2.3 The wine example

O			P		
		Responses	**Responses**	**Main Thesis**	0
				(Consuming) Date-wine (*nabīdh*) is forbidden (*ḥarām*)[a]	
				! $\mathcal{H}$(*far*ʿ)	
1	Why?	? 0	¿1, ¿! 2	Isn't drinking grape-wine (*khamr*) forbidden by the Quran? [b]	2
				$\mathcal{H}$(*aṣl*)?	
3	Yes, it is forbidden.	! 2	¿3, ¿! 4	Isn't grape-wine a drink made of fruit-juice which contains *euphoric intensity* (*shiddat muṭriba*)?	4
	! $\mathcal{H}^{S}$(*aṣl*)			*aṣl*: $\mathcal{P}$?	
5	Yes	! 4	¿ 3(5), ¿! 6	So, according to your moves 3 and 5, the presence of euphoric intensity occasions the proscription of consuming grape-wine. Right?	6
	aṣl: $\mathcal{P}$			ʿ*illa*(*aṣl*): $\mathcal{H}^{\mathcal{P}}$(*aṣl*)?	
7	*muṭālaba*!	? 6	! 7	ʿ*aks*: Before the occurrence of the euphoric intensity, the lawfulness of consuming a drink made of fruit-juice is the object of consensus.	8
	Justify!			! ($\forall x$: $\neg\mathcal{P}$)$\neg\mathcal{H}(x)$	

(continued)

Table 2.3 (continued)

				ṭard: After the euphoric intensity occurs [*i.e.*, when it becomes wine] and nothing else occurs, the proscription of consuming a drink made of fruit-juice is the object of consensus.	
				(ratification of) *ʿaks*: When the euphoric intensity of a drink made of fruit-juice falls away [*i.e.*, when it becomes vinegar] and nothing else falls away, it is the object of consensus that it should not be forbidden.	
				$! (\forall x: \mathcal{P})\mathcal{H}(x)$	
				taʾthīr: Therefore, the presence of the *ḥukm* is due to the presence of the *waṣf*, and the absence of the *ḥukm* is due to its absence	
				$! (\forall x: \mathcal{P}\vee\neg\mathcal{P}) \{[(\forall y: \mathcal{P}_{\mathcal{D}})\ w^{\vee}(y) =_{\{\mathcal{P}\vee\neg\mathcal{P}\}} x \supset \mathcal{H}(y)]\wedge (\forall z: \neg\mathcal{P}_{\mathcal{D}})\ s^{\vee}(z) =_{\{\mathcal{P}\vee\neg\mathcal{P}\}} x \supset \neg\mathcal{H}(z)]\}$	
9	Given these arguments I concede your previous request	! 6 (8)	¿9, ¿! 10	Isn't *nabīdh* a drink made of fruit-juice which contains 'euphoric intensity'?	10
	$! (\forall x: \mathcal{P}\vee\neg\mathcal{P}) \{[(\forall y: \mathcal{P})\ w^{\vee}(y) =_{\{\mathcal{P}\vee\neg\mathcal{P}\}} x \supset \mathcal{H}(y)]\wedge (\forall z: \neg\mathcal{P})\ s^{\vee}(z) =_{\{\mathcal{P}\vee\neg\mathcal{P}\}} x \supset \neg\mathcal{H}(z)]\}$			*farʿ*:$\mathcal{P}$?	
11	Yes, I agree	! 10	? 9	If it is the case that date-wine contains euphoric intensity, and, given 9, should this not lead you to endorse as a consequence its interdiction?	12
	farʿ: $\mathcal{P}$			*farʿ*:$\mathcal{P}$	
13	Indeed, the presence of euphoric intensity should occasion its interdiction.	! 12	! 1	So, this provides the justification for the thesis you were asking for with your first move: The branch-case falls under the ruling because it instantiates the property you just endorsed as constituting the occasioning factor.	14
	ap(*farʿ*.$t^{\mathcal{P}}$): $\mathcal{H}$(*farʿ*)			*'illa*(*farʿ*): $\mathcal{H}^{\mathcal{P}}$(*farʿ*)	
	ilzām				

[a]The original text deploys the word *ḥarām*. This notion, the opposite of *ḥalāl*, refers (in this context) to the interdiction of consuming certain food

[b]It is sanctioned in the Quran that wine is *ḥarām* (forbidden [to be consumed]):

يَا أَيُّهَا الَّذِينَ آمَنُوا إِنَّمَا الْخَمْرُ وَالْمَيْسِرُ وَالأَنصَابُ وَالأَزْلاَمُ رِجْسٌ مِنْ عَمَلِ الشَّيْطَانِ فَاجْتَنِبُوهُ لَعَلَّكُمْ تُفْلِحُونَ

(O you believers! Wine, gambling, altars and divining arrows are filth, made up by Satan. Therefore, refrain from it, so that you may be succesful). [Q.S: 5: 90]

Table 2.4 The wine example and the deployment of *mu'āraḍa*

O			P		
		Responses	**Responses**	**Main Thesis**	0
				(Consuming) Date-wine is forbidden. ! $\mathcal{H}$(*far'*)	
1	Why?	? 0	¿1, ¿! 2	Isn't drinking grape-wine forbidden by the Quran? $\mathcal{H}$(*aṣl*)?	2
3	Yes, it is *ḥarām*. ! $\mathcal{H}^{S}$(*aṣl*)	! 2	¿3, ¿! 4	Isn't grape-wine made of pressed fruit-juice *aṣl*: $\mathcal{P}$?	4
5	Yes *aṣl*: $\mathcal{P}$	! 4	¿3,(5),! 6	So, according to your moves 3 and 5, the proscription of consuming grape-wine is caused by the fact that it is made of pressed fruit-juice. Right? *'illa*(*aṣl*): $\mathcal{H}^{\mathcal{P}}$(*aṣl*)?	6
7	I am far from being convinced. I rather think that the cause of its interdiction is that it is one of the drinks containing euphoric intensity ($\mathcal{P}^{*}$) ! $\mathbb{V}$ *'illa*(*aṣl*): $\mathcal{H}^{\mathcal{P}*}$(*aṣl*)	? 6	?7	*muṭālaba*! Justify!	8
	START OF THE SUB-PLAY ------------------------------			**START OF THE SUB-PLAY** ------------------------------	
9	Vinegar is made of pressed juice-fruit. Isn't it? *aṣl**: $\mathcal{P}$?	¿ 8, ¿! 9	! 9	Indeed. *aṣl**: $\mathcal{P}$	10
11	Given 6, you must agree that being a pressed juice is efficient property for sanctioning pressed juices as *ḥarām*. Right? $(\forall x: \mathcal{P}\vee\neg\mathcal{P})\ \{[(\forall y: \mathcal{P})\ w^{\vee}(y) =_{\{\mathcal{P}\vee\neg\mathcal{P}\}} x\supset \mathcal{H}(y)]\wedge (\forall z: \neg\mathcal{P})\ s^{\vee}(z) =_{\{\mathcal{P}\vee\neg\mathcal{P}\}} x\supset \neg\mathcal{H}(z)]\}$?	¿ 6, ¿! 11	! 11	Yes ! $(\forall x: \mathcal{P}\vee\neg\mathcal{P})\ \{[(\forall y: \mathcal{P})\ w^{\vee}(y) =_{\{\mathcal{P}\vee\neg\mathcal{P}\}} x\supset \mathcal{H}(y)]\wedge (\forall z: \neg\mathcal{P})\ s^{\vee}(z) =_{\{\mathcal{P}\vee\neg\mathcal{P}\}} x\supset \neg\mathcal{H}(z)]\}$	12
13	But, given that you just agreed that vinegar is made of pressed juice, (according to the *ṭard* -component of your assertion) it should be *ḥarām* *aṣl**: $\mathcal{P}$	? 12	! 13	Indeed ***ap***(*aṣl**.$t^{\mathcal{P}}$): $\mathcal{H}$(*aṣl**)	14

(continued)

Table 2.4 (continued)

15	But its consumption is not forbidden. Is it? $! \neg\mathcal{H}(aṣl^*)$?	¿ 14, ¿! 15	! 15	Yes it is not *ḥarām* $! \neg\mathcal{H}^{S}$ $(aṣl^*)$	16
17	! *tanāquḍ* 14–16 You contradict yourself	? 16		I concede!	18
19	Herewith my argument for the relevance of $\mathcal{P}^*$ *ʿaks*: Before the occurrence of the euphoric intensity, the lawfulness of consuming a drink made of fruit-juice is the object of consensus. $! (\forall x: \neg\mathcal{P}^*)\neg\mathcal{H}(x)$ *ṭard*: After the euphoric intensity occurs [*i.e.*, when it becomes wine] and nothing else occurs, the proscription of consuming a drink made of fruit-juice is the object of consensus. (ratification of) *ʿaks*: When the euphoric intensity of a drink made of fruit-juice falls away [*i.e.*, when it becomes vinegar] and nothing else falls away it is the object of consensus that it should not be forbidden. $! (\forall x: \mathcal{P}^*)\mathcal{H}(x)$ *taʾthīr*: Therefore, the presence of the *ḥukm* is due to the presence of the $\mathcal{P}$, and the absence of the *ḥukm* is due to its absence $! (\forall x: \mathcal{P}^*\vee\neg\mathcal{P}^*) \{[(\forall y: \mathcal{P}^*) w^{\vee}(y) =_{\{\mathcal{P}^*\vee\neg\mathcal{P}^*\}} x \supset \mathcal{H}^{S}(y)] \wedge (\forall z: \neg\mathcal{P}^*) s^{\vee}(z) =_{\{\mathcal{P}^*\vee\neg\mathcal{P}^*\}} x \supset \neg\mathcal{H}^{S}(z)]\}$ And it certainly applies to our root-case: ***ʻap***$(aṣl.f^{\mathcal{P}*})$: $\mathcal{H}^{S}(aṣl)$	! 8			
	END OF THE SUB-PLAY ------------------------------			**END OF THE SUB-PLAY** ------------------------------	
21	Yes, it does.	! 20	¿ 19, ¿! 20	I concede your argument in favour of singling out euphoric intensity as the relevant property, but then	20

(continued)

Table 2.4 (continued)

				you should admit that our branch-case *nabīdh* in fact instantiates this property. Does it?	
	*far*ʿ: $\mathcal{P}^*$			*far*ʿ: $\mathcal{P}^*$?	
23	Indeed!	! 22	? 19	If it is the case that date-wine contains euphoric intensity, and, given your endorsement at move 19 of ! $(\forall x{:}\ \mathcal{P}^*\vee\neg\mathcal{P}^*)\ \{[(\forall y{:}\ \mathcal{P}^*)\ w^{\vee}(y) =_{\{\mathcal{P}^*\vee\neg\mathcal{P}^*\}} x \supset \mathcal{H}^{S}(y)]\wedge(\forall z{:}\ \neg\mathcal{P}^*)\ s^{\vee}(z) =_{\{\mathcal{P}^*\vee\neg\mathcal{P}^*\}} x \supset \neg\mathcal{H}^{S}(z)]\}$ Should this not lead to the interdiction of our branch-case?	22
	ap(*far*ʿ,$t^{\mathcal{P}*}$): $\mathcal{H}$(*far*ʿ)			*far*ʿ: $\mathcal{P}^*$	
			! 1	So, this provides the justification for the thesis you were asking for with your first move: The branch-case falls under the ruling because it instantiates the property you just helped to identify as the one determining the occasioning factor.	24
				ʿ*illa*(*far*ʿ): $\mathcal{H}^{\mathcal{P}*}$ (*far*ʿ)	
	ilzām				

This yields the following tree displaying the winning-strategy. Since as explained in the following section, the strategy is being conceived as a recapitulation of the "correct" moves, the unsuccessful attempts are deleted:

0. **P**! $\mathcal{H}$(*far*ʿ)
1. **O** Why [?0]
2. **P** $\mathcal{H}$(*aṣl*)?
3. **O**! $\mathcal{H}^{S}$(*aṣl*)
4. **P** *aṣl*: $\mathcal{P}^*$?
5. **O** *aṣl*: $\mathcal{P}^*$
6. **P** ʿ*illa*(*aṣl*): $\mathcal{H}^{\mathcal{P}*}$(*aṣl*)?
7. **O**! $(\forall x{:}\ \mathcal{P}^*\vee\neg\mathcal{P}^*)\ \{[(\forall y{:}\ \mathcal{P}^*) w^{\vee}(y) =_{\{\mathcal{P}^*\vee\neg\mathcal{P}^*\}} x \supset \mathcal{H}^{S}(y)]\wedge(\forall z{:}\ \neg\mathcal{P}^*)\ s^{\vee}(z) =_{\{\mathcal{P}^*\vee\neg\mathcal{P}^*\}} x \supset \neg\mathcal{H}^{S}(z)]\}$
8. **P** *far*ʿ: $\mathcal{P}^*$?

9. **O** *far*ʿ: $\mathscr{P}^*$
10. **P** *far*ʿ: $\mathscr{P}^*$ [?7]
11. **O** ***ap***[*far*ʿ.$t^{\mathscr{P}*}$]: $\mathscr{H}^{S}$(*far*ʿ)
12. **P** *ʿilla*(*far*ʿ): $\mathscr{H}^{\mathscr{P}*}$(*far*ʿ) (! 1. answer to the request of justification in the second move)

2.4.4 The Main Rules of the Dialogical Framework for Qiyās al-ʿIlla

The dialogical approach to logic is not a specific logical system but rather a framework rooted on a rule-based approach to meaning in which different logics can be developed, combined and compared.[84]

More precisely, in a dialogue two parties argue about a thesis respecting certain fixed rules. The player that states the thesis is called Proponent (**P**), and his rival, who contests the thesis, is called Opponent (**O**). Dialogues are designed in such a way that each of the plays end after a finite number of moves with one player winning, while the other loses.

Actions or moves in a dialogue are often understood as speech-acts involving *declarative utterances or statements* and *interrogative utterances or requests*.

The point is that the rules of the dialogue do not operate on expressions or sentences isolated from the act of uttering them.

The rules are divided into particle rules or rules for logical constants (*Partikelregeln*) and structural rules (*Rahmenregeln*).

Particle rules provide an abstract description of how the game can proceed locally: they specify the way a formula can be challenged and defended according to its main logical constant. In this way the particle rules govern the local level of meaning (of logical constants – but it can be extended to non-logical ones). Strictly speaking, the expressions occurring in the table above are not actual moves because they feature formula schemata and the players are not specified. Moreover, these rules are indifferent to any particular situations that might occur during the game. For these reasons we say that the description provided by the particle rules is abstract.

The structural rules determine the development of a dialogue game and they govern the moves involving elementary statements.

---

[84]In the following sections we present only a simplified and adapted form of the Dialogical Framework, called *Immanent Reasoning* – see Rahman/McConaughey/Klev/Clerbout (2018). For a more complete presentation see the chapter IV of the present book. The main original papers are collected in Lorenzen/Lorenz (1978) – see too Lorenz (2010a,b), Felscher (1985), Krabbe (2006). For an account of recent developments see Rahman/Keiff (2005), Keiff (2009), Rahman/Tulenheimo (2009), Rückert (2011), Clerbout (2014a,b). The most recent work links dialogical logic and Constructive Type Theory, see Clerbout/Rahman (2015) and Rahman/Clerbout/Redmond (2017).

2.4.4.1 Local Meaning

It is presupposed in standard dialogical systems that the players use well-formed formulas. The well formation can be checked at will, but only with the usual meta reasoning by which the formula is checked to indeed observe the definition of a wff. We want to enrich the system by first allowing players to enquire on the status of expressions and in particular to ask if a certain expression is a proposition. We thus start with dialogical rules explaining the formation of propositions.

Moreover, we extend the first-order language assumed in standard dialogical logic by adding two labels **O** and **P**, standing for the players of the game, and the two symbols '!' and '?'. When the identity of the player does not matter, we use the variables **X** or **Y** (with $\mathbf{X} \neq \mathbf{Y}$).

A move $\mathbb{M}$ is an expression of the form '**X**-*e*', where *e* is one of the forms specified by the particle rules.

Local meaning: Formation

Statement	Challenge	Defence
X $A \vee B$: **prop**	**Y** $?_{F\vee 1}$ Or **Y** $?_{F\vee 2}$	**X** A: **prop** / **X** B: **prop**
X $A \wedge B$: **prop**	**Y** $?_{F\wedge 1}$ Or **Y** $?_{F\wedge 2}$	**X** A: **prop** / **X** B: **prop**
X $A \supset B$: **prop**	**Y** $?_{F\supset 1}$ Or **Y** $?_{F\supset 2}$	**X** A: **prop** / **X** B: **prop**
X $\neg A$: **prop**	**Y** $?_{F\neg}$	**X** A: **prop**
X $(\forall x: A)\, B(x)$: **prop**	**Y** $?_{F\forall 1}$ Or **Y** $?_{F\forall 2}$	**X** A: **set** / **X** $B(x)$: **prop** $(x{:}A)$
X $(\exists x: A)\, B(x)$: **prop**	**Y** $?_{\exists 1}$ Or **Y** $?_{F\exists 2}$	**X** A: **set** / **X** $B(x)$: **prop** $(x{:}A)$

Besides the formation rules, the rules described by the local meaning for some statement π indicate those moves that constitute the *canonical argumentation form of the local reason* specific to the statement/set at stake in π.

Because our deployment expressions come from Constructive-Type Theory, the language contains expressions such as the following (further expressions are provided in the section on terminology in the main text):

X! *A*	Player **X** claims that he *can produce* some *local reason* for *A*.
X *p*: *A*	Player **X** states that *p* instantiates *A*. In other words, player **X** states that *p* provides a *local reason* for *A*.
X p_i: $B(p_j)$	Player **X** states that p_i provides a *local reason* for *B* given that *the antagonist* **Y** states that p_j provides a *local reason* for *A*, and given that ***B***(*x*): **prop** (*x*:*A*).

Similarly

X p_i: $B(p_j)$	Player **X** states that p_i provides a *local reason* for *B* given that it is *he himself* (**X**), who states that p_j provides a *local reason* for *A*, and given that ***B***(*x*): **prop** (*x*:*A*). Sometimes, when the context requires it, we add the indications p_i^X: $B(p_j^Y)$ or p_i^X: $B(p_j^X)$.

Synthesis of Local Reasons

The **synthesis rules** of local reasons determine how to produce a local reason for a statement; they include rules of interaction indicating how to produce the local reason that is required by the proposition (or set) in play, that is, they indicate what kind of dialogical action –what kind of move – must be carried out, by whom (challenger or defender), and what reason must be brought forward.

Synthesis rules for local reasons

	Move	Challenge	Defence
Conjunction	**X !** $A \wedge B$	**Y** ? $L^{\wedge}$ or **Y** ? $R^{\wedge}$	**X** p_1: A (resp.) **X** p_2: B
Existential quantification	**X** ! $(\exists x{:}\ A)B(x)$	**Y** ? $L^{\exists}$ or **Y** ? $R^{\exists}$	**X** p_1: A (resp.) **X** p_2: $B(p_1)$
Disjunction	**X !** $A \vee B$	**Y** $?^{\vee}$	**X** p_1: A or **X** p_2: B
Implication	**X !** $A \supset B$	**Y** p_1: A	**X** p_2: B
Universal quantification	**X** ! $(\forall x{:}\ A)B(x)$	**Y** p_1: A	**X** p_2: $B(p_1)$
Negation	**X !** $\neg A$ Also expressed as **X !** $A \supset \bot$	**Y** p_1: A	**X** p_2: $\bot$

Analysis of Local Reasons

Apart from the rules for the synthesis of local reasons, we need rules that indicate how to parse a complex local reason into its elements: this is the *analysis* of local reasons. In order to deal with the complexity of these local reasons and formulate general rules for the analysis of local reasons (at the play level), we introduce certain operators that we call *instructions*, such as $L^{\vee}(p)$ or $R^{\wedge}(p)$. To the standard particle rules (the local rules for logical constants) we also add rules for the operators $\mathbb{F}$ and $\mathbb{V}$ adapted to the purposes of our present study.

Let us introduce these instructions and the analysis of local reasons with an example: player **X** states the implication $(A \wedge B) \supset B$. According to the rule for the synthesis of local reasons for an implication, we obtain the following:

Move	**X** ! $(A \wedge B) \supset B$
Challenge	**Y** p_1: $A \wedge B$

Recall that the synthesis rule prescribes that **X** must now provide a local reason for the consequent; but instead of defending his implication (with **X** $p_2 : B$ for instance), **X** can choose to parse the reason p_1 provided by **Y** in order to force **Y** to provide a local reason for the right-hand side of the conjunction that **X** will then be able to copy. In other words, **X** can force **Y** to provide the local reason for B out of the local reason p_1 for the antecedent $A \wedge B$ of the initial implication. The analysis rules prescribe how to carry out such a parsing of the statement by using *instructions*.

The rule for the analysis of a local reason for the conjunction $p_1 : A \wedge B$ will thus indicate that its defence includes expressions such as

- the left instruction for the conjunction, written $L^{\wedge}(p_1)$, and
- the right instruction for the conjunction, written $R^{\wedge}(p_1)$.

These instructions can be informally understood as carrying out the following step: for the defence of the conjunction $p_1 : A \wedge B$ separate the local reason p_1 in its left (or right) component so that this component can be adduced in defence of the left (or right) side of the conjunction.

Let us now proceed to present the **Analysis rules** for the usual logical constants.

Analysis rules for local reasons

	Move	Challenge	Defence
Conjunction	**X**p: $A \wedge B$	**Y** ? $L^{\wedge}$ or **Y** ? $R^{\wedge}$	**X** $L^{\wedge}(p)$: A (resp.) **X** $R^{\wedge}(p)$: B
Existential quantification	**X**p: $(\exists x: A)B(x)$	**Y** ? $L^{\exists}$ or **Y** ? $R^{\exists}$	**X** $L^{\exists}(p)$: A (resp.) **X** $R^{\exists}(p)$: $B(L^{\exists}(p))$
Disjunction	**X**p: $A \vee B$	**Y** ?$^{\vee}$	**X** $L^{\vee}(p)$: A or **X** $R^{\vee}(p)$: B
Implication	**X**p: $A \supset B$	**Y** $L^{\supset}(p)$: A	**X** $R^{\supset}(p)$: B
Universal quantification	**X**p: $(\forall x: A)B(x)$	**Y** $L^{\forall}(p)$: A	**X** $R^{\forall}(p)$: $B(L^{\forall}(p))$
Negation	**X**p: $\neg A$ Also expressed as **X**p: $A \supset \bot$	**Y** $L^{\neg}(p)$: A **Y** $L^{\supset}(p)$: A	**X** $R^{\neg}(p)$: $\bot$ **X** $R^{\supset}(p)$: $\bot$ Which amounts to stating **X** ! $\bot$[a]

[a] The general point of deleting the instruction in **X** $R^{\supset}(p)$: $\bot$ is that instructions occurring in expressions stating **falsum** keep un-resolved – see below structural rule SR3 on resolutions, item 3.

Special Denominations for *Qiyās al-ʿIlla*

Expressions "*p*" in "*p*: *A*" stand for either some branch-case *farʿ* or some root-case *aṣl*

Statement	Challenge	Defence
Synthesis **X** ! $\mathcal{P}_{\mathcal{D}}\vee\neg\mathcal{P}_{\mathcal{D}}$	**Y** $?^{\vee}$	**X** p_1: $\mathcal{P}_{\mathcal{D}}$ or **X** p_2: $\neg\mathcal{P}_{\mathcal{D}}$
Analysis **X** p: $\mathcal{P}_{\mathcal{D}}\vee\neg\mathcal{P}_{\mathcal{D}}$	**Y** $?^{\vee}$	**X** $wuj\bar{u}d^{\vee}(p)$: $\mathcal{P}_{\mathcal{D}}$ or **X** $salb^{\vee}(p)$: $\neg\mathcal{P}_{\mathcal{D}}$
Synthesis **X** ! $(\forall x: \mathcal{P}_{\mathcal{D}})\, \mathcal{H}(x)$ **X** ! $(\forall x: \neg\mathcal{P}_{\mathcal{D}})\, \neg\mathcal{H}(x)$	**Y**p_1: $\mathcal{P}_{\mathcal{D}}$ **Y**q_1: $\neg\mathcal{P}_{\mathcal{D}}$	**X** p_2: $\mathcal{H}(p_1)$ **X** q_2: $\neg\mathcal{H}(q_1)$
Analysis **X** p: $(\forall x: \mathcal{P}_{\mathcal{D}})\, \mathcal{H}(x)$ **X** q: $(\forall x: \neg\mathcal{P}_{\mathcal{D}})\, \neg\mathcal{H}(x)$	**Y** $L^{\forall}(p)$: $\mathcal{P}_{\mathcal{D}}$ **Y** $L^{\forall}(q)$: $\neg\mathcal{P}_{\mathcal{D}}$	**X** *ṭard*(p): $\mathcal{H}(L^{\forall}(p))$ **X** *ʿaks*(q): $\neg\mathcal{H}(L^{\forall}(q))$
Synthesis **X** ! $(\forall x: \mathcal{P}_{\mathcal{D}}\vee\neg\mathcal{P}_{\mathcal{D}})\ \{\, [\, (\forall y: \mathcal{P}_{\mathcal{D}})\ wuj\bar{u}d^{\vee}(y)$ $=_{\{\mathcal{P}\mathcal{D}\vee\neg\mathcal{P}\mathcal{D}\}} x \supset \mathcal{H}(y)\,] \wedge [\, (\forall z: \neg\mathcal{P}_{\mathcal{D}})\ salb^{\vee}(z)$ $=_{\{\mathcal{P}\mathcal{D}\vee\neg\mathcal{P}\mathcal{D}\}} x \supset \neg\mathcal{H}(z)]\, \}$	**Y**p_1: $\mathcal{P}_{\mathcal{D}}$	**X** *taʾthīr*$^{\mathcal{P}}$: $\{\, [\, (\forall y: \mathcal{P}_{\mathcal{D}})\ wuj\bar{u}d^{\vee}(y) =_{\{\mathcal{P}\mathcal{D}\vee\neg\mathcal{P}\mathcal{D}\}} p_1 \supset \mathcal{H}(y)\,]$ $\wedge [\, (\forall z: \neg\mathcal{P}_{\mathcal{D}})\ salb^{\vee}(z) =_{\{\mathcal{P}\mathcal{D}\vee\neg\mathcal{P}\mathcal{D}\}} p_1 \supset \neg\mathcal{H}(z)\,]\, \}$ (similar for **Y** q_1: $\neg\mathcal{P}_{\mathcal{D}}$)
Analysis **X** p: $(\forall x: \mathcal{P}_{\mathcal{D}}\vee\neg\mathcal{P}_{\mathcal{D}})\ \{\, [\, (\forall y: \mathcal{P}_{\mathcal{D}})\ wuj\bar{u}d^{\vee}(y)$ $=_{\{\mathcal{P}\mathcal{D}\vee\neg\mathcal{P}\mathcal{D}\}} x \supset \mathcal{H}(y)\,] \wedge [\, (\forall z: \neg\mathcal{P}_{\mathcal{D}})\ salb^{\vee}(z)$ $=_{\{\mathcal{P}\mathcal{D}\vee\neg\mathcal{P}\mathcal{D}\}} x \supset \neg\mathcal{H}(z)]\, \}$	**Y** $L^{\forall}(p)$: $\mathcal{P}_{\mathcal{D}}$	**X** . $L^{\forall}(p)$.*taʾthīr*$^{\mathcal{P}}$: $\{\, [\, (\forall y: \mathcal{P}_{\mathcal{D}})\ wuj\bar{u}d^{\vee}(y) =_{\{\mathcal{P}\mathcal{D}\vee\neg\mathcal{P}\mathcal{D}\}} L^{\forall}(p)$ $\supset \mathcal{H}(y)\,] \wedge [\, (\forall z: \neg\mathcal{P}_{\mathcal{D}})\ salb^{\vee}(z)$ $=_{\{\mathcal{P}\mathcal{D}\vee\neg\mathcal{P}\mathcal{D}\}} L^{\forall}(p) \supset \neg\, \mathcal{H}(z)\,]\, \}$ (similar for **Y** $L^{\forall}(q)$: $\neg\mathcal{P}_{\mathcal{D}}$)

Actually in the dialogues, we write **X**. ***ap***[$L^{\forall}(p)$.*taʾthīr*$^{\mathcal{P}}$] instead of **X**. [$L^{\forall}(p)$.*taʾthīr*$^{\mathcal{P}}$]. Strictly speaking; the former expression corresponds to the strategy level (see section on strategies below), whereas the latter corresponds to the play level. This use assumes that the player **X** has indeed a winning strategy.

Special Moves for *Qiyās al-ʿIlla*

Tanāquḍ

Statement	Challenge	Defence
X ! A (or p_i: A) move m … **X** ! $\neg A$ (or p_j: $\neg A$) move n	**Y** ! *tanāquḍ m-n* The antagonist indicates the contradiction	**X** ! I concede

The Operator $\mathbb{F}$[85]

In uttering the formula $\mathbb{F}A$ the argumentation partner **X** claims that he can find a counterexample during a play where the antagonist **Y** asserts A.

The antagonist **Y** challenges $\mathbb{F}A$ by asserting that A can be challenged successfully. Thus, through this challenge **Y** obliges **X** to open a *sub-play* where he (**X**) states A.

- The rules for synthesis and analysis follow those of

Y! $\neg A$
fulfilling the distribution of duties and rights prescribed for the role of **Y** in the sub-play.

In other words, the local meaning of the operator $\mathbb{F}A$ reduces to stating the negation of the propostion under its scope. However, this statement might change his duties in relation to the Socratic Rule

	Challenge	Defence
X ! $\mathbb{F}A$	**Y** ?F	
	Sub-play $\mathfrak{D}_1$	*Sub-play* $\mathfrak{D}_1$
	Y ! A **Y** must play under the restriction of the *Socratic-Rule* in the sub-play	**X** $?_A$(he challenges A)
		The local reason for the operator is the local reason that encodes a play for the negation of A.

[85]Cf. Rahman/Rückert (2001, pp. 113–116).

The Operator $\mathbb{V}$

In uttering the formula $\mathbb{V}A$ the argumentation partner **X** claims that he can win a play where he (**X**) asserts A.

The antagonist **Y** responds by challenging **X** to open a *sub-play* where he (**X**) defends A.

- The rules for synthesis and analysis follow those of

X! A
fulfilling the distribution of duties and rights prescribed for the role of **X** in the sub-play.

	Challenge	**Defence**
X ! $\mathbb{V}A$	Y: ?$\mathbb{V}$	
	Sub-play $\mathfrak{D}_1$	*Sub-play* $\mathfrak{D}_1$
	Y $?_A$(he challenges A) **Y** must play under the restriction of the *Socratic Rule*	**X** ! A
		The local reason for the operator is the local reason that encodes a play for A.

Qiyās al-ʿilla also require the following moves prescribed by the **development rules** specific to the dialectical framework underlying this form of *qiyās*.

Requests
Our framework for *qiyās al-ʿilla* includes moves by means of which players can request the contender to endorse some particular assertion. The general form of a request and the response is the following:

$$\mathbf{X}\ A?$$

$$\mathbf{Y}!\ A$$

If the request has a form that indicates sources, it **must** be endorsed by the respondent

$$\mathbf{X}\ p^{\mathbb{S}} : A? \quad \mathbf{X}!\ A^{\mathbb{S}}?$$

$$\mathbf{Y}\ p^{\mathbb{S}} : A \quad \mathbf{Y}!\ A^{\mathbb{S}}$$

(Since in the glosses of the examples, the backing from the sources is made explicit; we often do not add them explicitly to the notation).

This general form of request might trigger a different form of answer if it involves the endorsement of a particular occasioning factor. In such a case, the following responses are possible:

X *'illa(aṣl)*: $\mathcal{H}^{\mathcal{P}}$*(aṣl)*?

Cooperative criticism	**Destructive Criticisms**	**Asking for Justification**	**Endorsing the request by asserting the efficiency of the property $\mathcal{P}$**
Y ! *mu'āraḍa*	Y ! *qalb* or Y ! *naqḍ* or Y ! *kasr* or Y ! *fasād al-waḍ'* **or** 'Y ! *'adam al -ta'thīr*	Y ! *muṭālaba*	Y ! $(\forall x: \mathcal{P}_{\mathcal{D}} \vee \neg\mathcal{P}_{\mathcal{D}})$ $\{ [(\forall y: \mathcal{P}_{\mathcal{D}})$ $wujūd^{\vee}(y) =_{\{\mathcal{P}\mathcal{D}\vee\neg\mathcal{P}\mathcal{D}\}} x \supset \mathcal{H}(y)]$ $\wedge [(\forall z: \neg\mathcal{P}_{\mathcal{D}})\ salb^{\vee}(z)$ $=_{\{\mathcal{P}\mathcal{D}\vee\neg\mathcal{P}\mathcal{D}\}} x \supset \neg\mathcal{H}(z)] \}$

Which of the options are available is determined by the rules prescribing the overall development of a play for *qiyās al-'illa*. We proceed to describe the development of the first three responses, the development of the fourth one (the universal) having already been described above.

1. ***Muṭālaba***

   This move presupposes that player **X** (usually the Proponent) requested the contender to endorse that the property $\mathcal{P}$ is the relevant one for occasioning the ruling of the root-case.

   That is, it presupposes the following request:

   X! *'illa(aṣl)*: $\mathcal{H}^{\mathcal{P}}$*(aṣl)*?
   Y! *muṭālaba*

   X must be able to bring forward arguments showing that the property satisfies *ṭard* $((\forall x{:}\mathcal{P})\mathcal{H}(x))$, *'aks* $((\forall x{:}\neg\mathcal{P})\neg\mathcal{H}(x))$. If he succeeds he can state the further assertion:

$$\mathbf{X}\,!\ (\forall x : \mathcal{P}_{\mathcal{D}} \vee \neg\mathcal{P}_{\mathcal{D}})\ \big\{[(\forall y : \mathcal{P}_{\mathcal{D}})\ wujūd^{\vee}(y) =_{\{\mathcal{P}\mathcal{D}\vee\neg\mathcal{P}\mathcal{D}\}} x \supset \mathcal{H}(y)] \wedge \big[(\forall z : \neg\mathcal{P}_{\mathcal{D}})\ salb^{\vee}(z) =_{\{\mathcal{P}\mathcal{D}\vee\neg\mathcal{P}\mathcal{D}\}} x \supset \neg\mathcal{H}(z)\big]\big\}$$

2. ***Mu'āraḍa*** **or cooperative criticism**

This move presupposes the same request as before. That is, the deployment of cooperative criticism presupposes the following request:

X *'illa(aṣl)*: $\mathcal{H}^{\mathcal{P}}$*(aṣl)*?

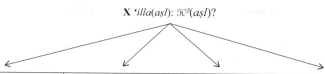

First step. The challenger refuses to endorse the requested assertion and starts by asserting that the relevant factor for the root-case at stake is the property $\mathcal{P}^{*}$ rather than $\mathcal{P}$. However, the Opponent believes that the main thesis is correct though it was poorly defended

! **Y** $\mathbb{V}$ *ʿilla(aṣl)*: $\mathcal{H}^{\mathcal{P}*}$*(aṣl)*

Second step. If the assertion of **Y** is rooted in the sources, **X** must accept it and the play will continue. If it is not based on the sources **X** responds by challenging **Y** to open a *sub-play* where the latter must defend his thesis.

X! *muṭālaba*

Third step. In the sub-play, before providing the required justification, the challenger might first choose to force **X** to accept that there is a root-case that contradicts the defender's choice of $\mathcal{P}$ as relevant for the juridical ruling at stake. Driving **X** to contradiction is carried out by means of the following move:

START OF A SUB-PLAY.X'S CONTRADICTION
Y searches for a new root-case to which $\mathcal{P}$. applies.
Y *aṣl**: $\mathcal{P}$**?**
X *aṣl**: $\mathcal{P}$
Y forces **X** to agree that according to the presupposition $\mathcal{P}$ has the efficiency required for producing the ruling
Request
Y ! $(\forall x: \mathcal{P}_{\mathfrak{D}} \vee \neg\mathcal{P}_{\mathfrak{D}})\ \{\ [\ (\forall y: \mathcal{P}_{\mathfrak{D}})\ wuj\bar{u}d^{\vee}(y) =_{\{\mathcal{P}\mathfrak{D} \vee \neg\mathcal{P}\mathfrak{D}\}} x \supset \mathcal{H}(y)\ ] \wedge [\ (\forall z: \neg\mathcal{P}_{\mathfrak{D}})\ salb^{\vee}(z) =_{\{\mathcal{P}\mathfrak{D} \vee \neg\mathcal{P}\mathfrak{D}\}} x \supset \neg\mathcal{H}(z)\ ]\ \}?$
Response Endorsing it
X ! $(\forall x: \mathcal{P}_{\mathfrak{D}} \vee \neg\mathcal{P}_{\mathfrak{D}})\ \{\ [\ (\forall y: \mathcal{P}_{\mathfrak{D}})\ wuj\bar{u}d^{\vee}(y) =_{\{\mathcal{P}\mathfrak{D} \vee \neg\mathcal{P}\mathfrak{D}\}} x \supset \mathcal{H}(y)\ ] \wedge [\ (\forall z: \neg\mathcal{P}_{\mathfrak{D}})\ salb^{\vee}(z) =_{\{\mathcal{P}\mathfrak{D} \vee \neg\mathcal{P}\mathfrak{D}\}} x \supset \neg\mathcal{H}(z)\ ]\ \}$
Based on this endorsement of **X, Y** then forces **X** to contradict himself in relation to the applicability of the ruling to the new-root case. Once the contradiction occurs **Y** indicates the contradictory moves and **X** must concede.
Y ! *tanāquḍ* **n-m**
(where **n** and **m** are moves of **X** where two contradictory statements have been asserted)
X ! I concede
START OF THE CONSTRUCTIVE CONTRIBUTION WITHIN THE SUB-PLAY.
After **X's** contradiction, the Opponent now starts his constructive contribution by displaying the efficiency of a new property. Herewith he answers to the request of justification.
X concedes and this ends the sub-play

Fourth step. Back to the main play:

X (usually the Proponent) accepts the suggestion developed in the constructive fragment of the sub-play and deploys it for the justification of the thesis.

The tree displaying the winning strategy will delete the unsuccessful attempts and also the justification of the sub-play.

3. **Destructive Criticisms**

This move also presupposes the same kind of request as before:

$$\mathbf{X}!\text{`}illa(a\d{s}\mathrm{l}) : \mathcal{H}^{\mathcal{P}}(a\d{s}\mathrm{l})?$$

However, contrary to cooperative criticism the Opponent aims to refute the main thesis. We will be more succinct in the description since after the description of the cooperative criticism and after the examples in the main text, the development is quite straightforward.

$$\mathbf{O}!\mathbb{F}\ (\forall x : \mathcal{P})\ \mathcal{H}(x)\ (\boldsymbol{qalb})$$

The Opponent is committed to a sub-play where he brings forward a root-case of which it is recorded that an opposite ruling to the claimed ruling applies. Hence the root-case is presented as a counterexample to the Proponent's claim that every $\mathcal{P}$ falls under the ruling $\mathcal{H}$ and in particular to the claim that this ruling applies to the branch-case.

$$\mathbf{O}!\mathbb{F}\ (\forall x : \mathcal{P})\ \mathcal{H}(x), \text{given } a\d{s}\mathrm{l}^* : \mathcal{P}, \mathcal{H}^{S*}(a\d{s}\mathrm{l}^*), \text{and}\neg(\mathcal{H}(a\d{s}\mathrm{l}^*) \wedge \mathcal{H}^*(a\d{s}\mathrm{l}^*))\ (\boldsymbol{naq\d{d}})$$

The Opponent is committed to a sub-play where he brings forward a root-case of which it is recorded that a different ruling to the claimed ruling applies and both rulings are incompatible. Hence the root-case is presented as a counterexample to the Proponent's assertion that every $\mathcal{P}$ falls under the ruling $\mathcal{H}$ and in particular to the claim that this ruling applies to the branch-case.

$$\mathbf{O}!\mathbb{F}\ (\forall y : \{ y : \mathcal{P}_{\mathcal{D}} \mid \mathcal{P}^*(y)\})\ \mathcal{H}(y)\ (\boldsymbol{kasr})$$

Given P's claim that the relevant property is in fact the compound $\{ y: \mathcal{P}_{\mathcal{D}} | \mathcal{P}^*(y)\}$ (it could be also composed by more than two properties), then the Opponent is committed to a sub-play where he brings forward a root-case that enjoys one of the components $\mathcal{P}_{\mathcal{D}}$ but is recorded falling under the scope $\mathcal{H}^*$, rather than the claimed $\mathcal{H}$, and it is the case that the remaining property (or cluster of properties) cannot induce the ruling $\mathcal{H}$.[86]

[86]See our comments on the doubts on the validity of this rule in 4.2.3.

$$\mathbf{O}!\mathbb{F}\ (\forall x : \mathcal{P})\ \mathcal{H}(x)\ (\textit{\textbf{fasād al}} - \textit{\textbf{waḍʿ}})$$

The Opponent is committed to a sub-play where he brings forward a root-case of which it is recorded in the sources that a property assumed in the thesis to apply to the branch-case occasions in fact, the opposite ruling to the one stated by the Proponent. In other words, the Opponent brings forward an *ʿilla* that destroys the thesis.

$$\mathbf{O}!\mathbb{F}\ (\forall x : \mathcal{P})\mathcal{H}(x) \wedge (\forall x : \neg\mathcal{P})\neg\mathcal{H}(x)\ \ (\textit{\textbf{ʿadam al}} - \textit{\textbf{taʾthīr}})$$

The Opponent is committed to a sub-play where he brings forward a root-case which constitutes a counterexample to the efficiency of the proposed property asserted by the Proponent**.** The counterexample refutes at least one of the constituents of the conjunction.

2.4.4.2 Global Meaning

2.4.4.2.1 Structural Rules

In the dialogical approach, validity is defined via the notion of *winning strategy*, where winning strategy for **X** means that for any choice of moves by **Y**, **X** has at least one possible move at his disposal such that he (**X**) wins:

Validity (definition): A proposition is valid in a certain dialogical system iff **P** has a winning strategy for this proposition.

In the present context we will deploy a variant of the structural rules. Before providing them, let us fix the following notions:

Play: A *play* is a legal sequence of moves, *i.e.*, a sequence of moves which observes the game rules. Particle rules are not the only rules which must be observed in this respect. In fact, it can be said that the second kind of rules, namely, the *structural rules* are those giving the precise conditions under which a given sequence is a play.

Dialogical game: The *dialogical game* for φ, written $\mathbb{D}(\varphi)$, is the set of all plays with φ being the *thesis* (see the Starting rule below).[87]

The ***structural rules*** are the following:

SR0 (Starting rule). Any dialogue starts with the Opponent stating initial concessions, if any, and the Proponent stating the thesis. After that the players each choose a positive integer called *repetition rank*.

[87] For a formal formulation see Clerbout (2014a,b).

- The *repetition rank* of a player restricts the number of challenges he can play in reaction to a single move.

SR1i (Classical game-playing rule). Players move alternately. After the repetition ranks have been chosen, each move is a challenge or a defence in reaction to a previous move and in accordance with the particle rules.

SR1ii (Intuitionistic game-playing rule). Players move alternately. After the repetition ranks have been chosen, each move is a challenge or a defence in reaction to a previous move and in accordance with the particle rules.
Players can only answer against the ***last non-answered*** challenge by the adversary.[88]

SR2 (Socratic Rule).[89] **P** cannot make an elementary statement if **O** has not stated it before, except in the thesis.
An elementary statement is either an elementary proposition with implicit local reason, or an elementary proposition and its local reason (not an instruction).

Challenges against elementary statements with implicit local reasons take the form:

$$\mathbf{X} \, ! \, A$$

$$\mathbf{Y} \, ?_{reason}$$

$$\mathbf{X} \, a : A$$

where A is an elementary proposition and a is a local reason. For more details see structural rules for Immanent Reasoning SR5 in the chaper IV of the present book. In the context of dialogues for ***qiyās*** it can take the form:

$$\mathbf{X} \, ! \, A$$

$$\mathbf{Y}_{why}?$$

$$\mathbf{X} \, a : A$$

[88]This last clause is known as the *Last Duty First* condition, and is the clause which makes dialogical games suitable for Intuitionistic.Logic, hence the name of this rule.

[89]This, rule, as extensively discussed in Sect. 2.3.2.1 is one of the most salient characteristics of dialogical logic. In previous literature on dialogical logic this rule has been called the *copy-cat rule or Socratic rule* and it introduces a kind of asymmetry in the distribution of roles. Clearly, if the ultimate grounds of a dialogical thesis are elementary statements and if this is implemented by the use of the copy-cat rule, then the development of a dialogue is in this sense necessarily asymmetric. Indeed, if both contenders were restricted by the copy-cat rule no elementary statement can ever be uttered. Thus, we implement the copy-cat rule by designating one player, called the *Proponent*, whose utterances of elementary statements are restricted by this rule. It is the win of the Proponent that provides the dialogical notion of validity.

Resolution of Instructions

1. A player may ask his adversary to carry out the prescribed instruction and thus bring forward a suitable local reason in defence of the proposition at stake. Once the defender has replaced the instruction with the required local reason we say that the instruction has been resolved.
2. The player index of an instruction determines which of the two players has the right to choose the local reason that will resolve the instruction.

   For example:

   X $L_{\wedge}(p)$: A
   Y? . . ./ $L_{\wedge}(p)$
   X p_1: A

The choice of a local reason for resolving an instruction is restricted by the distribution of rights and duties prescribed by the local rules.

Instructions occurring in expressions stating **falsum** have no resolution. In fact, The player stating $\mathcal{I}(p)$: $\perp$ gives up and therefore loses the play. For more details see structural rules for Immanent Reasoning SR3 and SR4 in the chapter IV of the present book.

SR3 (The overall development of a dialogue for *qiyās al-ʿilla*). We describe this rule below.

SR4 (Winning rule). This structural rule requires some additional terminology:

- ***Terminal play***: A play is called *terminal* when it cannot be extended by further moves in compliance with the rules.
- ***X-terminal***: We say it is **X**-*terminal* when the last move in the play is an **X**-move.

Player **X** wins the play ζ only if it is **X**-terminal, unless he states $\perp$. The player who states falsum loses the play.

Strategy: A *strategy* for player **X** in $\mathbb{D}$ (φ) is a function which assigns an **X**-move M to every non terminal play ζ having a **Y**-move as last member such that extending ζ with M results in a play.

X-winning-strategy: An *X-strategy* is *winning* if playing according to it leads to **X**-terminal play no matter how **Y** moves.

Winning-strategy resulting from a cooperative move: Winning strategies constituted by plays where cooperative moves took place will disregard the unsuccessful attempts and also the justification of the sub-play. More precisely, it will proceed as if the Proponent has chosen the property resulting from the sub-play. Accordingly, the winning strategy will include moves where the Proponent rather than the Opponent asserted the efficiency of the relevant property

Let us now come back to SR3 and describe the overall development of a dialogue (a less detailed form has been already deployed above):

SR3

The overall development of a dialogue for *qiyās al-ʿilla*

Preliminary Remark:

Recall our discussion in the introduction to section 4 regarding the strategic aims of the dialogue ***qiyās***. The main point of that discussion is that, despite the strategic aims of the debate, the development of such dialogues is based on **running of actual plays**. Accordingly, the strategic reason of the main assertion on the efficiency of the proposed property is left implicit. In short, the strategic reason can be specified only after the plays have been run and the sequence of moves constituting the winning strategy has been described. We call such a procedure *recapitulation* (see the introduction to 4.4.2 and particularly our remark on the strategic reason for the main assertion in 4.4.2.2).

1. A dialogical play for *qiyās al-ʿilla* starts with the Proponent claiming that some specific legal ruling applies to a certain branch-case.

2. **P** ! $\mathcal{H}$(*farʿ*)

3. After agreement on the finiteness of the argument to be developed, the Opponent will launch a challenge to the assertion by asking for justification.

4. **O** Why?

The Proponent's aim is to develop an argument in such a way that it forces the Opponent to concede the justification of the challenged assertion (see step 13). In other words **P** will try **O** to concede

O ***ap***[*farʿ*. *taʾthīr*$^{\mathcal{P}}$]: $\mathcal{H}$(*farʿ*)

which will allow **P** to make the move

P *ʿilla*(*farʿ*): $\mathcal{H}$(*farʿ*), that justifies the main thesis.

5. In order to develop his argument, the Proponent will start by choosing (to the best of his juridical knowledge) a suitable root-case from the sources for which the ruling at stake has been applied. The move consists in the Proponent forcing the Opponent to acknowledge this fact.

6. Since the evidence comes from the sources the Opponent is forced to concede it.

Steps 3 and 4 yield:

P $\mathcal{H}^{\mathbb{S}}$(*aṣl*)?

O ! $\mathcal{H}^{\mathbb{S}}$(*aṣl*)

The "$\mathbb{S}$" in "$\mathcal{H}^{\mathbb{S}}$" indicates that there is evidence from the *sources* that the ruling $\mathcal{H}$ applies to the root-case.

7. Once conceded, the Proponent will start by choosing (to the best of his juridical and epistemological knowledge) a suitable property (that should lead to the relevant occasioning factor). The move consists in the Proponent forcing the Opponent to acknowledge that the root-case instantiates that property. Recall that here we adopt al-Baṣrī's and al-Shīrāzī's practice of keeping only those plays where the Opponent responds positively to this form of request.

P *aṣl*: $\mathcal{P}$?

O *aṣl*: $\mathcal{P}$

SR3 **The overall development of a dialogue for *qiyās al-ʿilla***
8. Once the Opponent concedes that both the ruling and the selected property apply to the root-case, the Proponent will ask the Opponent to concede that the property just selected is the one that constitutes the relevant occasioning factor. The request can indicate the sources or not.
9. **P** *ʿilla(aṣl)*: $\mathcal{H}$*(aṣl)*?
If the *ʿilla* has been determined by the sources the Opponent must accept by endorsing the efficiency of the property. This endorsement commits the Opponent to assert the universal $\mathbf{O} ! (\forall x: \mathcal{P}_{\mathcal{D}} \vee \neg\mathcal{P}_{\mathcal{D}}) \{ [(\forall y: \mathcal{P}_{\mathcal{D}})\ wuj\bar{u}d^{\vee}(y) =_{\{\mathcal{P}\mathcal{D} \vee \neg\mathcal{P}\mathcal{D}\}} x \supset \mathcal{H}(y)] \wedge [(\forall z: \neg\mathcal{P}_{\mathcal{D}})\ salb^{\vee}(z) =_{\{\mathcal{P}\mathcal{D} \vee \neg\mathcal{P}\mathcal{D}\}} x \supset \neg\mathcal{H}(z)] \}$. If there is no explicit backing from the sources the Opponent can ask for justification (*muṭālaba*), cooperate in such a justification or *strongly* reject it.
10. If the Opponent asks for a justification, the Proponent will switch to the development of a dialogue of the form *qiyās al-ʿilla al-khafī* and will develop an argument towards establishing its efficiency. In other words, the Proponent must be able to bring forward arguments showing that the property satisfies *ṭard* and *ʿaks*. These duties commit the Proponent to assert $\mathbf{P} ! (\forall y: \mathcal{P}_{\mathcal{D}})\mathcal{H}(y))$ and $\mathbf{P}! (\forall z: \neg\mathcal{P}_{\mathcal{D}}) \neg\mathcal{H}(z)$. Both assertions lead to the further assertion $\mathbf{O} ! (\forall x: \mathcal{P}_{\mathcal{D}} \vee \neg\mathcal{P}_{\mathcal{D}}) \{ [(\forall y: \mathcal{P}_{\mathcal{D}})\ wuj\bar{u}d^{\vee}(y) =_{\{\mathcal{P}\mathcal{D} \vee \neg\mathcal{P}\mathcal{D}\}} x \supset \mathcal{H}(y)] \wedge [(\forall z: \neg\mathcal{P}_{\mathcal{D}})\ salb^{\vee}(z) =_{\{\mathcal{P}\mathcal{D} \vee \neg\mathcal{P}\mathcal{D}\}} x \supset \neg\mathcal{H}(z)] \}$, that establishes *taʾthīr* (the efficiency of the property $\mathcal{P}$ for causing the juridical decision $\mathcal{H}$, for any concrete case satisfying $\mathcal{P}$).
11. If the Proponent does not succeed, the play stops unless the Opponent decides to cooperate as described in the next step.
12. The Opponent might react by deciding to cooperate by first proposing a more precise formulation of the property advanced or by proposing a new property for the constitution of the occasioning factor. This will trigger a sub-play where the Opponent will defend the choice of an alternative property following the procedure prescribed for a *muʿāraḍa*-move or constructive criticism. Once the sub-play ended, the play proceeds to step 12. A *muʿāraḍa*-move assumes (1) that the choice of the root-case and the choice of ruling are relevant for the thesis, despite the fact that the Proponent chooses the wrong property for determining the occasioning factor, and (2) that the branch-case instantiates the "right" (newly proposed) property.
The launching of a constructive criticism by **O** will be indicated with the following notation
$\mathbf{O} ! \mathbf{V}$ *ʿilla(aṣl)*: $\mathcal{H}^{\mathcal{P}*}$*(aṣl)*
where the "V" indicates that **O** proposes to develop an argument for establishing $\mathcal{P}*$ rather than $\mathcal{P}$ as the relevant property.

SR3

The overall development of a dialogue for *qiyās al-ʿilla*

13. The Opponent might also react by *strongly* rejecting the Proponent's proposal. We distinguish two cases that we call (1) *Destruction of the thesis*. The main target of this form of objection is the thesis rather than only objecting to the Proponent's proposal for determining the *ʿilla*. In such a case it is he, the Opponent, who has to bring forward a counterexample from the sources. This will trigger a sub-play where the Opponent develops his counter argumentation, following the prescriptions for one of the forms of destructive criticism, namely: *qalb* (reversal), *naqḍ* (inconsistency), or *kasr* (breaking apart). (2) *Destruction of the ʿilla*. The counter-argument involves bringing forward objections against the proposed *waṣf* proposed as determining the *ʿilla*, following the prescriptions for attacks of the forms *fasād al-waḍʿ* (invalidity of occasioned status) or *ʿadam al-taʾthīr* (lack of efficiency). If the Opponent succeeds, the play stops.

14. If, after the justification, the Opponent concedes that the property determines the occasioning factor for the ruling of the root-case, then the same moves as in step 7 follow. In other words, the Opponent commits himself to assert the universal

O ! $(\forall x: \mathcal{P}_{\mathcal{D}} \vee \neg\mathcal{P}_{\mathcal{D}})$ { [$(\forall y: \mathcal{P}_{\mathcal{D}})$ $wuj\bar{u}d^{\vee}(y) =_{\{\mathcal{P}_{\mathcal{D}} \vee \neg\mathcal{P}_{\mathcal{D}}\}} x \supset \mathcal{H}(y)$] $\wedge$ [$(\forall z: \neg\mathcal{P}_{\mathcal{D}})$ $salb^{\vee}(z) =_{\{\mathcal{P}_{\mathcal{D}} \vee \neg\mathcal{P}_{\mathcal{D}}\}} x \supset \neg\mathcal{H}(z)$] }.

15. After the Opponent's assertion of the universal stated in the previous step, the Proponent will ask the Opponent to acknowledge that the property also applies to the branch-case – recall (again) that here we adopt al-Baṣrī's and al-Shīrāzī's practice of keeping only those plays where the Opponent responds positively to this form of request. Request and answer will be expressed by means of the following notation:

P *farʿ*: $\mathcal{P}$? (or $\mathcal{P}$*)

O *farʿ*: $\mathcal{P}$ (or $\mathcal{P}$*)

16. After the Opponent concedes that the property does apply to the branch case, and since the Opponent also concedes that the property is the one that characterizes the relevant occasioning factor, the Proponent will ask the Opponent to acknowledge that the branch-case falls under the ruling at stake. This move forces the Opponent to concede the challenged thesis. A play ends if there are no other moves allowed. If the Proponent's defence is successful the play will end by a move where he indicates that the Opponent has finished by endorsing the thesis under scrutiny.

P *farʿ*: $\mathcal{P}$ (challenging the universal that expresses the *ṭard*-condition)

O ***ap***[*farʿ.taʾthīr*$^{\mathcal{P}}$]: $\mathcal{H}$(*farʿ*)

P *ʿilla*(*farʿ*): $\mathcal{H}$(*farʿ*)

(answer to the request for justification of the thesis that can be glossed as: you just stated the justification of the thesis you asked for)

Schema of the Development of a Dialogue for *Qiyās al-'Illa*

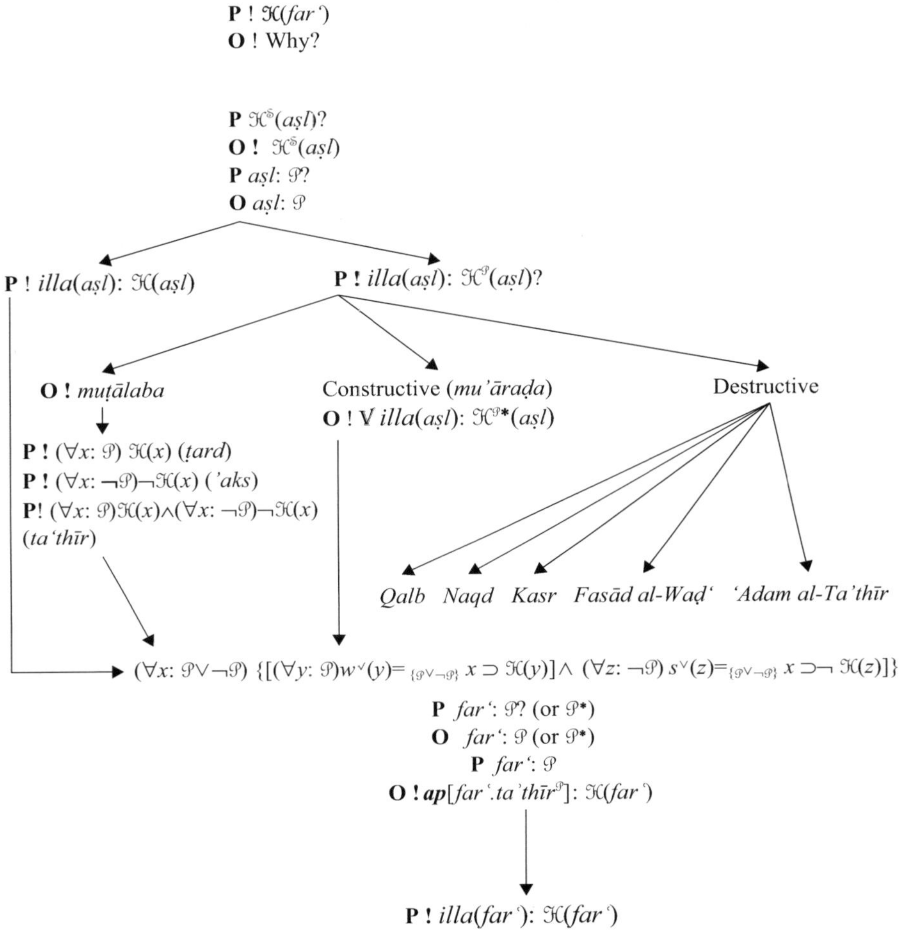

2.4.4.2.2 The Constitution of Strategies

While building the core of a *winning* **P**-strategy, local reasons are linked not only to the local meaning of expressions but also to their justification. This cannot be achieved while considering single plays.

Consider, for example, the case of a **P**-conjunction such that the Proponent claims that it has a (winning) strategic reason for it. Single plays cannot provide a way to check if a conjunction is justified; this would require **P** to win the play for the two conjuncts. However, if the repetition rank chosen by the Opponent is 1, then in no single play can **P** bring forward the strategic reason for the whole conjunction. It is only within the tree that displays the winning-strategy that both plays can be brought together as two branches with a common root. Indeed, if we think of the tree as developed through the plays, the root of the tree will not explicitly display the information gathered while developing the plays. When a play starts it is just a *claim*. Only at the end of the construction-process of the relevant plays will **P** be able to have the knowledge required to *assert* the thesis.

Similarly, in the case of a disjunction, we will only be able to display the strategic reason correspondent to the choice that yielded the canonical argumentation form of the strategic reason after the choices involving the defence have been made. More generally:

- The *assertion* of the thesis that makes explicit the reason resulting from the plays is a *recapitulation* of the result achieved after running the relevant plays, after **P**'s initial statement of that thesis. This is what the canonical argumentation form of a reason is at the strategic level, and this is what renders the dialogical formulation of a canonical proof-object. We call those reasons that constitute a winning strategy *global reasons*.

In the case of material implication (and universal quantification), a winning **P**-strategy literally displays the procedure by which the Proponent chooses the local reason for the consequent *depending* on the local reason chosen by the Opponent for the antecedent. What the canonical argumentation form of a global reason does is to make explicit the relevant *choice-dependence* by means of a *recapitulation* of the thesis.

This corresponds to the general description of proof-objects for material implications and universally quantified formulas in CTT: a method which, given a proof-object for the antecedent, yields a proof-object for the consequent. The dialogical interpretation of this functional dependence amounts to rendering the canonical argumentation form of a global reason for **P**! $A \supset B$ as **P** $p_j[\![p_i{}^{\mathbf{O}}]\!]$: $A \supset B$ that expresses that if **P** is looking to make his claim legitimate he must be able to assert the consequent for any reason that the Opponent brings forward to back his (the Opponent's) own assertion of the antecedent. Thus, the global reason for the material implication $A \supset B$ is the "strategic-reason" **P** $p_j[\![p_i{}^{\mathbf{O}}]\!]$. In fact, the CTT-framework prescribes the notation $\lambda(x^{\mathbf{O}})b^{\mathbf{P}}(x)$: $A \supset B$, that is, the lambda-abstract of the function $p(x)$: B (see the chapter IV of the present book). However, here we use instead $p_j[\![p_i{}^{\mathbf{O}}]\!]$: $A \supset B$ in order to stress the dialogical interdependence.

Similar holds for a universal, **P**-strategic reasons must be built (*synthesis* of **P**-strategic reasons); they constitute the justification of a statement by providing certain information—choice-dependences—that are essential to the relevant plays issuing from the statement: strategic reasons are a recapitulation of the building of a winning strategy, directly inserted into a play. Thus a strategic reason for a **P**-statement on the universal **P**! $(\forall x: A)\ B(x)$ has the form $p_j{}^{\mathbf{P}}[\![p_i{}^{\mathbf{O}}]\!]$ (where $p_j{}^{\mathbf{P}}$: $B(p_i{}^{\mathbf{O}})$ and $p_i{}^{\mathbf{O}}$: A) and indicates that **P**'s choice p_j for defending the right constituent of the universal, is dependent upon **O**'s choice of p_i.

Strategic reasons for **P** are the dialogical formulation of CTT proof-objects, and the canonical argumentation form of strategic reasons correspond to canonical proof-objects. Since in this section we are seeking a notion of winning strategy that corresponds to that of a CTT-demonstration, and since these strategies have being identified to be those where **P** wins, we will only describe the synthesis of strategic reasons for **P**– for a complete presentation of all the rules see the chapter IV of the present book.

Synthesis of strategic reasons for P:

	Move	**Synthesis of local reasons**		**Synthesis of strategic reasons Canonical Argumentation form**
		Challenge	**Defence**	
Conjunction	$\mathbf{P}\ !\ A \wedge B$	$\mathbf{O}\ ?\ L^{\wedge}$ or $\mathbf{O}\ ?\ R^{\wedge}$	$\mathbf{P}\ p_1: A$ (resp.) $\mathbf{P}\ p_2: B$	$\mathbf{P} < p_1, p_2 >: A \wedge B$
Existential quantification	$\mathbf{P}\ !\ (\exists x: A)B(x)$	$\mathbf{O}\ ?\ L^{\exists}$ or $\mathbf{O}\ ?\ R^{\exists}$	$\mathbf{P}\ p_1: A$ (resp.) $\mathbf{P}\ p_2: B(p_1)$	$\mathbf{P} < p_1, p_2 >: (\exists x: A)B(x)$
Disjunction	$\mathbf{P}\ !\ A \vee B$	$\mathbf{O}\ ?^{\vee}$	$\mathbf{P}\ p_1: A$ or $\mathbf{P}\ p_2: B$	$\mathbf{P}\ p_1: A \vee B$ or $\mathbf{P}\ p_2: A \vee B$
Implication	$\mathbf{P}\ !\ A \supset B$	$\mathbf{O}\ p_1: A$	$\mathbf{P}\ p_2: B$	$\mathbf{P}\ p_1{}^{\mathbf{P}}[\![p_i{}^{\mathbf{O}}]\!]: A \supset B$ (where $p_j{}^{\mathbf{P}}: B$ and $p_i{}^{\mathbf{O}}: A$)
Universal quantification	$\mathbf{P}\ !\ (\forall x: A)B(x)$	$\mathbf{O}\ p_1: A$	$\mathbf{P}\ p_2: B(p_1)$	$\mathbf{P}\ p_1{}^{\mathbf{P}}[\![p_i{}^{\mathbf{O}}]\!]: (\forall x: A)B(x)$ (where $p_j{}^{\mathbf{P}}: B(p_i{}^{\mathbf{O}})$ and $p_i{}^{\mathbf{O}}: A$)
Negation	$\mathbf{P}\ !\ A \supset \bot$	$\mathbf{O}\ p_1: A$ ... $\mathbf{O}\ !\ \bot$ (stating the antecedent leads eventually to **O** giving up)	–	$\mathbf{P}\ p_j{}^{\mathbf{P}}[\![p_i{}^{\mathbf{O}}]\!]\ [\![p_i{}^{\mathbf{O}}]\!]: A \supset \bot$ The method encoded by $p_1{}^{\mathbf{P}}[\![p_i{}^{\mathbf{O}}]\!]$ will never be never be carried out. Indeed, since this method provides a winning strategy, **P** will force **O** to state **falsum** himself (on the grounds of the move $\mathbf{O}\ p_1: A$), before $p_j{}^{\mathbf{P}}$ comes into play.

Strategic Reasons for the Main Assertion

The notation

taʾthīr$^{\mathcal{P}}$ $[\![p_i{}^{\mathbf{Y}}]\!]$

Indicates that the process (the function) *ta'thīr*$^{\mathscr{P}}$ is dependent upon the p_i chosen by **Y**

$\boldsymbol{ap}[p_1, ta\text{'}th\bar{\imath}r^{\mathscr{P}}]$: $\mathcal{H}(p_1)$

Indicates that when p_1 is chosen by the challenger *ta'thīr*$^{\mathscr{P}}$ confirms the efficiency of property $\mathscr{P}$.

Statement	Challenge	Defence
Synthesis		
X! $(\forall x: \mathscr{P}_{\mathscr{D}} \vee \neg\mathscr{P}_{\mathscr{D}})$ $\{ [(\forall y: \mathscr{P}_{\mathscr{D}})$ $wuj\bar{u}d^{\vee}(y) =_{\{\mathscr{P}\mathscr{D}\vee\neg\mathscr{P}\mathscr{D}\}} x \supset \mathcal{H}(y)] \wedge$ $[(\forall z: \neg\mathscr{P}_{\mathscr{D}})\ salb^{\vee}(z) =_{\{\mathscr{P}\mathscr{D}\vee\neg\mathscr{P}\mathscr{D}\}} x \supset$ $\neg\mathcal{H}(z)]\}$	**Y** p_i: $\mathscr{P}_{\mathscr{D}}$	'*ta'thīr*$^{\mathscr{P}}$ $[\![p_i{}^{\mathbf{Y}}]\!]$: $\{[(\forall y: \mathscr{P}_{\mathscr{D}})\ wuj\bar{u}d^{\vee}(y) =_{\{\mathscr{P}\mathscr{D}\vee\neg\mathscr{P}\mathscr{D}\}} p_i \supset$ $\mathcal{H}(y)] \wedge [(\forall z: \neg\mathscr{P}_{\mathscr{D}})\ salb^{\vee}(z) =_{\{\mathscr{P}\mathscr{D}\vee\neg\mathscr{P}\mathscr{D}\}}$ $p_i \supset \neg\mathcal{H}(z)]\}$ (similar for **Y** q_i: $\neg\mathscr{P}_{\mathscr{D}}$)
Analysis		
X p: $(\forall x: \mathscr{P}_{\mathscr{D}} \vee \neg\mathscr{P}_{\mathscr{D}})$ $\{[(\forall y: \mathscr{P}_{\mathscr{D}})$ $wuj\bar{u}d^{\vee}(y) =_{\{\mathscr{P}\mathscr{D}\vee\neg\mathscr{P}\mathscr{D}\}} x \supset \mathcal{H}(y)] \wedge$ $[(\forall z: \neg\mathscr{P}_{\mathscr{D}})\ salb^{\vee}(z) =_{\{\mathscr{P}\mathscr{D}\vee\neg\mathscr{P}\mathscr{D}\}} x \supset$ $\neg\mathcal{H}(z)]\}$	**Y** $L^{\supset}(p)^{\mathbf{Y}}=p_1$: $\mathscr{P}_{\mathscr{D}}$	$R^{\supset}(p)=p_1.ta\text{'}th\bar{\imath}r^{\mathscr{P}}$ ⇓ **X** $\boldsymbol{ap}[p_1.ta\text{'}th\bar{\imath}r^{\mathscr{P}}]$: $\mathcal{H}(p_1)$: $\{[(\forall y: \mathscr{P}_{\mathscr{D}})\ wuj\bar{u}d^{\vee}(y) =_{\{\mathscr{P}\mathscr{D}\vee\neg\mathscr{P}\mathscr{D}\}} p_1 \supset$ $\mathcal{H}(y)] \wedge [(\forall z: \neg\mathscr{P}_{\mathscr{D}})\ salb^{\vee}(z) =_{\{\mathscr{P}\mathscr{D}\vee\neg\mathscr{P}\mathscr{D}\}}$ $p_1 \supset \neg\mathcal{H}(z)]\}$ (similar for **Y** q_1: $\neg\mathscr{P}_{\mathscr{D}}$)
Notice that in the development of a play "p" will be left implicit (see remark below)		In practice we skip the equality steps.

Remark

As discussed above, the strategic reason of the main assertion on the efficiency of the proposed property is left implicit – it will be made explicit through the equality that "resolves" the instruction to apply the process *ta'thīr*$^{\mathscr{P}}$ to p_1 only after the winning strategy has been developed. The point is that during a play, the player who brings forward such an assertion *claims* to be able to provide a strategic reason rather than commiting himself to be already in possession of one. In short, the strategic reason can be specified only after the plays have been run and the sequence of moves constituting the winning strategy has been described.

2.5 Conclusions

The meaning of *ijtihād* in Islamic jurisprudence presupposes that the notion of law is dynamic in nature. This dynamic was put into work in the process of the development of *uṣūl al-fiqh* that occurred in the conceptual venue that Young (2017) calls the *dialectical forge*.

In such a dialectical setting premises of legal theory were continually produced, tested and reproduced in order to yield a deeper systematization. To put it another way, it seems that the dialectical forge is not only the venue but also is a dialectical engine which powered the process by which the legal theory was continuously forged and refined. Moreover, unlike other dialectical frameworks– such as the

Obligationes,[90] the focus of the dialectical forge is on developing methods of dialectical interaction aimed at the winning of knowledge and meaning, beyond the rhetoric purposes of a legal trial or debate. This gave *jadal* a crucial epistemological role in the pursuit of truth.[91]

In this context, Islamic jurists studied and developed several instruments suitable for implementing the dialectical forge. One of the most important of these instruments is *qiyās*, that constitutes the subject of our study. The aim of this form of inference is to provide a rational ground for the application of a *ḥukm* to a given case not yet considered by the original juridical sources. As a product of legal theory shaped by the dialectical forge, it is fair to say that a dialogical framework such as that developed in the present study provides a suitable setting in order to delve into the structure and meaning underlying the legal notion of *qiyās*. The dialogical framework displays three of the hallmarks of this form of inference.

First, the interaction of heuristic with logical steps. This interaction was displayed by two main steps:

1. finding the root-case from which the occasioning factor can be inferred;
2. linking the root-case logically with the branch-case by means of a generalization that links the occasioning factor with the relevant juridical ruling.

Second, the dynamics underlying the extension of the legal terms involved. This dynamics is displayed by the intertwining of confirmations and refutations that contribute to establish the most suitable conclusion in relation to the consideration of a new case.

Third, the unfolding of parallel reasoning as symmetry in action. Parallel reasoning is about unfolding the process by the means of which symmetries are constituted.

The third point, reasoning by symmetry, takes us to the second main part of the present study.

References

Al-Baṣrī, Abū al-Ḥusayn. (1964). *Kitāb al-qiyās al-sharʿī*. In *idem*, *Kitāb al-muʿtamad fī uṣūl al-fiqh*. Vol. 2. (Muḥammad Ḥamīd Allāh, Muḥammad Bakīr, and Ḥasan Ḥanafī, Eds.). Damascus: al-Maʿhad al-ʿIlmī al-Faransī li'l-Dirāsāt al-ʿArabiyya bi-Dimash.

Al-Juwaynī, 'Abd al-Malik ibn 'Abd Allāh. (1979). In F. Ḥ. Maḥmūd (Ed.), *Al-Kāfiya fī al-jadal*. Cairo: Maṭba'at 'Īsā al Bābi al-Ḥalabī.

Al-Namla, 'Abd al-Karīm b. 'Alī b. Muḥammad. (1999). *Al-Muhadhdhab fī 'ilm uṣūl al-fiqh al-muqārin*. Riyadh: Maktabat al-Rushd.

Al-Shīrāzī, Abū Isḥāq. (1987). *Al-Maʿūna fī al-jadal*. ('Alī b. ʿAbd al-ʿAzīz al-ʿUmayrīnī. Al-Safāh, Ed.). Kuwait: Manshūrāt Markaz al-Makhṭūṭāt wa-al-Turāth.

Al-Shīrāzī, Abū Isḥāq. (2003). *Al-Lumaʿ fī uṣūl al-fiqh*. Beirut: Dār al-Kutub al-'Ilmiyah.

[90] Duthil-Novaes (2007) interprets *Obligationes* as games of *consistency-checking*. This is definetely not the aim of *qiyās*.

[91] Hallaq (1987a).

Al-Shīrāzī, Abū Isḥāq. (2016). *Mulakhkhaṣ fī al-jadal*. Retrieved February 1, 2016 from https://upload.wikimedia.org/wikisource/ar/e/ea/الملخص_في_الجدل_خ.pdf.

Aristotle (1984). *The complete works of Aristotle. The revised Oxford translation*. (J. Barnes, Trans. & Ed.). Princeton: Princeton University Press.

Bartha, P. F. A. (2010). *By parallel reasoning. The construction and evaluation of analogical arguments*. Oxford: Oxford University Press.

Castelnérac, B., & Marion, M. (2009). Arguing for inconsistency: Dialectical games in the academy. In G. Primiero & S. Rahman (Eds.), *Acts of knowledge: History, philosophy and logic* (pp. 37–76). London: College Publications.

Cellucci, C. (2013). *Rethinking logic: Logic in relation to mathematics, evolution and method*. Dordrecht: Springer.

Clerbout, N. (2014a). First-order dialogical games and tableaux. *Journal of Philosophical Logic, 43*(4), 785–801.

Clerbout, N. (2014b). *La Semantiques Dialogiques. Notions Fondamentaux et Éléments de Metathéorie*. London: College Publications.

Clerbout, N., & Rahman, S. (2015). *Linking game-theoretical approaches with constructive type theory: Dialogical strategies as CTT-demonstrations*. Dordrecht: Springer.

Crubellier, M., McConaughey, M., Marion M., & Rahman, S. (2019). Dialectic, the Dictum de omni and Ecthesis. *History and Philosophy of Logic*. In print.

David, J. (2010). Legal comparability and cultural identity: The case of legal reasoning in Jewish and Islamic traditions. *Electronic Journal of Comparative Law*, vol. 14.1, http://www.ejcl.org.

David, J. (2014). *Jurisprudence and theology*. Dordrecht: Springer.

Davidson, D. (1980). *Essays on actions and events*. Oxford: Clarendon Press.

Duthil-Novaes, C. (2007). *Formalizing medieval logical theories*. Dordrecht: Springer.

Felscher, W. (1985). Dialogues as a foundation for intuitionistic logic. In D. Gabbay & F. Guenthner (Eds.), *Handbook of philosophical logic* (Vol. 3, pp. 341–372). Dordrecht: Kluwer.

Gili, L. (2015). Alexander of Aphrodisias and the Heterdox dictum de omni et de nullo. *History and Philosophy of Logic, 36*(2), 114–128.

Ginzburg, J. (2012). *The interactive stance*. Oxford: OUP.

Granström, J. G. (2011). *Treatise on intuitionistic type theory*. Dordrecht: Springer.

Hallaq, W. (1985). The logic of legal reasoning in religious and non-religious cultures: The case of Islamic law and common law. *Cleveland State Law Review, 34*, 79–96.

Hallaq, W. (1987a). A tenth-eleventh century treatise on juridical dialectic. *The Muslim World, 77*(3–4), 151–282.

Hallaq, W. (1987b). The development of logical structure in Islamic legal theory. *Der Islam*, 64/1, pp. 42–67.

Hallaq, W. (1993). *Ibn Taymiyya against the Greek logicians*. Oxford: Clarendon Press.

Hallaq, W. (1997). *A history of Islamic legal theories: An introduction to Sunnī Uṣūl al-Fiqh*. Cambridge, NY: Cambridge University Press.

Hallaq, W. (2004). *Continuity and change in Islamic law*. Cambridge, NY: Cambridge U. Press.

Hallaq, W. (2009a). *The origins and evolution of Islamic law*. Cambridge, NY: Cambridge University Press.

Hallaq, W. (2009b). *Sharīʿa: Theory, practice, transformation*. Cambridge, NY: Cambridge University Press.

Hodges, W. (1998). The laws of distribution for syllogisms. *Notre Dame Journal of Formal Logic, 39*(2), 221–230.

Keiff, L. (2009). Dialogical logic. In Edward, N (ed.), *The Stanford encyclopedia of philosophy*. Zalta. URL http://plato.stanford.edu/entries/logic-dialogical/

Klev, A. M. (2018). *A brief introduction to constructive type theory*. In S. Rahman, Z. McConaughey, A. Klev and N. Clerbout (2018, chapter II).

Krabbe, E. C. (2006). Dialogue Logic. In D. M. Gabbay & J. Woods (Eds.), *Handbook of the history of logic* (Vol. 7, pp. 665–704). Amsterdam: Elsevier.

Lorenz, K. (2000). Sinnbestimmung und Geltungssicherung. First published under the title “Ein Beitrag zur Sprachlogik”. In G.-L. Lueken (Ed.), *Formen der Argumentation* (pp. 87–106). Leipzig: Akademisches Verlag.

Lorenz, K. (2010a). *Logic, language and method: On polarities in human experience*. Berlin/New York: De Gruyter.

Lorenz, K. (2010b). *Philosophische Variationen: Gesammelte Aufsätze unter Einschluss gemeinsam mit Jürgen Mittelstraß geschriebener Arbeiten zu Platon und Leibniz*. Berlin/New York: De Gruyter.

Lorenzen, P., & Lorenz, K. (1978). *Dialogische logik*. Darmstadt: Wissenschaftliche Buchgesellschaft.

Marion, M., & Rückert, H. (2015). Aristotle on universal quantification: A study from the perspective of game semantics. *History and Philosophy of Logic, 37*(3), 201–209.

Martin-Löf, P. (1984). *Intuitionistic type theory. Notes by Giovanni Sambin of a series of lectures given in Padua, June 1980*. Naples: Bibliopolis.

Martin-Löf, P. (1996). On the meanings of the logical constants and the justifications of the logical laws. *Nordic Journal of Philosophical Logic, 1*, 11–60.

Martin-Löf, P. (2012). *Aristotle's distinction between apophansis and protasis in the light of the distinction between assertion and proposition in contemporary logic*. Workshop "Sciences et Savoirs de l'Antiquité à l'Age classique". Lecture held at the laboratory SPHERE–CHSPAM, Paris VII. Seminar organized by Ahmed Hasnaoui.

Martin-Löf, P. (2015). Is logic part of normative ethics?. Lecture held at the research unit *Sciences, normes, décision (FRE 3593)*, Paris, May 2015. Transcription by Amsten Klev.

Miller, L. B. (1984). *Islamic disputation theory: A study of the development of dialectic in Islam from the tenth through fourteenth centuries*. Princeton: Princeton University. (Unpublished dissertation).

Nordström, B., Petersson, K., & Smith, J. M. (1990). *Programming in Martin-Löf's type theory: An introduction*. Oxford: Oxford University Press.

Nordström, B., Petersson, K., & Smith, J. M. (2000). Martin-Löf's type theory. In S. Abramsky, D. Gabbay, & T. S. E. Maibaum (Eds.), *Handbook of logic in computer science. Volume 5: Logic and algebraic methods* (pp. 1–37). Oxford: Oxford University Press.

Parsons, T. (2014). Articulating medieval logic. Oxford: Oxford University Press.

Peregrin, J. (2014). *Inferentialism. Why rules matter*. New York: Plagrave MacMillan.

Plato. (1997). *Plato. Complete works*. (Jhon M. Cooper, Tans. & Ed.). Indianapolis IN: Hackett.

Popek, A. (2012). Logical dialogues from middle ages. In C. B. Gómez, S. Magnier, & F. J. Salguero (Eds.), *Logic of knowledge. Theory and applications* (pp. 223–244). London: College Publications.

Primiero, G. (2008). *Information and knowledge*. Dordrecht: Springer.

Rahman, S., & Iqbal, M. (2018). Unfolding parallel reasoning in Islamic jurisprudence. Epistemic and dialectical meaning within Abū Isḥāq al-Shīrāzī's system of co-relational inferences of the occasioning factor. *Cambridge Journal for Arabic Sciences and Philosophy, 28*, 67–132.

Rahman, S., & Keiff, L. (2005). On how to be a dialogician. In D. Vanderveken (Ed.), *Logic, thought and action* (pp. 359–408). Dordrecht: Kluwer.

Rahman, S., & Rückert, H. (2001). Dialogical connexive logic. *Synthese, 125*(1–2), 105–139.

Rahman, S., & Tulenheimo, T. (2009). From games to dialogues and back: Towards a general frame for validity. Games: Unifying logic, language and philosophy. O. Majer, A. Pietarinen T. Tulenheimo. Dordrecht: Springer, pp. 153–208.

Rahman, S., Clerbout, N., & Redmond, J. (2017). Interaction and equality. The dialogical interprepretation of CTT (In Spanish). ***Critica***.

Rahman, S., McConaughey, Z., Klev, A., & Clerbout, N. (2018). *Immanent reasoning. A plaidoyer for the play level*. Dordrecht: Springer.

Ranta, A. (1988). Propositions as games as types. *Synthese, 76*, 377–395.

Ranta, A. (1994). *Type-theoretical grammar*. Oxford: Clarendon Press.

Rückert, H. (2011). *Dialogues as a dynamic framework for logic*. London: College Publications.

Sundholm, G. (2009). A century of judgement and inference, 1837–1936: Some strands in the development of logic. In L. Haaparanta (Ed.), *The development of modern logic* (pp. 263–317). Oxford: Oxford University Press.

Sundholm, G. (2012). "Inference versus consequence" revisited: Inference, conditional, implication. *Synthese, 187*, 943–956.

Sundholm, G. (2013). *Inference and consequence in an interpeted language.* Talk at the Workshop PROOF THEORY AND PHILOSOPHY, Groningen, December 3–5, 2013.

Tahiri, H. (2008). The birth of scientific controversies: The dynamic of the Arabic tradition and its impact on the development of science: Ibn al-Haytham's challenge of Ptolemy's *Almagest*. The Unity of science in the Arabic tradition. Ed. S. Rahman, T. Street and H. Tahiri. Dordrecht: Springer, pp. 183–225.

Tahiri, H. (2014). Al Kindi and the universalization of knowledge through mathematics. *Revista de Humanidades de Valparaíso*, (4), 81–90.

Tahiri, H. (2015). *Mathematics and the mind. An introduction to Ibn Sīnā's theory of knowledge.* Dordrecht: Springer.

Tahiri, H. (2018). When the present misunderstands the past. How a modern Arab intellectual reclaimed his own heritage. *Cambridge Journal for Arabic Sciences and Philosophy, 28*(1), 133–158.

Weiss, B. G. (1992). *Search for God's law, Islamic jurisprudence in the writings of Sayf al-din al-Amidi*. Salt Lake City: University of Utah Press.

Weiss, B. G. (1998). *The Spirit of Islamic law*. Athens/London: The University of Georgia Press.

Young, W. E. (2017). *The dialectical forge. Juridical disputation and the evolution of Islamic law.* Dordrecht: Springer.

Chapter 3
Qiyās al-Dalāla and *Qiyās al-Shabah*: al-Shīrāzī's System of Correlational Inferences by Indication and Resemblance

The present chapter examines al-Shīrāzī's classification of correlational inferences by indication (*qiyās al-dalāla*) and resemblance (*qiyās al-shabah*) based on pinpointing specific relevant parallelisms between rulings or resemblances between properties. These forms of inferences, sometimes broadly referred to as arguments by analogy (or better by the Latin denomination arguments *a pari*) are put into action when there is absence of knowledge of the occasioning factor grounding the application of a given ruling. These forms of correlational inferences should make the process of transferring the relevant juridical ruling from the root-case to the branch-case plausible. The plausibility of a conclusion attained by parallelism between rulings (*qiyās al-dalāla*) is considered to be of a higher epistemic degree than the conclusion obtained by resemblances based on sharing properties (*qiyās al-shabah*). Conclusions obtained by either *qiyās al-dalāla* or *qiyās al-shabah* have a lower degree of epistemic plausibility than conclusions inferred by the deployment of *qiyās al-'illa*.

It is worth mentioning that al-Shīrāzī can be identified as the main developer if not the inventor of the system of correlational inferences based on drawing parallelisms between rulings (*qiyās al-dalāla*).

Furthermore, both *qiyās al-dalāla* and *qiyās al-shabah* can perhaps be seen as the first antecedents of *arguments from precedent case* and *arguments by analogy*, two central forms of reasoning in contemporary American and British Common Law.

3.1 Introduction: On al-Shīrāzī's Classification of *Qiyās al-Dalāla* and *Qiyās al-Shabah*

As extensively discussed previously, in the context of Law *qiyās* is a form of inference by means of which the application of a ruling (*ḥukm*) from a case already sanctioned by juridical sources, which is called *aṣl* (the root-case), is extended to

S. Rahman et al., *Inferences by Parallel Reasoning in Islamic Jurisprudence*, Logic, Argumentation & Reasoning 19, https://doi.org/10.1007/978-3-030-22382-3_3

cover a case not yet considered, which is called *far'*(the branch-case). Let us stress here that the *general aim* of applying this form of inference is to provide the means for identifying the juridical ground, called *'illa* or the occasioning factor, that justifies transferring the ruling from the root-case to the branch-case.

> والقياس حمل فرع على أصل بعلة واجراء حكم الأصل على الفرع [1]
>
> *Qiyās* is the linking of a branch-case with a source-case by way of an occasioning factor, and the application of the ruling of the source-case to the branch-case.[2]

In other words, generally speaking, *qiyās* is the instrument for making the rationale behind a juridical ruling apparent.

In the case of the so-called *qiyās al-'illa* the occasioning factor can be learned either.

- because the sources explicitly (*jalī*) identify the relevant property; or
- because, though the sources do not contain an explicit description of the property determining the *'illa*, it comes out as *evident* (*wāḍiḥ*), by hermeneutical examination of the texts; or
- because, when it is neither explicit nor apparent after a hermeneutical study, but hidden or *latent* (*khafī*), it is made apparent by an epistemological enquiry. This enquiry should aim at (a) isolating some property, (b) assessing if it has the required efficiency (*ta'thīr*) for determining the occasioning factor for the relevant ruling, and (c) determining if the isolated property also applies to the branch-case.

The association of an occasioning factor to a ruling obtained by *qiyās al-'illa* can be said to be *direct*, in the sense that the conclusion is achieved by identifiying and making explicit the link between the case under study and the *'illa* causing the ruling claimed to apply to the branch-case.

However, in many cases (if not in most of them), the property sources do not provide sufficient evidence for identifying the *'illa*, even if the methods mentioned above are applied. In such situations, the inferential system called *qiyās al-dalāla*[3] is put into action, providing ways to link the root-case and the branch-case by means of some form of *indication* (*dalāla*) that supports transferring the relevant juridical ruling from the root-case to the branch-case.

> وأما قياس الدلالة فهو أن يحمل الفرع على الأصل بضرب من الشبه غير العلة التي علق الحكم عليها في الشرع. وهذا ضرب من القياس لا تعرف صحته إلا بالاستدلال بالأصول. [4]
>
> *As for Qiyās al-Dalāla, it is that one that links the branch-case with the source-case by way of a type of resemblance other than the occasioning factor upon which the ruling is*

---

[1]See al-Shīrāzī (2016), *Mulakhkhaṣ fī al-jadal*, fol. 5a.

[2]Cf. Young (2017, p. 109).

[3]Some other jurists also called it *qiyās al-shabah*. However, for al-Shirazi *qiyās al-shabah* denominates a subtype of *qiyās al-dalāla*. Moreover, as we discuss further on, al-Shirazi seems to be inclined to consider *qiyās al-shabah* as a separate form of *qiyās*.

[4]See al-Shīrāzī, *Mulakhkhaṣ fī al-jadal*, fol. 5a.

made contingent in God's Law. The validity of this type of correlational inference is not known except by way of drawing indication from the authoritative source-cases.[5]

More precisely, in the absence of knowledge of an occasioning factor grounding the ruling, the task is to isolate some specific forms of parallelism that *indicate* that the transference (from the root-case to the branch-case) of the relevant ruling can be carried out. However, *indication* does not provide the means for establishing a "direct" link to the *'illa* in the sense mentioned before.

Actually, in his *Mulakhkhaṣ* al-Shīrāzī classifies *qiyās* into two general types:

qiyās al-'illa, where the occasioning factor is known, and

qiyas al-dalāla, where it is not known. In his *Mulakhkhaṣ*, *qiyas al-shabah* (correlational inference by resemblance) is set as a particular case of *qiyās al-dalāla*.

However, in his further work al-Shīrāzī distinguishes between *qiyās al-dalāla* and *qiyas al-shabah* as two separate forms. The distinction deepens in *al-Luma'* where clearly he classifies *qiyas al-shabah* as a third type of *qiyās.*[6]

In fact, though *qiyās al-dalāla* and *qiyas al-shabah* are both based on establishing parallelisms, the notion of resemblance deployed by *qiyās al-dalāla* is quite different from that one deployed by *qiyās al-shabah.*

Indeed, whereas the notion of resemblance deployed by *qiyās al-dalāla* requires making it apparent that root-case and branch-case share some structural parallelism, in the sense that each of both cases fall under the scope of a pair of *rulings* linked by some structural relation (either of specification or of sheer parallelism), the kind of resemblance deployed by *qiyas al-shabah* amounts to pointing out one or more relevant *properties* shared by the root- and the branch-case.

In short, whereas the conclusion drawn in an inference of the form *qiyās al-dalāla* is based on the **resemblance between two rulings,** the conclusion drawn by an inference of the form *qiyas al-shabah* is based on the **resemblance of *aṣl* and *far'***.

We took the option to follow the approach adopted in *al-Luma'* and therefore, in the present study, we classify *qiyās al-shabah* as a form of inference different from *qiyās al-dalāla.* On our view this strategy provides a fertile ground for a close examination of the epistemological notions involved in the systems of *qiyas al-dalāla* and *al-shabah.*[7]

---

[5]Cf. Young (2017, p. 115).

[6]Abū Isḥāq al-Shīrāzī (2003, pp. 99-101).

[7]For the dialectical structure of *qiyās al-'illa*, see the chapter II of the present book and Rahman/Iqbal (2018).

3.2 *Qiyās al-Dalāla*

Qiyās al-dalāla amounts to the task of pointing out some what, by extending the original terminology, we migh call *indicators,* that support transferring some specific juridical ruling applied to a root-case to the branch-case. Al-Shīrāzī, who is well aware of the difficulty of establishing a form of inference that lies between one where the occasioning factor is known and one exclusively based on some form of resemblance or analogy, provides an example that should highlight the fine distinction.[8] His example can be put in the following way:

That some being is a living being (*al-ḥayā*) can be inferred by observing that this being experiences senses (*al-iḥsās*), suffers pain (*ta'allum*) and undergoes processes of growth (*al-numuww*).

Clearly, senses, pain and growth are **not** actually the factors occasioning the living, but one can recognize that a certain being is a living one because of these three *life-indicators*. Those indicators are dependent upon some *'illa,* which though it is unknown, is the source of their efficiency for indicating the presence of life.

Thus, in absence of the knowledge of the *'illa* we might deploy those indicators when we have to decide if some being is or not a living one – because if a being fails to have one of those indicators it cannot be said (in principle) to be a living one, and because if it has the properties described by the indicators, then the claim that it is indeed a living being is plausible. Another example is that some peculiar smell is always present when alcohol is, but this smell does not occasion the interdiction of wine.

If the indicators are close together, in the sense that both always occur together, then the hypothesis that both are linked to a common occasioning factor wins support. Thus, the closer the indicators are, the stronger the justification for the transference from the known case to the new case is.

Now, when we move to the juridical case the idea is that the *indicators* of *qiyās al-dalāla* are rulings. Indeed, the form of inference typical of *dalāla* is based on the idea of establishing a relationship between the ruling under consideration $\mathcal{H}$ and a second ruling $\mathcal{H}^*$ such that both apply to the root-case.

More precisely, since whenever $\mathcal{H}^*$ applies to the root-case the ruling $\mathcal{H}$ also applies, and if $\mathcal{H}^*$ also applies to the branch-case, we can say that the presence of the relationship of those rulings in relation to the root-case *indicates* (rather than *occasions*) that the application of ruling $\mathcal{H}$ can also be transferred to the branch-case. The rationale underlying the transference is that,

- whatever the *'illa* for the ruling $\mathcal{H}^*$ is, this must be the same as the one occasioning $\mathcal{H}$.

---

[8]Abū Isḥāq al-Shīrāzī (1988, p. 806). Notice that this strategy deploys a comparison.

In other words, the ultimate grounding of the transference is that while applying the ruling to the new case, we rely on the (unknown) occasioning factor binding both indicators.

In fact, al-Shīrāzī emphasizes in several texts, such as in the *Sharḥ al-Luma'*, that *ṭard* and *'aks*, usually linked to the efficiency test underlying *qiyās al- 'illa*, are to be included as parts of the process of finding in the sources the suitable pair of rulings.

However, in the context of *qiyās al-dalāla* the logical structure of *ṭard* and *'aks* is quite different to the one they have in *qiyās al- 'illa*, since the juridical sanction at work cannot be defined as a function from an (occasioning) property to that sanction.

Intuitively, the idea is that in order to test if the ruling $\mathcal{H}$ applies to the branch-case, evidence from the sources should witness that when this ruling applies to the root-case then another ruling $\mathcal{H}^*$ also applies to the branch-case, whereby the first and the second stand in a structural relation of either specification (*khaṣīṣa*) or bi-implication (*naẓīr*).

The different structural relations between both rulings feature the subdivision of *qiyās al-Dalāla* into two main kinds of different epistemic degree, called, precisely, *khaṣīṣa* and *naẓīr*. Arguments based on specification have a higher degree of epistemic degree that those based on bi-implication since, as discussed in the following section, specification indicates a semantic dependence of ruling $\mathcal{H}$ upon its counterpart $\mathcal{H}^*$.

Given two rulings as applied to the root-case it is said that the relation is one of.

khaṣīṣa or *special characteristic*, when the relationship has the form general/particular (or more precisely of *specification*);

The relation is one of.

naẓīr when the relationship between both rulings is that of a parallelism between legal sanctions of the same degree of specification (and both can be seen as subsets of a same set).

The following schema displays the structure underlying *qiyās al-dalāla* (Schema 3.1):

In order to extract from the diagram the underlying *jadal*-structure, we need to read the arrows as dialectical actions or argumentative moves. Let us now spell out each of those moves in the diagram:

- the first and second actions (the arrow linking 0 with 1 and 1 with 2) express the *heuristic moves* of finding both a suitable root-case relevant for the sought ruling $\mathcal{H}$ and a second ruling $\mathcal{H}^*$ linked by some common (not identified) occasioning factor;
- the third action (the arrow linking 2 with 3) represents the result of establishing that the second ruling $\mathcal{H}^*$ also applies to the branch-case.
- despite the fact that the occasioning factor of the root-case is unknown, we have nevertheless the indication that the application of the rulings $\mathcal{H}^*$ and $\mathcal{H}$ to the root-case are close together (dash 4). Moreover, since the second ruling also applies to the branch-case, we can infer by this indication – rather than with certainty

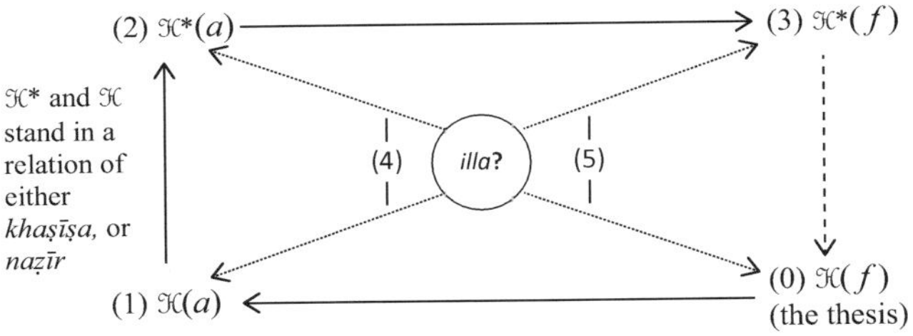

Notational keys:
"$\mathcal{H}^*(a)$" can be glossed as "Ruling $\mathcal{H}^*$ applies to the root-case"
"$\mathcal{H}(a)$" can be glossed as "Ruling $\mathcal{H}$ applies to the root-case"
"$\mathcal{H}^*(f)$" can be glossed as "Ruling $\mathcal{H}^*$ applies to the branch-case"
"$\mathcal{H}(f)$" can be glossed as "Ruling $\mathcal{H}$ applies to the branch-case"
"*illa*?" can be glossed as "Rulings $\mathcal{H}$ and $\mathcal{H}^*$ are both dependent upon an unknown occasioning factor *illa*" The pointed arrows express the dependence of the indicators (i.e., the rulings $\mathcal{H}$ and $\mathcal{H}^*$) upon the *illa*.

Schema 3.1 *Qiyās al-Dalāla*

(dotted arrow from 3 to 0) – that the first ruling also applies to the branch-case. Dash 5 expresses that the inference from 3 to 0 replicates the link (dash 4) established between the two rulings for the root-case.

3.2.1 Khaṣīṣa, Shahādat al-Uṣūl *and the First Type of* Qiyās al-Dalāla

احدها ان يستدلّ بخصيصة من خصائص الشيء عليه[9]

[the first type] is one that employs one of the particularities of a thing (khaṣīṣa min khaṣāiṣ al- shay') as an indication for that thing (al- shay').

Khaṣīṣa When one ruling $\mathcal{H}^*$ is said to be a *khaṣīṣa* of a second ruling $\mathcal{H}$, the indication that the second ruling can be transferred from the root-case to the branch-case is based on the fact that $\mathcal{H}^*$ can be shown to be a specification of $\mathcal{H}$ by means of some additional qualification. This leads us to speak of *particular* and *general ruling*.

For example, given the pair:

Fasting during Ramaḍān is obligatory
Intent is obligatory while fasting during Ramaḍān

[9]Abū Isḥāq al-Shīrāzī (1987, p. 37).

The second ruling is to be considered as *particular* in relation to the first due to the additional qualification "intent" which specifies the obligation targeted, namely, the intention to fast.

This brings to the fore one crucial condition for applying ***qiyās al-dalāla*** based on *khaṣīṣa,* namely the *interdependency of the rulings.* Let us discuss this point in detail.

Khaṣīṣa *and* Shahādat al-Uṣūl

فأجلاها أن يستدل بخصيصة من خصائص الحكم على ثبوت ذلك الحكم، وذلك مثل أن يستدل الشافعي في سجود التلاوة أنه نفل فيقول: (سجود يجوز فعله على الراحلة من غير عذر فكان نفلا كسائر سجود النفل). فاستدل بجواز فعله على الراحلة من غير عذر على كونه نفلا لأن جواز فعله على الراحلة مع عدم العذر من خصيصة النوافل. ألا ترى أن سجود الصلاة لما كان واجبا لم يجز فعله على الراحلة من غير عذر؟[10]

The strongest qiyās al-dalāla (the first type) is that one employs one of the ruling's particularities as indication for the confirmation of that ruling. And that is like the argumentation of Shāfiʿī on prostration of Quran recital that it is supererogatory (non-obligatory), by saying: "prostration which is allowed to be performed on the vehicle during travelling without validating excuse is supererogatory (non-obligatory), like all prostrations of supererogatory prayers." Thus, they argue its supererogatory-status by way of its allowed-status to be performed on the vehicle during travelling, because it (the allowed-status to be performed on the vehicle during travelling) is the particularity of supererogations. Don't you see that if prostration of prayers is obligatory, then it is not allowed to be performed on the vehicle during travelling without validating excuse?

In the context of *qiyās al-dalāla* in general al-Shīrāẓī and al-Baghdādī speak of the *sources as* (*providing*) *testimony* (*shahādat al-uṣūl*) of the relationship between the two rulings.[11] As already mentioned, the closer the relationship between both rulings, the stronger the indication grounding the transference from the root-case to the branch-case.

This is precisely what motivates looking for a general-particular relationship between the two rulings required for the application of *qiyās al-dalāla*. Indeed, if *khaṣīṣa* can be established, then the relation is so close that it is likely that the (unknown) occasioning factor which produced the particular ruling is the same as the factor occasioning the general one.

- Now, a close examination of the examples of *khaṣīṣa* and commentaries on them suggests that, generally speaking, the specification expressed by the particular rule is conceived as a **restriction of the domain of application of the general rule**. Thus, particular-general applies in the first place to the domain of application.

This has consequences for the formulation of the conditions of co-presence and co-exclusiveness.

---

[10] Abū Isḥāq al-Shīrāzī (1988, pp. 809-810).

[11] See Abū Isḥāq al-Shīrāzī (2003, p. 112); and al-Khaṭīb al-Baghdādī (1421H, p. 520).

Unfortunately, though in the *Sharḥ al-Luma*ʻal-Shīrāzī explicitly emphasizes *ṭard* and *ʻaks* as parts of *shahādat al-uṣūl* for *qiyās al-dalāla* in general,[12] he does not explain explicitly how *ṭard* and *ʻaks* should be applied to the first type of *qiyās al-dalāla*.

However, if we study al-Shīrāzī's own examples for the use of *khaṣīṣa*, it comes out that the main target of his study are those cases where the particular ruling prescribes *a specific way to perform an action* of the kind that constitutes the domain of application of the general rule. Moreover, the specific way at work is a *non-canonical* way to perform an action. Certainly, if the specification of the domain of application amounts to pinpointing some canonical ways to perform the kind of action falling under the ruling, the exercise would reduce to simply subsuming the particular to the general.

Thus, if we study al-Shīrāzī's own examples, co-presence and co-exclusiveness take the following form:

- *ṭard*: We say that the relation of specification satisfies *co-presence* when the following holds: If the sources provide evidence that ruling $\mathcal{H}^*$ allows some particular, non-canonical way to perform an undertaking of type $\mathcal{a}$ (such as those prostrations allowed to be performed on the back of a camel), then the sources also provide evidence that the ruling $\mathcal{H}$ sanctions performances of this kind of action (e.g. prostrations) as non-obligatory in general, and that this includes non-canonical performances. So canonical performances $\mathcal{C}$ and not-canonical performances $\mathcal{C}^\circ$ are not incompatible.
- *ʻaks*: We say that the relation of specification satisfies *co-exclusiveness* when the following holds: If the ruling $\mathcal{H}^*$ sanctions that some undertaking of type $\mathcal{a}$ is forbidden to be performed in some specific, non-canonical way (such as those prostrations forbidden to be performed on the back of a camel), then the sources also provide evidence that the general ruling $\mathcal{H}$ sanctions that performing that kind of action is obligatory $\mathcal{a}$ (it is not allowed not to perform it). Furthermore, the sources also make it evident that the obligation sanctioned by $\mathcal{H}$ entails that the non-canonical way of performing specified by $\mathcal{H}^*$ is forbidden.

Thus, co-presence and co-exclusiveness involve distinguishing within the domain of application $\mathcal{a}$ two different subsets of actions, those that are allowed and those that are forbidden in relation to some specific form of carrying those actions out.

Accordingly, showing that the condition *ṭard* is satisfied for the general ruling $\mathcal{H}$ and the particular ruling $\mathcal{H}^*$ requires.

> Finding in the sources that the particular ruling $\mathcal{H}^*$ *allows* (henceforth "**L**" stands for *allowed*) some root-case a, an action of the type $\mathcal{a}$, to be carried out in a non-canonical way.

[12]Al-Shīrāzī (1988, p. 860).

Making it explicit that the general form of this particular ruling presupposes that its domain of application are those actions of the type $\mathcal{a}$ that, when carried out in a non-canonical manner, are allowed by the general ruling $\mathcal{H}$:

$\mathcal{H}^*(x, y, z)$: *prop* (x: $\mathcal{a}$, y: $\mathcal{C}(x) \vee \mathcal{C}^\circ(x)$, z: $\mathcal{H}(x, \mathbf{right}^\vee(y))$)[13]
or with explicit modality
$\mathbf{L}^*(x, y, z)$: *prop* (x: $\mathcal{a}$, y: $\mathcal{C}(x) \vee \mathcal{C}^\circ(x)$, z: $\mathbf{L}(x, \mathbf{right}^\vee(y))$), given $\mathcal{a}$: *set* and y: $\mathcal{C}(x) \vee \mathcal{C}^\circ(x)$: *prop* ($x$: $\mathcal{a}$).

(In plain words, $\mathcal{H}^*$ is constituted by those elements of the right side of the disjunction $\mathcal{C}(x) \vee \mathcal{C}^\circ(x)$; that is, the set of non-canonical performances $\neg\mathcal{C}_a$, included in the ruling $\mathcal{H}$ and prescribed by both rulings as non-obligatory).[14]

Thus, if the particular ruling allows some undertaking to be performed in a non-canonical form, then this presupposes that also the general ruling does. Moreover, the latter presupposes that the general ruling allows some undertaking to be carried out, it also allows it to be carried out in both ways, canonical and non-canonical. So in fact, strictly speaking we should extend **L** to both a canonical and a non-canonical performance of the same kind action. For the sake of simplicity, we leave this further precission out.

Showing that the condition *'aks* is satisfied concerns considering (within the domain of application $\mathcal{a}$) the case of forbidden actions, and this requires.

Finding in the sources that the particular ruling $\mathcal{H}^*$ *forbids* (henceforth "$\neg$**L**" stands for *not-allowed* or *forbidden*) some root-case a^*, an action of the type $\mathcal{a}$ from being carried out in a non-canonical way.

Making it explicit that the general form of this particular ruling presupposes that its domain of application are those actions of the type $\mathcal{a}$ that, when carried out in a non-canonical manner, are forbidden by the general ruling $\mathcal{H}$:

$\mathcal{H}^*(x, y, z)$: *prop* (x: $\mathcal{a}$, y: $\mathcal{C}(x) \vee \mathcal{C}^\circ(x)$, z: $\mathcal{H}(x, \mathbf{right}^\vee(y))$).
or with explicit modality
$\neg\mathbf{L}^*(x, y, z)$: *prop* ($x$: $\mathcal{a}$, y: $\mathcal{C}(x) \vee \neg\mathcal{C}(x)$, z: $\neg\mathbf{L}(x, \mathbf{right}^\vee(y))$).

(In plain words, $\mathcal{H}^*$ is constituted by those elements of the right side of the disjunction $\mathcal{C}_a \vee \neg\mathcal{C}_a$, that is, the set of non-canonical performances $\neg\mathcal{C}_a$ included in the ruling $\mathcal{H}$ and prescribed by both rulings as forbidden (not-allowed)

This also presupposes that when the general ruling sanctions that performing some undertaking is obligatory (henceforth "**O**" stands for *obligatory*), it also forbids this undertaking from being carried out in a non-canonical form.

---

[13]In plain words, ruling $\mathcal{H}^*$ is dependent upon ruling $\mathcal{H}$ which applies to cases of the type A. See the explanation of hypotheticals with multiple hypotheses in the appendix to the present book.

[14]Recall that, as mentioned in Sect. 2.3.1.2, the expression "$\mathbf{right}^\vee(x)$" stands for the operator that selects the right proof-object of a disjunction.

In other words, the task of showing that *ṭard* is satisfied also consists in making it explicit that the formation of

$\mathcal{H}(a^*)$: or with explicit modality $\mathbf{O}(a^*)$, whereby a^*: $\mathcal{A}$,

presupposes the formation rules

$\mathbf{O}(x, y)$: *prop* (x: $\mathcal{A}$, y: $\mathcal{C}(x)$), given $\mathcal{A}$: *set* and y: $\mathcal{C}(x)$: *prop* (x: $\mathcal{A}$).
$\neg\mathbf{L}(x, z)$: *prop* (x: $\mathcal{A}$, z: $\mathcal{C}^\circ(x)$).

If we come back to the general structure, the formal steps underlying a correlational inference by *khaṣīṣa* can thus be described in the following way:

- Establishing by examining the sources that one ruling, that applies to both branch-case and root-case, is a specification of a more general one (that applies to the root-case).
- Establishing by examining the sources that there is enough evidence for asserting that both the deontic force (being allowed, obligatory or forbidden) and the juridical consequences of the particular ruling stem from the general one. This amounts to establishing that both co-presence and co-exclusiveness are satisfied.
- The establishment of *ṭard* and *'aks* allows (1) the efficiency (*ta'thīr*) to be assessed of the *khaṣīṣa* –link between both rulings, (2) making it explicit that the concrete applications of the particular ruling to the root- and the branch-case, and of the general ruling to the root-case, instantiate a general form linking both rulings. This crucial move amounts to the act of *grasping the universal* in the concrete applications recorded by the sources. In other words, by examining the formation rules underlying the concrete applications of the ruling, the general form of the rulings becomes apparent.[15]
- Establishing that whatever the occasioning factor of the general ruling is, it must be the same as that of the particular ruling. That is,

  if $\mathcal{H}^*$ is a specification of $\mathcal{H}$ and
  if there is some (unknown) occasioning factor for the latter, i.e.
  z: (*'illa*(z): $\mathcal{H}$)

  ---

  then this occasioning factor also causes the ruling
  z: (*'illa*(z): $\mathcal{H}^*$)

[15]This move can be seen as related to Averroes' notion of *ibdāl* or substitution of the general by the particular (see Bou Akl (2019, pp. 50–62). However, as discussed in our preface, al-Shīrāzī's general conception of *qiyās* (*not only of the kind al-dalāla*) goes the other way round: while examining the form of the substituted instance, the general substitutional form comes to the fore.

whereby the expression "*z*" indicates that there is a *hypothesis* or *open assumption*, as explained in part II of the present study. However, we actually do not know what the occasioning factor is.

- Justifying! $\mathcal{H}$(*far'*)[16]

The main thesis is just the claim that the general ruling applies to the branch-case. It requires a justification, that is, a proof-object for the proposition $\mathcal{H}$(*far'*). Moreover, the justification will require it to be shown that the branch-case encodes some inner structure. One way to think about the branch-case occurring in $\mathcal{H}$(*far'*) is as its being a non-canonical proof-object that will be brought to its canonical form during the inferential moves. Implementing this requires some more notation. In order to limit this, when occurring in an inference, we will deploy the notation "*far'*" for its non-canonical form and "*f,y, ..., z*" for its canonical form. The same applies to the root-case.
Given

z: (*'illa*(x): $\mathcal{H}$)
z: (*'illa*(x): $\mathcal{H}$): $\mathcal{H}^*$)
$\mathbf{L}^*(x, y, z)$: *prop* (x: α, y: $\mathcal{C}(x) \vee \mathcal{C}^\circ(x)$, z: $\mathbf{L}(x, \mathbf{right}^\vee(y))$)

the following holds:

! $\mathbf{L}^*(f, b, c)$
for
b: $\mathcal{C}(f) \vee \mathcal{C}^\circ(f)$
c: $\mathbf{L}(f, \mathbf{right}^\vee(b))$

The latter is the explicit justified form of the thesis, which is encoded by the expression

$$dal\bar{a}la^{\,\mathcal{H}\ *\text{-}khaṣīṣa\text{-}\mathcal{H}} = c\text{: } \mathbf{L}(f,b)$$ [17]

(In plain words, the justification of the thesis is the proof-object c, which is equal to the proof-object that encodes a demonstration of the proposition that the branch-case is allowed to be carried out in a non-canonical way. The demonstration encoded deploys the correlational inference of *khaṣīṣa* to the pair of rulings $\mathcal{H}$ and $\mathcal{H}^*$.)

The following diagram expresses one typical example for this form of *qiyās al-dalāla* – the graphical presentation is based on that of Young (2017, p. 116). The example requires the richer structure discussed above.

---

[16] An alternative reconstruction would stress the fact that both the root- and the branch-case are identical in relation to the rulings, and then conclude by substitution. However, this option makes the distinction between *qiyas al-dalāla* and *qiyas al-shabah* less clear-cut.

[17] Recall that the injection $\mathbf{right}^\vee(b)$: $\mathcal{C}(f) \vee \mathcal{C}^\circ(f)$ yields b: $\mathcal{C}(f)$.

The root-case *aṣl*: *Prostration of Supererogatory prayer*		**The branch-case** *far'*: *Prostration of Qu'rān recital*[a]
$\mathbf{L}^*(a, b, c)$	⟷	$\mathbf{L}^*(f, b, c)$
It (prostration of supererogatory prayer) is allowed to be performed on the back of a camel while travelling without validating excuse ('udhr)		*It (prostration of Qu'rān recital) is allowed to be performed on the back of a camel while travelling without validating excuse ('udhr)*
c: $\mathbf{L}(a, b)$	⟶	c: $\mathbf{L}(f, b)$
Prostration of supererogatory prayer is non-obligatory		*Prostration of Qu'rān recital is non-obligatory*

[a]The branch-case *Sujūd al-tilāwa* – sanctioned as non-obligatory by the ruling $\mathcal{H}$ – is the prostration performed after reciting *"the verses of prostration"*. There are 14 verses of prostration in the Qur'an

The particular specification $\mathcal{H}^*(x, y, z)$: *prop* (x: $\mathcal{a}$, y: $\mathcal{C}(x) \vee \mathcal{C}^{\circ}(x)$, z: $\mathcal{H}(x, \mathbf{right}^{\vee}(y))$) at stake in this example is the following:

"$\mathbf{L}(x)$" (which presupposes "$\mathbf{L}(x)$: *prop* (x: $\mathcal{a}$)") stands for *"non-obligatory undertakings* of the type $\mathcal{a}$ *(prostration)."*

"$\mathbf{L}^*(x,y, z)$" stands for "*undertakings of the type* $\mathcal{a}$ *(x) to be performed on the back of a camel while travelling without validating excuse (y), are allowed (z)*"

"a" stands for the root-case "*sujūd-prostration of supererogatory prayer*", which is one of actions allowed to be performed in a non-canonical way. The term *supererogatory* corresponds to the modality *recommendable action* (*mustaḥabb*) and applies to actions that are rewarded if performed but neither sanctioned nor rewarded if not performed (see our remark on deontic modalities below).

"f" stands for the branch-case "*sujūd-prostration of Qu'rān recital*".

"b" stands for some evidence from the sources that undertakings of the type $\mathcal{a}$ can be performed either in canonical or non-canonical form.

"c" stands for some evidence from the sources that the general ruling, which allows actions of the type $\mathcal{a}$, includes non-canonical undertakings of that type.

The analysis of Young (2017, pp. 116–117) is slightly different from ours. Indeed, while discussing this example, Young (2017, p. 116) underlines the resemblance of $\mathcal{H}^*(a)$ and $\mathcal{H}^*(f)$ and thus also the similarity of $\mathcal{H}(a)$ and $\mathcal{H}(f)$, instead of relying on the force of the inference in the relation of specification.[18]

The resemblance is, of course, important, but in the further elucidations of *al-Luma'* al-Shīrāzī completes the explanation by stressing that the transference obtains its epistemic force from the fact that the second ruling $\mathcal{H}^*(a)$ specifies the first $\mathcal{H}(a)$ in some particular way, and that the resemblance is rooted in such particular form of specification:

> *[the first type of qiyās al-dalāla] is that one which employs one of the ruling's particularities (khaṣīṣa min khaṣāiṣ al-ḥukm) as indication for the ruling (al-ḥukm).*[19]

[18]However, in other parts of Young's book there is a discussion of this point but not in relation to that example, such as Young (2017, pp. 94–95 and p. 105).

[19]al-Shīrāzī (2003, p. 100).

Remark On Obligatory and Permissible Actions

It is important to keep in mind that in Islamic jurisprudence (and ethics) deontic modalities such as **obligatory** and **permissible** take the form of *heteronomous imperatives*, defined with the help of the qualifications **Reward** and **Sanction**.

So **obligatory** is the set of all those actions rewarded when performed and sanctioned when omitted.

A useful logical analysis of this formulation yields:[a]

$b(x)$: $[\,(\forall y: A_1)\ \mathbf{left}^{\vee}(y)=_{\{H\}}x \supset R(y)\,] \wedge [\,(\forall z: \neg A)\ \mathbf{right}^{\vee}(z)=_{\{H\}}x \supset S_1(z)\,]\ (x: A \vee \neg A)$

whereby $\{H\}$ is a short-form for the hypothesis $A \vee \neg A$.

The hypothetical assertion can be glossed as follows:

All those performances of an action of type A identical to the ones chosen (by agent ***g****) to be performed (i.e., if the leftside of the disjunction has been chosen to be performed), are to be* ***rewarded****; and All those cases omitting to perform an action of type A identical to the ones chosen (by agent* ***g****) to be omitted (i.e., if the right side of the disjunction ¬A has been chosen to be performed), are to be* ***sanctioned****.*

If we elaborate this analysis for the five main deontic modalities in Islamic jurisprudence we obtain:[b]

***wājib, farḍ, lāzim* (*obligatory*):** If we do it we are rewarded. If we do not do it we are sanctioned.

$b_1(x)$: $[\,(\forall y: A_1)\ \mathbf{left}^{\vee}(y)=_{\{H1\}}x \supset R_1(y)\,] \wedge [\,(\forall z: \neg A_1)\ \mathbf{right}^{\vee}(z)=_{\{H1\}}x \supset S_1(z)\,]\ (x: A_1 \vee \neg A_1)$.

***ḥarām, maḥẓūr* (*forbidden*):** If we do it we are sanctioned. If we do not do it we are rewarded.

$b_2(x)$: $[\,(\forall y: A_2)\ \mathbf{left}^{\vee}(y)=_{\{H2\}}x \supset S_2(y)\,] \wedge [\,(\forall z: \neg A_2)\ \mathbf{right}^{\vee}(z)=_{\{H2\}}x \supset R_2(z)\,]\ (x: A_2 \vee \neg A_2)$.

***mubāḥ mustaḥabb* (*recommended*):** If we do it we are rewarded. If we do not do it we are neither sanctioned nor rewarded.

$b_3(x)$: $[\,(\forall y: A_3)\ \mathbf{left}^{\vee}(y)=_{\{H3\}}x \supset R_3(y)\,] \wedge [\,(\forall z: \neg A_3)\ \mathbf{right}^{\vee}(z)=_{\{H3\}}x \supset (\neg S_3(z) \wedge \neg R_3(z))]$ $(x: A_3 \vee \neg A_3)$.

***mubāḥ makrūh* (*reprehensible*):** If we do not do it we are rewarded. If we do it we are neither sanctioned nor rewarded.

$b_4(x)$: $[\,(\forall y: A_4)\ \mathbf{left}^{\vee}(y)=_{\{H4\}}x \supset (\neg S_4(y) \wedge \neg R_4(y))] \wedge [\,(\forall z: \neg A_4)\ \mathbf{right}^{\vee}(z)=_{\{H4\}}x \supset R_4(z)]$ $(x: A_4 \vee \neg A_4)$.

***mubāḥ mustawin* (*purely permissible*):** If we do it we are neither sanctioned nor rewarded. If we do not do it we are neither sanctioned nor rewarded.

$b_5(x)$: $[\,(\forall y: A_5)\ \mathbf{left}^{\vee}(y)=_{\{H5\}}x \supset (\neg S_5(y) \wedge \neg R_5(y))] \wedge [\,(\forall z: \neg A_5)\ \mathbf{right}^{\vee}(z)=_{\{H5\}}x \supset$ $(\neg S_5(z) \wedge \neg R_5(z))\,]\ (x: A_5 \vee \neg A_5)$.

In the present book we will not display the logical form of the deontic modalities we just mentioned, but the reader should take into consideration that expressions such as *set of obligatory undertaking of the type A*, should be read as standing for the formulation set of all those actions rewarded when performed and sanctioned when omitted.

[a]See Rahman/Granström/Farjami (2019) and Rahman/Zidani/Young (2019).

[b]See Ibn Ḥazm (1926–1930, vol. 3, p. 77); idem (1959, p. 86; 2003, pp. 83–4).

Let us now discuss the second form of *qiyās al-dalāla*.

3.2.2 **Naẓīr, Shahādat al-Uṣūl** *and the Second Type of* **Qiyās al-Dalāla**

والضرب الثاني أن يستدل بحكم يشاكل حكم الفرع ويجري مجراه على حكم الفرع ثم يقيس ذلك على أصل.[20]

The second type is that one employs a ruling that resembles the branch-case's ruling and runs the same course as the branch-case's ruling as indication for the branch-case's ruling; then one correlates that with a source-case.

Naẓīr

The procedure might be described as follows:

1. We wish to find out if some branch-case-ruling $\mathcal{H}$(*far'*) (*ḥukm al-far'*) applies, but no occasioning factor can be learned from the sources. However, by reviewing the sources we discover that there is another ruling $\mathcal{H}^*$(*far'*) that resembles very closely the branch-case-ruling under consideration (*ḥukm yushākil ḥukm al-far'*).
2. A new visit into the sources shows that, in relation to some relevant root-case, we also discover that the two rulings mentioned above, i.e., $\mathcal{H}(x)$ and $\mathcal{H}^*(x)$, can be seen as different specifications of a general ruling from which their deontic force and juridical consequence stem (take the example of two different valid forms of divorce-declarations of a Muslim; though different, they can be seen as subsets of the set of divorce-declarations – so that their juridical consequences stem from the fact that they are divorce-declarations). In other words, both rulings can be said to be of the same juridical type and always run together (*yajriyān majran wāḥidan*); and thus one of the rulings can be said to be the parallel (*naẓīr*)[21] of the other.
3. Actually, from the sources we learn that there is evidence that this parallelism can be generalized beyond the one established for the root-case. The parallelism between $\mathcal{H}(a)$ and $\mathcal{H}^*(a)$ is so close that they can thus be considered as almost equal (*taswiya*) – or more precisely, one of the two rulings holds if and only if the other one does.
4. Establishing that whatever the occasioning factor of one of the rulings is, it must be the same as that of the other.
5. Hence, if there is indeed enough evidence that (i) from the point of view of their juridical effect both rulings $\mathcal{H}(x)$ and $\mathcal{H}^*(x)$ run together, and (ii) given $\mathcal{H}(a)$, $\mathcal{H}^*(a)$, and $\mathcal{H}^*(f)$, it follows that $\mathcal{H}(x)$ also applies to the branch-case f.

---

[20]See al-Shīrāzī, *Mulakhkhaṣ fī al-jadal*, fol. 5a.

[21]In fact, like the term *khaṣīṣa* in the first type, al-Shīrāzī does not employ the term *naẓīr* in the *Mulakhkhaṣ*, however, he does use it in the *Ma'ūna* and in the *al-Luma'*.

Step 4 hinges on the assumption of the *sameness* of both rulings in *general*, not only in relation to the root-case.

If we formulate this in the language of CTT, the formal steps underlying the process just described is roughly the following:

- Establishing that both rulings involve the same underlying ***set***.

  $\mathcal{H}^*(x)$: *prop* (x: $\mathcal{D}$).
  $\mathcal{H}(x)$: *prop* (x: $\mathcal{D}$)

- Establishing by examining the root-case and the sources that (in relation to the deontic force and juridical effects determined by the underlying set) there is enough evidence for asserting that if one is the case then so is the second and vice-versa.[22]

  $(\forall x: \mathcal{D})\ \mathcal{H}(x) \supset \subset \mathcal{H}^*(x)$
  Notice that the task of showing the bi-implication amounts to showing that *ṭard* and *'aks* are satisfied.

- Inferring the ruling under consideration for the branch-case

$$\frac{(\forall x{:}\mathcal{D})\ \mathcal{H}(x) \supset\subset \mathcal{H}^*(x)\ \textit{\textbf{true}} \qquad \mathcal{H}^*(f)\ \textit{\textbf{true}}}{\mathcal{H}(f)\ \textit{\textbf{true}}}$$

The standard example of al-Shīrāzī requires special care. On one hand, the example suggests that both the root-case and the branch-case involve a kind of general terms such as "Muslim" and "non-Muslim", while on the other the rulings involved are constituted by some specific forms of divorce-declarations sanctioned as valid irrespective of whether they are perfomed by a Muslim or a non-Muslim.

Indeed, the main example of 'al-Shīrāzī concerns deciding about the legal validity of an old form of divorce-declaration called *ẓihār*[23] when performed by a non-Muslim (*Dhimmī*)[24] given that it is known from the sources that a standard form of divorce-declaration called *ṭalāq* is legally valid when performed by both Muslims and non-Muslims. If we follow the texts of our author, it looks as if the example involves.

root-case: *Muslim,*
branch-case: *(some) Non-Muslim*

[22]This again involves the process of grasping the universal by examining the particular

[23]See Fyzee (1964, p. 154).

[24]*Dhimmī* is a historical term referring to non-Muslim citizens of an Islamic state.

Parallel rulings for the root-case

Base-ruling established by the sources *Ṭalāq-declaration-is-valid of Muslim* ***Naẓīr.* Thesis to be grounded** *Ẓihār-declaration-is-valid of Muslim*

Parallel rulings for the branch-case

Base-ruling established by the sources *Ṭalāq-declaration-is-valid of non-Muslim* ***Naẓīr.* Thesis to be grounded** *Ẓihār-declaration-is-valid of non-Muslim*

Now, as mentioned above, the general structure of this form of *qiyās* requires both forms of divorce to be understood as being specifications of an underlying set.

In this example, the idea is that the propositional function *valid ṭalāq-declaration* is a subset of the set *divorce-declarations* $\mathfrak{D}$. The same applies to the formation of *ẓihār*(*x*).

	(*x*: *divorce-declaration*)
	...
divorce-declaration: **set**	*ṭalāq*(*x*) ∧ *Valid* (*x*): *prop*
	(*x*: *divorce-declaration*)
	...
divorce-declaration: **set**	*ẓihār* (*x*) ∧ *Valid* (*x*): *prop*

Moreover, we should also bring to the fore that *divorce-declarations* are brought forward by Humans, instances of which include *Muslims* and *non-Muslims*, so that the fully explicit formation of.

Valid divorce-declaration of the kind ṭalāq brought forward by x,
Valid divorce-declaration of the kind ẓihār brought forward by x,

if written in linear form, is:

valid (*x*, *y*, *z*) *prop* (*x*: *Human*, *y*: *divorce-declaration*(*x*), *z*: *ṭalāq*(*x*, *y*)).
valid (*u*, *v*, *w*) *prop* (*u*: *Human*, *v*: *divorce-declaration*(*u*), *w*: *ẓihār* (*u*, *v*)).

In plain words, *valid* qualifies *ṭalāq-declarations* that are *divorce-declarations* brought forward by some *Human* (the same applies to *ẓihār-declarations*).[25]

If we use our usual notation of juridical rulings we obtain:

$\mathcal{H}(x, y, z)$ "*ṭalāq-declaration of x is a valid divorce-declaration*"
$\mathcal{H}^*(u, v, w)$ "*ẓihār-declaration of u is a valid divorce-declaration*"

[25] See the explanation of hypotheticals with multiple hypotheses in the appendix to the present book.

Hence, as expected, the whole point is to establish the relevant parallelism. This, as mentioned above, requires two complementary steps:

1. Establishing that both are subsets specifying an underlying set – in our case-study, the set of *valid divorce-declarations.* This amounts to the examination of the formation rules involved.
2. Establishing that whenever one of the rulings is legally valid, so is the other.[26]

The second step relates to co-presence and co-absence, which we will discuss in the following section. However, before going into that issue let us briefly discuss an alternative possible reconstruction.

Despite the fact that in the *al-Luma'* al-Shīrāzī indicates that the branch-case and the root-case are *Non-Muslim* and *Muslim,* the formulation, particularly in the *Mulakhkhaṣ*, might lead one to conceive that both the root-case and the branch-case split in two subcases, rendering a four-folded structure:

Root-cases
ṭalāq-declaration of Muslim
ẓihār-declaration of Muslim

Branch-cases
ṭalāq-declaration of non-Muslim
ẓihār-declaration of non-Muslim

Parallel rulings for the root-case:
ṭalāq-declaration of Muslim is *legally-valid*
ẓihār-declaration of Muslim is *legally-valid*

Parallel rulings for the branch-case:
ṭalāq-declaration of non-Muslim is *legally-valid*
ẓihār-declaration of non-Muslim is *legally-valid*

This is, in essence, the interpretation followed by Young (2017, p. 117), who bases his reconstruction on the *Mulakhkhaṣ* rather than on the *al-Luma'*. Notice that this reconstruction also requires establishing a resemblance between the "twin root-cases". This brings *qiyas al-dalāla* closer to *qiyas al-shabah.*

Since, as discussed above, we prefer to keep *qiyas al-dalāla* and *al-shabah* apart, and because of our reconstruction of the deployment of *naẓīr* in *al-Luma',* we stick with the two-fold structure.

[26]Notice that in the case of *khaṣīṣa* both steps have the same objective, namely establishing a formation rule that makes it apparent that one of the rulings is a specification of the other.

The following diagram condenses our two-fold view on the main moves behind a *qiyas al-dalāla* by means of *naẓīr*:

The root-case *aṣl*: *Muslim*		The branch-case *far'*: *non-Muslim*
$\mathcal{H}^*(a,q,r)$:	⟷	$\mathcal{H}^*(f,d,t)$:
ṭalāq is valid (of Muslim)		*ṭalāq is valid (of non-Muslim)*
(ṭalāq-declaration of a Muslim is a valid divorce-declaration)		*(ṭalāq-declaration of a non-Muslim is a valid divorce-declaration)*
$\mathcal{H}(a,q',r')$:	⟶	$\mathcal{H}(f,d',t')$:
ẓihār is valid (of Muslim)		*ẓihār is valid (of non-Muslim)*
(ẓihār-declaration of a Muslim is a valid divorce-declaration)		*(ẓihār-declaration of a non-Muslim is a valid divorce-declaration)*

The formation assumed is the following:

$\mathcal{H}^*(f,d,t)$:
valid (*x*, *y*, *z*) *prop* (*x*: *Human*, *y*: *divorce-declaration*(*x*), *z*: *ṭalāq*(*x*, *y*)).
non-muslim: *Human*, *d*: *divorce-declaration*(*non-muslim*), *t*: *ṭalāq*(*non-muslim*, *d*)

$\mathcal{H}^*(a,q,r)$:
valid (*x*, *y*, *z*) *prop* (*x*: *Human*, *y*: *divorce-declaration*(*x*), *z*: *ṭalāq*(*x*, *y*)).
muslim: *Human*, *q*: *divorce-declaration*(*muslim*), *r*: *ṭalāq*(*muslim*, *q*)

$\mathcal{H}(f,d',t')$
valid (*u*, *v*, *w*) *prop* (*u*: *Human*, *v*: *divorce-declaration*(*u*), *w*: *ẓihār* (*u*,*v*)).
non-muslim: *Human*, *d'*: *divorce-declaration*(*non-muslim*), *t'*: *ẓihār* (*non-muslim*, *d'*)

$\mathcal{H}(a,d',t')$
valid (*u*, *v*, *w*) *prop* (*u*: *Human*, *v*: *divorce-declaration*(*u*), *w*: *ẓihār* (*u*,*v*)).
muslim: *Human*, *d'*: *divorce-declaration*(*muslim*), *t'*: *ẓihār* (*muslim*, *d'*)

***Naẓīr*, *Shahādat al-Uṣūl* and Inferring the Conclusion.**

In the case where the indication is based on *naẓīr*, the *mujtahid* must verify that the sources provide evidence that if the ruling $\mathcal{H}$ applies, then $\mathcal{H}^*$ also does (co-presence), and that if the first does not apply, then neither does the second (co-exclusiveness). Only then can the equality (*taswiya*) of the ruling be considered.

Thus in this form of correlational inference, establishing the equality (*taswiya*) between both rulings amounts to establishing their efficiency (*ta'thīr*).

In our example, the point is to show that.

for all whose *ṭalāq*-declarations are valid-divorce-declarations, then their performances of *ẓihār* –declarations also are (*ṭard*) (*man ṣaḥḥa ṭalāquhu ṣaḥḥa ẓihāruhu*); and that dually for all whose performances of *ṭalāq*- declarations are not valid-divorce-declarations, then their performances of *ẓihār* –declarations are not valid either (*ʿaks*). For example: if a *ṭalāq*- declaration is performed by a mad-man, and is therefore not legally valid, then neither is the *ẓihār*–declaration performed by a mad-man.

Let us assume that the examination of various cases like that of a mad-man, a child and so on, leads to generalizing the parallelism of the rulings not only in relation to the root-case but also in general, so that we obtain the fully explicit notation:

It is ***true*** that all those humans who perform a valid *ṭalāq*-declaration also perform a valid *ẓihār* one, and it is also ***true*** that all those humans who perform a valid *ẓihār*-declaration also perform a *ṭalāq*-declaration.

For the sake of simplicity, let us further assume that some *divorce-declarations, ṭalāq-declarations* and *ẓihār-declarations,* have been fixed for the debate.

d, d': *divorce-declaration*
t: *ṭalāq-declaration*
t': *ẓihār -declaration*

Hence, once the following have been established:

$! (\forall x: Human)\{ valid(x,d,t) \supset valid(x,d',t')\}$ ***true*** (*ṭard*)
$! (\forall x: Human)\{ \neg valid(x,d,t) \supset \subset \neg valid(x,d',t')\}$ ***true*** (*ʿaks*)

then the main premise holds:

$(\forall z: Human)\ (valid(z,d,t) \supset \subset valid(z,d',t'))$ ***true*** (*taʾthīr*)

Let us also further assume that *non-muslim* has been selected to eliminate the quantifier:

non-muslim: Human

The main final step of the inference that leads to the searched conclusion is then:

$$\frac{(\forall z: Human)\ (valid(z,d,t) \supset\subset valid(z,d',t'))\ \textbf{true} \qquad valid(non\text{-}muslim,d,t)\ \textbf{true}}{valid(non\text{-}muslim,d',t')\ \textbf{true}}$$

In the dialectical practice, the way to show that two pair of rulings are associated by a ***naẓīr***-relation requires finding some root-case and then make explicit the relation by displaying the logical of form of both rulings and asserting their bi-implication.

3.3 *Qiyās al-Shabah*

والضرب الثالث هو أن يحمل الفرع على أصل بضرب من الشبه[27]

"The third type (or qiyās al-shabah) is that one that links the branch-case with a source-case, by way of a type of resemblance."

Unlike *qiyās al-dalāla*, the targeted conclusion is inferred by establishing a resemblance (*al-shabah*) between the root- and the branch-case in relation to some relevant set of properties or rulings.[28]

Notice that identifying the relevant properties (or rulings) does not amount here to establishing the efficiency (*ta'thīr*) required to become an occasioning factor; the only role of these properties (or rulings) is to provide a set in relation to which *aṣl* and *far'* can be said to be similar. Thus, if the set in question is a pair of rulings, those rulings are structured neither by a *khaṣīṣa*-relation nor by a *naẓīr*-relation.[29]

Briefly, parallel reasoning displayed by *qiyās al-shabah* is based on a mere resemblance without any association, direct or indirect, with the occasioning factor (*'illa*). Therefore, jurisprudents disagreed on the validity of such a type of *qiyās*; even when accepted, its epistemological strength was considered as the weakest.

Al-Shabah.

The procedure of deploying similarity might be described as follows.

1. We wish to find out if some branch-case-ruling $\mathcal{H}(f)$ applies, but no occasioning factor can be learned from the sources, nor is there a way to identify some kind of indication. However by reviewing the sources we discover that this ruling applies to a root-case $\mathcal{H}(a)$.
2. A close inspection of both the root-case and the branch-case shows that they share a set of properties or rulings that are juridically relevant.
3. Given this set and its juridical relevance, root-case and branch-case are taken to be identical (within the set).
4. Given the (assumed) identity of *aṣl* and *far'*, the occurrence of the root-case in $\mathcal{H}(a)$ can be substituted with the branch-case and the searched conclusion $\mathcal{H}(f)$ is obtained.

Step 4 hinges on the assumption of identifying a suitable set that provides the sameness-condition required by the substitution. The problem is that, on one hand, applying *qiyās al-shabah* requires identifying a relevant set of properties, while on the other hand, those properties are not sufficient to provide the occasioning factor.

---

[27] al-Shīrāzī, *Mulakhkhaṣ fī al-jadal*, fol. 5a.

[28] See Abū Isḥāq al-Shīrāzī (2003, p. 100; 1988, p. 812).

[29] It looks as if this type of *qiyās* is very close to Aristotle's *argument from likeness (homoiotes).*

Thus, the selected properties must be somehow relevant for ruling albeit the fact that they provide neither enough elements for identifying the juridical ground underlying the ruling, nor a way to assume that some common juridical ruling (even if not known) is at work.

This underlies the rejection of this form of inference by many jurists including al-Shīrāzī. Indeed, although, as mentioned above, al-Shīrāzī followed the Shāfi'ī school in acknowledging and studying the application of *qiyās al-shabah*, his own opinion was that it is not a valid (*lā yaṣiḥḥ*) form of inference because it is based neither on an *'illa* nor on an indication (*dalāla*) of the *'illa*.[30]

Notice that, despite the problem of singling out a suitable set of properties (or rulings) required by *qiyās al-shabah*, the study of the examples existing in the literature shows that this system imposes quite strong conditions for its application: the properties grounding the analogy must be **exactly the same** for both the root- and the branch-case.[31]

The underlying dialectical moves underlying *qiyās al-shabah* can be schematized by means of the following informal diagram:

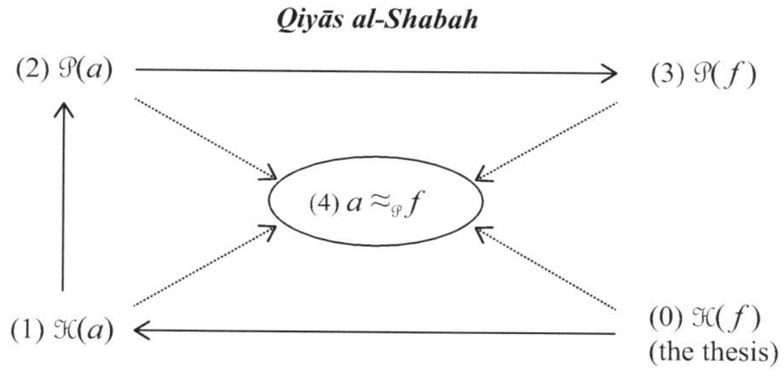

Let us spell out the main moves as depicted in the diagram:

- the first action (the solid arrow linking 0 with 1) amounts to the heuristic move of finding a suitable root-case;
- the second and the third (the solid arrows linking 1 with 2 and 2 with 3) indicate the result of finding out a set of properties or ruling(s) shared by the root-case and the branch-case. Let "$\mathcal{P}$" stand for the selected set of properties (or ruling(s));

[30] Cf. Abū Isḥāq al-Shīrāzī, *al-Luma' fī uṣūl al-fiqh*, p. 101.

[31] This is different to the main conceptions of analogy nowadays where the properties on both sides (the target case and the known case) might be *similar* rather than exactly the same – see e.g. Bartha (2010) – we come back to this issue at the end chapter of the present book.

- The fourth action (two dash arrows linking 2 and 3 with 4) indicates the result of establishing the similarity of the root-case and the branch-case in relation to the set $\mathcal{P}$ – the notation "$a \approx_{\mathcal{P}} f$" expresses this similarity;
- The next (two dash arrows linking 4 with 1and 0) indicates the result of inferring by analogy by means of substituting the root-case with the branch-case in (1) based on the similarity established in (4).

The inferential structure of *Qiyās al-Shabah*.

The inferential structure of this form of *qiyās* deploys substitution of identicals. However, the *epistemic weakeness* of this form of *qiyās* is that we do not really know if they are identicals, but only taken to be so in relation to the property (or properties) $\mathcal{P}$. We indicate this weak form of identity with the notation $a \approx_{\mathcal{P}} f$.

Within the formal framework of CTT the inference of the conclusion is reached by applying a version of what is nowadays known as *Leibniz's substitution rule*:

$$\mathcal{P}(x): prop\ (x: \mathcal{D})$$

$$\ldots$$

$$\frac{a, f: \mathcal{D} \qquad \mathcal{P}(a)\ \textbf{\textit{true}} \qquad \mathcal{P}(f)\ \textbf{\textit{true}} \qquad a \approx_{\mathcal{P}} f\ \textbf{\textit{true}} \qquad \mathcal{H}(a)\ \textbf{\textit{true}}}{shabah^{\mathcal{H}^*\text{-}a\approx f\text{-}\mathcal{H}}: \mathcal{H}(f)}$$

Remarks

1. The main CTT notion deployed is a variant of *propositional identity*. Propositional identity is distinguished from *judgemental equality*: whereas the latter establishes (at the ontological level) a *real definition,* the former establishes identity in the form of a proposition and in relation to a set. For example, while a slave and a free person can be seen as identical in relation to some juridical properties that lead one to infer that the slave is allowed to own property, slave is not a definition of free person![32]
2. Notice that the form of the ruling is **not** $\mathcal{H}(x,y)$: *prop* (x: $\mathcal{D}$, y: $\mathcal{P}(x)$), which would establish the dependence of the ruling upon the property. The point is that, in the context of *qiyās al-shabah*, we really do not know if that property is sufficient for determining the occasioning factor. The main inferential step is actually a substitution based on an assumed identity between the root-and the branch-case.

Let us see very briefly one classical example of *qiyās al-shabah*, which deploys three properties. The diagram speaks for itself[33]:

---

[32]More precisely, within the framework of CTT real definitions establish what something is in relation to some canonical element of the set, and thus if two entities are definitionally equal a true proposition establishing the identity of both can be asserted. However, the inverse is not assured – see Ranta (1994, p. 52).

[33]See al-Shīrāzī, *Mulakhkhaṣ fī al-jadal*, fol. 5a, cf. Young (2017, p. 118).

The root-case *aṣl*: *The free person*		The branch-case *far'*: *The slave*
$\mathcal{P}1(a)$		$\mathcal{P}1(f)$
(the free person) is a human being to whom instructive communication is addressed (mukhāṭab)	⟷	*(the slave) is a human being to whom instructive communication is addressed (mukhāṭab)*
– Where $\mathcal{P}1(x)$: *prop* (*x*: *Human being*)		– Where $\mathcal{P}1(x)$: *prop* (*x*: *Human being*).
$\mathcal{P}2(a)$		$\mathcal{P}2(f)$
(the free person) is a human being who is rewarded (muthāb)	⟷	*(the slave) is a human being who is rewarded (muthāb)*
– Where $\mathcal{P}2(x)$: *prop* (*x*: *Human being*)		– Where $\mathcal{P}2(x)$: *prop* (*x*: *Human being*)
$\mathcal{P}3(a)$		$\mathcal{P}3(f)$
(the free person) is a human being who is punished ((mu'āqab)	⟷	*(the slave) is a human being who is punished (mu'āqab)*
– Where $\mathcal{P}3(x)$: *prop* (*x*: *Human being*)		– Where $\mathcal{P}3(x)$: *prop* (*x*: *Human being*)
$\mathcal{H}(a)$		$\mathcal{H}(f)$, given $a \approx_{\mathcal{P}} f$
(the free person) is a human being who is legally permitted to own	→	– Where "$\mathcal{P}$" stands for the conjunction $\mathcal{P}1(x) \wedge \mathcal{P}2(x) \wedge \mathcal{P}3(x)$: *prop* (*x*: *Human being*)
		(the slave) is a human being who is legally permitted to own
– Where $\mathcal{H}(x)$: *prop* (*x*: *Human being*)		– Where $\mathcal{H}(x)$: *prop* (*x*: *Human being*)

3.4 The Dialectical Structure of *Qiyās al-Dalāla* and *Qiyās al-Shabah*

Before developing the systematic presentation of the dialogical setting for these forms of correlational inferences, let us start by providing a presentation of the overall dialectical structure of *qiyās al-dalāla* and *qiyās al-shabah.*

This overall picture will be later integrated into the structural rules for the dialogues in Sect. 3.5. However, despite the fact that the reader will find this once more further on in our text, we will nevertheless present it here already in order to facilitate the reading of the examples that follow.

3.4.1 The Overall Development of a Dialogue for Qiyās al-Dalāla *and* Qiyās al-Shabah

1. A dialogical play starts with the Proponent setting the thesis that some specific legal ruling ($\mathcal{H}$) applies to a certain branch-case.

$$\mathbf{P}!\mathcal{H}(\mathit{far'})$$

The Proponent's aim is to develop an argument in such a way that it forces the Opponent to concede the justification of the thesis.

Remark: As pointed out before, the main thesis is just the claim that the general ruling applies to the branch-case. It requires a justification, that is, a proof-object for the proposition $\mathcal{H}$(*far'*). Moreover, the justification will require it to be shown that the branch-case encodes some inner structure. One way to think about the branch-case occurring in $\mathcal{H}$(*far'*) is as its being a non-canonical proof-object that will be brought to its canonical form during the inferential moves. Implementing this requires some more notation. In order to limit this, when occurring in an inference, we will deploy the notation "*far'*" for its non-canonical form and "*f,y, ..., z*" for its canonical form. The same applies to the root-case.

2. After agreement on the finiteness of the argument to be developed, the Opponent will launch a challenge to the assertion by asking for the occasioning factor justifying the thesis:

O *'illa*?

3. The Proponent's aim is to develop an argument in such a way that it forces the Opponent to concede the thesis. In case of *dalāla* but not *shabah* the Proponent will try to show that there are sufficient elements to *assume* that there is some underlying occasioning factor, *despite the fact that no precise occasioning factor can be found*. In order to develop his argument, the Proponent will start by choosing (to the best of his juridical knowledge) a root-case from the sources for which the ruling $\mathcal{H}$ has been applied and will ask the Opponent to endorse it.

P $\mathcal{H}$(*aṣl*)?

Remark: The main aim behind this move that motivates the whole argumentation consists in the Proponent forcing the Opponent to endorse the thesis because of some specific indications (in the case of *qiyās al-dalāla*) or resemblances (in the case of *qiyās al-shabah*) brought forward by the Proponent himself. The endorsement of the Opponent, at the **end** of the play – if such an endorsement takes place–, allows the Proponent to justify his thesis by bringing forward one of the following statements:

dalāla $^{\mathcal{H}*\text{-}khaṣīṣa\text{-}\mathcal{H}}$: $\mathcal{H}(f,b)$
($\mathcal{H}(f,b)$ is justified by the *khaṣīṣa*-relation between both rulings)

dalāla $^{\mathcal{H}*\text{-}naẓīr\text{-}\mathcal{H}}$: $\mathcal{H}(f,d,t)$
($\mathcal{H}(f)$ is justified by a *naẓīr*-relation between both rulings)

shabah $^{\mathcal{H}* \approx f\text{-}\mathcal{H}}$: $\mathcal{H}(f,b)$
($\mathcal{H}(f)$ is justified by a *shabah*-relation between root- and branch-case).

4. Since the evidence backing $\mathcal{H}$(*aṣl*) comes from the sources, the Opponent is forced to concede it.

O!$\mathcal{H}$(*aṣl*)

5. Once the Opponent has endorsed $\mathcal{H}$(*aṣl*), and given that the occasioning factor cannot be learned, the Proponent will look in the sources for another suitable ruling ($\mathcal{H}^*$). This new ruling also applies to the root-case. The Proponent will proceed by forcing the Opponent to acknowledge this.
6. If the Opponent concedes that both of the rulings $\mathcal{H}^*$ and $\mathcal{H}$ apply to the root-case, the Proponent will look to associate $\mathcal{H}^*$ with $\mathcal{H}$ when applied to the root-case by asking the Opponent to acknowledge that the ruling $\mathcal{H}^*$ is either a specification (*khaṣīṣa*) of the ruling $\mathcal{H}$ or a parallel (*naẓīr*) of the ruling $\mathcal{H}$. This launches a *qiyās* by indication (*dalāla*) – since indication by *khaṣīṣa* is a stronger indication than one by *naẓīr*, we will assume that the Proponent will start with the former. The *qiyās al-dalāla* will thus be launched by a move either of the form

   P $\mathcal{H}^*[x_1, \ldots x_n]$-*khaṣīṣa*-$\mathcal{H}[x]$? (requesting **O** to endorse a *khaṣīṣa-link*).
   or
   P $\mathcal{H}[x]$-*naẓīr*-$\mathcal{H}^*[x]$? (requesting **O** to endorse a *naẓīr-link*).

7. The Opponent might ask for justification (*muṭālaba*) of the proposed link or refuse it. The refusal amounts of drawing a distinction (*al-farq*) between the application of $\mathcal{H}^*$ to the root-case and the branch-case so that this ruling cannot be seen as a specification (or a parallel) of $\mathcal{H}$. If such an objection has been raised, a sub-play starts and a role reversal takes place where the Opponent must defend his arguments following the prescriptions of step 8 (or 9 in the case of *naẓīr*). Once the sub-play ends and the Proponent concedes defeat, the whole argument is re-written with the thesis justified by the sub-play.
8. If the Opponent asks for a justification of the claim that a *khaṣīṣa-relation* links both rulings, the Proponent must, *first*, be able to show that the particular-general relationship holds and *second*, bring forward evidence from the sources (*shahādat al-uṣūl*) that co-presence and co-exclusivennes apply to the link between those rulings – recall the formulation of co-presence and co-exclusiveness for the *khaṣīṣa-relation* given above. If the Proponent does not succeed and if the indication is not one of *naẓīr*, the play stops, unless it switches to *qiyās al-shabah*.
9. If the Opponent asks for a justification of the claim that a *naẓīr-relation* links both rulings, the Proponent must fulfil two main tasks. *First*, the Proponent must prove that both $\mathcal{H}$ and $\mathcal{H}^*$ are particular rulings that specify some underlying set $\mathcal{D}$ – and thus, that both can be taken to be equal in relation to the deontic force and juridical effects of the underlying general rule. *Second*, the Proponent must bring forward evidence from the sources (*shahādat al-uṣūl*) that the ruling $\mathcal{H}^*$ applies if and only if the ruling $\mathcal{H}$ does. In doing so, it is also established that, whatever the occasioning factor of one of the rulings is, it must be the same as that of the other. If the Proponent does not succeed, the play stops, unless, it switches to *qiyās al-shabah*.

10. Once the Opponent concedes that the ruling $\mathcal{H}^*$ stands in either a *khaṣīṣa* or a *naẓīr* relationship with $\mathcal{H}$, and since the ruling $\mathcal{H}^*$ does apply to the branch-case, the Proponent will ask the Opponent to acknowledge that the branch-case too falls under the ruling $\mathcal{H}$. So while conceding this the Opponent concedes the main thesis brought forward by the Proponent. This concession of the Opponent leads him to also concede that whatever the *'illa* for the ruling $\mathcal{H}^*$ is, it must be the same as that one occasioning $\mathcal{H}$.
11. If at the start (step 5) the play already applies *qiyās al-shabah*, or after unsuccessful attempts to apply *qiyās al-dalāla* switches to *qiyās al-shabah*, then the Opponent will be asked to concede that the set (of properties or ruling(s)) $\mathcal{P}$ which applies to the root-case also applies to the branch-case (the move of this request being: **P** $\mathcal{H}[x]$- *shabah*-$\mathcal{H}^*[x]$?).
12. If conceded, the Proponent can ask the Opponent to acknowledge that, given the similarity of root- and branch-case in relation to $\mathcal{P}$, then the application of the ruling $\mathcal{H}$ to the root-case can be transferred by analogy to the branch-case. This will lead to the Opponent conceding the main thesis.
13. If at step 11 the Opponent refuses to accept that the branch-case can be taken to be identical in relation to $\mathcal{P}$, the Opponent must be able to draw a distinction (*al-farq*) between the root-case and the branch-case. This move will trigger a sub-play and a role reversal takes place where the Opponent must defend the grounds for drawing this distinction.

3.4.2 *Some Examples of Dialogues for* Qiyās al-Dalāla *and* Qiyās al-Shabah

The notation, terminology and moves to be deployed in the following dialogues will be disclosed in the context of the plays. In the following section we will present a generalization of such kinds of dialogue.

A Dialogue for *Qiyās al-Dalāla* I: The Deployment of *Khaṣīṣa*

Here we deploy the same notational conventions as those of the schematic diagram above:

The particular specification $\mathcal{H}^*(x, y, z)$: *prop* (x: $\mathcal{A}$, y: $\mathcal{C}(x) \vee \neg\mathcal{C}(x)$, z: $\mathcal{H}(x, \mathbf{right}^{\vee}(y))$) at stake in this example is the following:

"**L**(x)" (which presupposes "**L**(x): *prop* (x: $\mathcal{A}$)") stands for *"non-obligatory undertakings* of the type $\mathcal{A}$ *(prostration)."*

"**L***(x,y, z)" stands for *"undertakings of the type* $\mathcal{A}$ *(x) to be performed on the back of a camel while travelling without validating excuse (y) are allowed (z)".*

"a" stands for the root-case *"sujūd-prostration of supererogatory prayer"*, which is one of the actions allowed to be performed in a non-canonical way. The term *supererogatory* corresponds to the modality *recommendable action* (*mustaḥabb*) and applies to actions that are rewarded if performed but neither sanctioned nor rewarded if not performed (see our remark on deontic modalities below).

"*f*" stands for the branch-case "*sujūd-prostration of Qu'rān recital*".

"*b*" stands for some evidence from the sources that undertakings of the type *a* can be performed either in canonical or non-canonical form.

"*c*" stands for some evidence from the sources that the general ruling, which allows actions of the type *a*, includes non-canonical undertakings of that type.

O			P		
		Responses	**Responses**	**Main Thesis**	0
				Sujūd al-tilāwa (*far'*) is not an obligatory undertaking ! $\mathcal{H}$(*far'*)	
1	Why? What is the *'illa?* *'illa*?	? 0 (challenges move 0)	¿1, ¿! 2 (responds to 1 with the request of endorsing 2)	According to the sources, supererogatory prayer (*aṣl*) is not an obligatory undertaking, is it? $\mathcal{H}$(*aṣl*)?	2
3	Yes, it is non-obligatory. ! $\mathcal{H}$(*aṣl*)	! 2 (responds to the request of move 2)	¿3, ¿! 4	Is supererogatory prayer one of those undertakings that are allowed to be performed on the back of a camel while travelling, without a validating excuse? $\mathcal{H}^*$(*aṣl*)?	4
5	Yes, it is. ! $\mathcal{H}^*$(*aṣl*)	! 4	¿5, ¿! 6	Is *sujūd al tilāwa* also allowed to be performed on the back of a camel while travelling, without a validating excuse? $\mathcal{H}^*$(*far'*)?	6
7	Yes, it is. ! $\mathcal{H}^*$(*far'*)	! 6	¿7(3,5), ¿!8	Don't you see that the relation of the allowed status of an undertaking to be performed on the back of a camel while travelling, without a validating excuse, to the non-obligatory status of that undertaking has the form particular-general? If we return to your assertions 3 and 5, can't we say that the second ruling is a specification of the first one? $\mathcal{H}^*[x_1, \ldots x_n]$-*khaṣīṣa*-$\mathcal{H}[x]$?	8

(continued)

O			P		
9	Justify! ***muṭālaba*!**	? 8	! 9	1) according to the sources (*shahādat al-uṣūl*), supererogatory prayers (a) are one of those undertakings allowed to be performed on the back of a camel while travelling, without a validating excuse, and the sources testimony too that all those kinds of undertakings are non-obligatory.	10
				! $\mathbf{L}^*(a,b,c)$ is the case and this presupposes that	
				$\mathbf{L}^*(x,y,z)$: *prop* (x: $\mathcal{a}$, y: $\mathcal{C}(x) \vee \neg\mathcal{C}(x)$, z: $\mathbf{L}(x, \mathbf{right}^{\vee}(y)))$	
				2) at the same time, according to the sources, obligatory undertakings, such as obligatory prayers (a^*), are not allowed to be performed on the back of a camel while travelling, without a validating excuse.	
				! $\neg\mathbf{L}^*(a^*,b^*,c^*)$ is the case. That is, those obligatory prayers a^*, that when carried out in a non-canonical manner are forbidden by $\mathcal{H}$ $(=:\mathbf{L})$, are also forbidden by $\mathcal{H}^*$ $((=:\mathbf{L}^*),)$. this presupposes that	
				$\neg\mathbf{L}^*(x^*,y^*,z^*)$: *prop* ($x^*$: $\mathcal{a}$, y^*: $\mathcal{C}(x) \vee \neg\mathcal{C}(x)$, z^*: $\neg\mathbf{L}(x, \mathbf{right}^{\vee}(y^*)))$.	
				This also presupposes the formation of $\mathbf{O}(a^*)$, where a^*: $\mathcal{a}$ is actually $\mathbf{O}(x, y)$: ***prop*** (x: $\mathcal{a}$, y: $\mathcal{C}(x)$)	
				$\neg\mathbf{L}(x, y)$: **Prop** (x: $\mathcal{a}$, y: $\mathcal{C}(x) \vee \mathcal{C}^{\circ}(x)$)	

(continued)

O			P		
11	Given these arguments I concede your previous request	! 8, (10). O endorses 8 after the sub-arguments developed in 10	? 11	If it is the case, and given that according to 7 *sujūd al tilāwa* is allowed to be performed on the back of a camel while travelling, without a validating excuse, and given your endorsement of the *khaṣīṣa*-relation between both rulings, should not this lead to the conclusion that branch- and root-case share the same *'illa*?	12
				you(7): $\mathcal{H}^*$(*far'*)	
				z: (*'illa*(x): $\mathcal{H}$)?	
	! $\mathcal{H}^*[x_1,\ldots x_n]$-*khaṣīṣa*-$\mathcal{H}[x]$			*z*: (*'illa*(x): $\mathcal{H}^*$)?	
13	I do endorse that whatever the *'illa* is, it must apply for both rulings.	! 12	¿13, ¿! 14	But then you should also acknowledge that the general form of the *khaṣīṣa*-relation between both rulings also applies to *f*: , and that it can be carried out in a non-canonical way, according to the general ruling, which allows those kind of actions to also be performed non-canonically. Hence you should endorse	14
	z: (*'illa*(x): $\mathcal{H}$)			**L**$^*(f,b,c)$?	
	z: (*'illa*(x): $\mathcal{H}^*$)				
15	I agree.	! 14	¿15, ¿! 16	Fine. Now, given this and your endorsement of the *khaṣīṣa*-relation, you should also endorse	16
	! **L**$^*(f,b,c)$			**L**(f, b)?	
13	Indeed, its allowed status to be performed on the back of a camel while travelling, without a validating excuse is the indication (*dalāla*) of the fact that it instantiates the factor occasioning the non-obligatory status.	! 16	! 1	So, this provides the justification for the thesis you were asking for with your first move: *sujūd al tilāwa* is not an obligatory undertaking. Thus, the relation of *khaṣīṣa* provides an indication that whatever the occasioning factor	14

(continued)

O			P		
				behind both rulings is, it is the same. Summing up; the justification of my thesis is grounded on an indication by *khaṣīṣa*.	
	! **L**(*f*, *b*)			*dalāla* $^{\mathcal{H}*\text{-}khaṣīṣa\text{-}\mathcal{H}}$ = *c*: **L**(*f*, *b*).	
	ilzām (I concede defeat)				

A Dialogue for *Qiyās al-Dalāla II*: the deployment of *Naẓīr*

O			**P**		
		Responses	**Responses**	*Dhimmī's ẓihār* is legally valid.[a]	0
				! $\mathcal{H}$(*far'*)	
1	Why? What is the *'illa?*	? 0	¿1, ¿! 2	Is Muslim's *ẓihār* legally valid?	2
	'illa?			$\mathcal{H}$(*aṣl*)?	
3	Yes, it is.	! 2	¿3, ¿! 4	Is Muslim's *ṭalāq* legally valid? [b]	4
	! $\mathcal{H}$(*aṣl*)			$\mathcal{H}^*$(*aṣl*)?	
5	Yes, it is.	! 4	¿5,! 6	Is *Dhimmī's ṭalaq* legally valid?	6
	! $\mathcal{H}^*$(*aṣl*)			$\mathcal{H}^*$(*far'*)?	
7	Yes, it is.	! 6	¿ 5 (3),! 8	If we return to your assertion 3 and 5, it is clear that the validity of *ṭalāq* and the validity of *ẓihār* are parallel (*naẓīr*) cases that run together. Right?	8
	! $\mathcal{H}^*$(*far'*)			$(\forall x: \mathfrak{D})\ \mathcal{H}(x) \supset\subset \mathcal{H}^*(x)$?	
9	Justify! ***muṭālaba*!**	? 8	! 9	$a^{1:}$ Don't you see that both the validity of the Muslim's *ṭalāq* and the validity of its *ẓihār* are two kinds of divorce-declarations in matrimony with the same deontic force and juridical consequences?	10
				So, both are applications of different forms of legally valid divorce-declarations?	
				In other words, don't you see that	
				$\mathcal{H}^*$(*dhimmī'*), and $\mathcal{H}^*$(*muslim*)	

(continued)

O			P		
				$\mathcal{H}$(*muslim*), share the following structure? *valid* (*x,y,z*) *prop* (*x*: *Human*, *y*: *divorce-declaration(x)*, *z*: *ṭalāq*(*x*, *y*)). *valid* (*x,y,z*) *prop* (*x*: *Human*, *y*: *divorce-declaration(x)*, *z*: *ẓihār*(*x*, *y*)).	
11	Can you develop your argument?	? 10 (8)	! 11	a^2: More generally, according to the sources, for all those whose *ṭalāq-declaration* is valid, their *ẓihār* is valid, such as the declaration of mature Muslims.	12
	muṭālaba!			In other words, the following holds: ! ($\forall x$: *Human*) $\{valid(x,d,t) \supset valid(x,d',t')\}$ ***true*** Assuming *d, d'*: *divorce-declaration* *t*: *ṭalāq-declaration* *t'*: *ẓihār -declaration* a^3: According to the sources, for all those whose *ṭalāq* is not valid, their *ẓihār* is not valid either, such as the declarations of children and madmen. Thus, the following holds (under the same assumptions as before): ! ($\forall x$: *Human*)$\{\neg valid(x,d,t) \supset \neg valid(x,d',t')\}$ ***true*** a^4: Therefore, by evidence of the sources (*shahādat al-uṣūl*) we can conclude that for those whose *ṭalāq* is valid, their *ẓihār* is valid, and for those whose *ṭalāq* is not valid, their *ẓihār* is not valid (*man ṣaḥḥa ṭalāquhu ṣaḥḥa ẓihāruhu*). ! ($\forall x$: *Human*)$\{valid(x,d,t) \supset \subset valid(x,d',t')\}$ ***true.***	
13	Given these arguments I concede your previous request.	! (8) 12	? 13(7), ¿! 14	If it is the case, and, given 7 that *Dhimmī's ṭalaq* is legally valid, should not this lead to validity of his *ẓihār*? moreover, we must also	14

(continued)

O			**P**		
				conclude that the relation of *naẓīr* provides an indication that whatever the occasioning factor behind both rulings is, it is the same.	
	! (∀*x*: 𝔇) ℋ(*x*) ⊃ ⊂ ℋ*(*x*)			*you*(7): ℋ*(*far*ʿ) *z*: (*ʿilla*(*x*): ℋ)? *z*: (*ʿilla*(*x*): ℋ*)?	
15	Indeed, the validity of *Dhimmī's ṭalaq* is an indication (*dalāla*) that the factor occasioning its validity is the same as that occasioning the validity of its *ẓihār*.	! 14	? 13, ¿! 16	Hence, given this and your endorsement of the *naẓīr*-relation between both rulings, you should also endorse	16
	z: (*ʿilla*(*x*): ℋ) *z*: (*ʿilla*(*x*): ℋ*)			ℋ(*f*,*d'*,*t'*)?	
17	I agree. The branch-case can be concluded as falling under ruling ℋ.	! 16		So, this provides the justification for the thesis you were asking for with your first move: *Dhimmī's ẓihār* is valid because of the validity of his *ṭalaq* that you just endorsed.	18
	! ℋ(*f*,*d'*,*t'*)			*dalāla*$^{ℋ\text{-}naẓīr\text{-}ℋ*}$: ℋ(*f*,*d'*,*t'*)	
19	*ilzām*				

[a]The term "*ẓihār*" – a component of the ruling H: "*ẓihār* is legally valid"– is an ancient form of divorce-statement by the husband. See above, no. 213.
[b]The term "*ṭalāq*" – a component of the ruling H*: "*ṭalāq* is legally valid" – is the standard form of divorce-statement by the husband.

Dialogue for *Qiyās al-Shabah*

O			P		
		Responses	**Responses**	The slave is legally permitted to own. ! ℋ(*far*ʿ)	0
1	Why? What is the *ʿilla?* *ʿilla*?	? 0 (challenges move 0)	¿1, ¿! 2 (responds to 1 with the request of endorsing 2)	Is the free person legally permitted to own? ℋ(*aṣl*)? [s]	2

(continued)

O			P		
3	Yes, it is.	! 2	¿3, ¿! 4	But a free person and a slave can be seen as being equal in relation to their right to own. Right?	4
	! $\mathcal{H}(a\d{s}l)$			$a \approx_{\mathcal{P}} f$? (where "$\mathcal{P}$" stands for the conjunction of properties	
				$\mathcal{P}\mathbf{1}(x) \wedge \mathcal{P}\mathbf{2}(x) \wedge \mathcal{P}\mathbf{3}(x)$ (x: *Human*)) establishing the right to own.	
5	Justify! ***muṭālaba!***	? 4	¿ 5, ¿! 6	The free person is a human being to whom instructive communication is addressed (*mukhāṭab*) ($\mathcal{P}\mathbf{1}$); and he can rewarded (*muthāb*) ($\mathcal{P}\mathbf{2}$) and punished (*mu'āqab*) ($\mathcal{P}\mathbf{3}$). Is that right?	6
				$\mathcal{P}\mathbf{1}(a) \wedge \mathcal{P}\mathbf{2}(a) \wedge \mathcal{P}\mathbf{3}(a)$?	
7	Yes, it is.	! 6	¿ 7, ¿! 8	The slave is also a human being to whom instructive communication is addressed; and is rewarded and punished. is it right?	8
	! $\mathcal{P}\mathbf{1}(a) \wedge \mathcal{P}\mathbf{2}(a) \wedge \mathcal{P}\mathbf{3}(a)$			$\mathcal{P}\mathbf{1}(f) \wedge \mathcal{P}\mathbf{2}(f) \wedge \mathcal{P}\mathbf{3}(f)$?	
9	Indeed.	! 8	¿ 9, ¿! 10	According to these endorsements, it seems reasonable to consider them identical in relation to $\mathcal{P}\mathbf{1\text{–}3}$, right?	10
	! $\mathcal{P}\mathbf{1}(f) \wedge \mathcal{P}\mathbf{2}(f) \wedge \mathcal{P}\mathbf{3}(f)$			Given:	
				you(7): $\mathcal{P}\mathbf{1}(a) \wedge \mathcal{P}\mathbf{2}(a) \wedge \mathcal{P}\mathbf{3}(a)$	
				you(9): $\mathcal{P}\mathbf{1}(f) \wedge \mathcal{P}\mathbf{2}(f) \wedge \mathcal{P}\mathbf{3}(f)$	
				$a \approx_{\mathcal{P}1\text{–}3} f$?	
11	I agree.	! 10	¿ 11, ¿! 12	If that is the case, and given 3 that the free person is legally permitted to own, should not this be similar to permission for the slave to own?	12
	! $a \approx_{\mathcal{P}1\text{–}3} f$			$\mathcal{H}(a/f)$?	

(continued)

O			P		
13	Indeed, according to their resemblance, the permission of the free person to own yields its analogous permission for the slave.	! 12	! 1	So, this provides the justification for the thesis you were asking for with your first move: The slave is permitted to own because it is analogous to such permission of the free person based their resemblance in relation to the set of properties $\mathcal{P}$.	14
	! $\mathcal{H}(f)$			! *shabah* $^{\mathcal{H}*\text{-}a \approx f\text{-}\mathcal{H}}$: $\mathcal{H}(f)$	
	ilzām				

3.5 A Dialogical Framework for *Qiyās al-Dalāla* and *Qiyās al-Shabah*

In our aim to facilitate the overview of the different parts of the book, in this part we will repeat the general introduction to dialogical logic of the last sections in the chapter II.

Moreover, in the chapter IV of the present volume we discuss more thoroughly the main notions involving the dialogical approach to Constructive Type Theory called *Immanent Reasoning* – see Rahman/McConaughey/Klev/Clerbout (2018).

3.5.1 *The Dialogical Approach to Logic*

The dialogical approach to logic is not a specific logical system but rather a framework rooted on a rule-based approach to meaning in which different logics can be developed, combined and compared.[34]

[34]In the following sections we present only a simplified and adapted form of the Dialogical Framework, called *Immanent Reasoning* – see Rahman/McConaughey/Klev/Clerbout (2018). For a more complete presentation see the chapter IV of the present book. The main original papers are collected in Lorenzen/Lorenz (1978) – see too Lorenz (2010a, b), Felscher (1985), Krabbe (2006). For an account of recent developments see Rahman/Keiff (2005), Keiff (2009), Rahman/Tulenheimo (2009), Rückert (2011), Clerbout (2014a, b). The most recent work links dialogical logic and Constructive Type Theory, see Clerbout/Rahman (2015) and Rahman/Clerbout/Redmond (2017).

More precisely, in a dialogue two parties argue about a thesis respecting certain fixed rules. The player that states the thesis is called Proponent (**P**), and his rival, who contests the thesis, is called Opponent (**O**). Dialogues are designed in such a way that each of the plays end after a finite number of moves with one player winning, while the other loses.

Actions or moves in a dialogue are often understood as speech-acts involving *declarative utterances or statements* and *interrogative utterances or requests*.

The point is that the rules of the dialogue do not operate on expressions or sentences isolated from the act of uttering them.

The rules are divided into particle rules or rules for logical constants (*Partikelregeln*) and structural rules (*Rahmenregeln*).

Particle rules provide an abstract description of how the game can proceed locally: they specify the way a formula can be challenged and defended according to its main logical constant. In this way the particle rules govern the local level of meaning (of logical constants – but it can be extended to non-logical ones). Strictly speaking, the expressions occurring in the table above are not actual moves because they feature formula schemata and the players are not specified. Moreover, these rules are indifferent to any particular situations that might occur during the game. For these reasons we say that the description provided by the particle rules is abstract.

The structural rules determine the development of a dialogue game and they govern the moves involving elementary statements.

3.5.1.1 Local Meaning

It is presupposed in standard dialogical systems that the players use well-formed formulas. The well formation can be checked at will, but only with the usual meta reasoning by which the formula is checked to indeed observe the definition of a wff. We want to enrich the system by first allowing players to enquire on the status of expressions and in particular to ask if a certain expression is a proposition. We thus start with dialogical rules explaining the formation of propositions.

Moreover, we extend the first-order language assumed in standard dialogical logic by adding two labels **O** and **P**, standing for the players of the game, and the two symbols '!' and '?'. When the identity of the player does not matter, we use the variables **X** or **Y** (with $\mathbf{X} \neq \mathbf{Y}$).

A move M is an expression of the form '**X**-*e*', where *e* is one of the forms specified by the particle rules.

Local meaning: Formation

Statement	Challenge	Defence
X $A \vee B$: **prop**	**Y** $?_{F\vee 1}$ Or **Y** $?_{F\vee 2}$	**X** A: **prop** **X** B: **prop**
X $A \wedge B$: **prop**	**Y** $?_{F\wedge 1}$ Or **Y** $?_{F\wedge 2}$	**X** A: **prop** **X** B: **prop**
X $A \supset B$: **prop**	**Y** $?_{F\supset 1}$ Or **Y** $?_{F\supset 2}$	**X** A: **prop** **X** B: **prop**
X $\neg A$: **prop**	**Y** $?_{F\neg}$	**X** A: **prop**
X $(\forall x: A)\ B(x)$: **prop**	**Y** $?_{F\forall 1}$ Or **Y** $?_{F\forall 2}$	**X** A: **set** **X** $B(x)$: **prop** $(x: A)$
X $(\exists x: A)\ B(x)$: **prop**	**Y** $?_{\exists 1}$ Or **Y** $?_{F\exists 2}$	**X** A: **set** **X** $B(x)$: **prop** $(x: A)$

Besides the formation rules, the rules described by the local meaning for some statement π indicate those moves that constitute the *canonical argumentation form of the local reason* specific to the statement/set at stake in π.

Because our deployment expressions come from Constructive-Type Theory, the language contains expressions such as the following (further expressions are provided in the section on terminology in the main text):

X! A Player **X** claims that he *can produce* some *local reason* for A.

X p: A Player **X** states that p instantiates A. In other words, player **X** states that p provides a *local reason* for A.

X p_i: B (p_j) Player **X** states that p_i provides a *local reason* for B given that *the antagonist* **Y** states that p_j provides a *local reason* for A, and given that ***B***(x): **prop** $(x: A)$.

Similarly

X p_i: $B(p_j)$ Player **X** states that p_i provides a *local reason* for B given that it is *he himself* (**X**), who states that p_j provides a *local reason* for A, and given that ***B***(x): **prop** $(x: A)$.

Synthesis of Local Reasons

The **synthesis rules** of local reasons determine how to produce a local reason for a statement; they include rules of interaction indicating how to produce the local reason that is required by the proposition (or set) in play, that is, they indicate what kind of dialogical action –what kind of move – must be carried out, by whom (challenger or defender), and what reason must be brought forward.

Synthesis rules for local reasons

	Move	Challenge	Defence
Conjunction	**X !** $A \wedge B$	**Y** ? $L^{\wedge}$ or **Y** ? $R^{\wedge}$	**X** p_1: A (resp.) **X** p_2: B
Existential quantification	**X** ! $(\exists x: A)B(x)$	**Y** ? $L^{\exists}$ or **Y** ? $R^{\exists}$	**X** p_1: A (resp.) **X** p_2: $B(p_1)$
Disjunction	**X !** $A \vee B$	**Y** $?^{\vee}$	**X** p_1: A or **X** p_2: B
Implication	**X !** $A \supset B$	**Y** p_1: A	**X** p_2: B
Universal quantification	**X** ! $(\forall x: A)B(x)$	**Y** p_1: A	**X** p_2: $B(p_1)$
Negation	**X !** $\neg A$ Also expressed as **X !** $A \supset \bot$	**Y** p_1: A	**X** p_2: $\bot$

Analysis of Local Reasons

Apart from the rules for the synthesis of local reasons, we need rules that indicate how to parse a complex local reason into its elements: this is the *analysis* of local reasons. In order to deal with the complexity of these local reasons and formulate general rules for the analysis of local reasons (at the play level), we introduce certain operators that we call *instructions*, such as $L^{\vee}(p)$ or $R^{\wedge}(p)$. To the standard particle rules (the local rules for logical constants) we also add rules for the operators F and V adapted to the purposes of our present study.

Let us introduce these instructions and the analysis of local reasons with an example: player **X** states the implication $(A \wedge B) \supset B$. According to the rule for the synthesis of local reasons for an implication, we obtain the following:

Move	**X** ! $(A \wedge B) \supset B$
Challenge	**Y** p_1: $A \wedge B$

Recall that the synthesis rule prescribes that **X** must now provide a local reason for the consequent; but instead of defending his implication (with **X** p_2 : B for instance), **X** can choose to parse the reason p_1 provided by **Y** in order to force **Y** to provide a local reason for the right-hand side of the conjunction that **X** will then be able to copy. In other words, **X** can force **Y** to provide the local reason for B out of the local reason p_1 for the antecedent $A \wedge B$ of the initial implication. The analysis rules prescribe how to carry out such a parsing of the statement by using *instructions*.

The rule for the analysis of a local reason for the conjunction p_1: $A \wedge B$ will thus indicate that its defence includes expressions such as.

- the left instruction for the conjunction, written $L^{\wedge}(p_1)$, and
- the right instruction for the conjunction, written $R^{\wedge}(p_1)$.

These instructions can be informally understood as carrying out the following step: for the defence of the conjunction p_1: $A \wedge B$ separate the local reason p_1 in its left (or right) component so that this component can be adduced in defence of the left (or right) side of the conjunction.

Let us now proceed to present the **Analysis rules** for the usual logical constants.

<u>**Analysis rules for local reasons**</u>

	Move	Challenge	Defence
Conjunction	**X**p: $A \wedge B$	**Y** ? $L^{\wedge}$ or **Y** ? $R^{\wedge}$	**X** $L^{\wedge}(p)$: A (resp.) **X** $R^{\wedge}(p)$: B
Existential quantification	**X**p: $(\exists x: A)B(x)$	**Y** ? $L^{\exists}$ or **Y** ? $R^{\exists}$	**X** $L^{\exists}(p)$: A (resp.) **X** $R^{\exists}(p)$: $B\ (L^{\exists}(p))$
Disjunction	**X**p: $A \vee B$	**Y** $?^{\vee}$	**X** $L^{\vee}(p)$: A or **X** $R^{\vee}(p)$: B
Implication	**X**p: $A \supset B$	**Y** $L^{\supset}(p)$: A	**X** $R^{\supset}(p)$: B
Universal quantification	**X**p: $(\forall x: A)B(x)$	**Y** $L^{\forall}(p)$: A	**X** $R^{\forall}(p)$: $B\ (L^{\forall}(p))$
Negation	**X**p: $\neg A$ Also expressed as **X**p: $A \supset \bot$	**Y** $L^{\neg}(p)$: A **Y** $L^{\supset}(p)$: A	**X** $R^{\neg}(p)$: $\bot$ **X** $R^{\supset}(p)$: $\bot$ Which amounts to stating **X** ! $\bot$[a]

[a]The general point of deleting the instruction in **X** $R^{\supset}(p)$: $\bot$ is that instructions occurring in expressions stating **falsum** keep un-resolved – see below structural rule SR3 on resolutions, item 3.

The Operator $\mathbb{F}$[35]

In uttering the formula $\mathbb{F}A$ the argumentation partner **X** claims that he can find a counterexample during a play where the antagonist **Y** asserts A.

The antagonist **Y** challenges $\mathbb{F}A$ by asserting that A can be challenged successfully. Thus, through this challenge **Y** obliges **X** to open a *sub-play* where he (**X**) states A.

- The rules for synthesis and analysis follow those of
- **Y**! $\neg A$
- fulfilling the distribution of duties and rights prescribed for the role of **Y** in the sub-play.

In other words, the local meaning of the operator $\mathbb{F}A$ reduces to stating the negation of the proposition under its scope. However, this statement might change his duties in relation to the Socratic Rule:

<table>
<tr><td rowspan="5">X ! $\mathbb{F}A$</td><td>Challenge</td><td>Defence</td></tr>
<tr><td>Y ?$\mathbb{F}$</td><td></td></tr>
<tr><td>Sub-play $\mathfrak{D}_1$</td><td>Sub-play $\mathfrak{D}_1$</td></tr>
<tr><td rowspan="2">Y ! A
Y must play under the restriction of the Socratic-Rule in the sub-play</td><td>X $?_A$(he challenges A)</td></tr>
<tr><td>The local reason for the operator is the local reason that encodes a play for the negation of A.</td></tr>
</table>

The Operator $\mathbb{V}$

In uttering the formula $\mathbb{V}A$ the argumentation partner **X** claims that he can win a play where he (**X**) asserts A.

The antagonist **Y** responds by challenging **X** to open a *sub-play* where he (**X**) defends A.

- The rules for synthesis and analysis follow those of
- **X**! A
- fulfilling the distribution of duties and rights prescribed for the role of **X** in the sub-play.

<table>
<tr><td rowspan="5">X ! $\mathbb{V}A$</td><td>Challenge</td><td>Defence</td></tr>
<tr><td>Y: ?$\mathbb{V}$</td><td></td></tr>
<tr><td>Sub-play $\mathfrak{D}_1$</td><td>Sub-play $\mathfrak{D}_1$</td></tr>
<tr><td rowspan="2">Y $?_A$(he challenges A)
Y must play under the restriction of the Socratic Rule</td><td>X ! A</td></tr>
<tr><td>The local reason for the operator is the local reason that encodes a play for A.</td></tr>
</table>

[35]Cf. Rahman/Rückert (2001, pp. 113–116).

3.5.1.2 Global Meaning

Structural Rules

In the dialogical approach, validity is defined via the notion of *winning strategy*, where winning strategy for **X** means that for any choice of moves by **Y**, **X** has at least one possible move at his disposal such that he (**X**) wins:

Validity (definition): A proposition is valid in a certain dialogical system iff **P** has a winning strategy for this proposition.

In the present context we will deploy a variant of the structural rules. Before providing them, let us fix the following notions:

Play: A *play* is a legal sequence of moves, *i.e.*, a sequence of moves which observes the game rules. Particle rules are not the only rules which must be observed in this respect. In fact, it can be said that the second kind of rules, namely, the *structural rules* are those giving the precise conditions under which a given sequence is a play.

Dialogical game: The *dialogical game* for φ, written D(φ), is the set of all plays with φ being the *thesis* (see the Starting rule below).[36]

The ***structural rules*** are the following:

SR0 (Starting rule). Any dialogue starts with the Opponent stating initial concessions, if any, and the Proponent stating the thesis. After that the players each choose a positive integer called *repetition rank*.

- The *repetition rank* of a player restricts the number of challenges he can play in reaction to a single move.

SR1i (Classical game-playing rule). Players move alternately. After the repetition ranks have been chosen, each move is a challenge or a defence in reaction to a previous move and in accordance with the particle rules.

SR1ii (Intuitionistic game-playing rule). Players move alternately. After the repetition ranks have been chosen, each move is a challenge or a defence in reaction to a previous move and in accordance with the particle rules.
Players can only answer against the ***last non-answered*** challenge by the adversary.[37]

SR2 (Socratic Rule).[38]**P** cannot make an elementary statement if **O** has not stated it before, except in the thesis.
An elementary statement is either an elementary proposition with implicit local reason, or an elementary proposition and its local reason (not an instruction).

---

[36]For a formal formulation see Clerbout (2014a,b).

[37]This last clause is known as the *Last Duty First* condition, and is the clause which makes dialogical games suitable for Intuitionistic Logic, hence the name of this rule.

[38]This rule is one of the most salient characteristics of dialogical logic – see structural rules in the chapter IV of the present work.

SR2.1 Challenging elementary sentences. Challenges against elementary statements with implicit local reasons take the form:

$$X!A$$

$$Y\ ?_{reason}$$

$$X\ a: A$$

where A is an elementary proposition and a is a local reason. For more details see structural rules for Immanent Reasoning SR5 in the chapter IV of the present book. In the context of dialogues for ***qiyās*** it can take the form:

$$X!A$$

$$Y_{why}?$$

$$X\ a: A$$

SR2.1.2 Responses to challenges against elementary statements other than the thesis. If **O** endorsed a statement of the form **O**! A at move n, **P** can state "*you*(i): A" which expresses that **P**'s reason for endorsing B is "you, the Opponent, have already endorsed B at move n". It can also take the form

$$\mathbf{P}!\ A$$
$$\mathbf{O}\ Why?$$
$$\mathbf{P}\ you(n): A\ (\text{assuming } \mathbf{O}\ a: A\ at\ n)$$

SR2.1.3 Responses to challenges against the thesis of a *qiyās*. **O**'s challenge to the thesis of a *qiyās dalāla* or *shabah* is described by SR3.

SR2.1.4 Resolution of instructions. A player may ask his adversary to carry out the prescribed instruction and thus bring forward a suitable local reason in defence of the proposition at stake. Once the defender has replaced the instruction with the required local reason we say that the instruction has been resolved.

The player index of an instruction determines which of the two players has the right to choose the local reason that will resolve the instruction.

For example:

$$\mathbf{X}\ L_{\wedge}(p): A$$
$$\mathbf{Y}?\ldots/\ L_{\wedge}(p)$$
$$\mathbf{X}\ p_1: A$$

The choice of a local reason for resolving an instruction is restricted by the distribution of rights and duties prescribed by the local rules. Instructions occurring in expressions stating **falsum** have no resolution. In fact, The player stating $\mathcal{I}(p)$: $\perp$ gives up and therefore loses the play. For more details see structural rules for Immanent Reasoning in the chapter IV of the present book.

SR2.1.5 Requests and endorsements for *qiyās al-dalāla* and *al-shabah*. *Qiyās al-dalāla* and *al-shabah* also require the following moves prescribed by the **development rules** specific to the dialectical framework underlying this form of *qiyās*.

SR2.1.5.1 Requests based on sources. If the request has a form that indicates sources, it **must** be endorsed by the respondent:

$$\mathbf{X}\ p^{\mathcal{S}}: A?\quad \mathbf{X}!A^{\mathcal{S}}?$$

$$\mathbf{Y}\ \ p^{\mathcal{S}}: A\quad \mathbf{Y}!A^{\mathcal{S}}$$

(Since in the glosses of the examples, the backing from the sources is made explicit, we often do not add them explicitly to the notation).

SR2.1.5.2 Special requests and endorsements

X $\mathcal{H}^*[x_1,\ldots x_n]$-*khaṣīṣa*-$\mathcal{H}[x]$?	**X** asks **Y** to endorse that specification $\mathcal{H}^*$ specifies $\mathcal{H}$.
Y *muṭālaba*!	Asking for argumentation
X $a_1.\ldots a_n$	Argumentation of **X** in order to show *first*, that the particular-general relationship holds between $\mathcal{H}^*(a)$ and a: $\mathcal{H}$; *second*, that according to the *sources* $\mathcal{H}$ applies iff $\mathcal{H}^*$ applies.
Y!! $\mathcal{H}^*[x_1,\ldots x_n]$-*khaṣīṣa*-$\mathcal{H}[x]$	**Y** endorses the request

X $(\forall x: \mathcal{D})\ \mathcal{H}(x) \supset\subset \mathcal{H}^*(x)$?	**X** asks **Y** to endorse that both rulings are in a *naẓīr*-relation
Y *muṭālaba*!	Asking for argumentation
X $a_1.\ldots a_n$	Argumentation of **X** in order to show *first*, that both $\mathcal{H}$ and $\mathcal{H}^*$ are particular rulings that specify some underlying set $\mathcal{D}$, and thus, that both can be said to be equal in relation to the deontic force and juridical effects of the underlying general ruling; *second*, that according to the *sources* $\mathcal{H}$ applies iff $\mathcal{H}^*$ applies.
Y! $(\forall x: \mathcal{D})\ \mathcal{H}(x) \supset\subset \mathcal{H}^*(x)$	**Y** endorses the request

X $a \approx_{\mathcal{P}} f$? (where "$\mathcal{P}$" stands for "$\mathcal{P}\mathbf{1}(x) \wedge, \ldots, \wedge \mathcal{P}\mathbf{n}(x)\ (x: \mathcal{P})$")?	**X** asks **Y** to endorse that root-case and branch-case are identical in relation to some conjunction of properties $\mathcal{P}$
Y *muṭālaba*!	Asking for argumentation
X $a_1.\ldots a_n$	Argumentation of **X** in order to show that the properties apply to the root-case and the branch-case.
Y! $a \approx_{\mathcal{P}} f$	**Y** endorses the request.
X $\mathcal{H}(a/f)$?	**X** asks **Y** to replace the root-case by the branch-case – Given the endorsement of the identity and given that **Y** also conceded $\mathcal{H}(a)$.
Y $\mathcal{H}(f)$	**Y** implements the requested substitution.

SR2.1.5.3 *Mu'ārada.* As already mentioned, the Opponent might ask for justification (*muṭālaba*) of the proposed link or refuse it. The refusal amounts to drawing a distinction (*al-farq*) between the application of $\mathcal{H}^*$ to the root-case and the branch-case so that this ruling can be seen neither as a specification nor a parallel of $\mathcal{H}$, since there is another alternative pair $\mathcal{H}^{\bullet\bullet}$, $\mathcal{H}^{\bullet}$, that (according to some sources $s^{\bullet}$ which have priority in relation to the sources (that ground **P**'s main thesis) applies to some root-case $a^{\bullet}$ but that contradicts the thesis $\mathcal{H}(f)$. We will assume that a refusal will be brought forward after the Proponent has developed his own argument. If such an objection has been raised, a sub-play starts and a role reversal takes place where the Opponent must defend his arguments.

Mu'ārada

P $\mathcal{H}^*[x_1,\ldots x_n]$-*khaṣīṣa*-$\mathcal{H}[x]$?	**P** asks **O** to endorse that specification $\mathcal{H}^*$ specifies $\mathcal{H}$.
O *muṭālaba*!	Asking for argumentation
P $a_1.\ldots.a_n$	Argumentation of **P** in order to show *first,* that the particular-general relationship holds between $\mathcal{H}^*(a)$ and a: $\mathcal{H}$, and second that according to the *sources* $\mathcal{H}$ applies iff $\mathcal{H}^*$ applies.
O *al-farq*	**O** refuses to endorse the requested assertion and states that a distinction is due.
P *muṭālaba*!	Now it is **P** who asks for justification
O V $\mathcal{H}^{\bullet\bullet}$ $[x_1,\ldots x_n]$-*khaṣīṣa*-$\mathcal{H}^{\bullet}[x]$	**O** launches a sub-play, where he proposes as his thesis the alternative pair of rulings $\mathcal{H}^{\bullet}$, $\mathcal{H}^{\bullet\bullet}$.
P *muṭālaba*?	**P** asks for justification
O $a_1.\ldots.a_n$	The sub-play continues as in a standard *khaṣīṣa* play.
O $\mathcal{H}^{\bullet\bullet}$ $[x_1,\ldots x_n]$-*khaṣīṣa*-$\mathcal{H}^{\bullet}[x]$?	**O** asks **P** to acknowledge the thesis of the sub-play.
P! $\mathcal{H}^{\bullet\bullet}$ $[x_1,\ldots x_n]$-*khaṣīṣa*-$\mathcal{H}^{\bullet}[x]$	**P** concedes in view of the evidence from the sources $s^{\bullet}$.
O $\mathcal{H}^{\bullet}(f,d',t')$?	**O** asks **P** to acknowledge that according to the sources $s^{\bullet}$ the branch-case falls under the scope of the general ruling $\mathcal{H}^{\bullet}$.
P! $\mathcal{H}^{\bullet}(f,d',t')$	**P** concedes.
O $(\mathcal{H}^{\bullet}(f,d',t') \wedge \mathcal{H}(\boldsymbol{f,d',t'})) \supset \bot$	**O** makes the point that the branch-case cannot fall under the same ruling (since this leads to a contradiction).
P ***Ifḥām***	**P** concedes defeat.
	After the objection and the constructive contribution of **O**, the *qiyās* is rewritten with the thesis *f*: $\mathcal{H}^{\bullet}$(*far'*) The tree displaying the winning strategy will delete the unsuccessful attempts and also the justification of the sub-play.

Similar sub-plays will be triggered by objections to the arguments in support of *naẓīr* or *shabah*.

SR3 (the Overall Development of a Dialogue for *Qiyās al-Dalāla* and *Qiyās al-Shabah*

1. A dialogical play starts with the Proponent setting the thesis that some specific legal ruling ($\mathcal{H}$) applies to a certain branch-case.

   $$\mathbf{P}!\mathcal{H}(far\text{'})$$

   The Proponent's aim is to develop an argument in such a way that it forces the Opponent to concede the justification of the thesis.

   Remark: As pointed out before, the main thesis is just the claim that the general ruling applies to the branch-case. It requires a justification, that is, a proof-object for the proposition $\mathcal{H}$(*far'*). Moreover, the justification will require it to be shown that the branch-case encodes some inner structure. One way to think about the branch-case occurring in $\mathcal{H}$(*far'*) is as its being a non-canonical proof-object that will be brought to its canonical form during the inferential moves. Implementing this requires some more notation. In order to limit this, when occurring in an inference, we will deploy the notation "*far'*" for its non-canonical form and "*f,y, ..., z*" for its canonical form. The same applies to the root-case.
2. After agreement on the finiteness of the argument to be developed, the Opponent will launch a challenge to the assertion by asking for the occasioning factor justifying the thesis:

   O *'illa*?

3. The Proponent's aim is to develop an argument in such a way that it forces the Opponent to concede the thesis. In case of *dalāla* but not *shabah* the Proponent will try to show that there are sufficient elements to *assume* that there is some underlying occasioning factor, *despite the fact that no precise occasioning factor can be found*. In order to develop his argument, the Proponent will start by choosing (to the best of his juridical knowledge) a root-case from the sources for which the ruling $\mathcal{H}$ has been applied and will ask the Opponent to endorse it.

   P $\mathcal{H}$(*aṣl*)?

   Remark: The main aim behind this move that motivates the whole argumentation consists in the Proponent forcing the Opponent to endorse the thesis because of some specific indications (in the case of *qiyās al-dalāla*) or resemblances (in the case of *qiyās al-shabah*) brought forward by the Proponent himself. The endorsement of the Opponent, at the **end** of the play – if such an endorsement takes place–, allows the Proponent to justify his thesis by bringing forward one of the following statements:

dalāla $^{\mathcal{H}*\text{-}khaṣīṣa\text{-}\mathcal{H}}$: $\mathcal{H}(f,b)$
($\mathcal{H}(f,b)$ is justified by the *khaṣīṣa*-relation between both rulings)

dalāla $^{\mathcal{H}*\text{-}naẓīr\text{-}\mathcal{H}}$: $\mathcal{H}(f,d,t)$
($\mathcal{H}(f)$ is justified by a *naẓīr*-relation between both rulings)

shabah $^{\mathcal{H}*\text{-}a \approx f\text{-}\mathcal{H}}$: $\mathcal{H}(f,b)$
($\mathcal{H}()$ is justified by a *shabah*-relation between root- and branch-case).

4. Since the evidence backing $\mathcal{H}(aṣl)$ comes from the sources, the Opponent is forced to concede it.

$$\mathbf{O}!\mathcal{H}(aṣl)$$

5. Once the Opponent has endorsed $\mathcal{H}(aṣl)$, and given that the occasioning factor cannot be learned, the Proponent will look in the sources for another suitable ruling ($\mathcal{H}^*$). This new ruling also applies to the root-case. The Proponent will proceed by forcing the Opponent to acknowledge this.
6. If the Opponent concedes that both of the rulings $\mathcal{H}^*$ and $\mathcal{H}$ apply to the root-case, the Proponent will look to associate $\mathcal{H}^*$ with $\mathcal{H}$ when applied to the root-case by asking the Opponent to acknowledge that the ruling $\mathcal{H}^*$ is either a specification (*khaṣīṣa*) of the ruling $\mathcal{H}$ or a parallel (*naẓīr*) of the ruling $\mathcal{H}$. This launches a *qiyās* by indication (*dalāla*) – since indication by *khaṣīṣa* is a stronger indication than one by *naẓīr*, we will assume that the Proponent will start with the former. The *qiyās al-dalāla* will thus be launched by a move either of the form

   P $\mathcal{H}^*[x_1,\ldots x_n]$-*khaṣīṣa*-$\mathcal{H}[x]$? (requesting **O** to endorse a *khaṣīṣa-link*)
   or
   P $\mathcal{H}[x]$-*naẓīr*-$\mathcal{H}^*[x]$? (requesting **O** to endorse a *naẓīr-link*)

7. The Opponent might ask for justification (*muṭālaba*) of the proposed link or refuse it. The refusal amounts to drawing a distinction (*al-farq*) between the application of $\mathcal{H}^*$ to the root-case and the branch-case so that this ruling cannot be seen as a specification (or a parallel) of $\mathcal{H}$. If such an objection has been raised, a sub-play starts and a role reversal takes place where the Opponent must defend his arguments following the prescriptions of step 8 (or 9 in the case of *naẓīr*). Once the sub-play ends and the Proponent concedes defeat, the whole argument is re-written with the thesis justified by the sub-play.
8. If the Opponent asks for a justification of the claim that a *khaṣīṣa-relation* links both rulings, the Proponent must, *first*, be able to show that the particular-general relationship holds and *second,* bring forward evidence from the sources (*shahādat al-uṣūl*) that co-presence and co-exclusivennes apply to the link between those rulings – recall the formulation of co-presence and co-exclusiveness for the *khaṣīṣa-relation* given above.

If the Proponent does not succeed and if the indication is not one of *naẓīr*, the play stops, unless it switches to *qiyās al-shabah.*

9. If the Opponent asks for a justification of the claim that a *naẓīr-relation* links both rulings, the Proponent must fulfil two main tasks. *First,* the Proponent must prove that both $\mathcal{H}$ and $\mathcal{H}^*$ are particular rulings that specify some underlying set $\mathcal{D}$ – and thus, that both can be taken to be equal in relation to the deontic force and juridical effects of the underlying general rule. *Second,* the Proponent must bring forward evidence from the sources *(shahādat al-uṣūl)* that the ruling $\mathcal{H}^*$ applies if and only if the ruling $\mathcal{H}$ does. In doing so, it is also established that, whatever the occasioning factor of one of the rulings is, it must be the same as that of the other. If the Proponent does not succeed, the play stops unless, it switches to *qiyās al-shabah.*
10. Once the Opponent concedes that the ruling $\mathcal{H}^*$ stands in either a *khaṣīṣa* or a *naẓīr* relationship with $\mathcal{H}$, and since the ruling $\mathcal{H}^*$ does apply to the branch-case, the Proponent will ask the Opponent to acknowledge that the branch-case too falls under the ruling $\mathcal{H}$. So while conceding this the Opponent concedes the main thesis brought forward by the Proponent. This concession of the Opponent leads him to also concede that whatever the *'illa* for the ruling $\mathcal{H}^*$ is, it must be the same as that one occasioning $\mathcal{H}$.

    Hence, the final steps for a successful play for the Proponent will have one of the following forms:

khaṣīṣa	***naẓīr***
P	**P**
you(*n*): $\mathcal{H}^*$(*far*ʿ)	*you*(*n*): $\mathcal{H}^*$(*far*ʿ)
z: (ʻ*illa*(*x*): $\mathcal{H}$)?	*z*: (ʻ*illa*(*x*): $\mathcal{H}$)?
z: (ʻ*illa*(*x*): $\mathcal{H}^*$)?	*z*: (ʻ*illa*(*x*): $\mathcal{H}^*$)?
O	**O**
z: (ʻ*illa*(*x*): $\mathcal{H}$)	*z*: (ʻ*illa*(*x*): $\mathcal{H}$)
z: (ʻ*illa*(*x*): $\mathcal{H}^*$)	*z*: (ʻ*illa*(*x*): $\mathcal{H}^*$)
P	**P**
$\mathbf{L}^*(f,b,c)$?	$\mathcal{H}(f,d',t')$?
O	**O**
! $\mathbf{L}^*(f,b,c)$	! $\mathcal{H}(f,d',t')$
P	**P**
$\mathbf{L}(f, b)$?	*dalāla*$^{\mathcal{H}\text{-}naz\bar{\imath}r\text{-}\mathcal{H}*}$: $\mathcal{H}(f,d',t')$
O	**O** *ilzām*
! $\mathbf{L}(f, b)$	
P	
dalāla$^{\mathcal{H}*\text{-}khas\bar{\imath}sa\text{-}\mathcal{H}} = c$: $\mathbf{L}(f, b)$	
O *ilzām*	

11. If at the start (step 5) already the play applies *qiyās al-shabah*, or after unsuccessful attempts to apply *qiyās al-dalāla* switches to *qiyās al-shabah*, then the

Opponent will be asked to concede that the set (of properties or ruling(s)) $\mathcal{P}$ which applies to the root-case also applies to the branch-case (the move of this request being: **P** $\mathcal{H}[x]$- *shabah*-$\mathcal{H}^*[x]$?).

12. If conceded, the Proponent can ask the Opponent to acknowledge that, given the similarity of root- and branch-case in relation to $\mathcal{P}$, then the application of the ruling $\mathcal{H}$ to the root-case can be transferred by analogy to the branch-case. This will lead to the Opponent conceding the main thesis. The end-moves are the following:

    al-shabah
    P
    you(n): $\mathcal{P}\mathbf{1}(a)\wedge \ldots .\mathcal{P}\mathbf{k}(a)$
    you(m): $\mathcal{P}\mathbf{1}(f)\wedge \ldots .\mathcal{P}\mathbf{k}(f)$
    $a \approx_{\mathcal{P}\,1\text{-k}} f$?
    O
    $!\; a \approx_{\mathcal{P}\,1\text{-k}} f$
    P
    $\mathcal{H}(a/f)$?
    O
    $\mathcal{H}(a/f)$?
    P
    shabah $^{\mathcal{H}*\text{-}a\, \approx\, f\text{-}\mathcal{H}}$: $\mathcal{H}(f)$
    O
    ilzām

13. If at step 11 the Opponent refuses to accept that the branch-case can be taken to be identical in relation to $\mathcal{P}$, the Opponent must be able to draw a distinction (*al-farq*) between the root-case and the branch-case. This move will trigger a sub-play and a role reversal takes place where the Opponent must defend the grounds for drawing this distinction (see section *mu'āraḍa* above).

SR4 (Winning rule). This structural rule requires some additional terminology:

Terminal play: A play is called *terminal* when it cannot be extended by further moves in compliance with the rules.

X-terminal: We say it is **X**-*terminal* when the last move in the play is an **X**-move.

Player **X** wins the play ζ only if it is **X**-terminal, unless he states $\perp$. The player who states **falsum** loses the play.

Strategy: A *strategy* for player **X** in D(φ) is a function which assigns an **X**-move M to every non-terminal play ζ having a **Y**-move as the last member such that extending ζ with M results in a play.

X-winning-strategy: An ***X***-*strategy* is *winning* if playing according to it leads to **X**-terminal play no matter how **Y** moves.

Winning-strategy resulting from a cooperative move: Winning strategies constituted by plays where cooperative moves took place will disregard the unsuccessful attempts and also the justification of the sub-play. More precisely, it will proceed as if the Proponent has chosen the relation between rulings resulting from the sub-play. Accordingly, the winning strategy will include moves where the Proponent rather than the Opponent asserts the efficiency of the relevant property

3.6 Conclusions

In the absence of knowledge of an occasioning factor grounding the application of a given ruling, *qiyās* forms of *dalāla* and *shabah* are put into action by pinpointing at specific relevant resemblances. These resemblances should make the process of transferring the relevant juridical ruling from the root-case to the branch-case plausible.

In fact, as mentioned above, though these forms of *qiyās* are based on establishing resemblances; the notion of resemblance deployed by *qiyās al-dalāla* is quite different from the one deployed by *qiyās al-shabah.* Indeed, whereas the notion of resemblance deployed by *qiyās al-dalāla* requires making it apparent that root-case and branch-case share some structural parallelism, in the sense that each of both cases fall under the scope of a pair of rulings linked by some structural relation, the kind of resemblance deployed by *qiyas al-shabah* amounts to pointing out one or more relevant properties shared by the root- and the branch-case.

Our use of some elements borrowed from CTT makes brings this to the fore. Indeed, the logical analisis of a thesis justified by a *khaṣīṣa*-link makes it apparent that the particular ruling is a specification of the general ruling.

Notice that the developed form of the branch-case of both of the rulings, namely $\mathbf{L}^*(f, b, c)$ and $\mathbf{L}(f, b)$, shows that the domain of application of the particular ruling, the triad (f, b, c), includes the local reason c that justifies the general ruling – c: $\mathbf{L}(f, b)$.

Similarly when the link is a *naẓīr*-link, the logical analysis shows that $\mathcal{H}^*(f, d,t)$ $\mathcal{H}(f,d',t')$ share the same domain d,d': *Divorce Declarations,* upon which the forms of divorce declaration *ṭalāq* and *ẓihār* are distinguished. Moreover, it is the shared domain that allows quantifying over the bi-implication! $(\forall x: Human)\{ valid(x,d, t) \supset \subset valid\ (x,d',t')\}$, the logical relation that characterizes the parallelism at work in the *qiyās dalāla* by *naẓīr.*

Notice too that on the contrary, that the logical form of the rulings involving *al-shabah* the only link is established is the one established by the posited identity $a \approx_{\wp\, 1\text{-k}} f$ between the branch- and the root-case.

What the dialogical framework adds is an instrument to show how the *indications* and *similarities* justifying a thesis of *qiyās dalāla* and *qiyās shabah* emerge as the result of a dynamic process that extends the domain of application of a ruling. This process as pointed out in our preface should not be understood as *abducing a ruling*.[39] Rather than abduction, the point is to be able to grasp the universal by examining its instantions. This requires the *forum* of a dialectical game where the Proponent is committed to put the indications and similarities justifying his thesis under the public scrutiny of the experts.

As we will discuss in the final remarks our book, it looks that the kind of inferences described are quite close to Paut Bartha's (2010, chapter 4) *Articulation Model* for Analogy in Sciences. This suggests that the scope of application of *qiyās dalāla* and *qiyās shabah* might include cases of inferences by parallelism within natural sciences.

References

Al-Baghdādī, al-Khaṭīb. (1421H). *Al-Faqīh wa al-mutafaqqih*. (Abū ʻAbd al-Raḥmān, Ed.). Saudi: Dār ibn Jauzī.

Al-Shīrāzī, Abū Isḥāq. (1987). *Al-Maʿūna fī al-jadal*. (ʻAlī b. ʿAbd al-ʿAzīz al-ʿUmayrīnī. Al-Safāh, Ed.). Kuwait: Manshūrāt Markaz al-Makhṭūṭāt wa-al-Turāth.

Al-Shīrāzī, Abū Isḥāq. (1988). *Sharḥ al-lumaʻ*. (Abd al-Majīd Turkī, Ed.). Beirut: Dār al-Gharb al-ʻIslāmī.

Al-Shīrāzī, Abū Isḥāq. (2003). *Al-Lumaʿ fī uṣūl al-fiqh*. Beirut: Dār al-Kutub al-ʻIlmiyah.

Al-Shīrāzī, Abū Isḥāq. (2016). *Mulakhkhaṣ fī al-jadal*. Retrieved February 1, 2019 from https://upload.wikimedia.org/wikisource/ar/e/ea/الملخص_في_الجدل_خ.pdf.

Bartha, P. F. A. (2010). *By parallel reasoning. The construction and evaluation of analogical arguments*. Oxford: Oxford University Press.

Bou Akl, Z. (2019). Averroes on juridical reasoning. In P. Adamson & M. Di Giovanni (Eds.), *Interpreting averroes*. Cambridge: Cambridge University Press.

Clerbout, N. (2014a). First-order dialogical games and tableaux. *Journal of Philosophical Logic, 43*(4), 785–801.

Clerbout, N. (2014b). *La Semantiques dialogiques. Notions Fondamentaux et Éléments de Metathéorie*. London: College Publications.

Clerbout, N., & Rahman, S. (2015). *Linking game-theoretical approaches with constructive type theory: Dialogical strategies as CTT-demonstrations*. Dordrecht: Springer.

Felscher, W. (1985). Dialogues as a foundation for intuitionistic logic. In D. Gabbay & F. Guenthner (Eds.), *Handbook of philosophical logic* (Vol. 3, pp. 341–372). Dordrecht: Kluwer.

Fyzee, A. A. A. (1964). *Outlines of Muhammadan law* (3rd ed.). Oxford: Oxford University Press.

Ibn Ḥazm. (1959). *Kitāb al-Taqrīb li-Ḥadd al-Manṭiq wa-l-Mudkhal ilayhi bi-l-alfāẓ al-ʿĀmmiyya wa-l-Amthila al-Fiqhiyya*. (Iḥsān ʿAbbās, Ed.). Beirut: Dār Maktabat al-Ḥayāt.

Ibn Ḥazm. (1926–1930). *Al-Iḥkām fī Uṣūl al-Aḥkām*. 8 vols. (Aḥmad Muḥammad Shākir, Ed.). Cairo: Maṭbaʿat al-Saʿāda.

Keiff, L. (2009). "Dialogical Logic". *The stanford encyclopedia of philosophy*. Ed. Edward Zalta, N. URL https://plato.stanford.edu/entries/logic-dialogical.

Krabbe, E. C. (2006). Dialogue logic. In D. Gabbay & J. Woods (Eds.), *Handbook of the history of logic* (Vol. 7, pp. 665–704). Amsterdam: Elsevier.

Lorenz, K. (2010a). *Logic, language and method: On polarities in human experience*. Berlin/New York: De Gruyter.

[39]For some illuminating paragraphs on this point see Zysow (2013, p. 197).

Lorenz, K. (2010b). *Philosophische Variationen: Gesammelte Aufsätze unter Einschluss gemeinsam mit Jürgen Mittelstraß geschriebener Arbeiten zu Platon und Leibniz*. Berlin/New York: De Gruyter.

Lorenzen, P., & Lorenz, K. (1978). *Dialogische Logik*. Darmstadt: Wissenschaftliche Buchgesellschaft.

Rahman, S., & Iqbal, M. (2018). Unfolding parallel reasoning in Islamic jurisprudence. Epistemic and dialectical meaning within Abū Isḥāq al-Shīrāzī's system of correlational inferences of the occasioning factor. *Cambridge Journal for Arabic Sciences and Philosophy, 28*, 67–132.

Rahman, S., & Keiff, L. (2005). On how to be a dialogician. In D. Vanderveken (Ed.), *Logic, thought and action* (pp. 359–408). Dordrecht: Kluwer.

Rahman, S., & Tulenheimo, T. (2009). From games to dialogues and Back: Towards a general frame for validity. In O. Majer, A. Pietarinen, & T. Tulenheimo (Eds.), *Games: Unifying logic, language and philosophy* (pp. 153–208). Dordrecht: Springer.

Rahman, S., Clerbout, N., & Redmond, J. (2017). Interaction and equality. The dialogical interpretation of CTT (In Spanish). ***Critica***. In print.

Rahman, S., Granström, J. G., & Farjami, A. (2019) legal reasoning and some logic after all. The lessons of the elders. In D. Gabbay, L. Magnani, W. Park and A-V. Pietarinen (eds.), *Natural arguments. A tribute to john woods*. In print.

Rahman, S., McConaughey, Z., Klev, A., & Clerbout, N. (2018). *Immanent reasoning. A plaidoyer for the play level*. Dordrecht: Springer.

Rahman, S., Zidani, F., & Young, W. E. (2019). Ibn Hazm on heteronomous imperative. Landmark in the history of the logical analysis of legal norms. In Armgardt, M. et al (eds.), *Legal reasoning contemporary and ancient perspectives*. Springer. Forthcoming.

Rückert, H. (2011). *Dialogues as a dynamic framework for logic*. London: College Publications.

Young, W. E. (2017). *The dialectical forge. Juridical disputation and the evolution of Islamic law*. Dordrecht: Springer.

Zysow, A. (2013). *The economy of certainty: An introduction to the typology of Islamic legal theory*. Atlanta: Lockwood Press.

Chapter 4
Dialogues, Reasons and Endorsement

Abstract The main aim of the present chapter is to provide a systematic overview on the dialogical framework called *Immanent Reasoning*. Moreover, we would like to suggest that, if we follow the dialogical insight that reasoning and meaning are constituted during interaction, and we develop this insight in a dialogical framework for Martin-Löf's Constructive Type Theory, a conception of knowledge emerges that has important links with Walter Young's (2017) concept of *Dialectical Forge* in the context of Islamic Law. Moreover, both the dialogical approach and the Dialectical Forge seem to be close to Robert Brandom's (1994, 2000) *inferential pragmatism*. The content of the present chapter is basically the same as in Rahman (2019).

4.1 Introduction

The present chapter aims at showing that, if we follow the dialogical insight that reasoning and meaning are constituted during interaction, and we develop this insight in a dialogical framework for Martin-Löf's Constructive Type Theory (CTT)°, a conception of knowledge emerges that has important links with Robert Brandom's (1994, 2000) *inferential pragmatism.*

Indeed according to Brandom (see for example, 2000, chapter 3) attribution of knowledge as determined by *games of giving and asking for reasons* is dependent upon three main conditions.[1]

In fact, the present chapter relies heavily on the main technical and philosophical results of Rahman/McConaugey/Klev/Clerbout (2018). However, some important modifications have been introduced, particularly in the conception of strategic objects. Many thanks to the reviewers, I owe the modifications to their suggestions

---

[1]The relation between dialogical logic and the games of asking and giving reasons has already been pointed out by (Keiff, 2007) and (Marion, 2006, 2009, 2010). See for example:

> *My suggestion is simply that dialogical logic is perfectly suited for a precisification of these 'assertion games'. This opens the way to a 'game-semantical' treatment of the 'game of giving and asking for reasons': 'asking for reasons' corresponds to 'attacks' in dialogical logic, while 'giving reasons' corresponds to 'defences'. In the Erlangen School, attacks*

S. Rahman et al., *Inferences by Parallel Reasoning in Islamic Jurisprudence*, Logic, Argumentation & Reasoning 19, https://doi.org/10.1007/978-3-030-22382-3_4

1. Attribution of those commitments engaged by an assertion
2. Attribution of those entitlements engaged by that assertion
3. Endorsing the assertion and the commitments and entitlements attached to it.

Our task now lies in developing *games of giving and asking for reasons* where some specific moves make explicit the fulfilment of the conditions mentioned above. In fact the dialogical framework already can be seen as displaying such kind of moves in the following way.

1. Commitment corresponds to the defensive move that one player is obliged to, when bringing forward some assertion
2. Entitlement correspond to the right of the adversary to attack that assertion
3. Endorsement corresponds to the so-called formal rule (also known as the Socratic rule).

Actually, as discussed further on in the present paper, in some recent talks Martin-Löf offered some insightful reflections on the contribution of the dialogical approach to the deontic and epistemic interface. More precisely, in his Oslo and Stockholm lectures, Martin-Löf's (2017a, b) condenses the dialogical view on commitments and entitlements that he declines respectively as on one hand *must-requests* (commitments or obligations) and on the other *may-requests* (or entitlements or rights) as follows[2]:

> [. . .] *So, let's call them rules of interaction, in addition to inference rules in the usual sense, which of course remain in place as we are used to them.*
> [. . .] *Now let's turn to the request mood. And then it's simplest to begin directly with the rules, because the explanation is visible directly from the rules. So, the rules that involve request are these, that if someone has made an assertion, then you may question his assertion, the opponent may question his assertion.*
>
> $$(Req1)\quad \frac{\vdash C}{?\vdash_{may} C}$$
>
> *Now we have an example of a rule where we have a may. The other rule says that if we have the assertion* $\vdash C$*, and it has been challenged, then the assertor must execute his knowledge how to do C.* [. . .].

were indeed described as 'rights' and defences as 'duties', so we have the following equivalences:

Right to attack ↔ *asking for reasons*
Duty to defend ↔ *giving reasons*

The point of winning 'assertion games', i.e., successfully defending one's assertion against an opponent, is that one has thus provided a justification or reason for one's assertion. Referring to the title of the book [Making it Explicit], *one could say that playing games of 'giving and asking for reasons' implicitly presupposes abilities that are made explicit through the introduction of logical vocabulary.* (Marion 2010, p. 490).

[2]Ansten Klev's transcription of Martin Löf (2017a, pp. 1-3, 7).

$$(Req1)\quad \frac{\vdash C \qquad ?\vdash C}{\vdash_{must} C'}$$

In relation to the third condition of Brandom, *endorsement*, it involves the use of assertions brought forward by the interlocutor. In this context Göran Sundholm (2013, p. 17) produced the following proposal that embeds Austin's remark (1946, p. 171) on assertion acts in the context of inference:

> *When I say* therefore, *I give others my authority for asserting the conclusion, given theirs for asserting the premisses.*

Herewith, the assertion of one of the interlocutors *entitles* the other one to endorse it. Moreover, in recent lectures, Per Martin-Löf (2015) used this dialogical perspective in order to escape a form of circle threatening the explanation of the notions of inference and demonstration. A demonstration may indeed be explained as a chain of (immediate) inferences starting from no premisses at all. That an inference

$$\frac{J_1 \ldots J_n}{J}$$

is valid means that one can make the conclusion (judgement J) evident on the assumption that $J_1, \ldots, J_n$ are known. Thus the notion of epistemic assumption appears when explaining what a valid inference is. According to this explanation however, we cannot take 'known' in the sense of *demonstrated*, or else we would be explaining the notion of inference in terms of demonstration when demonstration has been explained in terms of inference. Hence the threatening circle. In this regard Martin-Löf suggests taking 'known' here in the sense of *asserted*, which yields epistemic assumptions as judgements others have made, judgements whose responsibility others have already assumed. An inference being valid would accordingly mean that, given others have assumed responsibility for the premisses, I can assume responsibility for the conclusion.

Thus, when explaining the notion of immediate inference we are assuming, not that the premisses have been demonstrated but that they have been asserted by someone else, and this can be endorsed. In a dialogical setting we are thus imagined as acquiring certain knowledge on trust of the Opponent's assertions, on which basis the Proponent may make evident certain further pieces of knowledge. In this solution to the circularity threatening the explanations of demonstration and immediate inference Martin-Löf understands epistemic assumption as assertoric assumption. This goes in hand with Martin-Löf's further point that in the dialogical setting, the deontic force has priority over other layers

Thus, the dialogical framework already seems to offer a formal system where the main features of Brandom's epistemological games can be rendered explicit. However, the system so far does not make explicit the reasons behind an assertion. In order to do so we need to incorporate into the dialogical framework expressions standing for those reasons. This requires combining dialogical logic with Per Martin Löfs Constructive Type Theory (1984) in a more thorough way.

We call the result of such enrichment of the expressive power of the dialogical framework, *dialogues for immanent reasoning* precisely because *reasons* backing a statement, now *explicit* denizens of the object-language of plays, are *internal* to the development of the dialogical interaction itself – see Rahman/McConaugey/Klev/Clerbout (2018).[3]

However, despite the undeniable links of the dialogical framework to both CTT and Brandom's inferentialist approach to meaning there are also some significant differences that are at the center of the dialogical conception of meaning, namely the identification of a level of meaning, i.e. the play-level, that does not reduce to the proof-theoretical one. We will start by presenting the main features of dialogues for immanent reasoning and then we will come back to the general philosophical discussion on the play-level as the core of what is known as *dialogue-definiteness*.

The present paper does not discuss explicitly phenomenology, however, Mohammad Shafiei (2017) developed in his thesis: *Intentionnalité et signification: Une approche dialogique*, a thorough study of the bearing of the dialogical framework for phenomenology. Nevertheless, his work did not deploy the new development we call *immanent reasoning*. So, one might see our proposal as setting the basis for a further study linking phenomenology and the dialogical conception of meaning.

4.2 Local Reasons

Recent developments in dialogical logic show that the Constructive Type Theory approach to meaning is very natural to the game-theoretical approaches in which (standard) metalogical features are explicitly displayed at the object language-level.[4] This vindicates, albeit in quite a different fashion, Hintikka's plea for the fruitfulness of game-theoretical semantics in the context of epistemic approaches to logic, semantics, and the foundations of mathematics.[5]

From the dialogical point of view, the actions—such as choices—that the particle rules associate with the use of logical constants are crucial elements of their full-fledged (local) meaning: if meaning is conceived as constituted during interaction, then all of the actions involved in the constitution of the meaning of an expression should be made explicit; that is, they should all be part of the object-language.

This perspective roots itself in Wittgenstein's remark according to which one cannot position oneself outside language in order to determine the meaning of something and how it is linked to syntax; in other words, language is unavoidable: this is his Unhintergehbarkeit der Sprache. According to this perspective of Wittgensteins, language-games are supposed to accomplish the task of studying language from a perspective that acknowledges its internalized feature. This is what

[3]In fact, the present paper relies heavily on the main technical and philosophical results of Rahman/McConaugey/Klev/Clerbout (2018). However, some important modifications have been introduced, particularly in the conception of strategic objects. Many thanks to the reviewers of the present paper, I owe the modifications to their suggestions.

[4]Such as developed in Rahman/McConaugey/Klev/Clerbout (2018) and also in Clerbout/Rahman (2015).

[5]Cf. Hintikka (1973).

underlies the approach to meaning and syntax of the dialogical framework in which all the speech-acts that are relevant for rendering the meaning and the "formation" of an expression are made explicit. In this respect, the metalogical perspective which is so crucial for model-theoretic conceptions of meaning does not provide a way out. It is in such a context that Lorenz writes:

> *Also propositions of the metalanguage require the understanding of propositions,* [...] *and thus cannot in a sensible way have this same understanding as their proper object. The thesis that a property of a propositional sentence must always be internal, therefore amounts to articulating the insight that in propositions about a propositional sentence this same propositional sentence does not express a meaningful proposition anymore, since in this case it is not the propositional sentence that is asserted but something about it.*
>
> *Thus, if the original assertion (i.e., the proposition of the ground-level) should not be abrogated, then this same proposition should not be the object of a metaproposition* [...].[6]
>
> *While originally the semantics developed by the picture theory of language aimed at determining unambiguously the rules of "logical syntax" (i.e. the logical form of linguistic expressions) and thus to justify them* [...]*—now language use itself, without the mediation of theoretic constructions, merely via "language games", should be sufficient to introduce the talk about "meanings" in such a way that they supplement the syntactic rules for the use of ordinary language expressions (superficial grammar) with semantic rules that capture the understanding of these expressions (deep grammar).*[7]

Similar criticism to the metalogical approach to meaning has been raised by Göran Sundholm (1997, 2001) who points out that the standard model-theoretical semantic turns semantics into a meta-mathematical formal object in which syntax is linked to meaning by the assignation of truth values to uninterpreted strings of signs (formulae). Language does not express content anymore, but it is rather conceived as a system of signs that speak about the world—provided a suitable metalogical link between the signs and the world has been fixed.

Ranta (1988) was the first to link game-theoretical approaches with CTT. Ranta took Hintikka's (1973) Game-Theoretical Semantics (GTS) as a case study, though his point does not depend on that particular framework: in game-based approaches, a proposition is a set of winning strategies for the player stating the proposition. In game-based approaches, the notion of truth is at the level of such winning strategies. Ranta's idea should therefore in principle allow us to apply, safely and directly, instances of game-based methods taken from CTT to the pragmatist approach of the dialogical framework.

From the perspective of a general game-theoretical approach to meaning however, reducing a proposition to a set of winning strategies is quite unsatisfactory. This is particularly clear in the dialogical approach in which different levels of meaning are carefully distinguished: there is indeed the level of strategies, but there is also the level of plays in the analysis of meaning which can be further analysed into local, global and material levels. The constitutive role of the play level for developing a meaning-explanation has been stressed by Kuno Lorenz in his (2001) paper:

---

[6]Lorenz (1970, p. 75), translated from the German by Shahid Rahman.

[7]Lorenz (1970, p. 109), translated from the German by Shahid Rahman.

> *Fully spelled out it means that for an entity to be a proposition there must exist a dialogue game associated with this entity, i.e., the proposition A, such that an individual play of the game where A occupies the initial position, i.e., a dialogue D(A) about A, reaches a final position with either win or loss after a finite number of moves according to definite rules: the dialogue game is defined as a finitary open two-person zero-sum game. Thus, propositions will in general be dialogue-definite, and only in special cases be either proof-definite or refutation-definite or even both which implies their being value-definite.*
>
> *Within this game-theoretic framework* [. . .] *truth of A is defined as existence of a winning strategy for A in a dialogue game about A; falsehood of A respectively as existence of a winning strategy against A.*[8]

Given the distinction between the play level and the strategy level, and deploying within the dialogical framework the CTT-explicitation program, it seems natural to distinguish between local reasons and strategic reasons: only the latter correspond to the notion of proof-object in CTT and to the notion of strategic-object of Ranta. In order to develop such a project we enrich the language of the dialogical framework with statements of the form "$p : A$". In such expressions, what stands on the left-hand side of the colon (here p) is what we call a local reason; what stands on the right-hand side of the colon (here A) is a proposition (or set).

The local meaning of such statements results from the rules describing how to compose (synthesis) within a play the suitable local reasons for the proposition A and how to separate (analysis) a complex local reason into the elements required by the composition rules for A. The synthesis and analysis processes of A are built on the formation rules for A.

The most basic contribution of a local reason is its contribution to a dialogue involving an elementary proposition. Informally, we can say that if the Proponent **P** states the elementary proposition A, it is because **P** claims that he can bring forward a reason in defence of his statement, it is this reason that provides content to the proposition.

4.2.1 *Local Meaning and Local Reasons*

Statements in Dialogues for Immanent Reasoning

Dialogues are games of giving and asking for reasons; yet in the standard dialogical framework, the reasons for each statement are left implicit and do not appear in the notation of the statement: we have statements of the form **X** ! A for instance where A is an elementary proposition. The framework of dialogues for immanent reasoning allows to have explicitly the reason for making a statement, statements then have the form **X** $a : A$ for instance where a is the (local) reason **X** has for stating the proposition A. But even in dialogues for immanent reasoning, all reasons are not always provided, and sometimes statements have only implicit reasons for bringing the proposition forward, taking then the same form as in the standard dialogical

[8] Lorenz (2001, p. 258).

framework: **X** ! *A*. Notice that when (local) reasons are not explicit, an exclamation mark is added before the proposition: the statement then has an implicit reason for being made.

A statement is thus both a proposition and its local reason, but this reason may be left implicit, requiring then the use of the exclamation mark.

Adding Concessions
In the context of the dialogical conception of CTT we also have statements of the form.

$$\mathbf{X}!\pi(x_1, \ldots, x_n)\ [x_i : A_i].$$

where "π" stands for some statement in which $(x_1, \ldots, x_n)$ ocurs, and where $[x_i: A_i]$ stands for some condition under which the statement $\pi(x_1, \ldots, x_n)$ has been brought forward. Thus, the statement reads:

X states that $\pi(x_1, \ldots, x_n)$ under the condition that the antagonist concedes x_i: A_i.

We call *required concessions* the statements of the form $[x_i: A_i]$ that condition a claim. When the statement is challenged, the antagonist is accepting, through his own challenge, to bring such concessions forward. The concessions of the thesis, if any, are called *initial concessions*. Initial concessions can include formation statements such as *A*: *prop*, *B*: *prop*, for the thesis, $A \supset B$: *prop*.

Formation Rules for Local Reasons: An Informal Overview
It is presupposed in standard dialogical systems that the players use well-formed formulas (*wff*). The well formation can be checked at will, but only with the usual meta reasoning by which one checks that the formula does indeed observe the definition of a *wff*. We want to enrich our CTT-based dialogical framework by allowing players themselves to first enquire on the formation of the components of a statement within a play. We thus start with dialogical rules explaining the formation of statements involving logical constants (the formation of *elementary* propositions is governed by the Socratic rule, see the discussion above on material truth). In this way, the well formation of the thesis can be examined by the Opponent before running the actual dialogue: as soon as she challenges it, she is *de facto* accepting the thesis to be well formed (the most obvious case being the challenge of the implication, where she has to state the antecedent and thus explicitly endorse it). The Opponent can ask for the formation of the thesis before launching her first challenge; defending the formation of his thesis might for instance bring the Proponent to state that the thesis is a proposition, provided, say, that *A **is a set*** is conceded; the Opponent might then concede that *A is a **set***, but only after the constitution of *A* has been established, though if this were the case, we would be considering the constitution of an elementary statement, which is a material consideration, not a formal one.

These considerations yield the following condensed presentation of the logical constants (plus *falsum*), in which "$\mathcal{K}$" in $A\mathcal{K}B$" expresses a connective, and "$\mathcal{Q}$" in "$(\mathcal{Q}x: A)\ B(x)$" expresses a quantifier.

Formation rules, condensed presentation

	Connective	Quantifier	Falsum
Move	**X** $A \mathfrak{K} B$: *prop*	**X** $(\mathfrak{Q}x: A)\ B(x)$: *prop*	**X** $\perp$: *prop*
Challenge	**Y** $?_{F\kappa 1}$ and/or **Y** $?_{F\kappa 2}$	**Y** $?_{F\mathfrak{Q}1}$ and/or **Y** $?_{F\mathfrak{Q}2}$	—
Defence	**X** A: *prop* (resp.) **X** B: *prop*	**X** A: *set* (resp.) **X** $B(x)$: $prop(x: A)$	—

Synthesis of Local Reasons

The synthesis rules of local reasons determine how to produce a local reason for a statement; they include rules of interaction indicating how to produce the local reason that is required by the proposition (or set) in play, that is, they indicate what kind of dialogical action—what kind of move—must be carried out, by whom (challenger or defender), and what reason must be brought forward.

Implication For instance, the synthesis rule of a local reason for the implication $A \supset B$ stated by player **X** indicates:

(i) that the challenger **Y** must state the antecedent (while providing a local reason for it): **Y** p_1: A.[9]
(ii) that the defender **X** must respond to the challenge by stating the consequent (with its corresponding local reason): **X** p_2: B.

In other words, the rules for the synthesis of a local reason for implication are as follows:

Synthesis of a local reason for implication

	Implication
Move	**X** ! $A \supset B$
Challenge	**Y** p_1: A
Defence	**X** p_2: B

Notice that the initial statement (**X**! $A \supset B$) *does not* display a local reason for the claim the the implication holds: player **X** simply states that he has some reason supporting the claim. We express such kind of move by adding an *exclamation mark* before the proposition. The further dialogical actions indicate the moves required for producing a local reason in defence of the initial claim.

[9]This notation is a variant of the one used by Keiff (2004, 2009).

Conjunction The synthesis rule for the conjunction is straightforward:

Synthesis of a local reason for conjunction

	Conjunction
Move	**X** ! $A \wedge B$
Challenge	**Y** ? $L^{\wedge}$ or **Y** ? $R^{\wedge}$
Defence	**X** p_1: A (resp.) **X** p_2: B

Disjunction For disjunction, as we know from the standard rules, it is the defender who will choose which side he wishes to defend: the challenge consists in requesting of the defender that he chooses which side he will be defending. The point is that each choice is sufficient for defending the claim on the disjunction:

Synthesis of a local reason for disjunction

	Disjunction
Move	**X** ! $A \vee B$
Challenge	**Y** $?_{\vee}$
Defence	**X** p_1: A or **X** p_2: B

The General Structure for the Synthesis of Local Reasons

More generally, the rules for the synthesis of a local reason for a constant $\mathcal{K}$ is determined by the following triplet:

General structure for the synthesis of a local reason for a constant

	A constant $\mathcal{K}$	Implication	Conjunction	Disjunction
Move	**X** ! $\varphi[\mathcal{K}]$ *X claims that* ϕ	**X** ! $A \supset B$	**X** ! $A \wedge B$	**X** ! $A \vee B$
Challenge	*Y asks for the reason backing such a claim*	**Y** p_1: A	**Y** ? $L^{\wedge}$ or **Y** ? $R^{\wedge}$	**Y** $?_{\vee}$
Defence	**X** p: $\varphi[\mathcal{K}]$ *X states the local reason p for $\varphi[\mathcal{K}]$ according to the rules for the synthesis of local reasons prescribed for $\mathcal{K}$.*	**X** p_2: B	**X** p_1: A (resp.) **X** p_2: B	**X** p_1: A or **X** p_2: B

Analysis of Local Reasons

Apart from the rules for the synthesis of local reasons, we need rules that indicate how to parse a complex local reason into its elements: this is the *analysis* of local reasons. In order to deal with the complexity of these local reasons and formulate general rules for the analysis of local reasons (at the play level), we introduce certain operators that we call *instructions*, such as $L^{\vee}(p)$ or $R^{\wedge}(p)$.

Approaching the Analysis Rules for Local Reasons

Let us introduce these instructions and the analysis of local reasons with an example: player **X** states the implication $(A \wedge B) \supset B$. According to the rule for the synthesis of local reasons for an implication, we obtain the following:

Move	**X** ! $(A \wedge B) \supset B$
Challenge	**Y** p_1: $A \wedge B$

Recall that the synthesis rule prescribes that **X** must now provide a local reason for the consequent; but instead of defending his implication (with **X** $p_2 : B$ for instance), **X** can choose to parse the reason p_1 provided by **Y** in order to force **Y** to provide a local reason for the right-hand side of the conjunction that **X** will then be able to copy; in other words, **X** can force **Y** to provide the local reason for B out of the local reason p_1 for the antecedent $A \wedge B$ of the initial implication. The analysis rules prescribe how to carry out such a parsing of the statement by using *instructions*. The rule for the analysis of a local reason for the conjunction $p_1 : A \wedge B$ will thus indicate that its defence includes expressions such as.

- the left instruction for the conjunction, written $L^{\wedge}(p_1)$, and
- the right instruction for the conjunction, written $R^{\wedge}(p_1)$.

These instructions can be informally understood as carrying out the following step: for the defence of the conjunction $p_1 : A \wedge B$ separate the local reason p_1 on its left (or right) component so that this component can be adduced in defence of the left (or right) side of the conjunction.

Here is a play with local reasons for the thesis $(A \wedge B) \supset B$ using instructions:

	O			**P**	
				! $(A \wedge B) \supset B$	0
1	$m := 1$			$n := 2$	2
3	p_1: $A \wedge B$	0		$R^{\wedge}(p_1)$: B	6
5	$R^{\wedge}(p_1)$: B		3	? $R^{\wedge}$	4

P wins.

In this play, **P** uses the analysis of local reasons for conjunction in order to force **O** to state $R^{\wedge}(p_1) : B$, that is to provide a local reason[10] for the elementary statement B; **P** can then copy that local reason in order to back his statement B, the consequent of his initial implication. With these local reasons, we explicitly have in the object-language the reasons that are given and asked for and which constitute the essence of an argumentative dialogue.

The general structure for the analysis rules of local reasons

	Move	Challenge	Defence
Conjunction	**X** $p: A \wedge B$	**Y** ? $L^{\wedge}$ or **Y** ? $R^{\wedge}$	**X** $L^{\wedge}(p): A$ (resp.) **X** $R^{\wedge}(p): B$
Disjunction	**X** $p: A \vee B$	**Y** $?_{\vee}$	**X** $L^{\vee}(p): A$ or **X** $R^{\vee}(p): B$
Implication	**X** $p: A \supset B$	**Y** $L^{\supset}(p): A$	**X** $R^{\supset}(p): B$

Interaction Procedures Embedded in Instructions
Carrying out the prescriptions indicated by instructions require the following three interaction-procedures:

1. *Resolution of instructions*: this procedure determines how to carry out the instructions prescribed by the rules of analysis and thus provide an actual local reason.
2. *Substitution of instructions*: this procedure ensures the following; once a given instruction has been carried out through the choice of a local reason, say b, then every time the same instruction occurs, it will always be substituted by the same local reason b.
3. *Application of the Socratic rule*: the Socratic rule prescribes how to constitute equalities out of the resolution and substitution of instructions, linking synthesis and analysis together.

Let us discuss how these rules interact and how they lead to the main thesis of this study, namely that immanent reasoning is equality in action.

From Reasons to Equality: A New Visit to Endorsement
One of the most salient features of dialogical logic is the so-called, *Socratic rule* (or Copy-cat rule or rule for *the formal use of elementary propositions* in the

[10]Speaking of local reasons is a little premature at this stage, since only instructions are provided and not actual local reasons; but the purpose is here to give the general idea of local reasons, and instructions are meant to be resolved into proper local reasons, which requires only an extra step.

standard—that is, non-CTT—context), establishing that the Proponent can play an elementary proposition only if the Opponent has played it previously.

The Socratic rule is a characteristic feature of the dialogical approach: other game-based approaches do not have it and it relates to *endorsing* condition mentioned in the introduction. With this rule the dialogical framework comes with an internal account of elementary propositions: an account in terms of interaction only, without depending on metalogical meaning explanations for the non-logical vocabulary.

The rule has a clear Platonist and Aristotelian origin and sets the terms for what it is to carry out a *formal argument*: see for instance Plato's *Gorgias* (472b-c). We can sum up the underlying idea with the following statement:

> *There is no better grounding of an assertion within an argument than indicating that it has been already conceded by the Opponent or that it follows from these concessions.*[11]

What should be stressed here are the following two points:

1. formality is understood as a kind of *interaction*; and
2. formal reasoning *should not* be understood here as devoid of content and reduced to purely syntactic moves.

Both points are important in order to understand the criticism often raised against formal reasoning in general, and in logic in particular. It is only quite late in the history of philosophy that formal reasoning has been reduced to syntactic manipulation— presumably the first explicit occurrence of the syntactic view of logic is Leibniz's "pensée aveugle" (though Leibniz's notion was not a reductive one). Plato and Aristotle's notion of formal reasoning is neither "static" nor "empty of meaning". In the Ancient Greek tradition logic emerged from an approach of assertions in which meaning and justification result from what has been brought forward during argumentative interaction. According to this view, dialogical interaction is constitutive of meaning.

Some former interpretations of standard dialogical logic did understand formal plays in a purely syntactic manner. The reason for this is that the standard version of the framework is not equipped to express meaning at the object-language level: there is no way of asking and giving reasons for elementary propositions. As a consequence, the standard formulation simply relies on a syntactic understanding of *Copy-cat moves*, that is, moves entitling **P** to copy the elementary propositions brought forward by **O**, regardless of its content.

The dialogical approach to CTT (dialogues for immanent reasoning) however provides a fine-grain study of the contentual aspects involved in formal plays, much finer than the one provided by the standard dialogical framework. In dialogues for immanent reasoning which we are now presenting, a statement is constituted both by a proposition and by the (local) reason brought forward in defence of the claim that

[11]Recent researches on deploying the dialogical framework for the study of history of logic claim that this rule is central to the interpretation of dialectic as the core of Aristotle's logic – see Crubellier (2014, pp. 11-40) and Marion and Rückert (2015).

the proposition holds. In formal plays not only is the Proponent allowed to copy an elementary proposition stated by the Opponent, as in the standard framework, but he is also allowed to adduce in defence of that proposition the *same* local reason brought forward by the Opponent when she defended that same proposition. Thus immanent reasoning and equality in action are intimately linked. In other words, a formal play displays the *roots of the content* of an elementary proposition, and *not* a syntactic manipulation of that proposition.

Statements of definitional equality emerge precisely at this point. In particular reflexivity statements such as.

$p = p$: A.

express from the dialogical point of view the fact that if **O** states the elementary proposition A, then **P** can do the same, that is, play the same move and do it on the same grounds which provide the meaning and justification of A, namely p.

These remarks provide an insight only on simple forms of equality and barely touch upon the finer-grain distinctions discussed above; we will be moving to these by means of a concrete example in which we show, rather informally, how the combination of the processes of analysis, synthesis, and resolution of instructions lead to equality statements.

Example

Assume that the Proponent brings forward the thesis $(A \wedge B) \supset (B \wedge A)$:

	O			**P**	
				! $(A \wedge B) \supset (B \wedge A)$	0

Both players then choose their repetition ranks:

	O			**P**	
				! $(A \wedge B) \supset (B \wedge A)$	0
1	$m := 1$			$n := 2$	2

O must now challenge the implication if she accepts to enter into the discussion. The rule for the synthesis of a local reason for implication (provided above) stipulates that in order to challenge the thesis, **O** must state the antecedent *and provide a local reason for it*:

Synthesis of a local reason for conjunction

	O			**P**	
				! $(A \wedge B) \supset (B \wedge A)$	0
1	$m := 1$			$n := 2$	2
3	p_1: $A \wedge B$	0			

According to the same synthesis-rule **P** must now state the consequent, which he is allowed to do because the consequent is not elementary:

O			**P**		
				$! (A \wedge B) \supset (B \wedge A)$	0
1	$m := 1$			$n := 2$	2
3	p_1: $A \wedge B$	0		q: $B \wedge A$	4

The Opponent launches her challenge asking for the left component of the local reason q provided by **P**, an application of the rule for the *analysis* of a local reason for a conjunction described above.

Analysis of a local reason for conjunction

O			**P**		
				$! (A \wedge B) \supset (B \wedge A)$	0
1	$m := 1$			$n := 2$	2
3	p: $A \wedge B$	0		q: $B \wedge A$	4
5	? $L^\wedge$	4			

Assume that **P** responds immediately to this challenge:

O			**P**		
				$! (A \wedge B) \supset (B \wedge A)$	0
1	$m := 1$			$n := 2$	2
3	p: $A \wedge B$	0		q: $B \wedge A$	4
5	? $L^\wedge$	4		$L^\wedge(q)$: B	6

O will now ask for the *resolution of the instruction*:

Resolution of an instruction

O			**P**		
				$! (A \wedge B) \supset (B \wedge A)$	0
1	$m := 1$			$n := 2$	2
3	p: $A \wedge B$	0		q: $B \wedge A$	4
5	? $L^\wedge$	4		$L^\wedge(q)$: B	6
7	? .../$L^\wedge(q)$	6			

In this move 7, **O** is asking **P** to carry out the instruction $L^{\wedge}(q)$ by bringing forward the local reason of his choice. The act of choosing such a reason and replacing the instruction for it is called *resolving the instruction*.

In this case, resolving the instruction will lead **P** to bring forward an *elementary statement*—that is, a statement in which *both* the local reason and the proposition are elementary, which falls under the restriction of the Socratic rule. The idea for **P** then is to postpone his answer to the challenge launched with move 7 and to force **O** to choose a local reason first so as to copy it in his answer to the challenge. This yields a further application of the *analysis rule* for the conjunction:

		O			**P**		
					$! (A \wedge B) \supset (B \wedge A)$	0	
	1	$m := 1$			$n := 2$	2	
	3	$p: A \wedge B$	0		$q: B \wedge A$	4	
	5	$? L^{\wedge}$	4		$L^{\wedge}(q): B$	6	
	7	$? .../L^{\wedge}(q)$	6		$b: B$	12	
O responds according to the *analysis rule*	9	$R^{\wedge}(p): B$	3		$? R^{\wedge}$	8	**P** launches his challenge asking for the right side of the concession move 3
O responds to the challenge by choosing the local reason b	11	$b: B$	9		$? .../R^{\wedge}(p)$	10	**P** asks **O** to resolve the instruction by providing a local reason

P wins.

Move 11 thus provides **P** with the information he needed: he can then copy **O**'s choice to answer the challenge she launched at move 7.

Note: *It should be clear that a similar end will come about if **O** starts by challenging the right component of the conjunction statement, instead of challenging the left component.*

Analysis of the Example

Let us now go deeper in the analysis of the example and make explicit what happened during the play:

When **O** resolves $R^{\wedge}(p)$ with the local reason b (for instance) and **P** resolves the instruction $L^{\wedge}(q)$ with the same local reason, then **P** is not only stating b: B but he is doing this by choosing b as local reason for B, that is, by choosing *exactly the same* local reason as **O** for the resolution of $R^{\wedge}(p)$.

Let us assume that **O** can ask **P** to make his choice for a given local reason explicit. **P** would then answer that his choice for his local reason depends on **O**'s own choice: he simply copied what **O** considered to be a local reason for B, that is $R^{\wedge}(p)^{O} = b : B$. The application of the Socratic rule yields in this respect definitional equality. This rule prescribes the following response to a challenge on an elementary local reason:

When **O** challenges an elementary statement of **P** such as b: B, **P** must be able to bring forward a definitional equality such as **P** $R^{\wedge}(p) = b$: B.

Which reads:

P grounds his choice of the local reason b for the proposition B in **O**'s resolution of the instruction $R^{\wedge}(p)$. At the very end **P**'s choice is the *same local reason* brought forward by **O** for the same proposition B.

In other words, the definitional equality $R^{\wedge}(p)^{O} = b : B$ that provides content to B makes it explicit at the object-language level that an application of the Socratic rule has been initiated and achieved by means of dialogical interaction.

The development of a dialogue determined by immanent reasoning thus includes four distinct stages:

1. applying the rules of synthesis to the thesis;
2. applying the rules of analysis;
3. launching the Resolution and Substitution of instructions;
4. applying the Socratic rule.
5. We can then add a fifth stage: Producing the strategic reason.

While the first two steps involve local meaning, step 3 concerns global meaning and step 4 requires describing how to produce a winning strategy. Now that the general idea of local reasons has been provided, we will present in the next chapter all the rules together, according to their level of meaning.

4.2.2 The Dialogical Roots of Equality: Dialogues for Immanent Reasoning

In this section we will spell out a *simplified version* of the dialogues for immanent reasoning, that is, the dialogical framework incorporating features of Constructive Type Theory—a dialogical framework making the players' reasons for asserting a proposition explicit. The rules can be divided, just as in the standard framework, into rules determining local meaning and rules determining global meaning. These include:

1. Concerning *local meaning*
   (a) formation rules;
   (b) rules for the synthesis of local reasons; and
   (c) rules for the analysis of local reasons.
2. Concerning *global meaning*, we have the following (structural) rules:
   (a) rules for the resolution of instructions;
   (b) rules for the substitution of instructions;
   (c) equality rules determined by the application of the Socratic rules.

We will be presenting these rules in this order in the next two sections, along with the adaptation of the other structural rules to dialogues for immanent reasoning in the second section.

4.2.2.1 Local Meaning in Dialogues for Immanent Reasoning

4.2.2.1.1 The Formation Rules

The formation rules for *logical constants* and for *falsum* are given in the following table. Notice that a statement '⊥ : **prop**' cannot be challenged; this is the dialogical account for falsum '⊥' being by definition a proposition.

Formation rules

	Move	Challenge	Defence
Conjunction	**X** $A \wedge B$: ***prop***	**Y** ? $F_{\wedge 1}$ or **Y** ? $F_{\wedge 2}$	**X** A: ***prop*** (resp.) **X** B: ***prop***
Disjunction	**X** $A \vee B$: ***prop***	**Y** ? $F_{\vee 1}$ or **Y** ? $F_{\vee 2}$	**X** A: ***prop*** (resp.) **X** B: ***prop***
Implication	**X** $A \supset B$: ***prop***	**Y** ? $F_{\supset 1}$ or **Y** ? $F_{\supset 2}$	**X** A: ***prop*** (resp.) **X** B: ***prop***
Universal quantification	**X** $(\forall x: A)B(x)$: ***prop***	**Y** ? $F_{\forall 1}$ or **Y** ? $F_{\forall 2}$	**X** A: ***set*** (resp.) **X** $B(x)$: ***prop*** $[x: A]$
Existential quantification	**X** $(\exists x: A)B(x)$: ***prop***	**Y** ? $F_{\exists 1}$ or **Y** ? $F_{\exists 2}$	**X** A: ***set*** (resp.) **X** $B(x)$: ***prop*** $[x: A]$
Falsum	**X** ⊥: ***prop***	–	–

4.2.2.1.2 The Substitution Rule within Dependent Statements

The following rule is not really a formation-rule but is very useful while applying formation rules where one statement is dependent upon the other such as $B(x)$: ***prop*** $[x : A]$.[12]

[12] This rule is an expression at the level of plays of the rule for the substitution of variables in a hypothetical judgement. See Martin-Löf (1984, pp. 9-11).

Substitution rule within dependent statements (subst-D)

	Move	Challenge	Defence
Subst-D	**X** $\pi(x_1, \ldots, x_n)[x_i: A_i]$	**Y** $\tau_1: A_1, \ldots, \tau_n: A_n)$	**X** $\pi(\tau_1, \ldots, \tau_n)$

In the formulation of this rule, "π" is a statement and "τ_i" is a local reason of the form either $a_i : A_i$ or $x_i : A_i$.

A particular case of the application of Subst-D is when the challenger simply chooses the same local reasons as those occurring in the concession of the initial statement. This is particularly useful in the case of formation plays:

4.2.2.1.3 The Rules for Local Reasons: Synthesis and Analysis

Now that the dialogical account of formation rules has been clarified, we may further develop our analysis of plays by introducing local reasons. Let us do so by providing the rules that prescribe the synthesis and analysis of local reasons.

Synthesis rules for local reasons

	Move	Challenge	Defence
Conjunction	**X !** $A \wedge B$	**Y** ? $L^{\wedge}$ or **Y** ? $R^{\wedge}$	**X** $p_1: A$ (resp.) **X** $p_2: B$
Existential quantification	**X** ! $(\exists x: A)B(x)$	**Y** ? $L^{\exists}$ or **Y** ? $R^{\exists}$	**X** $p_1: A$ (resp.) **X** $p_2: B(p_1)$
Disjunction	**X !** $A \vee B$	**Y** ?$^{\vee}$	**X** $p_1: A$ (or) **X** $p_2: B$
Implication	**X !** $A \supset B$	**Y** $p_1: A$	**X** $p_2: B$
Universal quantification	**X** ! $(\forall x: A)B(x)$	**Y** $p_1: A$	**X** $p_2: B(p_1)$
Negation	**X !** $\bot A$ Also expressed as **X !** $A \supset \bot$	**Y** $p_1: A$	**X** $p_2: \bot$

Analysis rules for local reasons

	Move	Challenge	Defence
Conjunction	**X** p: $A \wedge B$	**Y** ? $L^{\wedge}$ or **Y** ? $R^{\wedge}$	**X** $L^{\wedge}(p)$: A (resp.) **X** $R^{\wedge}(p)$: B
Existential quantification	**X** p: $(\exists x: A)B(x)$	**Y** ? $L^{\exists}$ or **Y** ? $R^{\exists}$	**X** $L^{\exists}(p)$: A (resp.) **X** $R^{\exists}(p)$: $B(L^{\exists}(p))$
Disjunction	**X** p: $A \vee B$	**Y** $?^{\vee}$	**X** $L^{\vee}(p)$: A (or) **X** $R^{\vee}(p)$: B
Implication	**X** p: $A \supset B$	**Y** $L^{\supset}(p)$: A	**X** $R^{\supset}(p)$: B
Universal quantification	**X** p: $(\forall x: A)B(x)$	**Y** $L^{\forall}(p)$: A	**X** $R^{\forall}(p)$: $B(L^{\forall}(p))$
Negation	**X** p: $\neg A$ Also expressed as **X** p: $A \supset \bot$	**Y** $L^{\neg}(p)$: A **Y** $L^{\supset}(p)$: A	**X** $R^{\neg}(p)$: $\bot$ **X** $R^{\supset}(p)$: $\bot$ Which amounts to stating **X** ! $\bot$[a]

[a]The general point of deleting the instruction in **X** $R^{\supset}(p)$: $\bot$ is that instructions occurring in expressions stating **falsum** keep un-resolved – see below structural rule SR3 on resolutions, item 3

Anaphoric Instructions: Dealing with Cases of Anaphora

One of the most salient features of the CTT framework is that it contains the means to deal with cases of anaphora. For example anaphoric expressions are required for formalizing *Barbara* in CTT. In the following CTT-formalization of *Barbara* the projection fst(z) can be seen as the tail of the anaphora whose head is *z*:

$(\forall z : (\exists x : D)A)B[\text{fst}(z)]$ true	premise 1
$(\forall z : (\exists x : D)B)C[\text{fst}(z)]$ true	premise 2
$(\forall z : (\exists x : D)A)C[\text{fst}(z)]$ true	conclusion

In dialogues for immanent reasoning, when a local reason has been made explicit, this kind of anaphoric expression is formalized through instructions, which provides a further reason for introducing them. For example if p is the local reason for the first premise we have.

P p: $(\forall z: (\exists x: D)A(x))B(L^{\exists}(L^{\forall}(p)^{\mathbf{O}}))$.

However, since the thesis of a play does not bear an explicit local reason (we use the exclamation mark to indicate there is an implicit one), it is possible for a statement to be bereft of an explicit local reason. When there is no explicit local reason for a statement using anaphora, we cannot bind the instruction $L^{\forall}(p)^{\mathbf{O}}$ to a local reason p. We thus have something like this, with a blank space instead of the anaphoric local reason:

$$\mathbf{P}!(\forall z : (\exists x : D)A(x)\Big)B\Big(L^{\exists}(L^{\forall}()^{\mathbf{O}})\Big).$$

But this blank stage can be circumvented: the challenge on the universal quantifier will yield the required local reason: O will provide $a : (\exists x : D)A(x)$, which is the local reason for z. We can therefore bind the instruction on the missing local reason with the corresponding variable—z in this case—and write.

$$\mathbf{P}!(\forall z : (\exists x : D)A(x))B\Big(L^{\exists}\Big(L^{\forall}(z)^{\mathbf{O}}\Big)\Big).$$

We call this kind of instruction, Anaphoric instructions. For the substitution of Anaphoric instructions the following two cases are to be distinguished:

Substitution of Anaphoric Instructions 1
Given some Anaphoric instruction such as $L^{\forall}(z)^{\mathbf{Y}}$, once the quantifier $(\forall z : A)B(\ldots)$ has been challenged by the statement a: A, the occurrence of $L^{\forall}(z)^{\mathbf{Y}}$ can be substituted by a. The same applies to other instructions.

In our example we obtain:

$$\mathbf{P}!(\forall z : (\exists x : D)A(x))B\Big(L^{\exists}\Big(L^{\forall}(z)^{\mathbf{O}}\Big)\Big)$$

$$\mathbf{O}\; a : (\exists x : D)A(x)$$

$$\mathbf{P}\; b : B\Big(L^{\exists}\Big(L^{\forall}(z)^{\mathbf{O}}\Big)\Big)$$

$$\mathbf{O}?a/L^{\forall}(z)^{\mathbf{O}}$$

$$\mathbf{P}\; b : B\big(L^{\exists}(a)\big)$$

...

Substitution of Anaphoric Instructions 2
Given some Anaphoric instruction such as $L^{\forall}(z)^{\mathbf{Y}}$, once the instruction $L^{\forall}(c)$— resulting from an attack on the universal $\forall z$: φ — has been resolved with a: φ, then any occurrence of $L^{\forall}(z)^{\mathbf{Y}}$ can be substituted by a. The same applies to other instructions.

4.2.2.2 Global Meaning in Dialogues for Immanent Reasoning

We here provide the structural rules for dialogues for immanent reasoning, which determine the global meaning in such a framework. They are for the most part similar in principle to the precedent logical framework for dialogues; the rules concerning instructions are an addition for dialogues for immanent reasoning.

4.2.2.2.1 Structural Rules

SR0: Starting rule

The start of a formal dialogue of immanent reasoning is a move where **P** states the thesis. The thesis can be stated under the condition that **O** commits herself to certain other statements called initial concessions; in this case the thesis has the form ! A [$B_1, \ldots, B_n$], where A is a statement with implicit local reason and B_1, . . ., B_n are statements with or without implicit local reasons.

A dialogue with a thesis proposed under some conditions starts if and only if **O** accepts these conditions. **O** accepts the conditions by stating the initial concessions in moves numbered 0.1, . . ., 0.n before choosing the repetition ranks.

After having stated the thesis (and the initial concessions, if any), each player chooses in turn a positive integer called the repetition rank which determines the upper boundary for the number of attacks and of defences each player can make in reaction to each move during the play.

SR1: Development rule

The Development rule depends on what kind of logic is chosen: if the game uses intuitionistic logic, then it is SR1i that should be used; but if classical logic is used, then SR1c must be used.

SR1i: Intuitionistic Development rule, or Last Duty First

Players play one move alternately. Any move after the choice of repetition ranks is either an attack or a defence according to the rules of formation, of synthesis, and of analysis, and in accordance with the rest of the structural rules. Players can answer only against the *last non-answered* challenge by the adversary.

Note: This structural rule is known as the Last Duty First condition, and makes dialogical games suitable for intuitionistic logic, hence the name of this rule.

SR1c: Classical Development rule

Players play one move alternately. Any move after the choice of repetition ranks is either an attack or a defence according to the rules of formation, of synthesis, and of analysis, and in accordance with the rest of the structural rules.

If the logical constant occurring in the thesis is not recorded by the table for local meaning, then either it must be introduced by a nominal definition, or the table for local meaning needs to be enriched with the new expression.

*Note: The structural rules with SR1c (and not SR1i) produce strategies for classical logic. The point is that since players can answer to a list of challenges in any order (which is not the case with the intuitionistic rule), it might happen that the two options of a **P**-defence occur in the same play—this is closely related to the classical development rule in sequent calculus allowing more than one formula at the right of the sequent.*

SR2: Formation rules for formal dialogues
SR2i: Starting a formation dialogue

A formation-play starts by challenging the thesis with the formation request **O**?$_{\mathbf{prop}}$; **P** must answer by stating that his thesis is a proposition.

SR2ii: Developing a formation dialogue

The game then proceeds by applying the formation rules up to the elementary constituents of **prop/set**.

After that **O** is free to use the other particle rules insofar as the other structural rules allow it.

Note: The constituents of the thesis will therefore not be specified before the play but as a result of the structure of the moves (according to the rules recorded by the rules for local meaning).

SR3: Resolution of instructions

1. A player may ask his adversary to carry out the prescribed instruction and thus bring forward a suitable local reason in defence of the proposition at stake. Once the defender has replaced the instruction with the required local reason we say that the instruction has been resolved.
2. The player index of an instruction determines which of the two players has the right to choose the local reason that will resolve the instruction.
   (a) If the instruction $\mathcal{I}$ for the logical constant $\mathcal{K}$ has the form $\mathcal{I}^{\mathcal{K}}(p)^{\mathbf{X}}$ and it is **Y** who requests the resolution, then the request has the form **Y**? .../ $\mathcal{I}^{\mathcal{K}}(p)^{\mathbf{X}}$, and it is **X** who chooses the local reason.

(b) If the instruction $\mathcal{I}$ for the logic constant $\mathcal{K}$ has the form $\mathcal{I}^{\mathcal{K}}(p)^{\mathbf{Y}}$ and it is player **Y** who requests the resolution, then the request has the form **Y** p_{i} / $\mathcal{I}^{\mathcal{K}}(p)^{\mathbf{Y}}$, and it is **Y** who chooses the local reason.

3. Instructions occurring in expressions stating **falsum** have no resolution. In fact, the player stating $\mathcal{I}(p)$: $\bot$ gives up and therefore loses the play.

SR4: Substitution of instructions

Once the local reason b has been used to resolve the instruction $\mathcal{I}^{\mathcal{K}}(p)^{\mathbf{X}}$, and if the same instruction occurs again, players have the right to require that the instruction be resolved with b. The substitution request has the form $?b/\mathcal{I}_{\mathrm{k}}(p)^{\mathbf{X}}$. Players cannot choose a different substitution term (in our example, not even **X**, once the instruction has been resolved).
This rule also applies to functions.

SR5: Socratic rule and definitional equality

The following points are all parts of the Socratic rule, they all apply.

SR5.1: Restriction of P statements

P cannot make an elementary statement if **O** has not stated it before, except in the thesis.
An elementary statement is either an elementary proposition with implicit local reason, or an elementary proposition and its local reason (not an instruction).

SR5.2: Challenging elementary statements in formal dialogues

Challenges against elementary statements with implicit local reasons take the form:

$$X!A$$

$$Y\ ?_{reason}$$

$$X\ a : A$$

where A is an elementary proposition and a is a local reason.[13]

P cannot challenge **O**'s elementary statements, except if **O** provides an elementary initial concession with implicit local reason, in which case **P** can ask for a local reason, or in the context of transmission of equality.

SR5.3: Definitional equality

[13]Note that **P** is allowed to make an elementary statement only as a thesis (Socratic rule); he will be able to respond to the challenge on an elementary statement only if **O** has provided the required local reason in her initial concessions.

O may challenge elementary **P**-statements; **P** then answers by stating a definitional equality expressing the equality between a local reason and an instruction both introduced by **O** (for non-reflexive cases, that is when **O** provided the local reason as a resolution of an instruction), or a reflexive equality of the local reason introduced by **O** (when the local reason was not introduced by the resolution of an instruction, that is either as such in the initial concessions or as the result of a synthesis of a local reason). We thus distinguish two cases of the Socratic rule:

1. non-reflexive cases;
2. reflexive cases.

These rules do not cover cases of transmission of equality. The Socratic rule also applies to the resolution or substitution of functions, even if the formulation mentions only instructions.

SR5.3.1: Non-reflexive cases of the Socratic rule

We are in the presence of a *non-reflexive case* of the Socratic rule when **P** responds to the challenge with the indication that **O** gave the same local reason for the same proposition when she had to resolve or substitute instruction I.

Here are the different challenges and defences determining the meaning of the three following moves:

Non-reflexive cases of the Socratic rule

	Move	Challenge	Defence
SR5.3.1a	**P** a: A	**O** ? = a	**P** $I = a$: A
SR5.3.1b	**P** a: $A(b)$	**O** ? = $b^{A(b)}$	**P** $I = b$: D
SR5.3.1c	**P** $I = b$: D (this statement stems from **SR5.3.1b**)	**O** ? = $A(b)$	**P** $A(I) = A(b)$: *prop*

Presuppositions

(i) The response prescribed by SR5.3.1a presupposes that **O** has stated A or $a = b$: A as the result of the resolution or substitution of instruction I occurring in I: A or in I = b: A.

(ii) The response prescribed by SR5.3.1b presupposes that **O** has stated A and b: D as the result of the resolution or substitution of instruction I occurring in a: A (I).

(iii) SR5.3.1c assumes that **P** $I = b$: D is the result of the application of SR5.3.1b. The further challenge seeks to verify that the replacement of the instruction produces an equality in **prop**, that is, that the replacement of the instruction with a local reason yields an equal proposition to the one in which the instruction was not yet replaced. The answer prescribed by this rule presupposes that **O** has already stated $A(b)$: **prop** (or more trivially $A(I) = A(b)$: **prop**).

(iv) The **P**-statements obtained after defending elementary **P**-statements cannot be attacked again with the Socratic rule (with the exception of SR5.3.1c), nor with a rule of resolution or substitution of instructions.

SR5.3.2: Reflexive cases of the Socratic rule

We are in the presence of a *reflexive case* of the Socratic rule when **P** responds to the challenge with the indication that **O** adduced the same local reason for the same proposition, though that local reason in the statement of **O** is not the result of any resolution or substitution.

Attacks have the same form as those prescribed by SR5.3.1. Responses that yield reflexivity presuppose that **O** has previously stated the same statement or even the same equality.

The response obtained cannot be attacked again with the Socratic rule.

SR6: Transmission of Definitional Equality

Definitional Equality transmits by reflexivity, transitivity and symmetry.

SR7: Winning rule for plays

The player who makes the last move wins unless he states $\bot$. The player who states **falsum** loses the play.[14]

4.2.2.2.2 Resolution and the Justification of the Analysis Rules for Local Reasoning

Notice that the analysis rules for local reasons meet the justification criteria required by constructivist theories of meaning; but at the play level.

Indeed, according to the constructivist approach in order to justify an elimination rule it is necessary to make the conclusion evident, on the assumption that the premises of the rule are known. In the CTT framework this is achieved by showing

[14]See, above point 3 of SR3. At the strategy level the move **O**! $\bot$allows **P** to bring forward the strategic reason $you_{gave\ up}(n)$ in support for any statement that he has not defended before **O** stated $\bot$ at move n.

that, if d: C is the conclusion of an elimination rule, then d evaluates to a canonical element of C (i.e. d evaluates to an element occurring in the conclusion of an introduction rule for C). The procedure of evaluation consists in the unwinding of definitions (implemented by suitable equality rules), replacing defined expressions by their definientia.

In the dialogical setting justifying a rule of analysis at the play level for some claim **X** d: C amounts to the task of showing that the "resolution" (or execution) of the instruction(s) prescribed by that analysis-rule render those local reasons determined by the synthesis rule for the claim **X**! C. Moreover, the justification should show that the analysis rule for **X** d: C, does not contravene the distribution of rights and duties associated by the synthesis rule to the claim **X**! C. An informal argument for the justification of the analysis-rules for local reasons is straightforward

X $p : A \wedge B$. If player **X** states a conjunction backing it with local reason p, then the corresponding instructions once resolved, render back, what the synthesis rules prescribe, namely that **X** must provide a local reason for the left side, when the antagonist **Y** asks for the left. Similarly for the right side.

X $p : (\exists x : A)B(x)$. If player **X** states an existential backing it with local reason p, then the corresponding instructions once resolved, render back, what the synthesis rules prescribe, namely that **X** must provide a local reason for the left side, when the antagonist **Y** asks for the left. If the antagonist **Y** asks for the right side, **X** must provide a local reason for the right side (where the local reason for the left side, chosen by **X**, occurs). That is, if **X** $L^{\exists}(p) = p_1$: A, then **X** $R^{\exists}(p) = p_2$: $B(p_1)$.

X $p : A \vee B$. If player **X** states a disjunction backing it with local reason p, then the corresponding instructions once resolved, render back, what the synthesis rules prescribe, namely that **X** must choose if p provides a local reason either for the left side or the right side.

X $p : A \supset B$. If player **X** states an implication backing it with local reason p, then the corresponding instructions once resolved, render back, what the synthesis rules prescribe, namely that **X** must provide a local reason for the consequent of the implication, given that the antagonist **Y** provided a local reason for the antecedent.

X $p : (\forall x : A)B(x)$.If player **X** states a universal backing it with local reason p, then the corresponding instructions once resolved, render back, what the synthesis rules prescribe, namely that **X** must provide a local reason for the right side of the universal, given that the antagonist **Y** provided a local reason for the left side. That is, if **Y** $L^{\forall}(p) = p_1$: A, then **X** $R^{\forall}(p) = p_2$: $B(p_1)$.

The justification of the analysis rule for negation follows the argument for implication. The justification of **falsum** is vacuously satisfied since there is no synthesis rule for it – cf. Sundholm (2012). Moreover, from the dialogical point of view the meaning of **falsum**, since it is an elementary proposition, must actually be considered as a special case of the Socratic Rule (see rule SR7).

4.2.3 Content and Material Dialogues

As pointed out by Krabbe (1985, p. 297), *material dialogues* – that is, dialogues in which propositions have content – receive in the writings of Paul Lorenzen and Kuno Lorenz priority over formal dialogues: material dialogues constitute the *locus* where the logical constants are introduced. However in the standard dialogical framework, since both material and formal dialogues marshal a purely syntactic notion of the formal rule – through which logical validity is defined, this contentual feature is bypassed,[15] with this consequence that Krabbe and others after him considered that, after all, *formal* dialogues had priority over material ones.

As can be gathered from the above discussion, we believe that this conclusion stems from shortcomings of the standard framework, in which local reasons are not expressed at the object-language level. We thus explicitly introduced these local reasons in order to undercut this apparent precedence of a formalistic approach that makes away with the contentual origins of the dialogical project.

In fact, in principle, a local reason prefigures a material dialogue displaying the content of the proposition stated. This aspect makes up the ground level of the normative approach to meaning of the dialogical framework, in which *use*—or dialogical interaction—is to be understood as *use prescibed by a rule*; such a use is what Peregrin (2014, pp. 2–3) calls the *role of a linguistic expression*. Dialogical interaction is this *use*, entirely determined by rules that give it meaning: the linguistic expression of every statement determines this statement by the role it plays, that is by the way it is used, and this use is governed by rules of interaction. The meaning of elementary propositions in dialogical interaction thus amounts to their *role* in the kind of interaction that is governed by the Socratic and Global rules for material dialogues, that is by the specific formulations of the Socratic and Global rules for precisely those very propositions.

It follows that material dialogues are important not only for the general issue on the normativity of logic but also for rendering a language with *content*.

We cannot in the present writing fully develop these kind of dialogues, however we will present briefly the case of the set **Bool** which provides the elements to tackle the case of empirical propositions.[16] The latter allows for expressing classical truth-functions within the dialogical framework, and it has an important role in the CTT-approach to empirical propositions..[17] We invite the reader to visit the chapter

[15]Krabbe (1985, p. 297).

[16]Here again we thank to the reviewers who urged us to sketch at least an example of material dialogues.

[17]See Martin-Löf (2014).

on material dialogues in Rahman/McConaughey/Klev/Clerbout (2018), where discuss material dialogues that include sets of natural numbers and the set **Bool.**

4.2.3.1 The Set Bool and Empirical Propositions

Most of the literature differentiating the philosophical perspective underlying the work of Boole and the one of Frege focused on discussing either the different ways both authors understood the relation between logic and psychology or the links between mathematics and logic, or both. According to these studies, Boole's framework has been mainly conceived as a kind of psychologism and a programme for the mathematization of logic, contrasting as well with Frege's radical anti-psychologism as with his logicist project for the foundations of mathematics.

These comparative studies have also been combined with the contrast between model-theoretical approaches to meaning, with their associated notion of *varying domains of discourse*, versus inferentialist approaches to meaning, with a *fixed universe of discourse*. It might be argued that while the first approach could be more naturally understood as an offspring of the algebraic tradition of Boole-Schröder, the second approach could be seen as influenced by Frege's *Begriffsschrift*.[18]

However, from the point of view of contemporary classical logic, and after the meta-mathematical perspective of Gödel, Bernays, and Tarski, both Boole's and Frege's view on semantics are subsumed under the same formalization, according to which classical semantics amount to a function of interpretation between the sentences $\boldsymbol{S}$ of a given language $\boldsymbol{L}$ and the set of truth values $\{\mathbf{0}, \mathbf{1}\}$—let us call such a set the set **Bool**. This function assumes that the well-formed formulae of $\boldsymbol{S}$ are made dependent upon a domain—either a *local domain of discourse* (in the case of Tarski's-style approach to Boolean-algebra), or a *universal domain* (in the case of Frege). More precisely, this functional approach is based on a separation of cases that simply assumes that the quantifiers and connectives take propositional functions into classical propositions—for a lucid insight on this perspective's limitations see (Sundholm, 2006). In fact, the integration of both views within the same formal semantic closes a gap in Boole's framework, which was already pointed out by Frege: the links between the semantics of propositional and first-order logic.[19]

Constructive Type Theory includes a third (epistemic) paradigm in the framework allowing for a new way of dividing the waters between Boolean operators and logical connectives, and, at the same time, integrating them in a common inferential system in which each of them has a specific role to play. The overall paradigm at

[18]Recall the distinction of language *as the universal medium* and *as a calculus* (van Heijenoort, 1967).

[19]Frege points out that within Boole's approach there is no organic link between propositional and first-order logic: "*In Boole the two parts run alongside one another; so that one is like the mirror image of the other, but for that very reason stands in no organic relation to it*" (Frege G. , Boole's Logical Calculus and the Concept Script [1880/81], 1979).

stake is the Brouwer–Heyting–Kolmogorov conception of propositions as sets of proofs embedded in the framework in which, thanks to the insight brought forward by the Curry–Howard isomorphism (Howard, 1980), propositions are read as sets and as types.

In a nutshell, as already mentioned, within CTT the simplest form of a judgement (the categorical) is an expression of the form

$$a : B$$

where "B" is a proposition and "a" a proof-object on the grounds of which the proposition B is asserted to be true, standing as shorthand for.

"a provides evidence for B".

In other words, the expression "$a : B$", is the formal notation of the categorical judgement.

"The proposition B is true",

which is shorthand for

"There is evidence for B".

According to this view, a proposition is a set of elements, called proof-objects, that make the proposition B true. Furthermore, we distinguish between *canonical proof-objects* on the one hand, those entities providing a *direct evidence* for the truth the proposition B, and on the other hand *non-canonical proof-objects*, the entities providing indirect pieces of evidence for B.

This generalization also allows another third reading: a proposition is a *type* and its elements are instances of this type. If we follow this reading proof-objects are conceived as instantiations of the type. This type-reading naturally leads to Brouwer–Heyting–Kolmogorov's constructivism mentioned above: if a proposition is understood as the set of its proofs, it might be the case that we do not have any proof for that proposition at our disposal, but that we neither have a proof for its negation (thus, in such a framework, *third excluded* fails). Notice that the constructivist interpretation requires the intensional rather than the extensional constitution of sets—recall the Aristotelian view that no "form" ("type") can be conceived independently of its instances and reversewise.

Moreover CTT provides a novel way to render the meaning of the set $\{\mathbf{0}, \mathbf{1}\}$ as the type **Bool**. More precisely, the type **Bool** is characterized as the set of the canonical elements **0** and **1**. Thus, each non-canonical element is equal to one of them. But what kind of entities are those (non-canonical) elements that might be equal to **1** or **0**? Since in such a setting **1**, **0** and those equal to them are elements, they are not considered to be of the type proposition; they are rather providers of truth or falsity of a proposition (or a set, according to the Curry–Howard isomorphism between propositions, sets, and types): they are proof-objects that provide evidence for the assertion **Bool true**.

In order to illustrate our point here and to explicit the link with material dialogues, let us take an example outside of mathematics, for instance this *sentence*:

Bachir Diagne is from Senegal.

This sentence differs from the *proposition*, that is, what Frege called the *sense* or *thought* expressed by that sentence, which would be.

that Bachir Diagne is from Senegal

So if we take the sentence as expressing the proposition, then we might be able to bring forward some proof-object—some piece of evidence *a*, his passport or his birth certificate for instance—that renders the proposition *that Bachir Diagne is from Senegal* true. In such a case we have the assertion that the proposition is true on the grounds of the piece of evidence *a* (the passport), which we can write:

passport: *Bachir Diagne is from Senegal*

or, in a more general assertion:

That Bachir Diagne is from Senegal **true**
(*there is some piece of evidence that Bachir Diagne is from Senegal*)

In this fashion, if we take the sentence *Bachir Diagne is from Senegal* as related to a *Boolean object*, then this sentence triggers a procedure yielding a non-canonical element, say **X** (the proposition), of the set **Bool**. In such a case the sentence would not *express* a proposition, but it could be understood as an *answer* to the question:

Is Bachir Diagne from Senegal?

the answer being:

yes, *Bachir Diagne is from Senegal*

which would thus yield the outcome **1**. In other words, determining to which of the canonical elements, **1** or **0**, the non-canonical element **X** is equal, would require answering to the question *Is Bachir Diagne from Senegal*? Thus, in our case, we take it to be equal to **1**.[20] The procedure would amount to the following steps:

Is Bachir Diagne from Senegal ?

↓

yes, *Bachir Diagne is from Senegal*

↓

X = 1 : Bool

[20]For the interpretation of empirical propositions see (Martin-Löf, 2014).

The arrows indicate that determining to which of the elements **X** is equal actually is the result of an enquiry (in this case an empirical one). This is not only different from:

passport: Bachir Diagne is from Senegal

but it is also different from:

Bool true

Indeed, while $\mathbf{X} = \mathbf{1} : \mathbf{Bool}$ expresses one of the possible outcomes the non-canonical element **X** can take in **Bool**, **Bool true** expresses the fact that at least one element of the set **Bool** can be brought forward.

Thus, a distinction is drawn between the Boolean object **1** (one of the canonical elements of **Bool**) and the predicate **true** that applies to **Bool**.

Moreover, operations between elements of **Bool** would then not be the logical connectives introduced by natural deduction rules at the right hand side of the colon, but they would be operations between objects occurring at the left hand side of the colon. For example the disjunction "+" at left of the colon in

$$A + B = \mathbf{1} : \mathbf{Bool}\ (given\ A = \mathbf{1} : \mathbf{Bool})$$

stands for an operation between the non-canonical **Boolean** objects A and B; whereas the disjunction occurring at right of the colon in the assertion

$$b : A \vee B\ (given\ b : A)$$

expresses the familiar logical connective of disjunction, that is here true since a piece of evidence for one of the disjuncts is provided: the piece of evidence b for A.

Since **Bool** is a type, and since according to the Curry–Howard isomorphism, it is itself a proposition, we can certainly have both, propositional connectives as sets of proof-objects, and have them combined with Boolean operations. This allows us, for example, to demonstrate that each canonical element in **Bool** is identical either to **1** or **0**:

$$(\forall x : \mathbf{Bool})\boldsymbol{Id}(\mathbf{Bool}, x, \mathbf{1}) \vee \boldsymbol{Id}(\mathbf{Bool}, x, \mathbf{0})\ \boldsymbol{true}$$

4.2.3.2 Dialogical Rules for Boolean Operators

In the dialogical framework, the elements of **Bool** are responses to **yes-no** questions, so that each element of **Bool** is equal to ***yes*** or ***no***. Responses such as $b = \boldsymbol{yes}$ or $b = \boldsymbol{no}$ make explicit one of the possible origins of the answer ***yes*** (or ***no***), namely whether b is or not the case. Here are the Global (player independent) rules for synthesis, analysis, and equalities of the Boolean operators.

Global rules for Bool and Boolean operators in immanent reasoning

	Move	Challenge	Defence
Synthesis	**X ! Bool**	**Y** $?_{Bool}$	**X** ***yes*****: Bool** **X** ***no*****: Bool**
Analysis	**X** p: $C(c)$[c: **Bool**]	**Y** ? = $c^{\mathbf{Bool}}$	**X**c ***yes*****: Bool** **X**c ***no*****: Bool**
Equalities ***yes***	**X** c: ***yes*** : **Bool** … **X** p: $C(c)$[c: **Bool**]	**Y** ? $=_{reason}$ ***yes***	**X**p_1: C (***yes***)
no	**X** c: ***no*** : **Bool** … **X** p: $C(c)$[c: **Bool**]	**Y** ? $=_{reason}$ ***no***	**X**p_1: C (***no***)

Specific Socratic Rule for Bool and Boolean Operators

When **O** states a : **Bool**, she is stating that a is an element of **Bool**, that is, she is committing to a being either ***yes*** or ***no***; **P** may challenge this **O**-statement by requesting that she makes her commitment explicit and provides the equality $a =$ ***yes* : Bool** or $a =$ ***no* : Bool**. The following table provides the dialogical rule for this interaction; this rule is part of the Socratic rules because it is player dependent,[21] but it is a rule specific to **Bool** and the Boolean operators thus providing their specific meaning: this specific Socratic rule for **Bool** and the Boolean operators provides their material meaning.

Specific Socratic rule for Bool

	Move	Challenge	Defence
Specific Socratic rule for Bool	**O** a: **Bool**	**P** ? = $a^{\mathbf{Bool}}$	**O** a = ***yes*****: Bool** **O** a = ***no*****: Bool**

We can now introduce quite smoothly the rules for the classical truth-functional connectives as operations between *elements* of **Bool** (left-hand side of the colon), which are distinct from the usual propositional connectives (right-hand side of the colon). We leave the description for quantifiers to the diligence of the reader, whereby the universal quantifier is understood as a finite sequence of products, and, dually, the existential as a finite sequence of additions.

[21] For a discussion on player dependence and the way this feature divides the Structural rules and the Particle rules, see above.

The dialogical interpretation of the rules below is very close to the usual one: it amounts to the commitments and entitlements specified by the rules of the dialogue: if for instance the response is ***yes*** to a (left-hand side) product, then the speaker is also committed to answer ***yes*** to further questions on both of the components of that product. Here again, the meaning of the Boolean operators is provided by interaction, where *choice* is a fundamental feature.

Global rules for classical truth-functional operators

	Move	Synthesis of local reasons: Challenge	Synthesis of local reasons: Defence
Product	**X** $a \times b$: **Bool**	**Y** $? = a \times b$	**X** $(a \times b) =$ ***yes***: **Bool** / **X** $(a \times b) =$ ***no***: **Bool**
***Yes*-equality (product)**	**X** $(a \times b) =$ ***yes***: **Bool**	**Y** $?\ L^{\times}$ ***yes***	**X** $a =$ ***yes***: **Bool**
		Y $?\ R^{\times}$ ***yes***	**X** $b =$ ***yes***: **Bool**
***No*-equality (product)**	**X** $(a \times b) =$ ***no***: **Bool**	**Y** $?^{\times}$ ***no***	**X** $a =$ ***no***: **Bool** / **X** $b =$ ***no***: **Bool**
Addition	**X** $a + b$: **Bool**	**Y** $? = a + b$	**X** $a =$ ***yes***: **Bool** / **X** $b =$ ***yes***: **Bool**
***Yes*-equality (addition)**	**X** $(a + b) =$ ***yes***: **Bool**	**Y** $?^{+}$ ***yes***	**X** $a =$ ***yes***: **Bool** / **X** $b =$ ***yes***: **Bool**
***No*-equality (addition)**	**X** $(a + b) =$ ***no***: **Bool**	**Y** $?\ L^{+}$ ***no***	**X** $a =$ ***no***: **Bool**
		Y $?\ R^{+}$ ***no***	**X** $b =$ ***no***: **Bool**
Implication	**X** $a \rightarrow b$: **Bool**	**Y** $? = a \rightarrow b$	**X** $(a \rightarrow b) =$ ***yes***: **Bool** / **X** $(a \rightarrow b) =$ ***no***: **Bool**
***Yes*-equality (implication)**	**X** $(a \rightarrow b) =$ ***yes***: **Bool**	**Y** $a =$ ***yes***: **Bool**	**X** $b =$ ***yes***: **Bool**
		Y $b =$ ***no***: **Bool**	**X** $a =$ ***no***: **Bool**
***No*-equality (addition)**	**X** $(a \rightarrow b) =$ ***no***: **Bool**	**Y** $?\ L^{\rightarrow}$ ***no***	**X** $a =$ ***yes***: **Bool**
		Y $?\ R^{\rightarrow}$ ***no***	**X** $b =$ ***no***: **Bool**
Negation	**X** $\sim a$: **Bool**	**Y** $? \sim a$	**X** $\sim a =$ ***yes***: **Bool** / **X** $\sim a =$ ***no***: **Bool**
***Yes*-equality (negation)**	**X** $\sim a =$ ***yes***: **Bool**	**Y** $?^{\sim}$ ***yes***	**X** $a =$ ***no***: **Bool**
***No*-equality (negation)**	**X** $\sim a =$ ***no***: **Bool**	**Y** $?^{\sim}$ ***no***	**X** $a =$ ***yes***: **Bool**

4.2.3.3 Empirical Propositions

As already mentioned above, non-canonical elements of the set **Bool** can be used to study the meaning of empirical propositions, though what we need in particular is the notion of *empirical quantity*. This notion has been introduced by Martin-Löf in applying CTT to the empirical realm (Martin-Löf, 2014) : whereas quantities of mathematics and logic are determined by computation, empirical quantities are determined by experiments and observation. An example of a mathematical quantity is 2 + 2; it is determined by a computation yielding the number 4. An example of an empirical quantity is the colour of some object. This is not determined by computation; rather, one must look at the object under normal conditions.

In the dialogical framework, we can consider empirical quantities as answers to a question. For example, give the question.

Are Cheryl's Eyes Blue? The yes or no answer, obtained through some kind of empirical procedure received in a given context, can be defined over the set **Bool**, namely as being equal to ***yes*** or ***no***. The following question however might involve many different answers:

What Is the Colour of Cheryl's Eyes? If $\boldsymbol{X}$ stands for the empirical quantity *Colour of Cheryl's eyes*, we might define the possible answers over some finite set $\mathbb{N}^n$ of natural numbers:

- $\boldsymbol{X} = 1 : \mathbb{N}^n$ if Cheryl's eyes are brown
- $\boldsymbol{X} = 2 : \mathbb{N}^n$ if Cheryl's eyes are green
- $\boldsymbol{X} = 3 : \mathbb{N}^n$if Cheryl's eyes are blue

...

- $\boldsymbol{X} = n : \mathbb{N}^n$ if Cheryl's eyes are...

Certainly the question ***Are Cheryl's eyes blue?*** can also be defined over a larger set, if several degrees of colour are to be included as an answer, or alternatively degrees of certainty (definitely blue, quite blue, slightly blue...). Let us assume then another set $\mathbb{N}^j$ for the degree of colour:

$\boldsymbol{Y} = 0\_1 : \mathbb{N}^j$ if Cheryl's eyes are dark blue
$\boldsymbol{Y} = 0\_2 : \mathbb{N}^j$ if Cheryl's eyes are light blue.
$\boldsymbol{Y} = 0\_3 : \mathbb{N}^j$ if Cheryl's eyes are green-blue.

...

$\boldsymbol{Y} = 0\_j : \mathbb{N}^j$ if Cheryl's eyes are...

The general dialogical rule for an empirical quantity can thus be rendered:

General dialogical rule for an empirical quantity

	Move	Challenge	Defence
Empirical quantity	X $\boldsymbol{X}$: $\mathbb{N}^n$	Y ?= $\boldsymbol{X}$	X $m_1 = \boldsymbol{X}$: $\mathbb{N}^n$ … X $m_n = \boldsymbol{X}$: $\mathbb{N}^n$ (the defender chooses)

Notice that determining the value of the empirical quantity is an empirical procedure, specific to that quantity; the result of carrying out such a procedure is determined by the rules for that quantity. Moreover, the value of two different empirical quantities might be the same: the quantities only indicate that *the way of determining* the answer to the question might be the same. Take for example these two enquiries

1. *Did Jorge Luis Borges compose the poem "Ajedrez"?*
2. *Is Ibn al-Haytham the author of* Al-Shukūk ʿalā Batlamyūs *(Doubts Concerning Ptolemy)?*

These two enquiries involve determining the value of the empirical quantity $\boldsymbol{X}$ for (1) and $\boldsymbol{Y}$ for (2), which can be the same: they can both be ***yes*** for instance if the underlying set is **Bool.**

This leads to a Socratic rule specific to statements of the form $\boldsymbol{X}, \boldsymbol{Y}, \boldsymbol{Z} : \mathbb{N}^n$. For example, given the set $\mathbb{N}^n$, **P** can defend the challenges.

O? $= \boldsymbol{X}$ with the statement **P** $m_1 = \boldsymbol{X}{:}\mathbb{N}^n$
O? $= \boldsymbol{Y}$ with the statement **P** $m_2 = \boldsymbol{Y}{:}\mathbb{N}^n$
O? $= \boldsymbol{Z}$ with the statement **P** $m_3 = \boldsymbol{Z}{:}\mathbb{N}^n$

Incompatibility

A system of rules that targets the development of a more complex meaning network might include incompatibility rules formulated as challenges. Thus, instead of establishing the simple use of Copy-cat, the game might include more sophisticated rules specific to a particular empirical quantity. For example, if a player responded ***yes*** to the enquiry associated with $\boldsymbol{X}$.

3. *Did the Greek won in 480 BC the sea-battle take of Salamis*?

that is, if he stated ***yes*** $= \boldsymbol{X}$: **Bool**; this player might not be allowed to respond ***yes*** to the enquiry associated with $\boldsymbol{Z}$

4. *Did Xerxes won in 480 BC the sea-battle of Salamis?*

that is, he might not be entitled to further state ***yes*** $= \boldsymbol{Z}$: **Bool**. That is, the other player may challenge the right to answer both (3) and (4) with ***yes***:

5. *Both answers cannot be* ***yes****.*

that is, she can challenge his two statements by stating that $\neg(\boldsymbol{Id}(\textbf{Bool}, \boldsymbol{yes}, \boldsymbol{X}) \wedge \boldsymbol{Id}(\textbf{Bool}, \boldsymbol{yes}, \boldsymbol{Z}))$. The first player would then have to give up. This challenge would be calling upon some *formal incompatibility* between two statements.

Formal incompatibility

	Move	Challenge	Defence
Formal incompatibility	**P** $yes = \boldsymbol{X}$: **Bool** *and* **P** $yes = \boldsymbol{Z}$: **Bool**	**O** $\neg(Id(\text{Bool}, yes, \boldsymbol{X}) \wedge Id(\text{Bool}, yes, \boldsymbol{Z}))$	**P** *gives up*

But there is another kind of incompatibility challenge, calling upon *contentual incompatibility*. Consider for instance (4): if a player answers ***yes***, *Xerxes won in 480 BC the sea-battle of Salamis*, then the other player can challenge this through contentual incompatibility: the challenger simply states the formally incompatible answer to the challenged statement: $Id(\mathbf{Bool}, yes, \boldsymbol{X})$, *The Greek won in 480 BC the sea-battle of Salamis*. The challenged player must then give up.

Contentual incompatibility

	Move	Challenge	Defence
Contentual incompatibility	**P** $yes = \boldsymbol{Z}$: **Bool**	**O** $Id(\text{Bool}, yes, \boldsymbol{X})$	**P** *gives up*

Dependent Empirical Quantities

Another more sophisticated form of dealing with empirical quantities is to implement a structure where one empirical quantity might depend on another one. For example let us define the empirical quantity $\boldsymbol{Y}$ as the function $b(\boldsymbol{X})$: $\mathbb{N}_j^n$ $[\boldsymbol{X}: \mathbb{N}^n]$ such that

$$\boldsymbol{Y} : =_{df} b(\boldsymbol{X}) : \mathbb{N}_j^n \; [\boldsymbol{X} : \mathbb{N}^n]$$

$$b(\boldsymbol{X}) = j_i : \mathbb{N}^j, \text{ given } \boldsymbol{X} = n_m : \mathbb{N}^n$$

$$\ldots$$

$$b(\boldsymbol{X}) = j_k : \mathbb{N}^j, \text{ given } \boldsymbol{X} = n_n : \mathbb{N}^n, \text{ if} \ldots$$

Suppose we are interested in determining the meaning of some empirical propositions; this can involve for instance establishing that stating that something has a determinate colour (say, *red*) would presuppose that the player already answered the question whether the object at stake *is coloured or not*.

In this case also the rules of the game might include rules for challenging empirical quantities on the basis of a certain evaluation of another empirical quantity on which the first is dependent; this would be like challenging that something is red by denying that the empirical quantity that yields the evaluation ***X*** has a positive response to the question if the object at stake has a colour. We will stop here and invite again the reader to visit the book *Immanent Reasoning*.

The final section of the chapter on *Material dialogues* in Rahman/McConaughey/Klev/Clerbout (2018), discusses the epistemological notion of *internalization of content.*[22] In this respect, the dialogical framework can be considered as a formal approach to reasoning rooted in the dialogical constitution and "internalization" of content—including empirical content—rather than in the syntactic manipulation of un-interpreted signs.

This discussion on material dialogues provides a new perspective on Willfried Sellars' (1991, pp. 129–194) notion of *Space of Reasons*: the dialogical framework of immanent reasoning enriched with the material level should show how to integrate world-directed thoughts (displaying empirical content) into an inferentialist approach, thereby suggesting that immanent reasoning can integrate within the same epistemological framework the two conflicting readings of the Space of Reasons brought forward by John McDowell (2009, pp. 221–238) on the one hand, who insists in distinguishing world-direct thought and knowledge gathered by inference, and Robert Brandom (1997) on the other hand, who interprets Sellars' work in a more radical anti-empiricist manner.

The point is not only that we can deploy the CTT-distinction between *reason* as a premise and *reason* as a piece of evidence justifying a proposition, but also that the dialogical framework allows for distinguishing between the **objective justification level** targeted by Brandom (1997, p. 129) and the **subjective justification level** stressed by McDowell.

According to our approach the subjective feature corresponds to the play level, where a concrete player brings forward the statement *It looks red to me*, rather than *It is red*. The general epistemological upshot from these initial reflections is that, on our view, many of the worries on the interpretation of the *Space of Reasons* and on the shortcomings of the standard dialogical approach to meaning (beyond the one of logical constants) have their origin in the neglect of the play-level.

4.3 Strategic Reasons in Dialogues for Immanent Reasoning

The conceptual backbone on which rests the metalogical properties of the dialogical framework is the notion of strategic reason which allows to adopt a global view on all the possible plays that constitute a strategy. However, this global view should not

[22]By "internalization" we mean that the relevant content is made part of the setting of the game of giving and asking for reasons: any relevant content is the content displayed during the interaction. For a discussion on this conception of internalization – see Peregrin (2014, pp. 36-42).

be identified with the perspective common in proof theory: strategic reasons are a kind of recapitulation of what can happen for a given thesis and show the entire history of the play by means of the instructions. Strategic reasons thus yield an overview of the possibilities enclosed in a thesis—what plays can be carried out from it—, but without ever being carried out in an actual play: they are only a perspective on all the possible variants of plays for a thesis and not an actual play. In this way the rules of synthesis and analysis of strategic reasons provided below are not of the same nature as the analysis and synthesis of local reasons, they are not produced through challenges and their defence, but are a recapitulation of the plays that can actually be carried out.

The notion of strategic reasons enables us to link dialogical strategies with CTT-demonstrations, since strategic reasons (and not local reasons) are the dialogical counterpart of CTT proof-objects; but it also shows clearly that the strategy level by itself—the only level that proof theory considers—is not enough: a deeper insight is gained when considering, together with the strategy level, the fundamental level of plays; strategic reasons thus bridge these two perspectives, the global view of strategies and the more in-depth and down-to-earth view of actual plays with all the possible variations in logic they allow,[23] without sacrificing the one for the other.

This vindication of the play level is a key aspect of the dialogical framework and one of the purposes of the present study: other logical frameworks lack this dimension, which besides is not an extra dimension appended to the concern for demonstrations, but actually constitutes it, the heuristical procedure for building strategies out of plays showing the gapless link there is between the play level and the strategy level: strategies (and so demonstrations) stem from plays. Thus the dialogical framework can say at least as much as other logical frameworks, and, additionally, reveals limitations of other frameworks through this level of plays.

4.3.1 Introducing Strategic Reasons

Strategic reasons belong to the strategy level, but are elements of the object-language of the play level: they are the reasons brought forward by a player entitling him to his statement. Strategic reasons are a perspective on plays that take into account all the possible variations in the play for a given thesis; they are never actually carried out, since any play is but the actualization of only one of all the possible plays for the thesis: each individual play can be actualized but will be separate from the other individual plays that can be carried out if other choices are made; strategic reasons allow to see together all these possible plays that in fact are always separate. There will never be in any of the plays the complex strategic reason for the thesis as a result

[23]Among these variations can be counted cooperative games, non-monotony, the possibility of player errors or of limited knowledge or resources, to cite but a few options the play level offers, making the dialogical framework very well adapted for history and philosophy of logic.

of the application of the particle rules, only the local reason for each of the subformulas involved; the strategic reason will put all these separate reasons together as a recapitulation of what can be said from the given thesis.

Consider for instance a conjunction: the Proponent claims to have a strategic reason for this conjunction. This means that he claims that whatever the Opponent might play, be it a challenge of the left or of the right conjunct, the Proponent will be able to win the play. But in a single play with repetition rank 1 for the Opponent, there is no way to check if a conjunction is justified, that is if both of the conjuncts can be defended, since a play is precisely the carrying out of only one of the possible **O**-choices (challenging the left or the right conjunct): to check both sides of a conjunction, two plays are required, one in which the Opponent challenges the left side of the conjunction and another one for the right side. So a strategic reason is never a single play, but refers to the strategy level where all the possible outcomes are taken into account; the winning strategy can then be displayed as a tree showing that both plays (respectively challenging and defending the left conjunct and right conjunct) are won by the Proponent, thus justifying the conjunction.

Let us now study what strategic reasons look like, how they are generated and how they are analyzed.

A Strategic *perspective* on a Statement

In the standard framework of dialogues, where we do not explicitly have the reasons for the statements in the object-language, the particle rules simply determine the local meaning of the expressions. In dialogues for immanent reasoning, the reasons entitling one to a statement are explicitely introduced; the particle rules (synthesis and analysis of local reasons) govern both the local reasons and the local meaning of expressions. But when building the core of a winning **P**-strategy, local reasons are also linked to the justification of the statements—which is not the case if considering single plays, for then only one aspect of the statement may be taken into account during the play, the play providing thus only a partial justification.

Take again the example of a **P**-conjunction, say

$$\mathbf{P}\, w : A \wedge B.$$

In providing a strategic reason w for the conjunction $A \wedge B$, **P** is claiming to have a winning strategy for this conjunction, that is, he is claiming that the conjunction is absolutely justified, that he has a proper reason for asserting it and not simply a *local* reason for stating it. Assuming that **O** has a repetition rank of 1 and has stated both A and B prior to move i, two different plays can be carried out from this point, which we provide without the strategic reason:

Introducing strategic reasons: stating a conjunction

	O			P	
	Concessions			Thesis	0
1	$m := 1$			$n := 2$	2
…	…			…	…
…	…			$! A \wedge B$	i

Introducing strategic reasons: left decision option on conjunction

	O			P	
	Concessions			Thesis	0
1	$m := 1$			$n := 2$	2
…	…			…	…
…	…			$! A \wedge B$	i
$i+1$	$? \wedge_1$			$! A$	$i+1$

Introducing strategic reasons: right decision option on conjunction

	O			P	
	Concessions			Thesis	0
1	$m := 1$			$n := 2$	2
…	…			…	…
…	…			$! A \wedge B$	i
$i+1$	$? \wedge_2$	i		$! B$	$i+2$

So if **P** brings forward the strategic reason w to support his conjunction at move i, he is claiming to be able to win *both* plays, and yet the actual play will follow into only one of the two plays. Strategic reasons are thus a *strategic perspective* on a statement that is brought forward during actual plays.

An Anticipation of the Play and Strategy as Recapitulation

Since a strategic reason (w for instance) is brought forward during a play (say at move i), it is clear that the play has not yet been carried out fully when the player claims to be able to defend his statement against whatever challenge his opponent might launch: bringing forward a strategic reason is thus an anticipation on the outcome of the play.

But strategic reasons are not a simple claim to have a winning strategy, they also have a complex internal structure: they can thus be considered as recapitulations of the plays of the winning strategy produced by the heuristic procedure, that is the winning strategy obtained only after running all the relevant plays; this strategy-building process specific to the dialogical framework is a richer process than the one yielding CTT demonstrations—or proof theory in general—, since the strategic reasons will contain traces of *choice dependences*, which constitute their complexity.

Choice dependences link possible moves of a player to the choices made by the other player: a player will play this move if his opponent used this decision-option, that move if the opponent used that decision-option. In the previous example, the Proponent will play move $i + 2$ depending on the Opponent's decision at move $i + 1$, so the strategic object w played at move i will contain these two possible scenarios with the $i + 2$ **P**-move depending of the $i + 1$ **O**-decision. The strategic reason w is thus a *recapitulation* of what would happen if each relevant play was carried out. When the strategic reason makes clearly explicit this choice-dependence of **P**'s moves on those of **O**, we say that it is in a *canonical argumentation form* and is a recapitulation of the statement.

The rules for strategic reasons do not provide the rules on how to play but rather rules that indicate how a winning strategy has been achieved while applying the relevant rules at the play level. Strategic reasons emerge as the result of considering the optimal moves for a winning strategy: this is what a recapitulation is about.

The canonical argumentation form of strategic reasons is closely linked to the synthesis and analysis of local reasons: they provide the recapitulation of all the relevant local reasons that could be generated from a statement. In this respect following the rules for the synthesis and analysis of local reasons, the rules for strategic reasons are divided into synthesis and analysis of strategic reasons, to which we will now turn.

In a nutshell, the synthesis of strategic reasons provides a guide for what **P** needs to be able to defend in order to justify his claim; the analysis of strategic reasons provides a guide for the local reasons **P** needs to make **O** state in order to copy these reasons and thus defend his statement.

Assertions and Statements

The difference between local reasons and strategic reasons should now be clear: while local reasons provide a local justification entitling one to his statement, strategic reasons provide an absolute justification of the statement, which thus becomes an *assertion*.

The equalities provided in each of the plays constituting a **P**-winning strategy, and found in the analysis of strategic objects, convey the information required for **P** to play in the best possible way by specifying those **O**-moves necessary for **P**'s victory. This information however is not available at the very beginning of the first play, it is not made explicit at the root of the tree containing all the plays relevant for the **P**-winning strategy: the root of the tree will not explicitly display the information gathered while developing the plays; this information will be available only once the whole strategy has been developed, and each possible play considered. So when a play starts, the thesis is a simple statement; it is only at the end of the construction process of the strategic reason that **P** will be able to have the knowledge required to assert the thesis, and thus provide in any new play a strategic reason for backing his thesis.

The *assertion* of the thesis, making explicit the strategic reason resulting from the plays, is in this respect a *recapitulation* of the result achieved after running the relevant plays, after **P**'s initial simple statement of that thesis. This is what the canonical argumentation form of a strategic object is, and what renders the dialogical formulation of a CTT canonical proof-object.

It is in this fashion that dialogical reasons correspond to CTT proof-objects: introduction rules are usually characterized as the right to assert the conclusion from the premises of the inference, that is, as defining what one needs in order to be entitled to assert the conclusion; and the elimination rules are what can be inferred from a given statement. Thus, in the dialogical perspective of **P**-winning strategies, since we are looking at **P**'s entitlements and duties, what corresponds to proof-object introduction rules would define what **P** is required to justify in order to assert his statement, which is the synthesis of a **P**-strategic reason; and what corresponds to proof-object elimination rules would define what **P** is entitled to ask of **O** from her previous statements and thus say it himself by copying her statements, which is the analysis of **P**-strategic reasons. We will thus provide the rules for the synthesis and analysis of strategic reasons (always in the perspective of a **P**-winning strategy), followed by their corresponding CTT rule. We have in this regard a good justification of Sundholm's idea that inferences can be considered as involving an (*implicit*) *interlocutor*, but here at the strategy level.

4.3.2 Rules for the Synthesis of P-Strategic Reasons

P-strategic reasons must be built (*synthesis* of **P**-strategic reasons); they constitute the justification of a statement by providing certain information—choice-dependences—that is essential to the relevant plays issuing from the statement: strategic reasons are a recapitulation of the building of a winning strategy, directly inserted into a play. Thus a strategic reason for a **P**-statement on the universal **P**! $(\forall x: A)\ B(x)$ has the form $\lambda(x^{\mathbf{O}})b^{\mathbf{P}}(x)$, which indicates that **P** has some method $b(x)$, that delivers a winning strategy for $B(x)$,whatever local reason x **O** choses for stating the antecedent. Moreover, it indicates that **P**'s choice for defending the right constituent (its consequent) of the universal is dependent upon **O**'s choice for stating the antecedent.

Strategic reasons for **P** are the dialogical formulation of CTT proof-objects, and the canonical argumentation form of strategic reasons correspond to canonical proof-objects.

Synthesis of strategic reasons for P:

	Move	Synthesis of local reasons		Synthesis of strategic reasons Canonical Argumentation form
		Challenge	Defence	
Conjunction	**P !** $A \wedge B$	**O** ? $L^{\wedge}$ or **O** ? $R^{\wedge}$	**P** p_1: A (resp.) **P** p_2: B	**P** $<p_1, p_2>$: $A \wedge B$
Existential quantification	**P** ! $(\exists x{:}A)B(x)$	**O** ? $L^{\exists}$ or **O** ? $R^{\exists}$	**P** p_1: A (resp.) **P** p_2: $B(p_1)$	**P** $<p_1, p_2>$: $(\exists x{:}A)B(x)$
Disjunction	**P !** $A \vee B$	**O** $?^{\vee}$	**P** p_1: A or **P** p_2: B	**P** $\mathbf{i}(p_1)$: $A \vee B$ or **P** $\mathbf{j}(p_2)$: $A \vee B$ The strategic reason $\mathbf{i}(p_1)$ indicates that **P** has chosen, the left side to build a winning-strategy for the disjunction – $\mathbf{i}(p_1)$ amounts to **P**. choosing p_1 as strategic reason for the disjunction. Analogous holds for $\mathbf{j}(p_2)$, that indicates **P**'s choice for the right-side.
Implication	**P !** $A \supset B$	**O** p_1: A	**P** p_2: B	**P** $\lambda(x^{\mathbf{O}})b^{\mathbf{P}}(x)$: $A \supset B$ $\lambda(x^{\mathbf{O}})b^{\mathbf{P}}(x)$ indicates that **P** has some method $b(x)$, which delivers a winning strategy for the consequent whatever local reason x **O** choses for stating the antecedent.
Universal quantification	**P** ! $(\forall x{:}A)B(x)$	**O** p_1: A	**P** p_2: $B(p_1)$	**P** $\lambda(x^{\mathbf{O}})b^{\mathbf{P}}(x)$: $(\forall x{:}A)B(x)$ $\lambda(x^{\mathbf{O}})b^{\mathbf{P}}(x)$ indicates that **P** has some method $b(x)$, which delivers a winning strategy for $B(x)$, whatever local reason x **O** choses for stating the antecedent.
Negation	**P !** $A \supset \bot$	**O** p_1: A … **O !** $\bot$ (stating the antecedent leads eventually to **O** giving up)	–	**P** $\lambda(x^{\mathbf{O}})b^{\mathbf{P}}(x)$: $A \supset \bot$ The method $b(x)$ encoded by $\lambda(x^{\mathbf{O}})b^{\mathbf{P}}(x)$ will never be carried out. Indeed, since $\lambda(x^{\mathbf{O}})b^{\mathbf{P}}(x)$ provides a winning strategy, **P** will force **O** to state **falsum** himself (on the grounds of the move **O** p_1: A), before $b(x)$ comes into play.

Remark: For the case of negation, we must bear in mind that we are considering **P**-strategies, that is, plays in which **P** wins, and we are not providing particle rules with a proper challenge and defence, but we are adopting a strategic perspective on the reason to provide backing a statement; thus the response to an **O**-challenge on a negation cannot be **P !** $\bot$, which would amount to **P** losing.

4.3.3 Rules for the Analysis of P-Strategic Reasons

Analysis rules for P-strategic reasons

	Move	Analysis of local reasons		Analysis of P-strategic reasons
		Challenge	Defence	
Conjunction	**O** $p: A \wedge B$	**P** ? $L^{\wedge}$ or **P** ? $R^{\wedge}$	**O** $L^{\wedge}(p): A$ … **O** $L^{\wedge}(p) = p_1^{\mathbf{O}}: A$ (resp.) **O** $R^{\wedge}(p) : B$ … **O** $R^{\wedge}(p) = p_2^{\mathbf{O}} : B$	**O** $p: A \wedge B$ **P** ! $C(p)$ ⇓ **P** $c : C(\mathbf{fst}(p))$ (resp.) **O** $p: A \wedge B$ **P** ! $C(p)$ ⇓ **P** $d : C(\mathbf{snd}(p))$ The rules indicate that, given **O** $p: A \wedge B$, **P**'s winning strategy for $C(p)$ is dependent upon **O**'s choice for a local reason for the first (or second) element of the conjunction. Where **O** $\mathbf{fst}(p)=p_1^{\mathbf{O}}: A$, and Where **O** $\mathbf{snd}(p)=p_2^{\mathbf{O}}: B$.
Existential quantification	**O** $p: (\exists x{:}A)B(x)$	**P** ? $L^{\exists}$ or **P** ? $R^{\exists}$	**O** $L^{\exists}(p): A$ … **O** $L^{\exists}(p) = p_1^{\mathbf{O}}: A$ (resp.) **O** $R^{\exists}(p) : B(L^{\exists}(p)^{\mathbf{O}})$ … **O** $R^{\exists}(p) = p_2^{\mathbf{O}} : B(p_1^{\mathbf{O}})$	**O** $p: (\exists x{:}A)B(x)$ **P** ! $C(p)$ ⇓ **P** $c : C(\mathbf{fst}(p))$ (resp.) **O** $p: (\exists x{:}A)B(x)$ **P** ! $C(p)$ ⇓ **P** $d : C(\mathbf{snd}(p))$ Where **O** $\mathbf{fst}(p)=p_1^{\mathbf{O}}: A$, and Where **O** $\mathbf{snd}(p)=p_2^{\mathbf{O}}: B(p_1^{\mathbf{O}})$.
Disjunction	**O** $p\ : A \vee B$	**P** $?^{\vee}$	**O** $L^{\vee}(p)\ : A$ … **O** $L^{\vee}(p) = p_1^{\mathbf{O}}: A$ or **O** $R^{\vee}(p)\ : B$ … **O** $R^{\vee}(p) = p_2^{\mathbf{O}} : B$	**O** $p\ : A \vee B$ **O** $x^{\mathbf{O}}: A$ **O** $y^{\mathbf{O}}: B$ **P** ! $C(\mathbf{i}(x^{\mathbf{O}}))$ **P** ! $C(\mathbf{j}(y^{\mathbf{O}}))$ ⇓ ⇓ **P** d: $C(\mathbf{i}(x^{\mathbf{O}}))$ **P** e: $C(\mathbf{j}(y^{\mathbf{O}}))$ ⇓ **P** $\mathbf{D}(p, x^{\mathbf{O}}.d;\ y^{\mathbf{O}}.e)$: $C(p)$ The strategic reason $\mathbf{D}(p, x^{\mathbf{O}}.d;\ y^{\mathbf{O}}.e)$ indicates that **P**'s winning strategy for $C(p)$, is dependent upon **O**'s choices for the disjunction. In other words **P** $\mathbf{D}(\mathbf{i}(p_1), x^{\mathbf{O}}.d;\ y^{\mathbf{O}}.e) = d[p_1]$: $C(\mathbf{i}(p_1))$. Similarly **P** $\mathbf{D}(\mathbf{j}(p_2), x^{\mathbf{O}}.d;\ y^{\mathbf{O}}.e) = e[p_2]$: $C(\mathbf{j}(p_2))$.

Analysis rules for P-strategic reasons

	Move	Analysis of local reasons		Analysis of P-strategic reasons
		Challenge	**Defence**	
Implication	**O** $p: A \supset B$	**P** $L^{\supset}(p) : A$ … **P** $L^{\supset}(p) = p_1^{\mathbf{P}}$:	**O** $R^{\supset}(p): B$ … **O** $R^{\supset}(p) = p_2: B$	**O** $p: A \supset B$ **O** $p_1: A$ **P** ! B ⇓ **O** $p_1: A$ ⇓ **P** **ap**$(p, p_1^{\mathbf{P}}): B$ The strategic reason **ap**$(p, p_1^{\mathbf{P}})$ indicates that **P** can build a winning strategy for his claim **P** ! B, given that **O** stated $p_1: A$ and that on that ground **P** can deploy this assertion for a challenge on the implication, in order to force **O** to state the consequent. In other words: **P** **ap**$(p, p_1^{\mathbf{P}}) = p_2^{\mathbf{O}}: B$.
Universal quantification	**O** $p: (\forall x{:}A)B(x)$	**P** $L^{\forall}(p) : A$ … **P** $L^{\forall}(p) = p_1^{\mathbf{P}}: A$	**O** $R^{\forall}(p): B(L^{\forall}(p)^{\mathbf{P}})$ … **O** $R^{\forall}(p) = p_2: B(p_1^{\mathbf{P}})$	**O** $p: (\forall x{:}A)B(x)$ **O** $p_1: A$ **P** ! $B(p_1)$ ⇓ **P** $p_1: A$ ⇓ **P** **ap**$(p, p_1^{\mathbf{P}}): B(p_1)$ The strategic reason **ap**$(p, p_1^{\mathbf{P}})$ indicates that **P** can build a winning strategy for his claim **P** ! $B(p_1)$, given that **O** stated $p_1: A$ and that on that ground **P** can deploy this assertion for a challenge on the universal, in order to force **O** to state the consequent. In ther words: **P** **ap**$(p, p_1^{\mathbf{P}}) = p_2^{\mathbf{O}}: B(p_1)$.
Negation	**O** $p: A \supset \bot$	**P** $L^{\supset}(p) : A$ … **P** $L^{\supset}(p) = p_1^{\mathbf{P}}$:	**O** $R^{\supset}(p) : \bot$ … The instruction $R^{\supset}(p)$ keeps un-resolved	**O** $p: A \supset \bot$ **O** $p_1: A$ **P** ! C ⇓ **P** $p_1: A$ ⇓ **O** **ap**$(p, p_1^{\mathbf{P}}): \bot$ ⇓ **P** $you_{gave\ up}$(n): C The strategic reason **ap**$(p, p_1^{\mathbf{P}})$ indicates that **P** can build a winning strategy for C, given that **O** stated $p_1: A$ and that on that ground, **P** can deploy this assertion for a challenge on the implication, in order to force **O** to give up by stating **falsum**.

4.4 A Plaidoyer for the Play-Level

To some extent, the criticisms the dialogical approach to logic has been subject to provides an opportunity for clarifying its basic tenets. We will therefore herewith consider some recent objections raised against the dialogical framework in order to pinpoint some of its fundamental features, whose importance may not have appeared clearly enough through the main body of the paper; namely,

dialogue-definiteness,
player-independence, and
the dialogical conception of proposition.

Showing how and why these features have been developed, and specifying their point and the level they operate on, will enable us to vindicate the play level and thus disarm the objections that have been raised against the dialogical framework for having neglected this crucial level.

We shall first come back on the central notion of dialogue-definiteness and on the dialogical conception of propositions, which are essential for properly understanding the specific role and importance of the play level. We shall then be able to address three objections to the dialogical framework, due to a misunderstanding of the notion of *Built-in Opponent*, of the principles of dialogue-definiteness and of player-independence, and of the reflection on normativity that constitutes the philosophical foundation of the framework; all of these misunderstandings can be reduced to a misappraisal of the play level. We shall then go somewhat deeper in the normative aspects of the dialogical framework, according to the principle that logic has its roots in ethics.

4.4.1 Dialogue-Definiteness and Propositions

The dialogical theory of meaning is structured in three levels, that of the local meaning (determined by the particle rules for the logical constants), of the global meaning (determined by the structural rules), and the strategic level of meaning (determined by what is required for having a winning strategy). The material level of consideration is part of the global meaning, but with particular rules so precise that they determine only one specific expression (through a modified Socratic rule). A characteristic of the local meaning is that the rules are player independent: the meaning is thus defined in the same fashion for each player; they are bound by the same sets of duties and rights when they start a dialogue. This normative aspect is thus constitutive of the play level (which encompasses both the local meaning and the global meaning): it is even what allows one to judge that a dialogue is taking place. In this regard, meaning is immanent to the dialogue: what constitutes the meaning of the statements in a particular dialogue solely rests on rules determining interaction (the local and the global levels of meaning). The strategy level on the other hand is built on the play level, and the notion of demonstration operates on the strategy level (it amounts to having a winning strategy).

Two main tenets of the dialogical theory of meaning can be traced back to Wittgenstein, and ground in particular the pivotal notion of dialogue-definiteness:

1. the internal feature of meaning (the *Unhintergehbarkeit der Sprache*[24]), and
2. the meaning as mediated by language-games.

As for the first Wittgensteinian tenet, the internal feature of meaning, we already mentioned in the introduction that if we relate the notion of internalization of meaning with both language-games and fully-interpreted languages of CTT, then a salient feature of the dialogical approach to meaning can come to fore: the expressive power of CTT allows all these actions involved in the dialogical constitution of meaning to be incorporated as an explicit part of the object-language of the dialogical framework.

In relation to the second tenet, the inceptors of the dialogical framework observed that if language-games are to be conceived as mediators of meaning carried out by social interaction, these language-games must be games actually playable by human beings: it must be the case that *we can actually perform them*,[25] which is captured in the notion of dialogue-definiteness.[26] Dialogue-definiteness is essential for dialogues to be mediators of meaning, but it is also constitutive of what propositions are, as Lorenz clearly puts it:

> [...] *for an entity to be a proposition there must exist an individual play, such that this entity occupies the initial position, and the play reaches a final position with either win or loss after a finite number of moves according to definite rules.* (Lorenz, 2001, p. 258)

A proposition is thus defined in the standard presentation of dialogical logic as a dialogue-definite expression, that is, an expression *A* such that there is an individual play about *A*, that can be said to be lost or won after a finite number of steps, following given rules of dialogical interaction.[27]

---

[24]See *Tractatus Logico-Philosophicus*, 5.6.

[25]As observed by Marion (2006, p. 245), a lucid formulation of this point is the following remark of Hintikka (1996, p. 158) who shared this tenet (among others) with the dialogical framework:

> [Finitism] *was for Wittgenstein merely one way of defending the need of language-games as the sense that* [sic] *they had to be actually playable by human beings.* [...] *Wittgenstein shunned infinity because it presupposed constructions that we human beings cannot actually carry out and which therefore cannot be incorporated in any realistic language-game.* [...] *What was important for Wittgenstein was not just the finitude of the operations we perform in our calculi and other language-games, but the fact that* we can actually perform them. *Otherwise the entire idea of language-games as meaning mediators will lose its meaning. The language-games have to be humanly playable. And that is not possible if they involve infinitary elements. Thus it is the possibility of actually playing the meaning-conferring language-games that is the crucial issue for Wittgenstein, not finitism as such.*

[26]The fact that these language-games must be finite does not rule out the possibility of a (potentially) infinite number of them.

[27]While establishing particle rules the development rules have not been fixed yet, so we might call those expressions *propositional schemata*.

The notion of *dialogue-definiteness* is in this sense the backbone of the dialogical theory of meaning: it provides the basis for implementing the human-playability requirement and the notion of proposition.

Dialogue-definiteness sets apart rather decisively the level of strategies from the level of plays, as Lorenz's notion of dialogue-definite proposition does not amount to a set of winning strategies, but rather to an individual play. Indeed, a winning strategy for a player **X** is a sequences of moves such that **X** wins *independently of the moves of the antagonist*. It is crucial to understand that the qualification *independently of the moves of the antagonist* amounts to the fact that the one claiming *A* has to play under the restriction of the Copy-cat rule: if possessing a winning strategy for player **X** involves being in possession of a method (leading to the win of **X**) allowing to choose a move for any move the antagonist might play, then we must assume that the propositions brought forward by the antagonist are justified. There is a winning strategy if **X** can base his moves leading to a win by endorsing himself those propositions whose justification is rooted on **Y**'s authority. For short, the act of endorsing is what lies behind the so-called Copy-cat rule and structures dialogues for immanent reasoning: it ensures that **X** can win whatever the contender might bring forward in order to contest *A* (within the limits set by the game).

Furthermore, *refuting*, that is bringing up a strategy *against A*, amounts to the dual requirement: that the antagonist **Y** possess a method that leads to the loss of **X** ! *A*, whatever **X** is can bring forward, and that she can do it under the Copy-cat restriction:

> *X !A is refuted, if the antagonist **Y** can bring up a sequence of moves such that she (**Y**) can win playing under the Copy-cat restriction.*

Refuting is thus different and stronger than contesting: while *contesting* only requires that the antagonist **Y** brings forward at least one counterexample in a kind of play where **Y** does not need to justify her own propositions, *refuting* means that **Y** must be able to lead to the loss of **X**! *A, whatever **X**'s justification of his propositions might be*.

In this sense, the assumption that every play is a finitary open two-person zero-sum game does not mean that either there is a winning strategy for *A* or a winning strategy *against A*: the play level cannot be reduced to the strategy level.

For instance, if we play with the Last-duty first development rule **P** will lose the individual plays relevant for the constitution of a strategy for $A \vee \neg A$. So $A \vee \neg A$ is *dialogue-definite*, though there is no winning strategy *against* $A \vee \neg A$.

The distinction between the play level and the strategy level thus emerges from the combination of dialogue-definiteness and the Copy-cat rule.

The classical reduction of strategies against *A* to the falsity of *A* (by means of the saddle-point theorem) assumes that the win and the loss of a *play* reduce to the truth or the falsity of the thesis. But we claim that the existence of the play level and a loss in one of the plays introduces a qualification that is not usually present in the purely proof-theoretic approach; to use the previous example, we know that **P** does not have a winning strategy for $!A \vee \neg A$ (playing under the intuitionisitic development rule), but neither will **O** have one against it if she has to play under the Copy-cat rule herself (notice the switch in the burden of the restriction of the Copy-cat rule when *refuting* a thesis). Let us identify the player who has to play under the Copy-cat restriction by highlighting her moves:

<u>Play *against* **P** ! $A \vee \neg A$</u>

	O			**P**	
				! $A \vee \neg A$	0
1	$n := 1$			$m := 2$	2
3	$?_{\vee}$	0		! A	4
				P wins	

The distinction between the play and the strategy level can be understood as a consequence of introducing the notion of dialogue-definiteness which amounts to a win or a loss at the play level, though strategically seen, the proposition at stake may be (proof-theoretically) undecidable. Hence, some criticisms to the purported lack of dynamics to dialogical logic are off the mark if they are based on the point that "games" of dialogical logic are deterministic[28]: plays are deterministic in the sense that they are dialogue-definite, but strategies are not deterministic in the sense that for every proposition there would either be a winning strategy for it or a winning strategy *against* it.

Before ending this section let us quote quite extensively (Lorenz, 2001), who provides a synopsis of the historical background that lead to the introduction of the notion of dialogue-definiteness and the distinction of the deterministic conception of plays—which obviously operates at the level of plays—from the proof-theoretical undecidable propositions—which operate at the level of strategies:

> [...] *It was Alfred Tarski who, in discussions with Lorenzen in 1957/58, when Lorenzen had been invited to the Institute for Advanced Study at Princeton, convinced him of the impossibility to characterize arbitrary (logically compound) propositions by some decidable generalization of having a decidable proof-predicate or a decidable refutation-predicate.*
>
> [...] *It became necessary to search for some decidable predicate which may be used to qualify a linguistic entity as a proposition about any domain of objects, be it elementary or logically compound. Decidability is essential here, because the classical characterization of a proposition as an entity which may be true or false, has the awkward consequence that of an undecided proposition it is impossible to know that it is in fact a proposition. This observation gains further weight by L. E. J. Brouwer's discovery that even on the basis of a set of "value-definite", i.e., decidably true or false, elementary propositions, logical composition does not in general preserve value-definiteness. And since neither the property of being proof-definite nor the one of being refutation-definite nor properties which may be defined using these two, are general enough to cover the case of an arbitrary proposition, some other procedure had to be invented which is both characteristic of a proposition and satisfies a decidable concept. The concept looked for and at first erroneously held to be synonymous with argumentation*[29] *turned out to be the concept of dialogue about a*

---

28 For such criticisms — see Trafford (2017, pp. 86-88).

29 Lorenz identifies argumentation rules with rules at the strategy level and he would like to isolate the interaction displayed by the moves constituting the play level — see Lorenz (2010a, p.79). We

proposition A (which had to replace the concept of truth of a proposition A as well as the concepts of proof or of refutation of a proposition A, because neither of them can be made decidable). Fully spelled out it means that for an entity to be a proposition there must exist a dialogue game associated with this entity, i.e., the proposition A, such that an individual play of the game where A occupies the initial position, i.e., a dialogue D(A) about A, reaches a final position with either win or loss after a finite number of moves according to definite rules: the dialogue game is defined as a finitary open two-person zero-sum game. Thus, propositions will in general be dialogue-definite, and only in special cases be either proof-definite or refutation-definite or even both which implies their being value-definite. Within this game-theoretic framework where win or loss of a dialogue D(A) about A is in general not a function of A alone, but is dependent on the moves of the particular play D(A), truth of A is defined as existence of a winning strategy for A in a dialogue game about A; falsehood of A respectively as existence of a winning strategy against A. Winning strategies for A count as proofs of A, and winning strategies against A as refutations of A. The meta-truth of "either 'A is true' or 'A is false' " which is provable only classically by means of the saddlepoint theorem for games of this kind may constructively be reduced to the decidability of win or loss for individual plays about A. The concept of truth of dialogue-definite propositions remains finitary, and it will, as it is to be expected of any adequate definition of truth, in general not be recursively enumerable. The same holds for the concept of falsehood which is conspicuously defined independently of negation. (Lorenz, 2001, pp. 257–258).

4.4.2 The Built-in Opponent and the Neglect of the Play Level

In recent literature Catarina Duthil-Novaes (2015) and James Trafford (2017, pp. 102–105) deploy the term *internalization* for the proposal that natural deduction can be seen as having an internalized Opponent, thereby motivating the inferential steps. This form of internalization is called the *built-in Opponent*. The origin of this concept is linked to Göran Sundholm who, by 2000, in order to characterize the fundamental links between natural deduction and dialogical logic, suggested in his lectures and talks the idea that elimination rules can be read as the moves of an Opponent aimed at testing the thesis. Yet, since this reading was meant to link the strategy level with natural deduction, the concept of *built-in Opponent* inherited the same strategic perspective on *logical truth*. Thus, logical truth can be seen as the encoding of a process through which the Proponent succeeds in defending his assertion against a stubborn *ideal* interlocutor.[30]

deploy the term *argumentation-rule* for request-answer interaction as defined by the local and structural rules. It is true that nowadays argumentation-rules has even a broader scope including several kinds of communicative interaction and this might produce some confusion on the main goal of the dialogical framework which is in principle, to provide an argumentative understanding of logic rather than the logic of argumentation. However, once this distinction has been drawn nothing prevents to develop the interface dialogical-understanding of logic/logical structure of a dialogue. In fact, it is our claim that in order to study the logical structure of a dialogue, the dialogical conception of logic provides the right venue.

[30]With "ideal" we mean an interlocutor that always make the optimal choices in order to collaborate in the task of testing the thesis.

From the dialogical point of view however, the ideal interlocutor of the strategy level is the result of a process of selecting the relevant moves from the play level. Rahman/Clerbout/Keiff (2009), in a paper dedicated to the Festschrift for Sundholm, designate the process as *incarnation*, using Jean-Yves Girard's term. Their thorough description of the incarnation process already displays those aspects of the *cooperative endeavour*, which was formulated by Duthil Novaes (2015) and quoted by Trafford (2017, p. 102) as a criticism of the dialogical framework. Their criticism seems to rest on the idea that the dialogues of the dialogical framework are not truly cooperative, since they are reduced to constituting logical truth. If this is really the point of their criticism, it is simply wrong, for the play level would then be completely neglected: the intersubjective in-built and implicit cooperation of the *strategy* level (which takes care of inferences) grows out of the *explicit* interaction of players at the *play* level in relation to the formation-rules; accepting or contesting a local reason is a process by the means of which players cooperate in order to determine the meaning associated to the action-schema at stake.[31]

It is fair to say that the standard dialogical framework, not enriched with the language of CTT, did not have the means to fully develop the so-called material dialogues, that is dialogues that deal with content. Duthil Novaes (2015, p. 602)—but not Trafford (2017, p. 102)—seems to be aware that dialogues are a complex interplay of adversarial and cooperative moves,[32] even in Lorenzen and Lorenz' standard formulation. However, since she understands this interplay as triggered by the built-in implicit Opponent at the strategy level, Duthil Novaes suggestions or corrections motivated by reflections on the Opponent's role cannot be made explicit in the framework.[33]

---

[31]In fact, when Trafford (2017) criticizes dialogical logic in his chapter 4, he surprisingly claims that this form of dialogical interaction does not include the case in which the plays would be open-ended in relation to the logical rules at stake, though it has already been suggested—see for instance in (Rahman & Keiff, 2005, pp. 394-403)—how to develop what we called *Structure Seeking Dialogues* (SSD). Moreover, Keiff's (2007) PhD-dissertation is mainly about SSD. The idea behind SSD is roughly the following; let us take some inferential practice we would like to formulate as an action-schema, mainly in a teaching-learning situation; we then search for the rules allowing us to make these inferential practices to be put into a schema. For example: we take the third excluded to be in a given context a sound inferential practice; we then might ask what kind of moves **P** should be allowed to make if he states the third excluded as thesis. It is nonetheless true to say that SSD were studied only in the case of modal logic. Neither Trafford (2017) nor Duthil-Novaes (2015) nor Duthil-Novaes/French (2018) refer to previous and recent work on linear logic, dialogical paraconsistent logic and belief-revision – see, among others, Rahman/Carnielli (2000), Rahman (2001), Rahman (2002), Rahman/Keiff (2005), Keiff (2007), Keiff (2009), Rahman/Fiutek/Rückert (2010), Beirlaen/Fontaine (2016) and Barrio/Clerbout/Rahman (2018).

[32]To put it in her own words: "*the majority of dialogical interactions involving humans appear to be essentially cooperative, i.e., the different speakers share common goals, including mutual understanding and possibly a given practical outcome to be achieved.*" Duthil Novaes (2015, p. 602).

[33]See for instance her discussion of countermoves Duthil Novaes (2015, p. 602) : indefeasibility means that the Opponent has no available countermove: "A countermove in this case is the presentation of one single situation, no matter how far-fetched it is, where the premises are the

Duthil Novaes' (2015, pp. 602–604) approach leads her to suggest that monotonicity is a consequence of the role of the Opponent as a stubborn adversary, which takes care of the non-defeasibility of the demonstration at stake; from this perspective, she contends that the standard presentations of dialogical logic, being mostly adversarial or competitive, are blind to defeasible forms of reasons and are thus

> [. . .] *rather contrived forms of dialogical interaction, and essentially restricted to specific circles of specialists* (Duthil Novaes, 2015, p. 602).

But this argument is not compelling when considering the strategy level as being built from the play level: setting aside the point on content mentioned above, if we conceive the constitution of a strategy as the end-result of the complementary role of competition and cooperation taking place at the play level, we do not seem to need—at least in many cases—to endow the notion of inference with non-monotonic features. The play level is the level were cooperative interaction, either constructive or destructive, can take place until the definitive answer—given the structural and material conditions of the rules of the game—has been reached.[34] The strategy level is a recapitulation that retains the end result.

These considerations should also provide an end to Trafford's (2017, pp. 86–88) search for *open-ended* dialogical settings: open-ended dialogical interaction, to put it bluntly, is a property of the play level. Certainly the point of the objection may be to point out either that this level is underdeveloped in the literature—a fact that we acknowledge with the provisos formulated above—, or that the dialogical approach to meaning does not manage to draw a clean distinction between local and strategic meaning—the section on *tonk* below intends to make this distinction as clear as possible.

A further point is that according to a recent paper on the dialogical interpretation of the structural rules Duthil-Novaes and French (2018, p. 147) conclude that, from the dialogical point of view, this rule is the less compelling of the structural rules.[35] The problem stems from ignoring the play level and the distinction between a local-reason a and the proposition A backed by a. The way to understand reflexivity, roughly, is the following: **Proponent**! A (**P** claims that he has some reason for

case and the conclusion is not—a counterexample."The question then would be to know how to show that the Opponent has no countermove available. The whole point of building winning strategies from plays is to *actually construct* the evidence that there is no possible move for the Opponent that will lead her to win: that is a winning strategy. But when the play level is neglected, the question remains: how does one know the Opponent has no countermove available? It can actually be argued that the mere notion of countermove tends to blur the distinction between the level of plays and of strategies: a *counter*move makes sense if it is 'counter' to a winning strategy, as if the players were playing at the strategy level, but that is something we explicitly reject. At the play level, there are only simple *moves*: these can be challenges, defences, counterattacks, but *countermoves* do not make any sense.

[34]See Rahman (2015), Rahman/Iqbal (2018) and strategies as recapitulations of cooperative moves in the chapter II of the present book.

[35]Notice however, that Duthil-Novaes/French (2018, pp. 138) seem to assume reflexivity when they bring up an example for the transitivity of implication.

asserting *A)* **Opponent** *On what grounds?* If **O** asserted *A* before and brought forward, say, *a* as local reason, then **P** wins by responding: *my reason is the same as yours!* At the strategy level, the recapitulation of the moves leading to victory, we have **O** *a: A* and **P** *a: A*. But this is not what the play was about!

At this point of the discussion we can say that the role of the (built-in) Opponent in Lorenzen and Lorenz' dialogical logic has been fully misunderstood. Indeed, the role of *both interlocutors* (implicit or not) is not about assuring logical truth by checking the non-defeasibility of the demonstration at stake, but their role is about implementing both the dialogical definiteness of the expressions involved and the internalization of meaning.[36]

4.4.3 Pathological Cases and the Neglect of the Play Level

The notorious case of Prior's (1960) *tonk* has been several times addressed as a counterargument to inferentialism and also to the "indoor-perspective" of the dialogical framework. This also seems to constitute the background of how Trafford (2017, p. 86) for instance reproduces the circularity objection against the dialogical approach to logical constants. At this point of the discussion, Trafford (2017, pp. 86–88) is clearly aware of the distinction between the rules for local meaning and the rules of the strategy level, though he points out that the local meaning is vitiated by the strategic notion of justification. This is rather surprising as Rahman/Keiff (2005), Rahman/Clerbout/Keiff (2009), Rahman (2012) and Redmond/Rahman (2016) have shown it is precisely the case of *tonk* that provides a definitive answer to the issue.

In this respect, three well distinguished levels of meaning are respectively determined by specific rules:

- the local meaning of an expression establishes how a statement involving such an expression is to be attacked and defended (through the particle rules);
- the global meaning of an expression results from structural rules prescribing how to develop a play having this expression for thesis;
- the strategy rules (for **P**) determine what options **P** must consider in order to show that he does have a method for winning whatever **O** may do—in accordance with the local and structural rules.

It can in a quite straightforward fashion be shown (see below) that an inferential formulation of rules for *tonk* correspond to *strategic* rules that *cannot be constituted* by the formulation of *particle* rules. The player-independence of the particle rules—

[36]Notice that if the role of the Opponent in adversial dialogues is reduced to checking the achievement of logical truth, one would wonder what the role of the Opponent might be in more cooperation-featured dialogues: A *soft* interlocutor ready to accept weak arguments?

responsible for the branches at the strategy level—do not yield the strategic rules that the inferential rules for *tonk* are purported to prescribe.

For short, the dialogical take on *tonk* shows precisely how distinguishing rules of local meaning from strategic rules makes the dialogical framework immune to *tonk*. As this distinction is central to the dialogical framework and illustrates the key feature of player-independence of particle rules, we will now develop the argument; we will then be able to contrast this pathological *tonk* case to another case, that of the black-bullet operator.

The *tonk* Challenge and Player-Independence of Local Meaning
To show how the dialogical framework is immune to *tonk* through the importance and priority it gives to the play level, winning strategies are linked to semantic tableaux. According to the dialogical perspective, if tableaux rules (or any other inference system for that matter) are conceived as describing the core of strategic rules for **P**, then the tableaux rules should be justified by the play level, and not the other way round: the *tonk* case clearly shows that contravening this order yields pathological situations. We will here only need conjunction and disjunction for dealing with *tonk*.[37]

A systematic description of the winning strategies available for **P** in the context of the possible choices of **O** can be obtained from the following considerations: if **P** is to win against any choice of **O**, we will have to consider two main different dialogical situations, namely those

(a) in which **O** has uttered a complex formula, and those
(b) in which **P** has uttered a complex formula.

We call these main situations the **O**-cases and the **P**-cases, respectively. In both of these situations another distinction has to be examined:

(i) **P** wins by *choosing*

i.1. between two possible challenges *in the **O**-cases* (a), or
i.2. between two possible defences *in the **P**-cases* (b),

iff he can win with *at least one* of his choices.

(ii) When **O** can *choose*

ii.1. between two possible defences *in the **O**-cases* (a), or
ii.2. between two possible challenges *in the **P**-cases* (b),

P wins iff he can win *irrespective* of **O**'s choices.

The description of the available strategies will yield a version of the semantic tableaux of Beth that became popular after the landmark work on semantic-trees by

[37]Clerbout (2014a,b) worked out the most thorough method for linking winning strategies and tableaux.

Raymond Smullyan (1968), where **O** stands for **T** (left-side) and **P** for **F** (right-side), and where situations of type ii (and not of type i) will lead to a branching-rule.

<u>Semantic tableaux and P-winning strategies for conjunction and disjunction</u>

(**P**)-Chooses	(**O**)-Chooses
$\dfrac{(\mathbf{P})\ A \vee B}{\begin{array}{c}\langle \mathbf{O}? \rangle\ (\mathbf{P})A \\ \langle \mathbf{O}? \rangle\ (\mathbf{P})B\end{array}}$	$\dfrac{(\mathbf{P})\ A \wedge B}{\langle \mathbf{O}?\wedge_1 \rangle\ (\mathbf{P})A \mid \langle \mathbf{P}?\wedge_2 \rangle\ (\mathbf{P})B}$
The expressions of the form ⟨**X**...⟩ constitute interrogative utterances.	The expressions of the form ⟨**X**...⟩ constitute interrogative utterances.
$\dfrac{(\mathbf{O})\ A \wedge B}{\begin{array}{c}\langle \mathbf{P}?\wedge_1 \rangle \\ (\mathbf{O})A \\ \langle \mathbf{P}?\wedge_2 \rangle \\ (\mathbf{O})B\end{array}}$	$\dfrac{(\mathbf{O})\ A \vee B}{\begin{array}{c}\langle \mathbf{P}? \rangle \\ (\mathbf{O})A \mid (\mathbf{O})B\end{array}}$

However, as mentioned above, semantic tableaux are not dialogues. The main point is that dialogues are built bottom up, from local to global meaning, and from global meaning to validity. This establishes the priority of the play level over the winning strategy level. From the dialogical point of view, Prior's original *tonk* contravenes this priority.

Let us indeed temporarily assume that we can start not by laying down the local meaning of *tonk*, but by specifying how a winning strategy for *tonk* would look like with the help of **T**(left)-side and **F**(right)-side tableaux-rules (or sequent-calculus) for logical constants; in other words, let us assume that the tableaux-rules are necessary and sufficient to set the meaning of *tonk*.

Prior's *tonk* rules are built for half on the disjunction rules (taking up only its introduction rule), and for half on the conjunction rules (taking up only its elimination rule). This renders the following tableaux version for the undesirable tonk[38]:

$$\dfrac{(\mathbf{O})\ [\text{or } (\mathbf{T})]\ AtonkB}{(\mathbf{O})\ [(\mathbf{T})]\ B} \qquad , \qquad \dfrac{(\mathbf{P})\ [\text{or } (\mathbf{F})]\ AtonkB}{(\mathbf{P})\ [(\mathbf{F})]\ A}$$

Tonk is certainly a nuisance: if we apply the cut-rule, it is possible to obtain a closed tableau for **T***A*, **F***B*, for any *A* and *B*. Moreover, there are closed tableaux for both $\{\mathbf{T}A,\ Atonk \neg A\}$ and $\{\mathbf{T}A, \neg(Atonk \neg A)\}$.

From the dialogical point of view, the rejection of *tonk* is linked to the fact there is no way to formulate rules for its local meaning that meet the condition of being player-independent: if we try to formulate rules for local meaning matching the ones of the tableaux, the defence yields a different response, namely the tail of *tonk* if the defender is **O**, and the head of *tonk* if the defender is **P**:

[38] Cf. Rahman (2012, pp. 222-224).

O-tonk rule for challenge and defence

O-move	Challenge	Defence
O ! *AtonkB*	P $?_{tonk}$	O ! *B*

P-tonk rule for challenge and defence

P-move	Challenge	Defence
P ! *AtonkB*	O $?_{tonk}$	P ! *A*

The fact that we need two sets of rules for the challenge and the defence of a *tonk* move means that the rule that should provide the local meaning of *tonk* is *player-dependent*, which should not be the case.

Summing up, within the dialogical framework *tonk*-like operators are rejected because there is no way to formulate player-independent rules for its local meaning that justify the tableaux rules designed for these operators. The mere possibility of writing tableaux rules that cannot be linked to the play level rules shows that the play level rules are not vitiated by strategic rules.

This brief reflection on *tonk* should state our case for both, the importance of distinguishing the rules of the play level from those of the strategy level, and the importance of including in the rules for the local meaning the feature of *player-independence*: it is the player-independence that provides the meaning explanation of the strategic rules, not the other way round.

The Black-Bullet Challenge and Dialogue-Definiteness

Trafford (2017, pp. 37–41) contests the standard inferentialist approach to the meaning of logical constants by recalling the counterexample of Stephen Read, the *black-bullet* operator. Indeed, Read (2008, 2010) introduces a different kind of pathological operator, the black-bullet •, a zero-adic operator that says of itself that it is false. Trafford (2017, p. 39 footnote 35) suggests that the objection also extends to CTT; this claim however is patently wrong, since those counterexamples would not meet the conditions for the constitution of a type.[39] Within the dialogical framework, though player-independent rules for black-bullet can be formulated (as opposed to *tonk*), they do not satisfy dialogue-definiteness.

Let us have the following tableaux rules for the black-bullet, showing that it certainly is pathological: they deliver closed tableaux for both • and ¬•:

$$\frac{\textbf{(P)}\ \bullet}{\begin{array}{c}\langle \textbf{O}?\rangle \\ \textbf{(P)}\ \bullet\supset\bot\end{array}} \qquad\qquad \frac{\textbf{(O)}\ \bullet}{\begin{array}{c}\langle \textbf{P}?\rangle \\ \textbf{(O)}\ \bullet\supset\bot\end{array}}$$

[39]Klev (2017, p. 12 footnote 7) points out that the introduction rule of such kind of operator fails to be meaning-giving because the postulated canonical **set** Λ(*A*) occurs negatively in its premiss, and that the restriction avoiding such kind of operators have been already formulated by Martin-Löf (1971, pp. 182-183), and by Dybjer (1994).

We can in this case formulate the following player-independent rules:

Black-bullet player-independent particle rules

Move	Challenge	Defence
X ! $\bullet$	Y ?$\bullet$	X! $\bullet \supset \bot$

The black-bullet operator seems therefore to meet the dialogical requirement of player-independent rules, and would thus have local meaning. But if it does indeed have player-independent rules, the further play on the defence (which is a negation) would require that the challenger concedes the antecedent, that is black-bullet itself:

Deploying the black-bullet challenges

	Y			X	
	...			...	
				! $\bullet$	i
$i+1$	? $\bullet$	i		! $\bullet \supset \bot$	$i+2$
$i+3$	! $\bullet$	$i+2$			
			$i+3$	? $\bullet$	$i+4$

Obviously, this play sequence can be carried out indefinitely, regardless of which player initially states black-bullet. So the apparently acceptable player-independent rules for playing black-bullet would contravene dialogue-definiteness; and the only way of keeping dialogue-definiteness would be to give up player-independence![40]

4.4.4 Conclusion: The Meaning of Expressions Comes from the Play Level

The two pathological cases we have discussed, the *tonk* and the black-bullet operators, stress the difference between the play level and the strategy level and how the meaning provided by rules at the strategy level does not carry to the local meaning. Thus, from the dialogical point of view, the rules determining the meaning of any expression are to be rooted at the play level, and at this level *what is to be admitted and rejected as a meaningful expression amounts to the formulation of a player-*

[40] We could provide at the local level of meaning a set of player-independent rules, and add some special structural rule in order to force dialogue-definiteness—see Rahman (2012, p. 225); however, such kinds of rules would produce a mismatch in the formation of black-bullet: the formulation of the particle rule would have to assume that black-bullet is an operator, but the structural rule would have to assume it is an elementary proposition.

independent rule, that prescribe the constitution of a dialogue-definite proposition (where that expression occurs as a main operator).

Notice that if we include material dialogues the distinction between logical operators and non-logical operators is not important any more. If we enrich the dialogical framework with the CTT-language, this feature comes more prominently to the fore. What the dialogical framework adds to the CTT framework is, as pointed out by Martin-Löf (2017a, b), to set a pragmatic layer where normativity finds its natural place. Let us now discuss the notion of normativity.

4.5 Normativity and the Dialogical Framework

4.5.1 A New Venue for the Interface Pragmatics-Semantics

In his recent book, Jaroslav Peregrin (2014) marshals the distinction between the play level and the strategy level (that he calls *tactics*) in order to offer another insight, more general, into the issue of normativity mentioned at that start of our volume (Indeed, Peregrin understands the normativity of logic not in the sense of a prescription on *how to reason*, but rather as *providing the material by the means of which* we reason.

> *It follows from the conclusion of the previous section that the rules of logic cannot be seen as tactical rules dictating feasible strategies of a game; they are the rules constitutive of the game as such. (MP does not tell us how to handle implication efficiently, but rather what implication is.) This is a crucial point, because it is often taken for granted that the rules of logic tell us how to reason precisely in the tactical sense of the word. But what I maintain is that this is wrong, the rules do not tell us how to reason, they provide us with things with which, or in terms of which, to reason.* (Peregrin, 2014, pp. 228–229)

Peregrin endorses at this point the dialogical distinction between rules for plays and rules for strategies. In this regard, the prescriptions for developping a *play* provide the *material* for reasoning, that is, the material allowing a play to be developped, and without which there would not even be a play; whereas the prescriptions of the *tactical* level (to use his terminology) prescribe how to win, or how to develop a winning-strategy:

> *This brings us back to our frequently invoked analogy between language and chess. There are two kinds of rules of chess: first, there are rules of the kind that a bishop can move only diagonally and that the king and a rook can castle only when neither of the pieces have previously been moved. These are the rules constitutive of chess; were we not to follow them, we have seen (Section 5.5) we would not be playing chess. In contrast to these, there are tactical rules telling us what to do to increase our chance of winning, rules advising us, e.g., not to exchange a rook for a bishop or to embattle the king by castling. Were we not to follow them, we would still be playing chess, but with little likelihood of winning.* (Peregrin, 2014, pp. 228-229)

This observation of Peregrin plus his criticism on the standard approach to the dialogical framework, according to which this framework would only focus on *logical constants* (Peregrin, 2014, pp. 100, 106)—a criticism shared by many others since (Hintikka, 1973, pp. 77–82)—naturally leads to the main subject of our book, namely immanent reasoning, or linking CTT with the dialogical framework.

The criticism according to which the focus would be on logical constants and not on the meaning of other expressions does indeed fall to some extent on the standard dialogical framework, as little studies have been carried out on material dialogues in this basic framework[41]; but the enriched CTT language in material dialogues deals with this shortcoming.

Yet this criticism seems to dovetail this other criticism, summoned by Martin-Löf as starting point in his Oslo lecture:

> *I shall take up criticism of logic from another direction, namely the criticism that you may phrase by saying that traditional logic doesn't pay sufficient attention to the social character of language.* (Martin-Löf, 2017a, p. 1)

The focus on the social character of language not only takes logical constants into account, of course, but it also considers other expressions such as elementary propositions or questions, as well as the acts bringing these expressions forward in a dialogical interaction, like statements, requests, challenges, or defences—to take examples from the dialogical framework—and how these acts made by persons intertwine and call for—or put out of order—other specific responses by that person or by others. In this regard, the social character of language is put at the core of immanent reasoning through the normativity present in dialogues: normativity involves, within immanent reasoning, rules of interaction which allow us to consider assertions as the result of having intertwined rights and duties (or permissions and obligations). This central normative dimension of the dialogical framework at large, which stems from questionning what is actually being done when implementing the rules of this very framework, entails that objections according to which the focus would be only on logical constants will always be, from the dialogical perspective, slightly off the mark.

As mentioned in the introduction, in his Oslo and Stockholm lectures, Martin-Löf's (2017a, b) delves in the structure of the deontic and epistemic layers of statements within his view on dialogical logic. In order to approach this normative aspect which pervades logic up to its technical parts, let us discuss more thoroughly the following extracts of "Assertion and Request"[42]:

> [...] *we have this distinction, which I just mentioned, between, on the one hand, the social character of language, and on the other side, the non-social* [...] *view of language. But there is a pair of words that fits very well here, namely to speak of the monological conception of logic, or language in general, versus a dialogical one. And here I am showing*

[41]This kind of criticism does not seem to have been aware of (Lorenz, 1970, 2009, 2010a, 2010b), carrying out a thorough discussion on predication from a dialogical perspective, which discusses the interaction between perceptual and conceptual knowledge. However, perhaps it is fair to say that this philosophical work has not been integrated into the dialogical logic—we will come back to this subject below.

[42]Transcription of Martin-Löf (2017a, pp. 1-3, 7).

some special respect for Lorenzen, who is the one who introduced the very term dialogical logic.

The first time I was confronted with something of this sort was when reading Aarne Ranta's book Type-Theoretical Grammar *in* (1994). *Ranta there gave two examples, which I will show immediately. The first example is in propositional logic, and moreover, we take it to be constructive propositional logic, because that does matter here, since the rule that I am going to show is valid constructively, but not valid classically. Suppose that someone claims a disjunction to be true, asserts, or judges, a disjunction to be true. Then someone else has the right to come and ask him, Is it the left disjunct or is it the right disjunct that is true? There comes an opponent here, who questions the original assertion, and I could write that in this way:*

$$? \vdash A \vee B \; true$$

And by doing that, he obliges the original assertor to answer either that A is true that is, to assert either that A is true or that B is true, so he has a choice, and we need to have some symbol for the choice here.

$$(Dis) \quad \frac{\vdash A \vee B \; true \qquad ? \vdash A \vee B \; true}{\vdash A \; true \mid \vdash B \; true}$$

Ranta's second example is from predicate logic, but it is of the same kind. Someone asserts an existence statement,

$$\vdash (\exists x : A)B(x) \; true$$

and then someone else comes and questions that

$$? \vdash (\exists x : A)B(x) \; true$$

And in that case the original assertor is forced, which is to say, he must come up with an individual from the individual domain and also assert that the predicate B is true of that instance.

[...] *So, what are the new things that we are faced with here? Well, first of all, we have a new kind of speech act, which is performed by the\ oh, I haven't said that, of course I will use the standard terminology here, either speaker and hearer, or else respondent and opponent, or proponent and opponent, as Lorenzen usually says, so that's terminology but the novelty is that we have a new kind of speech act in addition to assertion.*

[...] *So, let's call them rules of interaction, in addition to inference rules in the usual sense, which of course remain in place as we are used to them.*

[...] *Now let's turn to the request mood. And then it's simplest to begin directly with the rules, because the explanation is visible directly from the rules. So, the rules that involve request are these, that if someone has made an assertion, then you may question his assertion, the opponent may question his assertion.*

$$(Req1) \quad \frac{\vdash C}{? \vdash_{may} C}$$

Now we have an example of a rule where we have a may. The other rule says that if we have the assertion $\vdash C$, and it has been challenged, then the assertor must execute his knowledge how to do C. And we saw what that amounted too in the two Ranta examples, *so I will write this schematically that he will continue by asserting zero, one, or more we have two in the existential case so I will call that schematically by C0.*

$$(Req2)\quad \frac{\vdash C \qquad ?\vdash C}{\vdash_{must}\, C'}$$

The Oslo and the Stockholm lectures of Martin-Löf (2017a, b) contain challenging and deep insights in dialogical logic, and the understanding of *defences as duties* and *challenges as rights* is indeed at the core of the deontics underlying the dialogical framework.[43] More precisely, the rules Req1 and Req2 do both, they condense the local rules of meaning, and they bring to the fore the normative feature of those rules, which additionally provides a new understanding for Sunholm's notion of *implicit interlocutor*: once we make explicit the role of the interlocutor, the deontic nature of logic comes out.[44] Moreover, as Martin-Löf points out, and rightly so, they should not be called *rules of inference* but *rules of interaction.*

Accordingly, a dialogician might wish to add players **X** and **Y** to Req2, in order to stress both that the dialogical rules do not involve inference but *interaction*, and that they constitute a new approach to the action-based background underlying Lorenzen's (1955) *Operative Logik*. This would yield the following, where we substitute the horizontal bar for an arrow[45]:

$$\text{(Req2)}\quad \begin{array}{ccc} \vdash^{X} C & & ?\vdash^{Y}_{may}\ C \\ & \Downarrow & \\ & ?\vdash^{X}_{must}\ C' & \end{array}$$

Such a rule does indeed condense the rules of local meaning, but it still does not express the choices while defending or challenging; yet it is the distribution of these choices that determines for example that the meaning of a disjunction is different from that of a conjunction: while in the former case (disjunction) the defender *must choose* a component, the latter (conjunction) requires of the challenger that, *her right to challenge is bounded to her duty to choose* the side to be requested (though she might further on request the other side). Hence, the rules for disjunction and conjunction (if we adapt them to Martin-Löf's rules) would be the following:

---

[43] See Lorenz (1981, p. 120), who uses the expressions *right to attack* and *duty to defend.*

[44] This crucial insight of Martin-Löf on dialogical logic and on the deontic nature of logic seems to underly recent studies on the dialogical framework which are based on Sundholm's notion of the *implicit interlocutor*, such as Duthil Novaes (2015) and Trafford (2017).

[45] In the context of Operative Logik operations are expressed by means of arrows of the form "⇒".

(Dis)
$$\begin{array}{ccc} \vdash^{X} D & & ?\ \vdash^{Y}_{may}\ \mathrm{D} \\ & \Downarrow & \\ & \vdash^{X}_{must}\ D' & \\ & \textit{choose} & \\ & \textit{one of the components} & \\ & \textit{of the disjunction } D & \end{array}$$

(Conj)
$$\begin{array}{ccc} \vdash^{X} C & & ?_{left}\ \vdash^{Y}_{may}\ \mathrm{C} \\ & \Downarrow & \\ & \vdash^{X}_{must}\ C' & \\ & \textit{assert} & \\ & \textit{the left of } C & \end{array}$$

(Conj)
$$\begin{array}{ccc} \vdash^{X} C & & ?_{right}\ \vdash^{Y}_{may}\ \mathrm{C} \\ & \Downarrow & \\ & ?\ \vdash^{X}_{must}\ C'' & \\ & \textit{assert} & \\ & \textit{the right of } C & \end{array}$$

These rules can be considered as inserting in the rules the back and forth movement described by Martin-Löf (2017a, p. 8) with the following diagram:

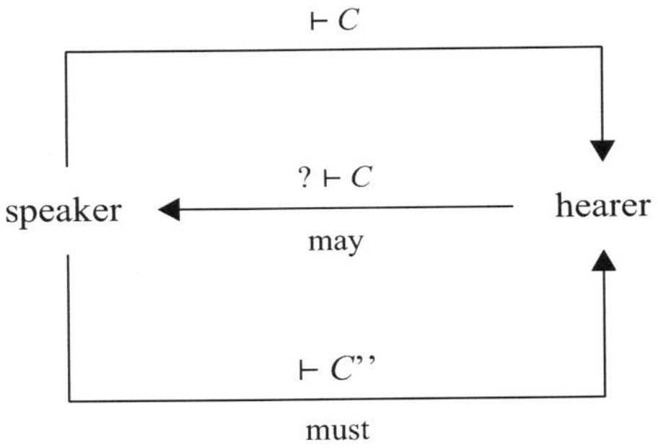

Notice however that these rules only determine the local meaning of disjunction and conjunction, not their global meaning. For example, while classical and constructive disjunction share the same rules of local meaning, they differ at the global level of meaning: in a classical disjunction the defender may come back on the choice he made for defending his disjunction, though in a constructive disjunction this is not allowed, once a player has made a choice he must live with it.

What is more, these rules are not rules of inferences (for example rules of introduction and elimination): they become rules of inference only when we focus on the choices **P** must take into consideration in order to claim that he has a winning strategy for the thesis. Indeed, as mentioned at the start of the present chapter strategy rules (for **P**) determine what options **P** must consider in order to show that he has a method for winning whatever **O** does, in accordance with the rules of local and global meaning.

The introduction rules on the one hand establish what **P** has to bring forward in order to assert it, when **O** challenges it. Thus in the case of a disjunction, **P** must *choose* and *assert* one of the two components. So, **P**'s obligation lies in the fact that he must choose, and so **P**'s *duty to choose* yields the introduction rule. Compare this with the conjunction where it is the *challenger* who has the *right to choose* (and who does not assert but request his choice). But in both cases, defending a disjunction and defending a conjunction, only one conclusion will be produced, not two: in the case of a conjunction, the challenger will ask one after the other (recall that it is an interaction taking place within a dialogue where each step alternates between moves of each of the players).

The elimination rules on the other hand prescribe what moves **O** must consider when she asserted the proposition at stake. So if **O** asserted a disjunction, **P** must be able to win whatever the choices of **O** be.

The case of the universal quantifier adds the *interdependence of choices* triggered by the *may*-moves and the *must*-moves: if the thesis is a universal quantifier of the form $(\forall x : A)\ B(x)$, **P** must assert $B(a)$, for *whatever a* **O** may chose from the domain A: this is what correspond to the introduction rule. If it is **O** who asserted the universal quantifier, and if she also conceded that, $a : A$, then **P** may challenge the quantifier by choosing $a : A$, *and request* of **O** that she asserts $B(a)$; this is how the elimination for the universal quantifier is introduced in the dialogical framework.

These distinctions can be made explicit if we enrich the first-order language of standard dialogical logic with expressions inspired by CTT. The first task is to introduce statements of the form "$p : A$". On the right-hand side of the colon is the proposition A, on the left-hand side is the *local reason p* brought forward to back the proposition *during a play*. The local reason is therefore *local* if the force of the assertion is limited to the level of plays. But when the assertion "$p : A$" is backed by a *winning strategy*, the judgement asserted draws its justification precisely from that strategy, thus endowing p with the status of a strategic reason that, in the most general cases, encodes an arbitrary choice of **O**.

The rock bottom of the dialogical approach is still the play level notion of dialogue-definiteness of the proposition, namely

> *For an expression to count as a proposition A there must exist an individual play about the statement* **X** *! A, in the course of which* **X** *is committed to bring forward a local reason to back that proposition, and the play reaches a final position with either win or loss after a finite number of moves according to definite local and structural rules.*

The deontic feature of logic is here built directly within the dialogical concept of statements about a proposition. More generally, the point is that, as observed by Martin-Löf (2017a, p. 9), according to the dialogical conception, logic belongs to the area of ethics.

One way of explaining how this important aspect has been overseen or misunderstood might be that the usual approaches to the layers underlying logic got the order of priority between the deontic notions and the epistemic notions the wrong way round.[46]

Martin-Löf's lectures propose a fine analysis of the inner and outer structure of the statements of logic from the point of view of speech-act theory, that put the order of priority mentioned above right; in doing so it pushes forward one of the most

[46]See (Martin-Löf, 2017b, p. 9).

cherished tenets of the dialogical framework, namely that *logic has its roots in ethics*.

In fact, Martin-Löf's insights on dialogical logic as re-establishing the historical links of ethics and logic provides a clear answer to Wilfried Hodges's (2008)[47] sceptical view in his section 2 as to what the dialogical framework's contribution is. Hodges's criticism seems to target the *mathematical* interest of a dialogical conception of logic, rather than a philosophical interest which does not seem to attract much of his interest.

In lieu of a general plaidoyer for the dialogical framework's philosophical contribution to the foundations of logic and mathematics, which would bring us too far, let us highlight these three points which result from the above discussions:

1. the dialogical interpretation of epistemic assumptions offers a sound venue for the development of inference-based foundations of logic;
2. the dialogical take on the interaction of epistemic and deontic notions in logic, as well as the specification of the play level's role, display new ways of implementing the interface pragmatics-semantics within logic.
3. the introduction of *knowing how* into the realm of logic is of great import (Martin-Löf, 2017a, b).

Obviously, formal semantics in the Tarski-style is blind to the first point, misunderstands the nature of the interface involved in the second, and ignores the third.

4.5.2 The Semantic and Communicative Interface in Dialogical Setting

The book *Logic, Language and Method. On Polarities in Human Experience*, published in 2010, includes papers written by Kuno Lorenz in a period extending over more than thirty years. These papers have planted the seeds for his further penetrating work (Lorenz, 2009, 2010a, b), which can be considered as philosophical variations on *Das Dialogische Prinzip* (2010b, pp. 509–520) underlying what is often known as *Dialogical Constructivism*.

In the framework of Dialogical Constructivism, the analysis of the notion of intersubjectivity starts by the study of a situation where two persons are engaged in the process of acquiring a common action-competence in a situation of teaching and learning[48]; what is at stake then is not simply mirroring an individual competence in another individual, but rather it is a *procedure* which incorporates from the very

[47] See also Hodges (2001) and Trafford (2017, pp. 87-88).

[48] The bibliographic background of this section is based mainly on (Lorenz, 2010a, pp. 2017-2018) chapter *Procedural Principles of the Erlangen School. On the Interrelation between the principles of method, of dialogue, and of reason.*

beginning this dialogical situation.[49] Immanent reasoning, being an offspring of Dialogical Constructivism, inherits its philosophical background and sensitivity. In this regard, the rules of the play level are not actualizations by themselves, but are rather procedures for actualizing some action consisting in dealing with an object or appropriating that object, be it in a situation of teaching and learning, or any dialogical situation.

A consequence of Lorenz's (2017b, pp. 509–520) general dialogical principle is that the interface semantics-pragmatics should be understood

1. neither as the result of the *semantization of pragmatics*—where deontic, epistemic, ontological, and temporal modalities become truth-functional operators;
2. nor as the result of the *pragmatization of semantics*—where a propositional kernel, when put into use, is complemented by moods yielding assertions, questions, commands and so on.

Lorenz's view (2010a, pp. 71–79) is that the differentiation of semantic and pragmatic layers is the result of the articulation within one and the same utterance: each utterance displays in principle both features: it *signifies* (semantic layer) and it *communicates* (pragmatic layer).

Take for example one-word sentences such as:

Rabbit!
Water!

With these utterances the speaker is conveying at the same time *what* the object is and *how* the object is. But while the first aspect (*what*) is related to *object-constitution*, the second (*how*) is related to *object-description;* or, if we use the terminology of Wittgenstein's *Tractatus* (1922), the first aspect relates to the *act of showing* and the second to the *act of saying*. Object-description is carried out by the use of predicates on an already constituted domain of objects. Lorenz recalls here Plato's *Cratylus* (388b), in which these two acts and their interdependence are distinguished as *naming* (which has the role of *indicating*) and *establishing* (with the role of *communicating*).[50]Lorenz's view is that each utterance of a sentence has this double nature, not only one-word sentences. Thus:

(a) *Sam is smoking*.

has both roles, indicating as well as communicating; though according to this analysis, uttering such a sentence does not yield any ambiguity: uttering it simply displays within one movement object-constitution (or construction) and object-description (or attribution).

While the first, object-constitution, involves differentiating parts of a whole (including the processes of partitioning a whole by synthesis and analysis), the

[49]The act of executing must be distinguished from taking the action as an object: while executing an action, actor and execution are said to be indistinguishable.

[50]In the previous section we briefly present the discussion of the *Cratylus* found in (Lorenz & Mittelstrass, 1967).

second, object-description, involves stating that a certain relation holds. In this regard, *attribution* is not a relation, but a means for stating that relations hold of objects. The usual procedure for representing attribution by using extensional class-membership relations thus blurs this distinction.

According to the language of immanent reasoning (borrowed from CTT),

(a) *Sam is smoking*

can be read as expressing either

(b) ! *Sam*: *Smoking*

or

(c) ! *d*(*Sam*): *Smoking*(*Sam*) (*Sam*: *Human*)

From the point of view of Lorenz's Dialogical Constructivism, me might say that the colon in both claims separates, using his words, the significative, particular, part of the expression from the communicative, universal, side of it, placed at the right side of the colon.

These considerations deserve further investigation, though this conclusion is not their place. But the point here is to stress that, according to the dialogical principle, pragmatization and semantization are two different aspects: $a : B$ and $B(a)$ are not the result of an ambiguity of some sort, but are simply two aspects, the semantic aspect and the pragmatic aspect.

4.6 Final Remarks

The play level is the level where meaning is forged: it provides the material with which we reason.[51] It reduces neither to the (singular) performances that actualize the interaction-types of the play level, nor to the "tactics" for the constitution of the schema that yields a winning strategy.

We call our dialogues involving rational argumentation *dialogues for immanent reasoning* precisely because *reasons* backing a statement, that are now *explicit* denizens of the object-language of plays, are *internal* to the development of the dialogical interaction itself.

More generally, the emergence of concepts, so we claim, are not only games of giving and asking for reasons (games involving *Why*-questions) they are also games that include moves establishing *how is it that the reason brought forward accomplishes the explicative task.* Dialogues for immanent reasoning are dialogical games of *Why* and *How*. Notice that the notion of dialogue-definiteness is not bound to knowing how *to win*—this is rather a feature that characterizes winning strategies; to master meaning of an implication, within the dialogical framework, amounts rather

[51]To use Peregrin's 2014, pp.228–229 words.

to *know how to* develop an *actual play for it*. In this context it is worth mentioning that during the Stockholm and Oslo talks on dialogical logic, Martin-Löf (2017a, b) points out that one of the hallmarks of the dialogical approach is the notion of *execution*, which—as mentioned in the preface—is close to the requirement *of bringing forward a suitable equality while performing an actual play*. Indeed from the dialogical point of view, an equality statement comes out as an answer to a question on the local reason *b* of the form *how*: *How do you show the efficiency of b as providing a reason for A*? In this sense the *how*-question presupposes that *b* has been brought-forward as an answer to a *why* question: *Why does A hold*? Thus, equalities express the way how to execute or carry out the actions encoded by the local reason; however, the actualization of a play-schema *does not require the ability of knowing how to win a play*. Thus, while execution, or *performance*, is indeed important the backbone of the framework lies in the *dialogue-definiteness notion of a play*.

The point of the preceding paragraph is that though actualizing and schematizing are processes at the heart of the dialogical construction of meaning, they should not be understood as performing two separate actions: through these actions we acquire the competence that is associated to the meaning of an expression by *learning* to play both, *the active* and *the passive* role. This feature of Dialogical Constructivism stems from Herder's view[52] that the cultural process is a process of education, in which teaching and learning always occur together: dialogues display this double nature of the cultural process in which concepts emerge from a complex interplay of *why* and *how* questions.. In this sense, as pointed out by Lorenz (2010a, pp. 140–147) the dialogical teaching-learning situation is where *competition,* the I-perspective, and *cooperation interact,* the You-perspective: both intertwine in collective forms of dialogical interaction that take place at the play level.

If the reader allows us to condense our proposal once more, we might say that the perspective we are trying to bring to the fore is rooted in the intimate conviction that meaning and knowledge are something we do together; our perspective is thus an invitation to participate in the open-ended dialogue that is the human pursuit of knowledge and collective understanding, since philosophy's endeavour is immanent to the kind of dialogical interaction that makes reason happen.

Acknowledgements I would like to thank the Laboratory STL: UMR-CNRS 8163 and to Leone Gazziero (STL), Laurent Cesalli (Genève), and Claudio Majolino (STL), leaders of the ANR-Project *SEMAINO*, for fostering the research leading to the present study.

Many thanks to Christina Weiss for her superb editorial work. My thanks also to Zoe McConaughey (STL), Steephen Eckoubili (STL) Clément Lion (STL) and Mohammad Shafiei (U. Shahid Beheshti) for fruitful discussions, and to the reviewers who suggested important improvements.

[52]See Herder (1960 [1772], Part II).

References

Austin, J. L. (1946). Other minds. *Aristotelian Soc Suppl, 20*, 148–187.

Barrio, E., Clerbout, N., & Rahman, S. (2018). Introducing consistency in a dialogical framework. *submitted*.

Beirlaen, M., & Fontaine, M. (2016). *Inconsistency-adaptive dialogical logic*. Logica Universalis.

Brandom, R. (1994). *Making it explicit*. Cambridge: Harvard University Press.

Brandom, R. (1997). A study guide. In W. Sellars (Ed.), *Empiricism and the philosophy of mind* (pp. 119–189). Cambridge MA: Harvard University Press.

Brandom, R. (2000). *Articulating reasons*. Cambridge: Harvard University Press.

Clerbout, N. (2014a). First-order dialogical games and tableaux. *Journal of Philosophical Logic, 43*(4), 785–801.

Clerbout, N. (2014b). *Étude sur quelques sémantiques dialogiques : Concepts fondamentaux et éléments de métathéorie*. London: College Publications.

Clerbout, N., & Rahman, S. (2015). *Linking game-theoretical approaches with constructive type theory: Dialogical strategies as CTT-demonstrations*. Dordrecht: Springer.

Crubellier, M. (2014). *Aristote, Premiers analytiques. Traduction, introduction et commentaire.* Garnier-Flammarion.

Duthil Novaes, C. (2015). A dialogical, multiagent account of the normativity of logic. *Dialectica, 69*(4), 587–609.

Duthil Novaes, C. & French, R. (2018). A dialogical, multiagent account of the normativity of logic. *Philosophical Issues, 28*(4), pp. 129–158.

Dybjer, P. (1994, July). Inductive families. Form asp Comput vol. 6, pp. 440–465. Formal Aspects of Computing, 6, 440–465.

Frege, G. (1979). Boole's logical calculus and the concept script [1880/81]. In K. Hermes & K. (Eds.), *Gottlob Frege posthumous Writtings* (pp. 9–52). Oxford: Basil Blackwell.

Herder, J. G. (1960 [1772]). Abhandulung über der Ursprung der Sprache. In E. Heintel, *Johann Gottfried Herder. Spachphilosophische Schriften.* (pp. 3–87). Hamburg: Felix Meiner.

Hintikka, J. (1973). *Logic, language-games and information: Kantian themes in the philosophy of logic*. Oxford: Clarendon Press.

Hintikka, J. (1996). *Ludwig Wittgenstein: Half truths and one-and-a-half truths*. Dordrecht: Kluwer.

Hodges, W. (2001). Dialogue foundations: A sceptical look. *Aristotelian Society Supplementary, 75*(1), 17–32.

Hodges, W. (2008). Logic and games. *Stanford encyclopedia of philosophy*.

Howard, W. A. (1980). The formulae-as-types notion of construction. In J. P. Seldin, & J. R. Hindley (Eds.), *To H. B. Curry: Essays on combinatory logic, lambda Calculus and formalism* (pp. 479–490). London: Academic.

Keiff, L. (2004). Heuristique formelle et logiques modales non normales. *Philosophia Scientiae, 8*(2), 39–59.

Keiff, L. (2007). Le Pluralisme dialogique: Approches dynamiques de l'argumentation formelle. Lille: PhD.

Keiff, L. (2009). *Dialogical logic*. (E. N. Zalta, Ed.) Retrieved from the Stanford encyclopedia of philosophy: http://plato.stanford.edu/entries/logic-dialogical

Klev, A. (2017). The justification of identity elimination in Martin-Löf's type theory. *Topoi*, 1–25.

Krabbe, E. C. (1985). Formal systems of dialogue rules. *Synthese, 63*, 295–328.

Lorenz, K. (1970). *Elemente der Sprachkritik. Eine Alternative zum Dogmatismus und Skeptizismus in der Analytischen Philosophie*. Frankfurt: Suhrkamp.

Lorenz, K. (1981). Dialogical logic. In W. Marciszewsku (Ed.), *Dictionary of logic as applied in the study of language* (pp. 117–125). The Hague: Martinus Nijhoff.

Lorenz, K. (2001). Basic objectives of dialogue logic in historical perspective. S. Rahman, & H. Rückert, (Eds.) *127*(1–2), 225–263.

Lorenz, K. (2009). *Dialogischer Konstruktivismus*. Berlin/New York: De Gruyter.

Lorenz, K. (2010a). *Logic, language and method: On polarities in human experiences*. Berlin/New York: De Gruyter.

Lorenz, K. (2010b). *Philosophische Variationen: Gesammelte Aufsätze unter Einschluss gemeinsam mit Jürgen Mittelstrass greschrievener Arbeiten zu Platon und Leibniz*. Berlin/New York: De Gruyter.

Lorenz, K., & Mittelstrass, J. (1967). On rational philosophy of language. The Programme in Plato's Cratylus reconsidered. *Mind, 76*(301), 1–20.

Marion, M. (2006). Hintikka on Wittgenstein: From language games to game semantics. In T. Aho & A.-V. Pietarinen (Eds.), *Truth and games: Essays in honour of Gabriel Sandu* (pp. 237–256). Helsinki: Acta Philosophica Fennica.

Marion, M. (2009). Why play logical games? In O. Majer, A. V. Pietarinen, & T. Tulenheimo (Eds.), *L. a. Games: Unifying logic*. Dordrecht: Springer.

Marion, M. (2010). Between saying and doing: From Lorenzen to Brandom and Back. In P. E. Bour, M. Rebuschi, & L. Rollet (Eds.), *Constructions: Essays in honour of Gerhard Heinzmann* (pp. 489–497). London: College Publications.

Marion, M., & Rückert, H. (2015). Aristotle on universal quantification: A study from the perspective of game semantics. *History and Philosophy of Logic, 37*(3), 201–209.

Martin-Löf, P. (1971). Hauptsatz for the intuitionistic theory of iterated inductive definitions. In J. E. Fenstad (Ed.), *Proceedings of the second Scandinavian logic symposium* (pp. 179–216). Amsterdam: North-Holland.

Martin-Löf, P. (1984). *Intuitionistic type theory. Notes by Giovanni Sambin of a series of lectures given in Padua, June 1980*. Naples: Bibliopolis.

Martin-Löf, P. (2014). *Truth of empirical propositions*. Lecture held at the University of Leiden, February 2014. Transcription by: Amsten Klev.

Martin-Löf, P. (2015). Is logic part of normative ethics? *Lecture Held at the research Unity Sciences, Normes, Décisions (FRE 3593), Paris, May 2015*. Transcription by:: Amsten Klev.

Martin-Löf, P. (2017a). Assertion and request. Lecture held at Oslo, 2017. Transcription by Ansten Klev.

Martin-Löf, P. (2017b). Assertion and request. *Lecture held at Stockholm*. Transcription by Ansten Klev.

McDowell, J. (2009). *Having the world in view: Essays on Kant, Hegel, and Sellars*. Harvard: Harvard University Press.

Peregrin, J. (2014). *Inferentialism. Why rules matter*. New York: Plagrave MacMillan.

Prior, A. (1960). The runabout inference-ticket. *Analysis, 21*, 38–39.

Rahman, S. (2001). On Frege's nightmare: A combination of intuitionistic, Free and paraconsistent logics. In H. Wansing, *Essays on non-classical logics* (pp. 61–90). New Jersey/London/Singapore/Hong Kong: World Scientific.

Rahman, S. (2002, October). "Un Desafío para las Teorías Cognitivas de la Competencia Lógica: Los Fundamentos Pragmáticos de la Semántica de la Lógica Linear". *Manuscrito, 25*(2), 381–432.

Rahman, S. (2012). Negation in the logic of first degree entailment and Tonk. A dialogical study. In S. Rahman, G. Primiero, & M. Marion (Eds.), *The realism-antirealism debate in the age of alternative logics* (pp. 213–250). Springer Netherlands.

Rahman, S. (2019). The logic of reasons and endorsement. In C. Weiss (Ed.), *Constructive semantics*, Springer. Chapter I. In print

Rahman, S., & Carnielli, W. (2000). The dialogical approach to paraconsistency. *Synthese, 125*(1–2), 201–232.

Rahman, S., & Clerbout, N. (2015). Constructive type theory and the dialogical turn : A new start for the Erlanger Konstruktivismus. In J. Mittelstrass & C. von Bülow (Eds.), *Dialogische Logik* (pp. 91–148). Münster: Mentis.

Rahman, S., & Iqbal, M. (2018). Unfolding parallel reasoning in Islamic Jurisprudence. Epistemic and dialectical meaning within Abū Isḥāq al-Shīrāzī's system of co-relational inferences of the occasioning factor. *Cambridge Journal of Arabic Sciences and Philosophy*, 28, 67–132.

Rahman, S., & Keiff, L. (2005). On how to be a dialogician. In D. Vanderveken (Ed.), *Logic, thought and action* (pp. 359–408). Dordrecht: Kluwer.
Rahman, S., Fiutek, V., & Rückert, H. (2010). A dialogical semantics for Bonanno's system of belief revision". In P. E. Bour, M. Rebuschi, L. Rollet (Eds.), *Construction* (pp. 315–334). London: College Publications.
Rahman, S., McConaughey, Z., Klev, A., & Clerbout, N. (2018). *Immanent reasoning. A plaidoyer for the play level*. Dordrecht: Springer.
Rahman, S., Clerbout, N., & Keiff, L. (2009). On dialogues and natural deduction. In G. Primiero & S. Rahman (Eds.), *Acts of knowledge: History, philosophy and logic: Essays dedicated to Göran Sundholm* (pp. 301–336). London: College Publications.
Rahman, S., Redmond, J., & Clerbout, N. (2017). "Interaction and Equality. The dialogical interprepretation of CTT" (In Spanish). *Critica, 49*(145), 51–91.
Ranta, A. (1988). Propositions as games as types. *Syntese, 76*, 377–395.
Read, S. (2008). Harmony and modality. In C. Dégremont, L. Kieff, & H. Rückert (Eds.), *Dialogues, logics and other strange things: Essays in honour of Shahid Rahman* (pp. 285–303). London: College Publications.
Read, S. (2010). General elimination harmony and the meaning of the logical constants. *Journal of Philosophical Logic, 39*, 557–576.
Redmond, J., & Rahman, S. (2016). Armonía Dialógica: tonk Teoría Constructiva de Tipos y Reglas para Jugadores Anónimos. *Theoria, 31*(1), 27–53.
Rückert, H. (2011). *Dialogues as a dynamic framework for logic*. London: College Publications.
Sellars, W. (1991). *Science, perception and reality*. Atascadero-California: Ridgeview Publishing Company.
Shafiei, M. (2017). *Intentionnalité et signification: Une approche dialogique*. Paris: PHD-thesis, Sorbonne.
Smullyan, R. (1968). *First-order logic*. New York: Springer.
Sundholm, G. (1997). Implicit epistemic aspects of constructive logic. *Journal of Logic, Language and Information, 6*(2), 191–212.
Sundholm, G. (2001). A Plea for logical atavism. In O. Majer (Ed.), *The Logica yearbook 2000* (pp. 151–162). Prague: Filosofía.
Sundholm, G. (2006). Semantic values for natural deduction derivations. *Synthese, 148*(3):623–638
Sundholm, G. (2012). "Inference versus Consequence" revisited: Inference, Consequence, Conditional, Implication. *Synthese, 187*(3):943–956.
Sundholm, G. (2013). Inference and Consequence in an Interpeted Language. Talk at *the workshop proof theory and philosophy*, Groningen, December 3–5, 2013.
Trafford, J. (2017). *Meaning in dialogue. An interactive approach to logic and reasoning*. Dordrecht: Springer.
van Heijenoort, J. (1967). Logic as calculus and logic as language. *Synthese, 17*, 324–330.
Young, W. E. (2017). *The dialectical forge. Juridical disputation and the evolution of Islamic law*. Dordrecht: Springer.
Wittgenstein, L. (1922). *Tractatus logico-philosophicus*. Lille: Kegan Paul.

Appendix: Some Basic Notions of Constructive Type Theory

Extracted from Chapter II *A brief introduction to constructive type theory* by **Ansten Klev** (in Rahman/McConaughey/Clerbout/Klev (2018)).

Martin-Löf's Constructive Type Theory (CTT) is a formal language developed in order to reason constructively about mathematics. It is thus a formal language conceived primarily as a tool to reason with rather than a formal language conceived primarily as a mathematical system to reason about. Constructive Type Theory is therefore much closer in spirit to Frege's ideography and to the language of Russell and Whitehead's Principia Mathematica than to the majority of logical systems ("logics") studied by contemporary logicians. Since CTT is designed as a language to reason with, much attention is paid to the explanation of basic concepts. This is perhaps the main reason why the style of presentation of CTT differs somewhat from the style of presentation typically found in, for instance, ordinary logic textbooks. For those new to the system it might be useful to approach an introduction, such as the one given below, more as a language course than as a course in mathematics.

Judgements and Categories

Statements made in Constructive Type Theory are called judgements. Judgement is thus a technical term, chosen because of its long pedigree in the history logic. (cf. e.g. (Martin-Löf 1996, 2011) and (Sundholm 2009)). Judgement thus understood is a logical notion and not, as it is commonly understood in contemporary philosophy, a psychological notion. As in traditional logic, a judgement may be categorical or hypothetical. Categorical judgements are conceptually prior to hypothetical judgements, hence we must begin by explaining them.

S. Rahman et al., *Inferences by Parallel Reasoning in Islamic Jurisprudence*, Logic, Argumentation & Reasoning 19, https://doi.org/10.1007/978-3-030-22382-3

Forms of Categorical Judgement

There are two basic forms of categorical judgement in CTT:

$$a : \mathcal{C}$$

$$a = b : \mathcal{C}$$

The first is read "a is an object of the category $\mathcal{C}$" and the second is read "a and b are identical objects of the category $\mathcal{C}$". Ordinary grammatical analysis of $a : \mathcal{C}$ yields a as subject, $\mathcal{C}$ as predicate, and the colon as copula. We thus call the predicate $\mathcal{C}$ in $a : \mathcal{C}$ a category. This use of the term 'category' is in accordance with one of the original meanings of the Greek katēgoria, namely as predicate. It is also in accordance with a common use of the term 'category' in current philosophy.[1] We require, namely, that any category $\mathcal{C}$ occurring in a judgement of CTT be associated with

- a criterion of application, which tells us what a $\mathcal{C}$ is; that a meets this criterion is precisely what is expressed in $a : \mathcal{C}$;
- a criterion of identity, which tells us what it is for a and b to be identical $\mathcal{C}$s; that a and b together meet this criterion is precisely what is expressed in $a = b : \mathcal{C}$.

What the categories of CTT are will be explained below.

In CTT any object belongs to a category. The theory recognizes something as an object only if it can appear in a judgement of the form $a : \mathcal{C}$ or $a = b : \mathcal{C}$. Since associated with any category there is a criterion of identity, we can recover Quine's (1969, p. 23) precept of "no entity without identity" as

- no object without category +
- no category without a criterion of identity.

Thus we derive Quine's precept from two of the fundamental principles of CTT. We shall have more to say later about the treatment of identity in CTT.

Neither semantically nor syntactically does $a : \mathcal{C}$ agree with the basic form of statement in predicate logic:

$$F(a)$$

In $F(a)$ a function F is applied to an argument a (in general there may be more than one argument). The judgement $a : \mathcal{C}$, by contrast, does not have function–argument form. In fact, the '$a : \mathcal{C}$'-form of judgement is closer to the 'S is P'-form of traditional syllogistic logic than to the function-argument form of modern, Fregean logic. Since we have required that the predicate $\mathcal{C}$ be associated with criteria of application and identity, the judgement $a : \mathcal{C}$ can only be compared with a special

[1] See, in particular, the definition of category given by Dummett (1973, pp. 75–76), which has been taken over by Hale and Wright (2001) for instance.

case of the '*S* is *P*'-form, for no such requirement is in general laid on the predicate *P* in a judgement of Aristotle's syllogistics—it can be any general term.

To understand the restriction that *P* be associated with criteria of application and identity, in terms of traditional logic, we may invoke Aristotle's doctrine of predicables from the Topics.[2] A predicable may be thought of as a certain relation between the *S* and the *P* in an '*S* is *P*'-judgement. Aristotle distinguishes four predicables: genus, definition, idion or proprium, and accident. That *P* is a genus of *S* means that *P* reveals a what, or a what-it-is, of the subject *S*; a genus of *S* may thus be proposed in answer to the question of what *S* is. The class of judgements of Aristotelian syllogistics to which judgements of the form $a : C$ may be compared is the class of judgements whose predicate is a genus of the subject. Provided the judgement $a : C$ is correct, the category C is namely an answer to the question of what a is; we may thus think of C as the genus of a. Aristotle's other predicables will not concern us here.

Being a natural number is in a clear sense a what of 7. The number 7 is also a prime number; but being prime is not a what of 7 in the sense that being a natural number is, even though 7 is necessarily, and perhaps even essentially, a prime number. Following Almog (1991) we may say that being prime is one of the hows of 7. This difference between the what and the how of a thing captures quite well the difference in semantics between a judgement $a : C$ of CTT and a sentence $F(a)$ of predicate logic. In the predicate-logical language of arithmetic we do not express the fact that 7 is a number by means of a sentence of the form $F(a)$. That the individual terms of the language of arithmetic denote numbers is rather a feature of the interpretation of the language that we may express in the metalanguage.[3] We do, however, say in the language of arithmetic that 7 is prime by means of a sentence of the form $F(a)$, for instance as **Pr**(7). It is therefore natural to suggest that by means of the form of statement $F(a)$ we express a how, but not the what, of the object a. The opposite holds for the form of statement $a : C$—by means of this we express the what, but not the how, of the object a. Thus, in CTT we do say that 7 is a number by means of a judgement, namely as $7 : \mathbb{N}$, where $\mathbb{N}$ is the category of natural numbers; but we do not say that 7 is prime by means of a similar judgement such as 7 : **Pr**. Precisely how we express in CTT that 7 is prime will become clear only later; it will then be seen that we express the primeness of 7 by a judgement of the form

$$p : \mathrm{Pr}(7)$$

where **Pr**(7) is a proposition and p is a proof of this proposition. The proposition **Pr** (7) has function-argument form, just as the atomic sentences of ordinary predicate logic.

[2](Barnes 1984), (Crubellier 2008).

[3]Compare Carnap's treatment of what he calls Allwörter ('universal words' in the English translation) in §§ 76, 77 of Logische Syntax der Sprache, (Carnap 1934).

Categories

The forms of judgement $a : C$ and $a = b : C$ are only schematic forms. The specific forms of categorical judgement employed in CTT are obtained from these schematic forms by specifying the categories of the theory. There is then a choice to be made, namely between what may be called a higher-order and a lower-order presentation of the theory. The higher-order presentation results in a somewhat conceptually cleaner theory, but the lower-order presentation is preferable for pedagogical purposes, both because it requires less machinery and because it is the style of presentation found in the standard references of Martin-Löf (1975b; 1982; 1984) and Nordström et al. (1990, ch. 4–16). We shall therefore follow this style of presentation. The categories are then the following. There is a category set of sets in the sense of Martin-Löf; and for any set A, A itself is a category. We therefore have the following four forms of categorical judgement:

$$A : \mathbf{set}$$

$$A = B : \mathbf{set}$$

and for any set A,

$$a : A$$

$$a = b : A$$

In the higher-order presentation the categories are **type** and α, for any **type** α. The higher-order presentation in a sense subsumes the lower-order presentation, since we have there, firstly, as an axiom **set**: **type**, hence **set** itself is a category; and secondly, there is a rule to the effect that if A:**set**, then A:**type**, hence also any **set** A will be a category. The higher-order presentation can be found in Nordström et al. (1990, ch. 19–20; 2000).

We have so far only given names to our categories. To justify calling **set** as well as any **set** A a category we must specify the criteria of application and identity of **set** and of A, for any **set** A. Thus we have to explain four things: what a **set** is, what identical sets are, what an element of a **set** A is, and what identical elements of a **set** A are. By giving these explanations we also explain the four forms of categorical judgement A: **set**, $A = B$: **set**, a: A, and $a = b$: A. Our explanations follow those given by Martin-Löf (1984, pp. 7–10).

We explain the form of judgement A: **set** as follows. A **set** A s defined by saying what a canonical element of A is and what equal canonical elements of A are. (Instead of 'canonical element' one can also say 'element of canonical form'.) What the canonical elements are, as well as what equal canonical elements are, of a **set** A is determined by the so-called introduction rules associated with A. For instance, the introduction rules associated with the **set** of natural numbers $\mathbb{N}$ are as follows.

$$0 : \mathbb{N} \quad 0 = 0 : \mathbb{N} \quad \frac{n : \mathbb{N}}{\mathbf{s}(n) : \mathbb{N}} \quad \frac{n = m : \mathbb{N}}{\mathbf{s}(n) = \mathbf{s}(m) : \mathbb{N}}$$

By virtue of these rules 0 is a canonical element of $\mathbb{N}$, as is $\mathbf{s}(n)$ provided n is a $\mathbb{N}$, which does not have to be canonical. Moreover, 0 is the same canonical element of $\mathbb{N}$ as 0, and $\mathbf{s}(n)$ is the same canonical element of $\mathbb{N}$ as $\mathbf{s}(m)$ provided $n = m : \mathbb{N}$. It is required that the specification of what equal canonical elements of a **set** A are renders this relation reflexive, symmetric, and transitive.

The form of judgement $A = B$: **set** means that from a's being a canonical element of A we may infer that a is also a canonical element of B, and vice versa; and that from a and b's being identical canonical elements of A we may infer that they are also identical canonical elements of B, and vice versa.

Thus we have given the criteria of application and identity for the category **set**. Suppose that A is a **set**. Then we know how the canonical elements of A are formed as well as how equal canonical elements of A are formed. The judgement a: A means that a is a programme which, when executed, evaluates to a canonical element of A. For instance, once one has introduced the addition function, +, and the definitions $1 = \mathbf{s}(0) : \mathbb{N}$ and $2 = \mathbf{s}(1) : \mathbb{N}$, one can see that 2 + 2 is an element of $\mathbb{N}$, since it evaluates to $\mathbf{s}(2 + 1)$, which is of canonical form. A canonical element of a **set** A evaluates to itself; hence, any canonical element of A is an element of A.

The judgement $a = b$: A presupposes the judgements a: A and b: A Hence, if we can make the judgement $a = b$: A, then we know that both a and b evaluate to canonical objects of A. The judgement $a = b$: A means that a and b evaluate to equal canonical elements of A. The value of a canonical element a of a **set** A is taken be a itself. Hence, if b evaluates to a, then we have $a = b$: A.

Thus we have given the criteria of application and identity for the category A, for any **set** A.

A note on terminology is here in order. 'Set' is the term used by Martin-Löf from (Martin-Löf 1984) onwards for what in earlier writings of his were called types.[4] A **set** in the sense of Martin-Löf is a very different thing from a **set** in the sense of ordinary axiomatic **set** theory. In the latter sense a **set** is typically conceived of as an object belonging to the cumulative hierarchy V. It is, however, this hierarchy V itself rather than any individual object belonging to V that should be regarded as a **set** in the sense of Martin-Löf. A **set** in the sense of Martin-Löf is in effect a domain of individuals, and V is precisely a domain of individuals. That was certainly the idea of Zermelo in his paper on models of **set** theory (Zermelo 1930): he there speaks of such models as Mengenbereiche, domains of sets. And Aczel (1978) has defined a **set** in the sense of Martin-Löf that is "a type theoretic reformulation of the classical conception of the cumulative hierarchy of types" (Aczel 1978, p. 61). It is in order to mark this difference in conception that we denote a **set** in the sense of Martin-Löf with boldface type, thus writing '**set**'.[5]

---

[4]This older terminology is retained for instance in Homotopy Type Theory (The Univalent Foundations Program 2013); what is there called a set (The Univalent Foundations Program 2013, p. Definition 3.1.1) is only a special case of a set in Martin-Löf's sense, namely a set over which every identity proposition has at most one proof.

[5]For a further discussion of the difference between Martin-Löf's notion and other notions of set, see (Granström 2011, pp. 53–63) and (Klev 2014a, pp. 138–140).

General Rules of Judgemental Equality

Recall that when defining a **set** A, it is required that the relation of being equal canonical elements then specified be reflexive, symmetric, and transitive. From the explanation of the form of judgement $a = b$: A, it is then easy to see that the relation of the so-called judgemental identity, namely the relation expressed to hold between a and b by means of the judgement $a = b$: A, is also reflexive, symmetric, and transitive. Thus the following three rules are justified.

$$\frac{a : A}{a = a : A} \qquad \frac{a = b : A}{b = a : A} \qquad \frac{a = b : A \quad b = c : A}{a = c : A}$$

The explanation of the form of judgement $A = B$:**set** justifies the same rules at the level of sets.

$$\frac{A : \mathbf{set}}{A = A : \mathbf{set}} \qquad \frac{A = B : \mathbf{set}}{B = A : \mathbf{set}} \qquad \frac{A = B : \mathbf{set} \quad B = C : \mathbf{set}}{A = C : \mathbf{set}}$$

They also justify the following two important rules.

$$\frac{a : A \quad A = B : \mathbf{set}}{a : B} \qquad \frac{a = b : A \quad A = B : \mathbf{set}}{a = b : B}$$

Propositions

The notion of proposition has already been alluded to above; and it is reasonable to expect that a system of logic should give some account of this notion. In CTT there is a category **prop** of propositions. The reason this category was not explicitly introduced above is that it is identified in CTT with the category **set**. Thus we have

prop = **set**

The identification of these two categories[6] is the manner in which the so-called Curry–Howard isomorphism (Howard 1980) is implemented in CTT. This "isomorphism" is one of the fundamental principles on which the theory rests.

When regarding A as a proposition, the elements of A are thought of as the proofs of A. Thus proof is employed as a technical term for elements of propositions. A proposition is, accordingly, identified with the **set** of its proofs. That a proposition is true means that it is inhabited.

By the identification of **set** and **prop** the meaning-explantion of the four basic forms of categorical judgement carries over to the explanation of the similar forms

[6] In the higher-order presentation this identification can be made in the language itself, namely as the judgement **prop** = **set** : **type**.

$$A : \mathbf{prop}$$

$$A = B : \mathbf{prop}$$

$$a : A$$

$$a = b : A$$

To define a **prop** one must lay down what are the canonical proofs of A and what are identical canonical proofs of A.That the propositions A and B are identical means that from a's being a canonical proof of A we may infer that it is also a canonical proof of B, and vice versa; and that from a and b's being identical canonical proofs of A we may infer that they are also identical canonical proofs of B, and vice versa. Thus, by the identification of **set** and **prop** we get for free a criterion of identity for propositions.

That a is a proof of A means that a is a method which, when executed, evaluates to a canonical proof of A. That a and b are identical proofs of A means that a and b evaluate to identical canonical proofs of A. Thus we have provided a criterion of identity for proofs.

Let us illustrate the concept of a canonical proof in the case of conjunction. A canonical proof of $A \wedge B$ is a proof that ends in an application of $\wedge$-introduction

$$\frac{\begin{matrix} D_1 & \quad & D_2 \\ A & \quad & B \end{matrix}}{A \wedge B}$$

where $\mathcal{D}_1$ is a proof of A and $\mathcal{D}_2$ a proof of B. An example of a non-canonical proof is therefore

$$\frac{\begin{matrix} D_1 & \quad & D_2 \\ C \supset A \wedge B & \quad & C \end{matrix}}{A \wedge B}$$

where $\mathcal{D}_1$ is a proof of $C \supset A \bigwedge B$ and $\mathcal{D}_2$ a proof of C.

The proofs occurring in the above illustration are in tree form. Proofs in the technical sense of CTT are not given in tree form, but rather as the subjects a of judgements of the form a: A, where A is a **prop**. Proofs in this sense are in effect terms in a certain rich typed lambda-calculus and they are often called proof-objects (this term was introduced by (Diller and Troelstra 1984)).

We may introduce a new form of judgement 'A *true*' governed by the following rule of inference

$$\frac{a\colon A}{A\ \mathit{true}}$$

Thus, provided we have found a proof a of A, we may infer A *true*. The conclusion A *true* can be seen as suppressing the proof a of A displayed in a: A.

Forms of Hypothetical Judgement

One of the characteristic features of Constructive Type Theory is that it recognizes hypothetical judgements as a form of statement distinct from the assertion of the truth of an implicational proposition $A \supset B$. In fact, hypothetical judgements are fundamental to the theory. It is, for instance, hypothetical judgements that give rise to the various dependency structures in CTT, by virtue of which it is a dependent type theory.

Assume A: **set**. Then we have the following four forms of hypothetical judgement with one assumption.

$$x : A \vdash B : \mathbf{set}$$
$$x : A \vdash B = C : \mathbf{set}$$
$$x : A \vdash b : B$$
$$x : A \vdash b = c : B$$

We have used the turnstile symbol, $\vdash$, to separate the antecedent, or assumption, of the judgement from the consequent. In (Martin-Löf 1984) the notation used is

$$B : \mathbf{set}\ (x : A)$$

for what we here write $x : A \vdash B : \mathbf{set}$. We read this judgement as "B is a **set** under the assumption x:A". Similar remarks apply to the other three forms of hypothetical judgement. Let us consider the more precise meaning-explantions of these forms of judgement.

A judgement of the form $x : A \vdash B : \mathbf{set}$ means that

$B[a/x] : \mathbf{set}$ whenever $a : A$, and
$B[a/x] = B[a'/x] : \mathbf{set}$ whenever $a = a' : A$.

Here '$B[a/x]$' signifies the result of substituting 'a' for 'x' in 'B'. Thus we may think of B as a function from A into **set**; or using a different terminology, B may be thought of as a family of sets over A. We are assuming that x is the only free variable in B and that A contains no free variables, hence that the judgement A: **set** holds categorically, that is, under no assumptions. It follows that $B[a/x]$ is a closed term, hence that $B[a/x]$: **set** holds categorically; by the explanation given of the form of categorical judgement A: **set** we therefore know the meaning of $B[a/x]$: **set**. Thus we see that the meaning of a hypothetical judgement is explained in terms of the meaning of categorical judgements. It holds in general that the meaning-explantion of hypothetical judgements is thus reduced to the meaning-explantion of categorical judgements.

The explanation of the form of judgement $x : A \vdash B : \mathbf{set}$ justifies the following two rules.

$$\frac{a : A \quad x : A \vdash B : \mathbf{set}}{B[a/x] : \mathbf{set}} \qquad \frac{a = a' : A \quad x : A \vdash B : \mathbf{set}}{B[a/x] = B[a'/x] : \mathbf{set}}$$

Note that by the second rule here, substitution into sets is extensional with respect to judgemental identity. That is to say, if we think of $x : A \vdash B : \mathbf{set}$ as expressing that B is a **set**-valued function (a family of sets), then B has the expected property that for identical arguments $a = a' : A$ we get identical values $B[a/x] = B[a'/x]$: **set**.

We note that the notion of substitution is here understood only informally and that the notation $B[a/x]$ belongs to the metalanguage. The notion of substitution can be made precise, and a notation for substitution introduced into the language of CTT itself; but it would take us too far afield to get into the details of that (cf. (Martin-Löf 1992) and (Tasistro 1993)).

A judgement of the form $x : A \vdash B = C : \mathbf{set}$ means that

$B[a/x] = C[a/x]$: **set** whenever a: A.

Hence, in this case we may think of B and C as identical families of sets over A. The explanation justifies the following rule.

$$\frac{a: A \qquad x: A \vdash B = C: \mathbf{set}}{B\ [a/x] = C\ [a/x]: \mathbf{set}}$$

A judgement of the form $x : A \vdash b : B$ means that

$b[a/x] : B[a/x]$ whenever $a : A$, and
$b[a/x] = b[a'/x] : B[a/x]$ whenever $a = a' : A$.

Here we are presupposing $x : A \vdash B : \mathbf{set}$, hence we know that $B[a/x] : \mathbf{set}$ whenever $a : A$, and therefore we also know the meaning of $b[a/x] : B[a/x]$ and $b[a/x] = b[a'/x] : B[a/x]$ whenever $a : A$ and $a = a' : A$. The judgement $x : A \vdash b : B$ can be understood as saying that b is a function from A into the family B; that is to say, b is a function that for any $a : A$ yields an element $b[a/x]$ of the **set** $B[a/x]$. The explanation justifies the following two rules.

$$\frac{a : A \quad x : A \vdash b : B}{b[a/x] : B[a/x]} \qquad \frac{a = a' : A \quad x : A \vdash b : B}{b[a/x] = b[a'/x] : B[a/x]}$$

Note that by the second rule here, substitution into elements of sets is extensional with respect to judgemental identity. That is to say, if we think of $x : A \vdash b : B$ as expressing that b is a function, then b has the expected property that for identical arguments $a = a' : A$ we get identical values $b[a/x] = b[a'/x] : B[a/x]$.

A judgement of the form $x : A \vdash b = c : B$ means that

$b[a/x] = c[a/x] : B[a/x]$ whenever $a : A$.

Thus, in this case, b and c are identical functions into the family B. The explanation justifies the following rule.

$$\frac{a: A \qquad x: A \vdash b = c: B}{b\,[a/x] = c[a/x]: B[a/x]}$$

Assumptions and Other Speech Acts

The notions of proposition, categorical judgement, and hypothetical judgement can be seen all of them to be presupposed by what is arguably the most natural interpretation of natural deduction derivations (Sundholm 2006). Consider the following natural deduction proof sketch:

$$\cfrac{\cfrac{\begin{matrix} A \\ D_1 \\ B \end{matrix}}{A \supset B} \qquad \begin{matrix} D_2 \\ A \end{matrix}}{B}$$

Here $\mathcal{D}_1$ is a proof of B from A, and $\mathcal{D}_2$ is a closed proof of A. Let us regard this natural deduction proof sketch as a representation of an actual mathematical demonstration and let us consider which speech acts the individual formulae here then represent.

The topmost A represents an assumption, namely the assumption that the proposition A is true.

The formula A that is the conclusion of $\mathcal{D}_2$ is the conclusion of a closed proof; this formula therefore represents the categorical judgement, or assertion, that A is true; the same considerations apply to $A \supset B$ and to the final conclusion B.

The B that is the conclusion of $\mathcal{D}_1$ represents neither an assumption nor a categorical assertion; it rather represents a hypothetical judgement, namely the judgement that B is true on the hypothesis that A is true.

The formula A occurring as a subformula in $A \supset B$ represents neither an assumption nor a categorical assumption nor a hypothetical judgement. It rather represents a proposition that is a part of a more complex proposition $A \supset B$, which in the given proof is asserted categorically to be true.

Thus we see that in order to make the semantics of natural deduction derivations explicit we should employ a notation that is able to distinguish not only propositions from judgements, but also categorical judgements from hypothetical judgements, and perhaps also assumptions from all of these. Assumptions can, however, be subsumed under hypothetical judgements, since we may regard the assumption of some categorical judgement J as the assertion of J on the hypothesis that J. In particular, the assumption of $a : A$ and the assumption that the proposition A is true may be analyzed as respectively:

$a : A \vdash a : A$ and $A\ true \vdash A\ true$

In CTT one can therefore make the semantics of the above natural deduction proof sketch explicit as follows

$$\cfrac{\cfrac{\begin{array}{c} A\ true \ \vdash\ A\ true \\ D_1 \\ A\ true\ \vdash\ B\ true \end{array}}{A \supset B\ true} \qquad \begin{array}{c} D_2 \\ A\ true \end{array}}{B\ true}$$

From the meaning-explantion of hypothetical judgements it is clear that the following rule is justified.

$$\frac{A\text{: }\mathbf{set}}{x\text{: }A \vdash x\text{: }A}$$

Nordström et al. (1990, p. 37) call this the rule of assumption, since it in effect allows us to introduce assumptions.

Hypothetical judgements with more than one assumption

The forms of hypothetical judgement where the number of hypotheses is $n > 1$ are explained by induction on n. We consider the case of $n = 2$ for illustration. We assume that $A_1 : \mathbf{set}$ and $x : A_1 \vdash A_2 : \mathbf{set}$. Thus A_1 is a **set** categorically, while A_2 is a family of **set**s over A_1. The four forms of judgement to be considered are the following.

$$\begin{array}{l} x : A_1, x_2 : A_2 \vdash B : \mathbf{set} \\ x : A_1, x_2 : A_2 \vdash B = C : \mathbf{set} \\ x : A_1, x_2 : A_2 \vdash b : B \\ x : A_1, x_2 : A_2 \vdash b = c : B \end{array}$$

The first of these judgements means that $B[a_1/x_1,\ a_2/x_2] : \mathbf{set}$ whenever $a_1 : A_1$ and $a_2 : A_2[a_1/x_1]$ and that $B[a_1/x_1,\ a_2/x_2] = B[a_1'/x_1,\ a_2'/x_2] : \mathbf{set}$ whenever $a_1 = a_1' : A_1$ and $a_2 = a_2' : A_2\ [a_1/x_1]$. Note that A_2 here in general may be a family of **set**s over A_1. Which member of the family the second argument a_2 is taken from depends on the first argument a_1. Thus B is a family of **set**s over A_1 and A_2, where A_2 itself may be a family of **set**s over A_1.

The meaning of the third judgement is that $b[a_1/x_1, a_2/x_2] : B[a_1/x_1, a_2/x_2]$ whenever $a_1 : A_1$ and $a_2 : A_2[a_1/x_1]$, and that $b[a_1/x_1, a_2/x_2] = b[a_1'/x_1, a_2'/x_2] : B[a_1/x_1, a_2/x_2]$ whenever $a_1 = a_1' : A_1$ and $a_2 = a_2' : A_2\ [a_1/x_1]$. Thus b is a binary function whose first argument is an element of A_1; if this element is a_1, then the second argument is an element of $A_2[a_1/x_1]$; if the second argument is a_2, then the value $b[a_1/x_1, a_2/x_2]$ is an element of $B[a_1/x_1, a_2/x_2]$.

Here one sees the complex dependency structures that can be expressed in CTT.It should be clear how the explanation of the second and fourth forms of judgement above, as well as the explanation for arbitrary n, should go.

Let J be any categorical judgement, that is, a judgement of one of the forms $B : \mathbf{set}$, $B = C : \mathbf{set}$, $b : B$, $b = b' : B$. In a hypothetical judgement

$$x_1 : A_1, \ldots, x_n : A_n \vdash J$$

we call the sequence of hypotheses $x_1 : A_1, \ldots, x_n : A_n$ a context. A judgement of the form

$$x_1 : A_1, \ldots, x_n : A_n \vdash B : \mathbf{set}$$

may thus be expressed by saying that B is a **set** in the context $x_1 : A_1, \ldots, x_n : A_n$. Let Γ be a context. From the meaning-explantion of hypothetical judgements one sees that rules of the following kind are justified.

$$\frac{\Gamma \vdash J \qquad \Gamma \vdash B\text{: }\mathbf{set}}{\Gamma, y\text{: } B \vdash J}$$

These rules may be called rules of weakening, in accordance with the terminology used in sequent calculus.

With the general hypothetical form of judgement explained we may introduce a notion of category in a wider sense, in effect what is called a category in (Martin-Löf 1984, p. 21–23). Let us write the four general forms of judgement in the style of Martin-Löf, namely as follows.

$$B : \mathbf{set}\ (x_1 : A_1, \ldots, x_n : A_n)$$
$$B = C : \mathbf{set}\ (x_1 : A_1, \ldots, x_n : A_n)$$
$$b : B\ (x_1 : A_1, \ldots, x_n : A_n)$$
$$b = c : B\ (x_1 : A_1, \ldots, x_n : A_n)$$

In a grammatical analysis of the first of these it is natural to view not only **set** but everything that is to the right of the colon, namely

$$\mathbf{set}\ (x_1 : A_1, \ldots, x_n : A_n)$$

as the predicate. The relation between the notions of predicate and category thus suggests that we may regard this as a category. Indeed, this may be regarded as the category of families of **set**s in n variables ranging over the **set**s or families of **set**s A_1, …, A_n, among which there may be dependency relations as explained for the case of $n = 2$ above. Likewise we may regard

$$B\ (x_1 : A_1, \ldots, x_n : A_n)$$

as a category. It is the category of n-ary functions from A_1, …, A_n into the family B (again keeping dependency relations in mind).

Thus we may extend the notion of category to include not only **set** and A for any A, but also n-ary families of **set**s and n-ary functions into a **set** A. Note that these are indeed categories in the present sense since they are associated with criteria of application and identity, namely through the explanation of the general forms of hypothetical judgement.

Rules

So far we have only the frame of a language, namely an explanation of its basic forms of statement as well as explanations of the basic notions of **set**, proposition, element of a **set**, and proof of a proposition. The frame is filled by the introduction of symbols signifying **sets**, operations for forming **sets**, and operations for forming elements of **sets**. These symbols are not explained one by one, but rather in groups. The meaning of the symbols in a given group is determined by rules of four kinds:

- Formation rules
- Introduction rules
- Elimination rules
- Equality, or computation, rules

The inclusion of formation rules in the language itself is a distinctive feature of CTT. The introduction and elimination rules are like those of Gentzen (1933), though generalized to the syntax of CTT so as also to cover the construction of proof-objects. The equality rules correspond to the reduction rules of Prawitz (1965). The best way of getting a grip on these notions is by looking at concrete examples, which we now proceed to do.

In the following we shall in most cases write $A[b, c]$ and $a[b, c]$, etc., instead of $A[b/x, c/y]$ and $a[b/x, c/y]$, etc. That is, for ease of readability we shall usually not mention the variables for which b, c, etc. are substituted in A, a, etc. Which variables are replaced will usually be clear from the context. Although variables are not mentioned, square brackets will still stand for substitution and not for function application.

Cartesian Product of a Family of Sets

Given a **set** A and a family B of **set**s over A we can form the product of B over A. That is the content of the Π-formation rule:

$$(\Pi\text{-form}) \qquad \frac{A: \mathbf{set} \qquad x: A \vdash B: \mathbf{set}}{(\Pi x: A)\, B: \mathbf{set}}$$

This rule lays down when we may judge that $(\Pi x : A)B$ is a **set**. There is a second Π-formation rule that lays down when we may judge that two **sets** of the form $(\Pi x : A)B$ are identical:

$$\frac{A = A': \mathbf{set} \qquad x: A \vdash B = B': \mathbf{set}}{(\Pi x: A)B = (\Pi x: A')B': \mathbf{set}}$$

All formation, introduction, and elimination rules are paired with identity rules of this kind, but we shall state these rules explicitly only in the present case of Π.

The conclusion of Π-formation says that $(\Pi x : A)B$ is a **set**. Since we have the right to judge that C is a **set** only if we can say what the canonical elements of C are, as well as what equal canonical elements of C are, we see that the rule of Π-formation requires justification.

The required justification is provided by the Π-introduction rules:

$$(\Pi\text{-intro})\quad \frac{x : A \vdash b : B}{\lambda x.\, b : (\Pi x : A)B} \qquad \frac{x : A \vdash b = b' : B}{\lambda x.\, b = \lambda x.\, b' : (\Pi x : A)B}$$

According to this rule a canonical element of $(\Pi x : A)B$ has the form $\lambda x.\, b$, where $b[a] : B[a]$ whenever $a : A$. Note that such a b is of a category different from the category of $\lambda x.\, b$. Namely, b is of category $B(x : A)$ whereas $\lambda x.\, b$ is of category $(\Pi x : A)B$. It was noted above that we may regard such a b as a function from A into the family B. We may think of $\lambda x.\, b$ as an individual that codes this function. The λ-operator is thus similar to Frege's course-of-values operator (cf. e.g. (Frege G. 1893, § 9)) which, given a function $f(x)$, yields an individual $\acute{\alpha}f(\alpha)$. Note, however, that $\lambda x.\, b$ belongs to a separate **set** $(\Pi x : A)B$ and not to the domain A of the function b; whence we cannot make sense of applying the function b to $\lambda x.\, b$, hence a contradiction along the lines of Russell's Paradox cannot be derived.

The role of the elements of $(\Pi x : A)B$ as codes of functions is made clear by the Π-elimination rule:

$$(\Pi\text{-Elim})\quad \frac{c : (\Pi x : A)B \quad a : A}{\mathbf{ap}(c, a) : B[a]} \qquad \frac{c = c' : (\Pi x : A)B \quad a = a' : A}{\mathbf{ap}(c, a) = \mathbf{ap}(c', a') : B[a]}$$

The conclusion of this rule asserts that $\mathbf{ap}(c, a)$ is an element of the **set** $B[a]$. Since we have the right to judge that c is an element of a **set** C only if we can specify how to compute c to a canonical element of C, we see that the rule of Π-elimination requires justification.

The required justification is provided by the rule of Π-equality, which specifies how $\mathbf{ap}(c, a)$ is computed in the case where c is of canonical form, namely $\lambda x.\, b$.

$$(\Pi\text{-eq})\qquad \frac{x{:}\ A \vdash b{:}\ B \qquad a{:}\ A}{\mathbf{ap}(\lambda x.\ b, a) = b[a]{:}\ B[a]}$$

We can now justify Π-elimination as follows. By the assumption $c : (\Pi x : A)B$ we know how to evaluate c to canonical form $\lambda x.\, b$, where $x : A \vdash b : B$; thus we have $c = \lambda x.\, b : (\Pi x : A)B$. But then also $\mathbf{ap}(c, a) = \mathbf{ap}(\lambda x.\, b, a) : B[a]$, so $\mathbf{ap}(c, a) = b[a] : B[a]$, whence the value of $\mathbf{ap}(c, a)$ is equal to the value of $b[a]$; by the assumption $x : A \vdash b : B$ we know how to find this value.

From the Π-equality rule we see that **ap** is an application operator; as such it is similar to the function $x \frown y$, satisfying the equation $\Delta \frown \acute{\alpha}f(\alpha) = f(\Delta)$, defined by Frege (1893, § 34).

We have now seen that the Π-introduction rules enable us to justify the Π-formation rule and that the Π-equality rule enables us to justify the Π-elimination rule. These relations of justification hold in general and not only in the case of Π.

The advantage of the higher-order presentation of CTT is most readily seen when we ask about the categories of Π, λ, and **ap**. Intuitively we may think of Π as a certain higher-order function that takes a **set** A and a family of **set**s B over A and yields a $(\Pi x : A)B$. But we have no means of naming the category of such a function in the language frame introduced here. In the higher-order presentation such a name is easily constructed; indeed we then express the category assignment of Π by means of the judgement $\Pi : (X : \mathbf{set})((X)\mathbf{set})\mathbf{set}$. Similar remarks apply to λ and **ap**, and in fact to all of the various symbols that we are now in the process of introducing into the language (apart from the constant sets $\mathbb{N}_n$ and $\mathbb{N}$ to be introduced below—these are of category **set**).

The Logical Interpretation of the Cartesian Product

Recall that **prop** = **set**. Hence we may regard a family B of **set**s over a **set** A as a family of propositions over A. A family of propositions over A is a function from A into the category of propositions; it is thus a propositional function.

Let us consider B as a propositional function over A and $(\Pi x : A)B$ as a proposition, and let us ask what a canonical proof of this proposition looks like. Such a canonical proof has the form $\lambda x.\, b$, where $x : A \vdash b : B$, and is in effect a code of the function b. This function b takes an element a of A and yields a proof $b[a]$ of the proposition $B[a]$. Keeping in mind the Brouwer–Heyting–Kolmogorov interpretation of the logical connectives (cf. e.g. (Troelstra and van Dalen 1988, pp. 9–10)), we see thus that $(\Pi x : A)B$, when regarded as a proposition, is the proposition $(\forall x : A)$ B, which intuitively says that all elements of A have the property B. Note that this proposition is not written $\forall xB$ as in ordinary predicate logic; rather, the domain of quantification, A, is explicitly mentioned.

On the understanding of Π as $\forall$, we can recover the rule of $\forall$-introduction from the rule of Π-introduction by employing the form of judgement 'C *true*' as follows.

$$\frac{x\colon A \vdash B \ \mathit{true}}{(\forall x\colon A)B \ \mathit{true}}$$

That is to say, if $B[a]$ is true whenever $a : A$, then $(\forall x : A)B$ is true. Let us also consider the version of $\forall$-introduction where the proof-objects have not been suppressed:

$$\frac{x\colon A \vdash b\colon B}{\lambda x.\, b\colon (\forall x\colon A)B}$$

Here we should think of b as an open proof of B, a proof depending on a parameter $x : A$. For instance, A may be the natural numbers, $\mathbb{N}$, and B may be the propositional function that for any element n of $\mathbb{N}$ yields the proposition that n is either even or odd; b is then a proof of the proposition that x is either even or odd, where x is a generic or arbitrary natural number. By binding x we get a proof $\lambda x.\, b$ of $(\forall x : A)B$ where x is no longer free; if x is the only free variable in b, then $\lambda x.\, b$ is a closed proof of $(\forall x : A)B$.

Since the domain of quantification is explicitly mentioned in $(\forall x : A)B$, it also has to be mentioned in the $\forall$-elimination rule:

$$\frac{(\forall x\colon A)B \ \mathit{true} \qquad a\colon A}{B[a]\mathit{true}}$$

Making the proof-objects explicit yields the following $\forall$-elimination rule.

$$\frac{c\colon (\forall x\colon A)B \qquad a\colon A}{\mathbf{ap}(c, a)\colon B[a]}$$

The rule says that if c is a proof of $(\forall x : A)B$ and $a : A$, then $\mathbf{ap}(c, a)$ is a proof of B $[a]$. The Π-equality rule can now be seen to correspond to the $\forall$-reduction of Prawitz (1965, p. 37) at the level of proof-objects. We shall illustrate this in the case of $\supset$, to which we now turn.

Suppose $B : \mathbf{set}$. Then, by weakening, $x : A \vdash B : \mathbf{set}$ holds. In this case an element of $(\Pi x : A)B$ codes a function from the **set** A to the **set** B. Since x is not free in B in this case, we may write $A \to B$ instead of $(\Pi x : A)B$, thereby also indicating that this is the function space from A to B. Regarding both A and B as propositions, and again keeping in mind the Brouwer–Heyting–Kolmogorov interpretation of the logical connectives, it is clear that $A \to B$ can be interpreted as the implication $A \supset B$.

The Π-introduction and elimination rules become $\supset$-introduction and elimination in this case. A canonical proof-object of $A \supset B$ has the form $\lambda x.\ b$, where b is an open proof from A to B. Given a proof of $c{:}A \supset B$ and a proof $a : A$, then $\mathbf{ap}(c, a)$ is a proof of B.

The Π-equality rule yields the following rule of $\supset$-equality.

$$\frac{x\colon A \vdash b\colon B \qquad a\colon A}{\mathbf{ap}(\lambda x.\ b, a) = b[a]\colon B}$$

Here a is a proof of A; b is an open proof of B from A; $\lambda x.\ b$ is a proof of $A \supset B$ obtained by extending b with one application of $\supset$-introduction; $\mathbf{ap}(\lambda x.\ b, a)$ is the proof of B got by applying $\supset$-elimination to $\lambda x.\ b$ and a; and $b[a]$ is a proof of B got from b by supplying it in the suitable sense with the proof a of A. The $\supset$-equality rule says that $\mathbf{ap}(\lambda x.\ b, a)$ and $b[a]$ are equal proofs of B. Using the standard notation of natural deduction this equality can be expressed as follows (where we write $\mathcal{D}_1$ instead of b and $\mathcal{D}_2$ instead of a).

$$\dfrac{\dfrac{\begin{matrix} A \\ D_1 \\ B \end{matrix}}{A \supset B} \qquad \begin{matrix} D_2 \\ A \end{matrix}}{B} \quad = \quad \begin{matrix} D_2 \\ A \\ D_1 \\ B \end{matrix}$$

By replacing '=' here with a sign for Prawitz's reduction relation, one sees that what is displayed here is just the rule of $\supset$-reduction. Thus the rule of $\supset$-equality can be read as saying that a proof containing a "detour" like that in the proof on the left hand side above is identical to the proof got by deleting this detour by means of a $\supset$-reduction.

Disjoint Union of a Family of Sets

Given a **set** A and a family B of **sets** over A we can form the disjoint union of the family B. That is the content of Σ-formation:

$$(\Sigma\text{-form}) \qquad \frac{A\colon \mathbf{set} \qquad x\colon A \vdash B\colon \mathbf{set}}{(\Sigma x\colon A)\,B\colon \mathbf{set}}$$

According to the rule of Σ-introduction, the canonical elements of $(\Sigma x : A)B$ are pairs:

$$(\Sigma\text{-intro}) \qquad \frac{a\colon A \qquad b\colon B[a]}{\langle a,\, b\rangle\colon (\Sigma x\colon A)\,B}$$

Assume A : **set**, $x : A \vdash B$: **set**. Then we may form $(\Sigma x : A)B$: **set**. Assume further that C is a family of sets over $(\Sigma x : A)B$, that is, assume $z : (\Sigma x : A)B \vdash C$: **set**. The rule of Σ-elimination is as follows:

$$(\Sigma\text{-elim}) \qquad \frac{c\colon (\Sigma x\colon A)\,B \qquad x\colon A,\, y\colon B \vdash d\colon C[\langle x,\, y\rangle]}{\mathbf{E}(c,\, xy.d)\colon C[c]}$$

We may think of the binary function d as a unary function on the canonical elements of $(\Sigma x : A)B$—it takes $\langle a, b\rangle$, where $a : A$ and $b : B[a]$, and yields an element $d[a, b]$ of $C[\langle a, b\rangle]$. The Σ-elimination rule provides us with a function $c \mapsto \mathbf{E}(c, xy.\, d)$ defined for all elements c (not only canonical ones) of $(\Sigma x : A)B$.

Two clarificatory remarks pertaining to Σ-elimination are in order here. The first remark concerns the premiss $x : A,\ y : B \vdash d : C[\langle x, y\rangle]$. By the preliminary assumption $z : (\Sigma x : A)B \vdash C$: **set**, the variable z, ranging over $(\Sigma x : A)B$, occurs (or, is allowed to occur) in C. Since $x : A,\ y : B \vdash \langle x, y\rangle : (\Sigma x : A)B$ holds by Σ-introduction, the substitution of $\langle x, y\rangle$ for z in C in the context $x : A$, $y : B$ makes sense. The second remark concerns the conclusion $\mathbf{E}(c, xy.\, d) : C[c]$. The operation **E** is variable-binding: it binds the free variables x and y in d. This is symbolized by prefixing d with x and y inside $\mathbf{E}(-, -)$.

The Σ-equality rule tells us how to compute $\mathbf{E}(c, xy.\, d)$ when c is in canonical form.

$$(\Sigma\text{-eq}) \qquad \frac{a\colon A \qquad b\colon B[a] \qquad x\colon A,\, y\colon B \vdash d\colon C[\langle x,\, y\rangle]}{\mathbf{E}(\langle a,\, b\rangle,\, xy.d) = d[a,\, b]\colon C\langle a,\, b\rangle}$$

The conclusion of Σ-elimination introduces a non-canonical element $\mathbf{E}(c, xy.\ d)$ in $C[c]$. To justify this rule we have to explain how to evaluate this non-canonical element to canonical form. This is done by reference to the Σ-equality rule. First evaluate $c : (\Sigma x : A)B$ to get a pair $\langle a, b \rangle$, where $a : A$ and $b : B[a]$. We have

$$\mathbf{E}(c, xy.d) = \mathbf{E}(\langle a, b \rangle, xy.d) = d[a, b] : C[\langle a, b \rangle]$$

by Σ-equality. By the premiss $x : A,\ y : B \vdash d : C[\langle x, y \rangle]$ we know how to compute $d[a, b]$ to obtain a canonical element of $C[\langle a, b \rangle]$; since $C[c] = C[\langle a, b \rangle] : \mathbf{set}$, this will also be a canonical element of $C[c]$.

By means of $\mathbf{E}$ we can define projection operations, which justifies our speaking of the canonical elements of $(\Sigma x : A)B$ as pairs. For the first projection we put $C = A$ and $d = x$ in the rule of Σ-elimination, thereby obtaining:

$$\frac{c\colon (\Sigma x\colon A)B \qquad x\colon A, y\colon B \vdash x\colon A}{\mathbf{E}(c, xy.\ x)\colon A}$$

By Σ-equality we have in this case:

$$\mathbf{E}(\langle a, b \rangle, xy.x) = x[a/x, b/y] = a : A$$

We may therefore define the first projection **fst** as follows.

$$c : (\Sigma x : A)B \vdash \mathbf{fst}(c) = \mathbf{E}(c, xy.x)$$

For the second projection we put $C = B[\mathbf{fst}(z)]$ and $d = y$ in the rule of Σ-elimination:

$$\frac{c\colon (\Sigma x\colon A)B \qquad x\colon A, y\colon B \vdash y\colon B\,[\mathbf{fst}(\langle x, y \rangle)]}{\mathbf{E}(c, xy.\ y)\colon B\,[\mathbf{fst}(c)]}$$

The second premiss here is valid since $x : A,\ y : B \vdash B[\mathbf{fst}(\langle x, y \rangle)] = B[x] = B : \mathbf{set}$ holds. By Σ-equality we have

$$\mathbf{E}(\langle a, b \rangle, xy.y) = y[a/x, b/y] = b : B[\mathbf{fst}(\langle a, b \rangle)]$$

But $\mathbf{fst}(\langle a, b \rangle) = a : A$, hence

$$B[\mathbf{fst}(\langle a, b \rangle)] = B[a] : \mathbf{set}$$

We therefore define the second projection by

$$c : (\Sigma x : A)B \vdash \mathbf{snd}(c) = \mathbf{E}(c, xy.y)$$

The following four rules are then justified

$$\frac{c : (\Sigma x : A)B}{\mathbf{fst}(c) : A} \qquad \frac{a : A \quad b : B[a]}{\mathbf{fst}(\langle a, b\rangle) = a : A}$$

$$\frac{c : (\Sigma x : A)B}{\mathbf{snd}(c) : B[\mathbf{fst}(c)]} \qquad \frac{a : A \quad b : B[a]}{\mathbf{snd}(\langle a, b\rangle) = b : B[a]}$$

The Logical Interpretation of the Disjoint Union of a Family of Sets

If we regard B as a propositional function over A, then (Σx:A)B can be regarded as the existentially quantified proposition $(\exists x : A)B$. A canonical proof of $(\exists x : A)B$ is a pair $\langle a, b\rangle$ where $a : A$ and $b : B[a]$; that is to say, a is a witness and b is a proof that a indeed has the property B. When suppressing proof-objects and employing the form of judgement *true*, the rule of Σ-elimination becomes ∃-elimination:

$$\frac{(\exists x{:}\ A)B \textit{ true} \qquad x{:}\ A, B \textit{ true} \vdash C \textit{ true}}{C \textit{ true}}$$

In ordinary natural deduction the assumption $x : A$ in the second premiss is usually not made explicit.

If B : **set** holds categorically, then the rules for Σ yield rules for ordinary Cartesian product. On the logical interpretation, the Cartesian product becomes conjunction. Indeed the Σ-formation and introduction rules then become:

$$\frac{A : \mathbf{prop} \quad B : \mathbf{prop}}{A \wedge B : \mathbf{prop}} \qquad \frac{a : A \quad b : B}{\langle a, b\rangle : A \wedge B}$$

The Σ-elimination rule, with and without proof-objects, becomes:

$$\frac{A \wedge B \textit{ true} \qquad A \textit{ true}, B \textit{ true} \vdash C \textit{ true}}{C \textit{ true}}$$

$$\frac{c{:}\ A \wedge B \qquad x{:}\ A, y{:}\ B \vdash d{:}\ C[\langle a, b\rangle]}{\mathbf{E}(c, xy.d){:}\ C[c]}$$

This is a generalization of the ordinary rules of ∧-elimination also found in Schroeder-Heister (1984, p. 1294). The ordinary rules are obtained as a special case by letting C be A or B. We remark that in the higher-order presentation a generalized elimination rule in this sense can also be given for Π Nordström et al. (Nordström et al. 1990, pp. 51–52); using this generalized elimination rule instead of the rule of Π-elimination presented above in fact yields a strictly stronger theory, as shown by Garner (2009).

Disjoint union of two **sets**

Given two **sets** we may form their disjoint union. That is content of the rule of +-formation.

$$(\text{+-form}) \qquad \frac{A\text{: } \mathbf{set} \qquad B\text{: } \mathbf{set}}{A + B\text{: } \mathbf{set}}$$

A canonical element of $A + B$ is an element of A or an element of B together with the information that it comes from A or B respectively. Thus there are two rules of +-introduction:

$$(\text{+-intro}) \qquad \frac{a\text{: } A}{\mathbf{i}(a)\text{: } A + B} \qquad \frac{b\text{: } B}{\mathbf{j}(b)\text{: } A + B}$$

Assume A : **set**, B : **set**, and $z : A + B \vdash C$: **set**. The rule of +-elimination is:

$$(\text{+-elim}) \qquad \frac{c\text{: } A + B \qquad x\text{: } A \vdash d\text{: } C[\mathbf{i}(x)] \qquad y\text{: } B \vdash e\text{: } C[\mathbf{j}(y)]}{\mathbf{D}(c, x.\ d, y.e)\text{: } C[c]}$$

The rule can be glossed as follows. Assume that C is a family of **set**s over $A + B$ and that we are given a function d which takes an $a : A$ to an element $d[a]$ of $C[\mathbf{i}(a)]$ and a function e which takes a $b : B$ to an element $e[b]$ of $C[\mathbf{j}(b)]$. Then $C[c]$ is inhabited for any $c : C$, namely by $\mathbf{D}(c, x.\ d, y.\ e)$. How to compute $\mathbf{D}(c, x.\ d, y.\ e)$ is determined by the +-equality rules. Since there are two +-introduction rules, there are also two +-equality rules.

$$(\text{+-eq}) \qquad \frac{a\text{: } A \qquad x\text{: } A \vdash d\text{: } C[\mathbf{i}(x)] \qquad y\text{: } B \vdash e\text{: } C[\mathbf{j}(y)]}{\mathbf{D}(\mathbf{i}(a), x.\ d, y.\ e) = d[a]\text{: } C[\mathbf{i}(a)]}$$

$$\frac{b\text{: } B \qquad x\text{: } A \vdash d\text{: } C[\mathbf{i}(x)] \qquad y\text{: } B \vdash e\text{: } C[\mathbf{j}(y)]}{\mathbf{D}(\mathbf{j}(b), x.\ d, y.\ e) = e[b]\text{: } C[\mathbf{j}(b)]}$$

In the logical interpretation + becomes disjunction $\vee$.

References

Aczel, P. (1978). The type theoretic interpretation of constructive set theory. In *Logic Colloquium '77* (pp. 55–66). Amsterdam: North-Holland.

Almog, J. (1991). The what and the how. *Journal of Philosophy*, *88*, 225–244.

Barnes, J. (1984). *The complete works of Aristotle. The revised Oxford translation.* Princeton: Princeton University Press.

Carnap, R. (1934). *Logische Syntax der Sprache*. Vienna: Julius Springer.
Crubellier, M. (2008). The programme of Aristotelian analytics. In Dégremont C., Keiff, L., & Rückert, H. (Eds.), *Dialogues, logics and other strange things. Essays in honour of Shahid Rahman* (pp. 103–129).
Diller, J., & Troelstra, A. (1984). Realizability and intuitionistic logic. *Synthese*, 60, 253–282.
Dummett, M. (1973). *Frege. Philosophy of language* (2nd (1981) ed.). London: Duckworth.
Frege, G. (1893). *Grundgesetze der Arithmetik*. Jena: Hermann Pohle.
Garner, R. (2009). On the strength of dependent products in the type theory of Martin-Löf. *Annals of Pure and Applied Logic, 160*, 1–12.
Gentzen, G. (1933). Untersuchungen über das logische Schliessen. *Mathematische Zeitschrift*, 39, 176–210.
Granström, J. G. (2011). *Treatise on intuitionistic type theory*. Dordrecht: Springer.
Hale, B., & Wright, C. (2001). To bury Caesar. In *The reason's proper study* (pp. 335–396). Oxford: Oxford University Press.
Howard, W. A. (1980). The formulae-as-types notion of construction. In J. P. Seldin & J. R. Hindley (Eds.), *To H. B. Curry: Essays on combinatory logic, lambda calculus and formalism* (pp. 479–490). London: Academic Press.
Klev, A. (2014). *Categories and logical syntax*. Leiden, The Netherlands: PhD.
Martin-Löf, P. (1975b). An intuitionistic theory of types: Predicative part. In H. E. Rose & J. C. Shepherdson (Eds.), *Logic Colloquium '73* (pp. 73–118). Amsterdam: North-Holland.
Martin-Löf, P. (1982). Constructive mathematics and computer programming. In J. L. Cohen & J. Los (Eds.), *Logic, methodology and philosophy of science VI, 1979* (pp. 153–175). Amsterdam: North-Holland.
Martin-Löf, P. (1984). *Intuitionistic type theory. Notes by Giovanni Sambin of a series of lectures given in Padua, June 1980*. Naples, Italy: Bibliopolis.
Martin-Löf, P. (1992). *Substitution calculus*. Lecture notes. http://archive-pml.github.io/martin-lof/pdfs/Substitution-calculus-1992.pdf
Martin-Löf, P. (1996). On the meanings of the logical constants and the justifications of the logical laws. *Nordic Journal of Philosophical Logic, 1*, 11–60.
Martin-Löf, P. (2011). *When did 'judgement' come to be a term of logic?* Lecture held at Ecole Normale Supérieure 14 October 2011. Video recording available: http://savoirs.ens.SR//expose.php?id¼481
Nordström, B., Petersson, K., & Smith, J. M. (1990). *Programming in Martin-Löf's type theory: An introduction*. Oxford: Oxford University Press
Prawitz, D. (1965). *Natural deduction*. Stockholm: Almqvist & Wiksell.
Quine, W. V. (1969). *Ontological relativity and other essays*. New York: Columbia University Press.
Schröder-Heister, P. (1984). A natural extension of natural deduction. *Journal of Symbolic Logic* 49: 1284–1300.
Sundholm, G. (2006). Semantic values for natural deduction derivations. *Synthese* 148: 623–638.

Sundholm, G. (2009). A century of judgement and inference, 1837–1936: Some strands in the development of logic. In *The development of Modern Logic*, by L (ed) Haaparanta, 264–317. Oxford: Oxford University Press.

Tasistro, A. (1993) *Formulation of Martin-Löf's theory of types with explicit substitutions.* Gothenburg, Master's thesis, Chalmers University of Technology.

The Univalent Foundations Program. (2013). *Homotopy type theory: Univalent foundations of mathematics.* Retrieved from http://homotopytypetheory.org/book.

Troelstra, A., and van Dalen, D. (1988). *Constructivism in mathematics.* Amsterdam: North-Holland.

Zermelo, E. (1930). Über Grenzzahlen und Mengenbereiche. *Fundamenta Mathematicae, 16.* 29–47.

Final Remarks and the Work Ahead

One crucial feature of the Islamic notion of Law that shaped the development of *uṣūl al-fiqh* is its dynamic nature. This dynamic was put into work in the conceptual venue that Young (2017) calls the *dialectical forge*. In such a dialectical setting premises of legal theory were continually produced, tested and reproduced in order to yield a deeper systematization. However, unlike other dialectical frameworks, the focus of the dialectical forge is on developing methods of interaction aimed at gaining knowledge and meaning, beyond the rhetoric purposes of a legal trial or debate. This gave *jadal* a crucial epistemological role in the pursuit of truth.[7]

In this context, Islamic jurists studied several instruments suitable for implementing the dialectical forge. One of the most important of these instruments is *qiyās*, which constitutes the subject of our study. The aim of this form of inference is to provide a rational ground for the application of a *ḥukm* to a given case not yet considered by the original juridical sources. As a product of legal theory shaped by interaction, it is fair to say that a dialogical framework, such as that developed in the present study provides a suitable setting in order to delve into the structure and meaning underlying the legal notion of *qiyās*. Indeed, the dialogical framework displays two of the hallmarks of this form of inference.

First, the interaction of heuristic and hermeneutic procedures with logical steps. This interface was displayed by two main steps: (1) finding the root-case from which the occasioning factor can be inferred; (2) linking the root-case logically with the branch-case by means of a general schema that constitutes the meaning of the ruling behind the root-case and that links the occasioning factor with the relevant juridical ruling.

Second, the dynamics underlying the extension of the legal terms involved. This dynamics is displayed by the intertwining of confirmations and refutations that

[7]Hallaq (1987a).

S. Rahman et al., *Inferences by Parallel Reasoning in Islamic Jurisprudence*, Logic, Argumentation & Reasoning 19, https://doi.org/10.1007/978-3-030-22382-3

contribute to establish the most suitable conclusion in relation to the consideration of a new case.

How does this framework contribute to contemporary legal reasoning and to parallel reasoning in general, beyond legal contexts?

Such a study is work in progress. Nevertheless, let us discuss briefly some of the points linked to such a generalization.

Let us start with some reflections on the contribution of the Islamic argumentation theory within *uṣūl al-fiqh* to contemporary legal reasoning, and more precisely in the case of Common Law. In fact Hallaq (1985) already pointed out the links between Common Law and *qiyās*. The following section can be seen as developing his remarks further.

What Qiyās Brings to Contemporary Legal Reasoning. Brief Remarks on Two Contemporary Accounts of Parallel Reasoning

Alchourrón on Arguments a pari

Nowadays, there is quite considerable literature on the use of analogy in contemporary legal reasoning, and particularly so within Common Law. One important example is the long and thorough paper of Scott Brewer (1996), however, curiously he does not mention one work that is a landmark on the issue, namely Alchourrón's (1961) paper *Los Argumentos Jurídicos a Fortiori y a Pari*, which as pointed out by himself was a reaction to Perelmann's mistrust of the use of formal logic within legal reasoning – a mistrust that had lasting influence in present-day legal reasoning.

Be that as it may, the main point of Alchourrón (1961, pp. 19–21) is that arguments by parallel reasoning, *a pari*, are based on what he calls the *inheritance* property of some legal qualification (such as obligatory, forbidden, etc) or more generally of a predicate. The idea is simple: if something is in a reflexive, transitive and symmetric relation to something else, and the legal qualification (or predicate) applies to the former, then it also applies to the latter. If the relation is indeed reflexive, transitive and symmetric we have a case of identity. Thus, inheritance in this case amounts to Leibniz's substitution rule.

Alchourrón's (1961, pp. 9–19) objective by deploying the term inheritance is to generalize it to what he identifies as the main forms of arguments by analogy in law. So we say that a legal qualification Q (or a predicate) enjoys the property of inheritance in regard to the relation R if, whenever it is verified that some Q can be said of x and it is the case that xRy, then Qy.

To put it in the terms of Islamic jurisprudence, there is inheritance when R allows *transferring* Q from the root-case (the known or precedent case) to the branch-case (the target cae). Certainly, as stressed by Alchourrón (1961, pp. 10–12), the problem is that this transference, when generalized for a relation, is usually not logically valid. In other words, if the relation is formulated very generally, the logical force of the transferrence is dependent upon the content of the predicate and the relation.

It is interesting to note that Alchourrón (1961) considers that there are only two main cases of analogy, *a pari*, and *a fortiori*. *A pari* corresponds to similarity and the use of substitution of identicals (or similars). Alchourrón's category of *a fortiori* (in legal reasoning) includes all those arguments in which the transference is based on a relation that is transitive and asymmetric.

Obviously, most of them are non-logically valid. Now, if we take it that the relation *R* is *a fortiori* and *a maiori ad minus* (infer the *smaller* from the *larger*), and the legal qualification, say *allowed*, enjoys the property of inheritance in regard to this relation (that is, if the transference from *x* to *y* rule holds for *Q* in regard to *R*), then, if the root-case *x* is allowed and *x* is (in some respect) *more than y*, then the branch-case *y* is also allowed – for example, if borrowing money with an interest rate of 12% is allowed, so is borrowing at an interest rater of 8%.

$$\frac{\begin{array}{l}\text{Allowed } x\\ x \text{ higher interest-than- } y\\ \text{Substitution (Allowed } x,\ x \text{ more-than } y)\end{array}}{\text{Allowed } (y/x)}$$

The same applies to *a minori ad maius* (infer the *larger* from *from the smaller*) – for example, if drinking small quantities of arak is forbidden while driving, then drinking large quantities of arak while driving is also interdicted. Clearly, all the logical force depends upon the content of the specific relation at stake, upon which the inheritance is defined.

Note that many of the jurists of the Islamic tradition, though they clearly identify the different forms of *a fortiori* arguments, do not classify them as being some form of correlational inferences; they rather consider them to be rooted in linguisitc methods that disclose the content of the relation at stake – see Hallaq (1985, pp. 80–85) and Young (2017, pp. 439–450).

More generally, the lesson to draw from the comparison of Alchourron's analyisis with the systems of correlational inferences by indication and resemblance of the Islamic tradition is that we might win inferential force if we add further conditions on the property of inheritance, namely: (1) *R* amounts to a relation of specification between two rulings *Q* and *Q*' (or legal quatlifications) or (2) *R* amounts to a relation of parallelism between two rulings *Q* and *Q*' (or legal quatlifications), or (3) *R* amounts to a relation of similarity between the known case and the target case.

Another way to understand Alchourrón's *inheritance relation* is that it does not involve any kind of substitution of identicals or similars, but it amounts to an inference-relation within a *generalization schema*. This will be the subject of discussion in the next section.

Scott Brewer and John Woods on Parallel Reasoning

As mentioned in the preface, Scott Brewer (1996, pp. 1003–1017) and John Woods (2013, pp. 273–281) developed an approach to parallel reasoning based on extracting a general reasoning schema for parallel reasoning (GRSP) from some specific rules. Woods (2015, p. 278) calls such a schema *generalization schema* (GS), while Brewer (1996, p. 1004) speaks of schemas of *exemplary reasoning* (ERS).

The legal context of both Brewer and Woods is *reasoning by precedent*, one of the hallmarks of Common Law. So the specific rules the GRS generalize are precedent cases recorded by the legal sources – let us deploy GRPS as a term that comprises both GS and ERS).

In fact, Woods (2015, pp. 275–277) seems to criticize approaches such as that of Brewer (1996, pp. 1003–1006). As we will discuss below the main concerns of Woods seem to be rooted on

1. how to understand a GRPS,
2. the passage from GRPS to legal ruligs, a passage that Brewer (1996, p. 1004) formulates with another rule called *analogy-warranting rule* (AWR), which transforms the schematic inference into an instance of a universal elimination rule. This deductivist approach, as acknowledged by Brewer (1996, p. 1006) himself; should in principle have problems in dealing with *defeasibility*.

However, if we have a close look at the logical structure behind Woods' GS and Brewer's ERS, it comes out that both can be seen as sharing the same meaning-constitution as the one that structures *qiyās al-'illa*. Moreover, the efficiency-test embedded in the system of correlational inferences by occasioning factor explains what AWR is about and why, despite the reluctance in Common Law to make rules explicit, an explicitation procedure such as the one displayed by *ta'thīr* is indeed a requirement for assuring the *tightness* of the properties Woods(2015, p.280) requires for a sound GS.

Actually Woods (2015) does not mention Brewer (1996) but Martin Golding (2001) who proposes a *causal* approach. We will focus on Brewer's approach in order to compare two in principle very different GRPS, the *deductivist* approach of Brewer (1996) and the *naturalist* approach of Woods (2015).

One of Brewer's (1996, pp. 1003–1007) main examples is the following case:

> [. . .] *valuables were stolen from a passenger's rented steamboat cabin. The issue in that case was whether the steamboat owner was strictly liable to the passenger for the loss (it having been decided below that neither the steamboat owner nor the passenger was negligent). Apparently, only a couple of cases were directly on point: one held that an innkeeper was strictly liable for the theft of boarders' valuables, while another held that a railroad company was not strictly liable to passengers for the theft of their valuables from open-berth sleeping-car trains. One might say that the legal issue was put to Judge O'Brien thus: in the "eyes of the law," was the steamboat sufficiently like an inn, on the one hand, or sufficiently like a railroad, on the other, to receive the same legal treatment?*

Reconstructed in accord with the schema presented above, the argument is as follows:
Target *(y) = the steamboat owner.*
Source *(x) = the innkeeper.*

Shared characteristics:
F: has a client who procures a room for specified reasons R (privacy, etc.).
G: has a tempting opportunity for fraud and plundering client.

Inferred characteristic:
H: is strictly liable.

Argument:

1. *y has F and G (target premise);*
2. *x has F and G (source premise);*
3. *x also has H (source premise)*
4. *AWR: if anything has F and G also has H, then everything that has F and G also has H;*
5. *Therefore, y has H.*

Brewer (1996, pp. 1004-1005).

If for the moment we leave the AWR out, at first sight the argument looks exactly like Woods (2015, p. 278) GS for a much discussed case in favour of abortion. In order to facilitate the comparison between ERS and GS let us answer the following questions:

What is a general reasoning schema for parallel reasoning?
What is inference within a GRSP?
What is a rule of law in reasoning by precedent?

In the formulation of an ERS, Brewer deploys the terminology: *shared characteristics*. This might suggest that what is at stake here is the similarity between the target and the source case, as in typical arguments by analogy (such as al-Shīrāzī (2003) *qiyās al-shabah*). However, notice that the argument in the quote above does **not** deploy substitution of identicals. In fact, as we suggested already, GRSP should be associated to *qiyās al-ʿilla*, i.e., let us recall, correlational inferences by occasioning factor, where the inference is carried out by a method (function) that *occasions* the legal ruling from some set of open assumptions (or schematic predicates).

The logical structure of Brewer's (1996) argument in the ERS quoted is based on the open assumptions *x and y have F, x and y have G,* and the propositional function *x also has H.* The cardinal step is to trigger an inference without assuming an identity relation. In order to do so, Brewer introduces AWR which accomplishes the task of embedding the step *if anything has F and G also has H* into a standard deductive framework, where *any* becomes *every*, that is, a universal quantifier that binds the variables of the open assumptions. Thus, AWR produces logically valid inferences. After all, the ERS do not rely on similarity of cases but in subsuming target- and source-case into a general universal rule.

Woods (2015 p. 278) speaks of *instantiating* a schema. For him, it is not at all about subsuming cases under the scope of a universal but rather instantiating a schema.

Clearly, instantiating a schema does not lead necessarily to logical validity. In fact, *if anything has F and G also has H* occurring in step four of Brewer's example quoted above can also be seen as an instantiation schema. Notice that within *if anything has F and G also has H* the distinction between the target *x* and the source *y* has been erased.

This suggests a first answer to the first of our questions, GRSP are instantiation schemas. Moreover, in relation to the second question, it is possible to produce an inference, provided these instantiation schemas are understood as making the conclusion inferentially dependent upon the premises. That is,

Let us provide two different reconstructions of

If anything has F and G also has H,

1. *H* and *G* are understood as being linked by a conjunction within an open assumption

   H(*x*) *true* (*x*: *F* ∧ *G*),
   that can be glossed as:

   x is liable if it instantiates both having a client who rents a room and having a tempting opportunity for fraud and plundering of client.

2. *H* and *G* are understood as being linked by a dependence relation. *Having a tempting opportunity for fraud and plundering of client* is restricted to *having a client who rents a room*

   H(*x*, *y*) *true* (*x*: *F*, *y*: *G*(*x*)),
   that can be glossed as: *Those x of whom G can be predicated (G(x)) are liable provided they instantiate F.*

   If we wish to have more a expressive structure we can go deeper into the structure:

   H(*u*,*v*) *true* (*u*: *Individuals*, *v*: *F*(*u*) ∧ *G*(*u*)
   x is liable if it instantiates an individual that is also an instance of those individuals having both F and G.

   H(*x*,*y*,*z*) *true* (*x*: *Individuals*, *y*: *F*(*y*), *z*: *G*(*x*,*y*))

   x is liable if it instantiates an individual that is also an instance of those individuals having G, provided they instantiate F (first).

Notice that even in the simpler version our analysis makes the liability dependent upon *F* and *G*. It is not liability in general, but that liability that is *inferentially* dependent upon *F* and *G*, and thus specific to having these properties.

How does this inferential structure of GRSP produce actual inferences? Well, by instantiating. The instrument of inference is a method that for any individual that instantiates the premises *F* and *G* takes us to the liability of this individual. The method is obviously a function; i.e. the dependent object that provides instances from open assumptions.

Let us now assume that a is an instantiation, then we obtain the following variants of the inference rules within an ERS underlying Brewer's example quoted above.

$$\frac{a: F \wedge G \qquad \begin{array}{c}(x: F \wedge G)\\ b(x): H(x)\end{array}}{b(a): H(a)} \qquad \frac{a: F,\ c: G(a) \qquad \begin{array}{c}(x: F,\ y: G(x)),\\ b(x, y): H(x, y)\end{array}}{b(a, c): H(a, c)}$$

These inference rules also make explicit how to produce inferences within Woods' framework. The following quote from Woods (2015, p. 259) provides the way to linking reasoning by precedent to our reconstruction:

> *We are now in a position to suggest a connection with legal precedents. A ruling on a specific set of facts originates a precedent for other facts when its* **ratio decendi** *instantiates a generalization schema which later facts also instantiate.*

Indeed, if we link this observation of Woods with our analysis of GS and instantiation, it emerges that the *ratio decendi* amounts to the *causative force* of the function $b(x)$ to trigger or *occasion* the legal ruling from the set of open assumptions (the condition or set of them) to the legal ruling.

It is important to keep in mind that if the process GS is to be considered a instantiation schema supporting inferences, the inferential structure must be based on open assumptions, not on premises. In other words, the function $b(x)$ defines the propositional functions:

$$b(x): H(x)\ (x: F \wedge G) \quad \text{or} \quad b(x,y): H(x)\ \mathit{true}\ (x: F,\ y: G(\mathrm{x}))$$

Let us deploy the terminology of *qiyās al-ʿilla* in the inference rule for GRSP, which stresses the *occasioning* or causative force of the function. This yields the following schema:

$$\mathit{ʿilla}(x): H(x)\ (x: F \wedge G) \quad \text{or} \quad \mathit{ʿilla}(x,y): H(x)\ (x: F,\ y: G(\mathrm{x})),$$

which leads to the inferential rules described above.

At this point of the discussion, the patient reader will have the impression of *déjà vu*. Indeed, according to our analysis the inferential structure of GRSP amounts to the one behind al-Shīrāzī (2003) *qiyās al-ʿilla* developed in chapter II of our book.

The idea is that when the judge delves into the content behind one specific rule that has been acknowledged by the legal sources as setting a precedent, the judge grasps the meaning as constituted by a schema that tightens inferential legal ruling and conditions. In other words, the judge presupposes that the propositional functions

$$H(x): \mathit{prop}\ (x: F \wedge G) \quad \text{Or} \quad H(x): \mathit{prop}\ (x: F,\ y: G(\mathrm{x})),$$

unify some set of cases that constituted a precedent – though the resulting generalization is not restricted to precedent cases.[8]

Moreover, according to Woods (2015, p. 279) the generalization schema is the legal rule itself, which judges are reluctant to make explicit. This yields an answer to our third question.

Notice that so far we have kept silent on Brewer's deductivist *analogy-warranting rule* AWR. Woods will certainly take exception to AWR, and if we follow the inferential schema described above we do not seem to need AWR at all.

However, one way to understand the role of this rule is to link it with *ta'thīr,* the possibility of testing if the applied instantiation schema does indeed manage to unify the relevant set of precedent cases put into action. In order to do so, we need to display the inferential structure behind AWR.

Inferentially speaking, the passage from the GS to the universal quantification is only a step away from the GS:

$$\frac{\begin{array}{c}(x\colon F \wedge G)\\ b(x) : H(x)\end{array}}{\lambda x.b(x)\colon (\forall x\colon F \wedge G)\, H(x)}$$

This is, in our view, the way to formulate Brewer's (1996, p. 1004) *analogy-warranting rule* AWR as emerging from an instantiation schema.

Nevertheless, this is only half of the story. As observed by Brewer (1996, pp. 1006–1016), AWR should be linked with the possibility of objecting to the relevance of the properties assumed by GRSP by means of a disanalogy.

Here again, al-Shīrāzī's (1987; 2003; 2016) insights help. As discussed in the chapter II of the present book, the idea is that *ta'thīr*, the test of efficiency, provides the means to test whether the property, or set of them, purported to be relevant for the juridical sanction at stake is indeed so.

The test declines into two complementary procedures: testing co-extensiveness or *ṭard* (if the property is present then the sanction too) and co-exclusiveness or *ʿaks* (if the property is absent then so is the juridical sanction – the consumption of vinegar is in principle not forbidden).

While co-extensiveness examines whether the legal qualification *H* follows from the verification of the presence of the property or set of properties, co-exclusiveness examines whether exemption from the legal qualification follows from the verification of the absence.

If we formulate AWR as such a kind of testing procedure, we need to have the following expansion of AWR:

[8]Notice that a GS might be based on putting together similar, rather than identical properties – see Woods (2015, p. 277).

- For every x, if it instantiates the property F (or set of them), then the legal qualification follows, if it does not instantiate F then the legal qualification does not apply (see part II of our book).

$$\lambda x.c\colon (\forall x\colon F\vee\neg F)\ \{[(\forall y\colon F)\ \mathit{left}^{\vee}(y) =_{\{F\vee\neg F\}} x \supset H(y)] \wedge [(\forall z\colon \neg F)\ \mathit{right}^{\vee}(z) =_{\{F\vee\neg F\}} x \supset \neg H(z)]\}.$$

Recall that the point of Brewer (1996, p. 1006) of introducing AWR is to unify some set of precedents specific to a giving ruling H. This is also the point of al-Shīrāzī's *ta'thīr*, where the testing amounts to unifying cases *recorded in the legal sources*. This, as mentioned in the preface, was al-Shīrāzī's way of answering to the antianalogists, a response that Brewer (1996, p. 1006) brings to the context of contemporary legal reasoning.

Accordingly, a disanalogy, that is, a counterexample to the claim that the presence of a property triggers the juridical ruling and its absence the failing of that ruling, can then defeat the use of some GRSP.

Woods (2015, p. 193) points out that in general, after a process, the legal verdicts are closed by *fiat*, though this does not mean that during the procedure the initial GS can not be contested. In our view this is related to the distinction between play level and strategy level. The latter, we claimed, should be understood as a *recapitulation* that settles the matter (see I.3 and I.4 above).

It is here that the dialogical approach comes on the scene: criticism amounts to a game of giving and asking for reasons during a fixed argumentative context. Recall that, as discussed in the chapter II, the argumentation theory of Islamic Jurisprudence included a rich set of both collaborative and destructive moves aimed at testing the relevance of some set of properties for some specific legal ruling.

The dialogical approach brings to the fore the dialectical stance on legal reasoning within classical Islam by providing a framework where inferential moves testing moves, and collaborative and destructive moves, aimed at grounding a legal qualification, can be unified.[9] More generally, the dialogical framework can even be understood as setting up a language-game in order to study the meaning-constitution of the terms involved during a legal argumentation.

Let us finish this section with the remark that in our framework, instantiating a GS is the way to *justify* a GS. Indeed, justifications are, in our framework, instances or tokens of a type. Moreover, as discussed in the chapter IV, *local reasons* or reasons brought forward during a play, should be distinguished from *strategic reasons*, or reasons that constitute (the justification of) a winning strategy either by establishing validity or by establishing the truth of material inferences). Thus, despite Woods' (2015, pp. 263–272) scepticism towards justification approaches, the instantiations at work in his own GS are, after all, either (local) reasons or justifications, that is, strategic reasons encoding a recapitulation of the process leading to the resulting legal ruling.

---

[9]As mentioned in our preface Miller (1984) was the first in suggesting to deploy dialogical logic in order to study Islamic argumentation theory.

Perhaps the problem comes from overseeing both

1. the difference between assertions brought forward to justify others and justifying objects, i.e.; truth-makers or proof-objects, and
2. ignoring the distinction of reasons brought forward in the context of a play (with all its material and temporal restrictions) and strategic reasons yielding logical validity. Notice that in our framework, *Immanent Reasoning,* even strategic reasons must **not** always be identified with justifications of logical validity (see the Chap. 4).

To use John Woods' (2015, p. 262) own words:
The defence now rests.

Beyond Legal Reasoning

As suggested in the conclusion of chap. III, a comparative study between contemporary theories of analogical reasoning such as Bartha's (2010, chap. 4) *Articulation Model* and the dialectical conception *qiyās* seems to offer a new promising research path. Such a study should launch the development of a general framework for parallel reasoning that comprises reasoning not only in Law but also in Natural and Social Sciences.[10]

Indeed, if we express the main features of *qiyās al-dalāla* and *qiyās al-shabah* in the terms of Paul Bartha's (2010, chap. 4) *Articulation Model*,[11] we might characterize these forms of correlational inferences as follows:

---

[10]Notice that Bartha's model introduces a *dialectical device* in order to test the epistemic strength of a purported analogy. His argument in support of the dialectical stance is very close to that of the inceptors of the *qiyās*. To that effect Bartha (2010, p. 5) writes:

I shall introduce a rhetorical device that will be useful throughout the book.

The philosophical argument is based on the assumption that justification for analogical reasoning, or at least the sort of justification that is of primary interest, should be public. It should be based on communicable experiences, models, and assumptions. This requirement certainly supports the thesis that justifiable analogical reasoning is capable of representation in argument form. It does not rule out the inclusion of visual information, such as diagrams, in the argument. The rhetorical device is to imagine that the analogical reasoning is presented by an enthusiastic advocate to a polite but moderately skeptical interlocutor, the critic. The reasoning succeeds if it survives the critic's scrutiny. The framework of advocate and critic helps to set a standard of justification that can be varied to reflect the demands of different settings. It also provides a vivid way to appreciate the requirement of publicity.

[11]See the diagram at the end of the present chapter. In a nutshell: the ***horizontal relations*** in Bartha's model are the relations of similarity (and difference) in the mapping between that source and the target domains (in our study-case the source domain is the root-case and the target domain the branch-case), while the ***vertical relations*** are those between the objects, relations, and properties within each domain.

Deploying *qiyās al-dalāla* assumes the *prior association* or *vertical links* (either in the form of a *khaṣīṣa*-relation or a *naẓīr*-relation) holding between two rulings that apply to the source case – i.e. the root-case – that is projected to hold in the target domain, i.e. the branch-case;

Deploying *qiyās al-shabah* is based merely on *horizontal* resemblances between the properties applying to both the source- and the target case, without, in principle, establishing any structure between the different properties used in the argument.

The prediction of Bartha's model (2010, pp. 24–26) coincides with those of the Islamic jurisprudents: conclusions achieved by means of *qiyās al-dalāla* are epistemically stronger than those achieved by deploying *qiyās al-shabah*.

However, notice that unlike the articulation model of Bartha, the vertical relations required by *qiyās al-dalāla* assume not only that the same kind of relation holds in both the source- and the target domain, but that the relations involve the *same rulings* (in Bartha's model rulings might be thought of as a kind of properties). In other words, Bartha's model allows that, to put it in the context of *qiyās*, instead of identical rulings we have *similar rulings* on both sides, and this similarity is established horizontally:

Bartha's Articulation Model[12]

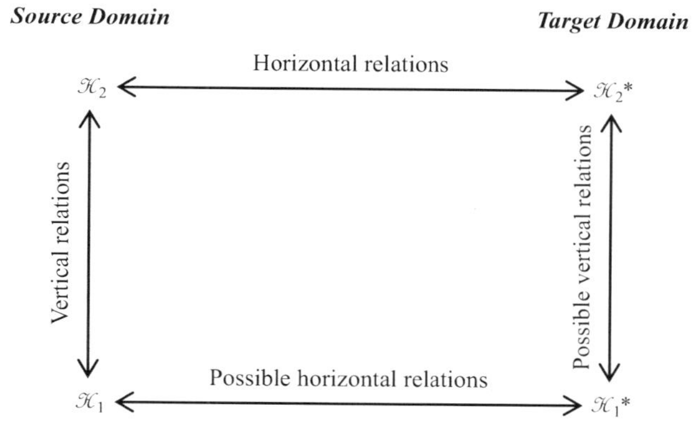

If we were to put it in the terms of Islamic jurisprudence, we might say that Bartha's model combines (several forms of) vertical relations between rulings,[13] with horizontal relations of similarity or *shabah* between those rulings (rather than between branch- and root-case): a combination that might sound intolerably weak for the higher aims of *uṣūl al-fiqh, where the* horizontal relations are constituted by the same rulings rather than by similar ones.

[12]Bartha (2010, p. 24). We slightly adapted the notation to facilitate the comparison: Bartha uses properties P and Q instead of rulings H_1 and H_2.

[13]Bartha's model conceives several forms of vertical relations not only of specification or parallelism. Whereas *naẓīr*-relation corresponds to the relation holding in Bartha's *correlative analogy*; and *khaṣīṣa*-relation seems to be close to the relation holding in his *explanatory analogy*, he also includes *predictive* and *functional forms* of vertical relations underlying respective analogies – see Bartha (2010, pp. 96-98).

A good start for the development of a general framework would be to study the effects of including Bartha's (2010, pp. 96–98) *predictive* and *functional* forms of vertical relations within the *qiyās*-model – though they might be closer to *qiyās* of the occasioning factor than to those of the indication or similarity.

Among all the learned disciplines, the law leads the way in its trust in the epistemic perspective for the shaping of regulated rational interaction. The Islamic juriconsults who developed the notion of *qiyās* learned this wisdom by delving into the roots of normativity underlying legal and moral rules. The result of their endeavour suggests exploring new synchronic and diachronic ways of approaching both the understanding and the practice of *parallel reasoning* in contexts of social and natural sciences.

Our final claim in this book is that *Immanent Reasoning*,[14] the recently developed approach to CTT, provides a bridge to launch such a study.

References

Alchourrón, C. E. (1961). Los Argumentos Jurídicos *a fortiori* y a Pari. *Revista Jurídica de Buenos Aires*, Vol. IV. pp. 177–199.

Al-Shīrāzī, Abū Isḥāq. (1987). *Al-Maʿūna fī al-jadal*. (ʿAlī b. ʿAbd al-ʿAzīz al-ʿUmayrīnī. Al-Safāh, Ed.). Kuwait: Manshūrāt Markaz al-Makhṭūṭāt wa-al-Turāth.

Al-Shīrāzī, Abū Isḥāq. (2003). *Al-Lumaʿ fī uṣūl al-fiqh*. Beirut: Dār al-Kutub al-ʿIlmiyah.

Al-Shīrāzī, Abū Isḥāq. (2016). *Mulakhkhaṣ fī al-jadal*. Retrieved February 1, 2016 from https://upload.wikimedia.org/wikisource/ar/e/ea/خ_الملخص_في_الجدل.pdf.

Bartha, P. F. A. (2010). *By Parallel Reasoning. The Construction and Evaluation of Analogical Arguments*. Oxford: Oxford University Press.

Brandom, R. (1994). *Making it Explicit*. Cambridge: Harvard University Press.

Brewer, S. (1996, March). Exemplary Reasoning: Semantics, Pragmatics, and the Rational Force of Legal Argument byAnalogy. *Harvard Law Review, 109*(5), 923–1028.

Golding, M. (2001). *Legal Reasoning*. Petersborough: Broadview Press.

Hallaq, W. (1985). The Logic of Legal Reasoning in Religious and Non-Religious Cultures: The Case of Islamic Law and Common Law". *Cleveland State Law Review,* 34, pp. 79–96.

Hallaq, W. (1987a). A Tenth-Eleventh Century Treatise on Juridical. *The Muslim World,* 77 3–4, pp. 151–282.

Rahman, S., McConaughey, Z., Klev, A., & Clerbout, N. (2018). *Immanent Reasoning or Equality in Action. A Plaidoyer for the Play Level*. Dordrecth: Springer.

Woods, J. (2015). *Is Legal Reasoning Irrational? An Introduction to the Epistemology of Law*. London: College Publications.

Young W. E. (2017). *The Dialectical Forge. Juridical Disputation and the Evolution of Islamic Law*. Dordrecht: Springer.

[14]See Rahman/McConaughey/Klev/Clerbout (2018).

Glossary of Some Relevant Technical Terms from Islamic Jurisprudence

ʿadam al-taʾthīr lack of efficiency (of the *ʿilla*, in occasioning the *ḥukm*)
ʿaks opposite; co-absence (of *ʿilla* and *ḥukm*) [as opposed to *ṭard*]
aṣl*, pl. *uṣūl lit. "root/stem/trunk"; [in *qiyās*] the authoritative, non-derived source-case whose *ḥukm* is known, and with which the *farʿ* is correlated; root-case; source-case; authoritative, divinely-sanctioned (or inspired) source-case; premise-principle [cf. *qāʿida*].
dalāla indication
dalīl*, pl. *adilla indicant drawn from an epistemically authoritative source
dawarān concomitance; co-presence and co-absence of *ʿilla* and *ḥukm* [cf. *jarayān*; *al-ṭard wa'l-ʿaks*]
faqīh*, pl. *fuqahāʾ jurist competent in *fiqh*
farʿ*, pl. *furūʿ lit. "branch"; [in *qiyās*] the derivative case whose *ḥukm* is determined by correlation with the *aṣl*; branch-case, derived case; substantive ruling determined via *ijtihād*
farq*, pl. *f urūq invalidating distinction, *qiyās*- invalidating difference
fasād al-waḍʿ invalidity of occasioned status
fiqh the jurist's "understanding" of God's Law, the fruit of *ijtihād*; a corpus of derived substantive law
ḥadīth*, pl. *aḥādīth Prophetic report, conveying a unit of Sunna with *isnād* and *matn*
ḥukm*, pl. *aḥkām ruling, norm (substantive, procedural, or methodological); [in *qiyās*] the ruling of the *aṣl* which the proponent seeks to transfer to the *farʿ*
ifḥām the silencing of a dialectical opponent
ijmāʿ consensus; Muslim communal and/or scholarly consensus on a particular *ḥukm*
ijtihād the attempted discovery of God's Law via exhaustive research and rational application of legal theoretical rules and methods; the cultivation of *furūʿ* from *uṣūl* via the principles developed in *uṣūl al-fi qh*

The list, including translation, is a selection of the list of Young (2017, pp. 609–614).

S. Rahman et al., *Inferences by Parallel Reasoning in Islamic Jurisprudence*, Logic, Argumentation & Reasoning 19, https://doi.org/10.1007/978-3-030-22382-3

***ʿilla*, pl. *ʿilal*[*inqiyās*]** the occasioning factor which gives rise to the *ḥukm*
ilzām the inexorable concession of a dialectical opponent
inqiṭā termination of the ***Jadal*** session.
istidlāl drawing indication; drawing forth a *dalīl* -indicant, as epistemic justification for the argued solution to the *mas'ala*; mode of argument from authoritative indicants
istinbāṭ rational inference
ithbāt confi rmation, affi rmation
iʿtirāḍ*, pl. *iʿtirāḍāt dialectical objection, critique
jadal dialectic; theory and practice of (juridical) dialectical disputation
jā'iz allowed, permitted
jalī clearly disclosed, perspicuous
jarayān concomitance; co-presence and co-absence of *ʿilla* and *ḥukm* [cf. *dawarān*; *al-ṭard wa'l-ʿaks*]
kasr breaking apart (the properties composing the *ʿilla*)
khafī latent, hidden
khaṣīṣa*, pl. *khaṣā'iṣ special characteristic
muʿāraḍa counter-indication (Q's bringing a counter- *dalīl* to oppose and supplant R's *dalīl*)
mujtahid jurist qualifi ed. to perform *ijtihād*
muṭālaba evidential demand; a demand for verification, justifi cation, etc.
naqḍ a dialectical charge of intra-doctrinal inconsistency
naṣṣ univocal source-text; unambiguous text; univocal formulation
naẓīr*, pl. *naẓā'ir parallel; one of two legal objects or categories whose corresponding rulings mirror each other
nuṭq divinely-sanctioned decree (as found in Qur'ān or Sunna)
qalb reversal (of the *qiyās*, to produce the contradictory *ḥukm*)
qiyās correlational inference
qiyās al-dalāla correlational inference of indication
qiyās al-ʿilla correlational inference of the occasioning factor
qiyās al-shabah correlational inference of resemblance
ra'y considered opinion
sabab reason, cause
shabah*, pl. *ashbāh resemblance
shahādat al-uṣūl testimony of the authoritative sources
Sharʿ / Sharīʿa G od's Law
taʿlīl justifying the occasioning factor; *ʿilla* -justifi cation
tanāquḍ intra-argument, logical contradiction
ṭard co-presence (of *ʿilla* and *ḥukm*) [as opposed to *ʿaks*]
al-ṭard wa'l-ʿaks concomitance; co-presence and co-absence of *ʿilla* and *ḥukm* [cf. *jarayān*; *dawarān*]
ta'thīr efficiency (in causing or occasioning something)
uṣūl al-fi qh Islamic legal theory
wāḍiḥ plainly-evident
waṣf*, pl. *awṣāf property, quality
ẓāhir most apparent meaning, sense, or interpretation

Bibliography

Aczel, P. (1978). The type theoretic interpretation of constructive set theory. In *Logic Colloquium '77* (pp. 55–66). Amsterdam: North-Holland.
Ahmed, R. (2010). *Islamic natural law theories*. New York: Oxford University Press.
Al-Baghdādī, al-Khaṭīb. (1421H). *Al-Faqīh wa al-mutafaqqih*. (Abū ‘Abd al-Raḥmān, Ed.). Saudi: Dār ibn Jauzī.
Al-Bājī, Abū al-Walīd. (2004). *Al-Minhāj fī tartīb al-ḥijāj*. Riyadh: Maktabat al-Rushd.
Al-Banjarī, Muhammad Arsyad. (1957). *Sabīl al-muhtadīn*. Riyadh: King Saud University.
Al-Banjarī, Muhammad Arsyad. (1983). *Tuḥfat al-rāghibīn*. Banjarmasin: Toko Buku Murni.
Al-Bāqillānī, Abū Bakr. (2012). *Al-Taqrīb wa al-irshād fī uṣūl al-fiqh*. Beirut: Dār al-Kutub al-‘Ilmiyya.
Al-Baṣrī, Abū al-Ḥusayn. (1964). *Kitāb al-qiyās al-sharʿī*. In *idem*, *Kitāb al-muʿtamad fī uṣūl al-fiqh*. Vol. 2. (Muḥammad Ḥamīd Allāh, Muḥammad Bakīr, and Ḥasan Ḥanafī, Eds.). Damascus: al-Maʿhad al-ʿIlmī al-Faransī li'l-Dirāsāt al-ʿArabiyya bi-Dimash.
Al-Baṣrī, Abū al-Ḥusayn. (1987). The Book of Juridical Qiyās. Trans. Wael Hallaq. *The Muslim World*, 77 3–4, pp. 207–228.
Al-Baṣrī, Abū al-Ḥusayn. (1995). *Al-Muʿtamad fī uṣūl al-fiqh*. Dār al-Kutub al-‘Ilmiyya.
Alchourrón, C. E. (1961). "Los Argumentos Jurídicos *a fortiori* y a Pari". *Revista Jurídica de Buenos Aires*, Vol. IV. pp. 177–199.
Al-Ghazālī, Abū Hāmid. (1324 H). *Al-Mustaṣfā min 'ilm al-uṣūl, 2* vols. Būlāq: al-Maṭba'a al-Amīrīyya.
Al-Ghazālī, Abū Ḥāmid. (1970). *Al-Mankhūl min ta'līqāt al-uṣūl*. (‘Abd al-Malik Ibn ‘Abd Allāh, Ed.). Damascus.
Al-Ghazālī, Abū Ḥāmid. (1993). *Al-Mustaṣfā fī 'ilm al-uṣūl*. (Ḥamzah ibn Zuhayr Ḥāfiẓ, Ed.). Medina: Ḥamzah ibn Zuhayr Ḥāfiẓ.
Al-Jaṣṣāṣ, Abū Bakr. (2000). *Uṣūl al-Jaṣṣāṣ al-Musammā al-Fuṣūl fī al-Uṣūl*. Beirut: Manshūrāt Muḥammad ‘Alī Bayḍūn.
Al-Juwaynī, ‘Abd al-Malik ibn ‘Abd Allāh. (1997). *Al-Burhān fī uṣūl al-fiqh*. (Salāh ibn Muḥammad ibn ‘Awīḍa, Ed.). Beirut: Dār al-Kutub al-‘Ilmiyya.
Al-Juwaynī, ‘Abd al-Malik ibn ‘Abd Allāh. (1979). *Al-Kāfiya fī al-jadal*. Ed. Fawqiya Ḥusayn Maḥmūd. Cairo: Maṭba‘at ‘Īsā al Bābi al-Ḥalabī.
Al-Juwaynī, ‘Abd al-Malik ibn ‘Abd Allāh. (2003). *Al-Talkhīs fī uṣūl al-fiqh*. (Muḥammad Ḥasan Ismā‘īl Shāfi‘ī, Ed.). Beirut: Dār al-Kutub al-‘Ilmīyya.
Al-Juwaynī, ‘Abd al-Malik ibn ‘Abd Allāh. (2007). *Nihāyat al-Maṭlab fī Dirāyat al-Madhhab*. Jeddah: Dār al-Minhāj.

S. Rahman et al., *Inferences by Parallel Reasoning in Islamic Jurisprudence*, Logic, Argumentation & Reasoning 19, https://doi.org/10.1007/978-3-030-22382-3

Al-Marghīnānī, 'Alī ibn Abī Bakr. (2000). *Al-Hidāya : Sharḥ bidāyat al-mubtadī*. Cairo: Dār al-Salām lil-Ṭiba'a wal-Nashr.

Al-Namla, 'Abd al-Karīm b. 'Alī b. Muḥammad. (1999). *Al-Muhadhdhab fī 'ilm uṣūl al-fiqh al-muqārin*. Riyadh: Maktabat al-Rushd.

Almog, J. (1991). The what and the how. *Journal of Philosophy, 88*, 225–244.

Al-Shīrāzī, Abū Isḥāq (1999) *Kitāb al-luma' fī uṣūl al-fiqh; Le livre des rais illuminant les fondements de la compréhension de la loi: traité de théorie légale musulmane*. (E. Chaumont Trans. & Ed.). Berkeley: Robbin.

Al-Shīrāzī, Abū Isḥāq. (1970). *Ṭabaqāt al-fuqahā*. Beirut: Dār al-Rā'id al-'Arabī.

Al-Shīrāzī, Abū Isḥāq. (1980). *Al-Tabṣira fī usūl al-fiqh*. (Muḥammad Ḥasan Hītū, Ed.). Damascus: Dār al-Fikr.

Al-Shīrāzī, Abū Isḥāq. (1987). *Al-Ma'ūna fī al-jadal*. ('Alī b. 'Abd al-'Azīz al-'Umayrīnī. Al-□afāh, Ed.). Kuwait: Manshūrāt Markaz al-Makhṭūṭāt wa-al-Turāth.

Al-Shīrāzī, Abū Isḥāq. (1988). *Sharḥ al-luma' fī uṣūl al-fiqh*. ('Abd al-Majīd Turkī, Ed.). Beirut: Dār al-Gharb al-Islāmī.

Al-Shīrāzī, Abū Isḥāq. (1992). *Al-Muhadhdhab fī fiqh al-Imām al-Shāfi'ī*. (Muḥammad al-Zuhaylī, Ed.). Damascus: Dār al-Qalam.

Al-Shīrāzī, Abū Isḥāq. (1995). *Al-Luma' fī uṣūl al-fiqh*. Beirut: Dār Ibn Kathīr.

Al-Shīrāzī, Abū Isḥāq. (2003). *Al-Luma' fī uṣūl al-fiqh*. Beirut: Dār al-Kutub al-'Ilmiyah.

Al-Shīrāzī, Abū Isḥāq. (2016). *Mulakhkhaṣ fī al-jadal*. Retrieved February 1, 2016 from https://upload.wikimedia.org/wikisource/ar/e/ea/خ_الملخص_في_الجدل.pdf.

Al-Subkī, Tāj al-Dīn. (1964). *Ṭabaqāt al-Shāfi'iyya al-kubrā*. (Maḥmūd Muḥammad Ṭanāḥī & 'Abd al-Fattāḥ Muḥammad al-Ḥulū eds.). Cairo: 'Isā al-Babīb al-Halabī.

Al-Zarkashī, Badr al-Dīn (1992). *Al-Baḥr al-muḥīt fī uṣūl al-fiqh*. ('Abd al-Qādir Al- 'Ānī, Ed.). Kuwait: Wizārat al-Awqāf wa'l-Shu'ūn al-Islāmiyya.

Austin, J. L. (1946). Other minds. *The Aristotelian Society Supplementary, 20*, 148–187.

Aristotle. (1984). *The complete works of Aristotle. The revised Oxford translation*. (J. Barnes, Trans. & Ed.). Princeton: Princeton University Press.

Barrio, E. A., Clerbout, N., & Rahman, S. (2018). Introducing consistency in a dialogical framework for paraconsistent logic. *IGPL*.-OUP. https://doi.org/10.1093/jigpal/jzy069.

Bartha, P. F. A. (2010). *By parallel reasoning. The construction and evaluation of analogical arguments*. Oxford: Oxford University Press.

Beirlaen, M., & Fontaine, M. (2016). Inconsistency-adaptive dialogical logic. *Logica Universalis, 10*(1), 99–134.

Bou Akl, Ziad. (2019). "Averroes on juridical reasoning" In Adamson, Peter., & Di Giovanni, Matteo (eds). Interpreting Averroes. Cambridge University Press, Cambridge.

Brandom, R. (1994). *Making it explicit*. Cambridge: Harvard University Press.

Brandom, R. (1997). "A Study Guide". In W. Sellars (Ed.), *Empiricism and the Philosophy of Mind* (pp. 119–189). Cambridge MA: Harvard University Press.

Brandom, R. (2000). *Articulating reasons*. Cambridge: Harvard University Press.

Brewer, S. (1996, March). Exemplary Reasoning: Semantics, Pragmatics, and the Rational Force of Legal Argument byAnalogy. *Harvard Law Review* 109(5): 923–1028.

Carnap, R. (1934). *Logische Syntax der Sprache*. Vienna: Julius Springer.

Castelnérac, B., & Marion, M. (2009). Arguing for inconsistency: Dialectical games in the academy. In G. Primiero & S. Rahman (Eds.), *Acts of knowledge: History, philosophy and logic* (pp. 37–76). London: College Publications.

Cellucci, C. (2013). *Rethinking logic: Logic in relation to mathematics, evolution and method*. Dordrecht: Springer.

Chaumont, E. (1991). Encore au sujet de l'Ash'arisme d'Abū Isḥāq Al-Shīrāzī. *Studia Islamica, 74*, 167–177.

Clerbout, N. (2014a). First-order dialogical games and tableaux. *Journal of Philosophical Logic, 43*(4), 785–801.

Clerbout, N. (2014b). *La Semantiques Dialogiques. Notions Fondamentaux et Éléments de Metathéorie*. London: College Publications.

Clerbout, N., & Rahman, S. (2015). *Linking game-theoretical approaches with constructive type theory: Dialogical strategies as CTT-demonstrations*. Dordrecht: Springer.

Crubellier, M. (2008). The programme of Aristotelian analytics. In C. Dégremont, L. Keiff, & H. Rückert (Eds.), *Dialogues, logics and other strange things. Essays in honour of Shahid Rahman* (pp. 103–129). London: College Publications.

Crubellier, M. (2014). *Aristote, Premiers analytiques. Traduction, introduction et commentaire*. Garnier-Flammarion.

Crubellier, M., McConaughey, M., Marion M., & Rahman, S. (2019). Dialectic, The Dictum de Omni and Ecthesis. *History and Philosophy of Logic*. In print.

David, J. (2010). Legal Comparability and Cultural Identity: The Case of Legal Reasoning in Jewish and Islamic Traditions. *Electronic Journal of Comparative Law*, vol. 14.1, http://www.ejcl.org.

David, J. (2014). *Jurisprudence and theology*. Dordrecht: Springer.

Davidson, D. (1980). *Essays on Actions and Events*. Oxford: Clarendon Press.

Diller, J., & Troelstra, A. (1984). Realizability and intuitionistic logic. *Synthese, 60*, 253–282.

Dummett, M. (1973). *Frege. Philosophy of language* (2nd (1981) ed.). London: Duckworth.

Duthil-Novaes, C. (2007). *Formalizing medieval logical theories*. Dordrecht: Springer.

Duthil Novaes, C. (2015). A dialogical, multiagent account of the normativity of logic. *Dialectica, 69*(4), 587–609.

Duthil Novaes, C., & French, R. (2018). A dialogical, multiagent account of the normativity of logic. *Philosophical Issues, 28*(4), 129–158.

Dybjer, P. (1994, July). Inductive families. *Formal Aspects of Computing, 6*: 440–465.

El Shamsy, A. (2007). The first Shāfiʿī: The traditionalist legal thought of Abū Yaʿqūb al-Buwaytī (d. 231/846). *Islamic Law and Society, 14*(3), 301–341.

Ephrat, D. (2000). *A learned Society in a Period of transition : The Sunni 'Ulama' of eleventh-century Baghdad*. Albany: State University of New York Press.

Felscher, W. (1985). Dialogues as a foundation for intuitionistic logic. In D. Gabbay & F. Guenthner (Eds.), *Handbook of Philosophical Logic* (Vol. 3, pp. 341–372). Dordrecht: Kluwer.

Frege, G. (1893). *Grundgesetze der Arithmetik*. Jena: Hermann Pohle.

Frege, Gottlob. (1979). "Boole's logical Calculus and the concept script [1880/81]". In Gottlob Frege posthumous Writtings, by Hermes, Kambartel and Kaulbach (eds), 9–52. Oxford: Basil Blackwell.

Fyzee, A. A. A. (1964). *Outlines of Muhammadan law* (3rd ed.). Oxford: Oxford University Press.

Garner, R. (2009). On the strength of dependent products in the type theory of Martin-Löf. *Annals of Pure and Applied Logic, 160*, 1–12.

Gentzen, G. (1933). Untersuchungen über das logische Schliessen. *Mathematische Zeitschrift, 39*, 176–210.

Gili, L. (2015). Alexander of Aphrodisias and the Heterdox dictum de omni et de nullo. *History and Philosophy of Logic, 36*(2), 114–128.

Ginzburg, J. (2012). *The interactive stance*. Oxford: OUP.

Golding, M. (2001). *Legal reasoning*. Petersborough: Broadview Press.

Goodman, N. (1976). *Languages of art*. Cambridge, MA: Hackett Publishing.

Granström, J. G. (2011). *Treatise on intuitionistic type theory*. Dordrecht: Springer.

Hale, B., & Wright, C. (2001). To bury Caesar. In *The reason's proper study* (pp. 335–396). Oxford: Oxford University Press.

Hallaq, W. (1985). The logic of legal reasoning in religious and non-religious cultures: The case of Islamic law and common law. *Cleveland State Law Review, 34*, 79–96.

Hallaq, W. (1987a). A tenth-eleventh century treatise on juridical dialectic. *The Muslim World, 77*(3–4), 151–282.

Hallaq, W. (1987b). The development of logical structure in Islamic legal theory. *Der Islam, 64/1*, 42–67.

Hallaq, W. (1993a). *Ibn Taymiyya against the Greek logicians*. Oxford: Clarendon Press.

Hallaq, W. (1997). *A history of Islamic legal theories: An introduction to Sunnī Uṣūl al-Fiqh*. Cambridge, NY: Cambridge University Press.

Hallaq, W. (2004). *Continuity and change in Islamic law*. Cambridge, NY: Cambridge University Press.

Hallaq, W. (2009a). *The origins and evolution of Islamic law*. Cambridge, NY: Cambridge University Press.

Hallaq, W. (2009b). *Sharīʿa: Theory, practice, transformation*. Cambridge, NY: Cambridge University Press.

Hallaq, W. B. (1993b). Was al-Shāfi'ī the master architect of Islamic jurisprudence? *International Journal of Middle East Studies, 25*(4), 587–605.

Herder, J. G. (1960 [1772]). Abhandulung über der Ursprung der Sprache. In E. Heintel (Ed.), *Johann Gottfried Herder. Spachphilosophische Schriften* (pp. 3–87). Hamburg: Felix Meiner.

Hintikka, J. (1973). *Logic, language-games and information: Kantian themes in the philosophy of logic*. Oxford: Clarendon Press.

Hintikka, J. (1996). *Ludwig Wittgenstein: Half truths and one-and-a-half truths*. Dordrecht: Kluwer.

Hītū, Muḥammad Ḥasan. (1980). *Al-Imām al-Shīrāzī : Ḥayātuhu wa-arā'uhu al-uṣūliyya*. Damascus: Dār al-Fikr.

Hodges, W. (1998). The Laws of distribution for syllogisms. *Notre Dame Journal of Formal Logic, 39*, 221–230.

Hodges, W. (2001). Dialogue foundations: A sceptical look. *Aristotelian Society Supplementary, 75*(1), 17–32.

Hodges, W. (2008). Logic and games. *Stanford Encyclopedia of Philosophy*.

Howard, W. A. (1980). The formulae-as-types notion of construction. In J. P. Seldin & J. R. Hindley (Eds.), *To H. B. Curry: Essays on combinatory logic, lambda calculus and formalism* (pp. 479–490). London: Academic.

Ibn al-Farrā', Abū Ya'la. (1990). *Al-'Udda fī uṣūl al-fiqh*. Riyadh: Sayr al-Mubārakī.

Ibn al-Jawzī, Abū al-Faraj (1992). *Al-Muntaẓam fī tārīkh al-mulūk wa'l-umam*. (Muḥammad 'Abd al-Qādir 'Aṭā & Muṣṭafā 'Abd al-Qādir 'Aṭā, Eds.). Beirut: Dār al-Kutub al-'Ilmiyya.

Ibn al-Qāṣṣ. (1999). *Al-Talkhīṣ*. ('Ādil Aḥmad 'Abd al-Mawjūd & 'Alī Muḥammad Mu'awwaḍ, Eds.). Mecca: Maktabat Nizār Muṣṭafā al-Bāz.

Ibn al-Salāḥ, al-Nawawī, and al-Mizzī. (1992). *Ṭabaqāt al-fuqahā' al-Shāfi'iyya*. (Muḥyī al-Dīn 'Alī Najīb, Ed.). Beirut: Dār al-Bashā'ir al-Islāmīya.

Ibn Fūrak, Abū Bakr. (1987). *Mujarrad maqālāt al-Shaykh Abī al-Ḥasan al-Ash'arī : Min imlā' al-Shaykh al-Imām Abī Bakr Muḥammad ibn al-Ḥasan ibn Fūrak (t. 406/1015)*. Beirut: Al-Tawzī' al-Maktaba al-Sharqiyya.

Ibn Kathīr, Ismaīl ibn 'Umar. *Ṭabaqāt al-Shāfi'iyya*. ('Abd al-Ḥafīz Manṣūr, Ed.). Beirut: Dār al-Madār al-Islamī.

Ibn Khallikān, Abū al-'Abbas. (1978). *Wafayāt al-ayān*. (Iḥsān 'Abbās, Ed.). Beirut: Dār al-Sādir.

Ibn Qāḍī Shuhba. (1987). *Ṭabaqāt al-Shāfi'iyya*. ('Abd al-'Alīm Khān & 'Abdallāh Anīs aṭ-Ṭabbā', Eds.). Beirut: 'Ālam al-Kutub.

Ibn Qudāma. (1998). *Rawḍā al-nāẓir wa-jannat al-munāẓir*. Beirut: Mu'assasa al-Rayyān.

Ibn Ḥazm (1959). *Kitāb al-taqrīb li-ḥadd al-manṭiq wa-l-mudkhal ilayhi bi-l-alfāẓ al-ʿāmmiyya wa-l-amthila al-fiqhiyya*. (Iḥsān ʿAbbās, Ed.). Beirut: Dār Maktabat al-Ḥayāt.

Ibn Ḥazm. (1926–1930). *Al-Iḥkām fī uṣūl al-aḥkām*. 8 vols. (Aḥmad Muḥammad Shākir, Ed.). Cairo: Maṭbaʿat al-Saʿāda.

Iqbal, M. (2019). *Arsyad al-Banjari's Approaches to Rationality: Argumentation and Sharia*. PhD-University of Lille Press: Lille. Forthcoming.

Iqbal, M. & Rahman, S. (2019). Arsyad al-Banjari's Dialectical Model for Integrating Indonesian Traditional Uses into Islamic Law. Arguments on *Manyanggar, Membuang Pasilih* and *Lahang*. Forthcoming.

Keiff, L. (2004). Heuristique formelle et logiques modales non normales. *Philosophia Scientiae, 8*(2), 39–59.

Keiff, L. (2007). *Le Pluralisme dialogique: Approches dynamiques de l'argumentation formelle.* Lille: PhD.

Keiff, L. (2009). *Dialogical Logic.* (E. N. Zalta, Ed.) Retrieved from *The Stanford Encyclopedia of Philosophy*: http://plato.stanford.edu/entries/logic-dialogical

Klev, A. (2014). *Categories and Logical Syntax.* Leiden: PhD.

Klev, A. (2017). The justification of identity elimination in Martin-Löf's type theory. *Topoi*, 1–25.

Krabbe, E. C. (1985). Formal Systems of Dialogue Rules. *Synthese, 63*, 295–328.

Krabbe, E. C. (2006). Dialogue Logic. In D. Gabbay & J. Woods (Eds.), *Handbook of the history of logic* (Vol. 7, pp. 665–704). Amsterdam: Elsevier.

Lorenz, K. (1970). *Elemente der Sprachkritik. Eine Alternative zum Dogmatismus und Skeptizismus in der Analytischen Philosophie.* Frankfurt: Suhrkamp.

Lorenz, K. (1981). Dialogical logic. In W. Marciszewsku (Ed.), *Dictionary of logic as applied in the study of language* (pp. 117–125). The Hague: Martinus Nijhoff.

Lorenz, K. (2000). Sinnbestimmung und Geltungssicherung. First published udner the title ›Ein Beitrag zur Sprachlogik‹ In: G.-L. Lueken (ed.), *Formen der Argumentation*, Leipzig: Akademisches Verlag, pp 87–106.

Lorenz, K. (2001). Basic objectives of dialogue logic in historical perspective. *Synthese, 127*(1–2), 225–263.

Lorenz, K. (2009). *Dialogischer Konstruktivismus.* Berlin/New York: De Gruyter.

Lorenz, K. (2010a). *Logic, language and method: On polarities in human experiences.* Berlin/New York: De Gruyter.

Lorenz, K. (2010b). *Philosophische Variationen: Gesammelte Aufsätze unter Einschluss gemeinsam mit Jürgen Mittelstrass greschriebener Arbeiten zu Platon und Leibniz.* Berlin/New York: De Gruyter.

Lorenz, K., & Mittelstrass, J. (1967). On rational philosophy of language. The Programme in Plato's Cratylus reconsidered. *Mind, 76*(301), 1–20.

Lorenzen, P., & Lorenz, K. (1978). *Dialogische Logik.* Damstadt: Wissenschaftliche Buchgesellschaft.

Lowry, J. E. (2007). *Early Islamic legal theory : The Risāla of Muḥammad ibn Idrīs al-Shāfiʿī.* Leiden/Boston: Brill.

Lucas, S. (2010). Principles of Traditionist jurisprudence reconsidered. *The Muslim World, 100*(1), 145–156.

Makdisi, G. (1984a). The juridical theology of Shāfiʿī: Origins and significance of Uṣūl al-Fiqh. *Studia Islamica, 59*, 5–47.

Makdisi, G. (1984b). *The rise of colleges: Institutions of learning in Islam and the west.* Edinburgh: Edinburgh University Press.

Marion, M. (2006). Hintikka on Wittgenstein: From language games to game semantics. In T. Aho & A.-V. Pietarinen (Eds.), *Truth and games: Essays in honour of Gabriel Sandu* (pp. 237–256). Helsinki: Acta Philosophica Fennica.

Marion, M. (2009). Why play logical games? In O. Majer, A. V. Pietarinen, & T. Tulenheimo (Eds.), *Logic and games: Unifying logic.* Dordrecht: Springer.

Marion, M. (2010). Between saying and doing: From Lorenzen to Brandom and Back. In P. E. Bour, M. Rebuschi, & L. Rollet (Eds.), *Constructions: Essays in honour of Gerhard Heinzmann* (pp. 489–497). London: College Publications.

Marion, M., & Rückert, H. (2015). Aristotle on universal quantification: A study from the perspective of game semantics. *History and Philosophy of Logic, 37*(3), 201–209.

Martin-Löf, P. (1971). Hauptsatz for the intuitionistic theory of iterated inductive definitions. In J. E. Fenstad (Ed.), *Proceedings of the second Scandinavian logic symposium* (pp. 179–216). Amsterdam: North-Holland.

Martin-Löf, P. (1975). An intuitionistic theory of types: Predicative part. In H. E. Rose & J. C. Shepherdson (Eds.), *Logic Colloquium '73* (pp. 73–118). Amsterdam: North-Holland.

Martin-Löf, P. (1982). Constructive mathematics and computer programming. In J. L. Cohen & J. Los (Eds.), *Logic, methodology and philosophy of science VI, 1979* (pp. 153–175). Amsterdam: North-Holland.

Martin-Löf, P. (1984). *Intuitionistic type theory. Notes by Giovanni Sambin of a series of lectures given in Padua, June 1980.* Naples: Bibliopolis.

Martin-Löf, P. (1992). *Substitution Calculus.* Lecture notes. http://archive-pml.github.io/martin-lof/pdfs/Substitution-calculus-1992.pdf

Martin-Löf, P. (1996a). On the meanings of the logical constants and the justifications of the logical Laws. *Nordic Journal of Philosophical Logic, 1*, 11–60.

Martin-Löf, P. (1996b). On the meanings of the logical constants and the justifications of the logical laws. *Nordic Journal of Philosophical Logic, 1*, 11–60.

Martin-Löf, P. (2011). *When did 'judgement' come to be a term of logic?* Lecture held at Ecole Normale Supérieure 14 October 2011.

Martin-Löf, P. (2012). *Aristotle's distinction between apophansis and protasis in the light of the distinction between assertion and proposition in contemporary logic.* Workshop "Sciences et Savoirs de l'Antiquité à l'Age classique". Lecture held at the laboratory SPHERE–CHSPAM, Paris VII. Seminar organized by Ahmed Hasnaoui.

Martin-Löf, P. (2014). Truth of Empirical Propositions. *Lecture held at the University of Leiden, February 2014.* Transcription by: Amsten Klev.

Martin-Löf, P. (2015). Is Logic Part of Normative Ethics? Lecture Held at the research unit *Sciences, Normes, Décisions (FRE 3593), Paris, May 2015.* Transcription by: Amsten Klev.

Martin-Löf, P. (2017a). Assertion and Request. *Lecture held at Oslo, 2017.* Transcription by Ansten Klev.

Martin-Löf, P. (2017b). Assertion and Request. *Lecture held at Stockholm.* Transcription by Ansten Klev.

Messick, B. (1996). *The calligraphic state: Textual domination and history in a Muslim society.* Berkeley: University of California Press.

McDowell, J. (2009). *Having the World in View: Essays on Kant, Hegel, and Sellars.* Harvard: Harvard University Press.

Miller, L. B. (1984). *Islamic disputation theory: A study of the development of dialectic in Islam from the tenth through fourteenth centuries.* Princeton: Princeton University. (Unpublished dissertation).

Mittermaier, A. (2010). *Dreams that matter: Egyptian landscapes of the imagination.* Berkeley: University of California Press.

Nordström, B., Petersson, K., & Smith, J. M. (1990). *Programming in Martin-Löf's type theory: An introduction.* Oxford: Oxford University Press.

Nordström, B., Petersson, K., & Smith, J. M. (2000). Martin-Löf's Type Theory. In Abramsky, S., Gabbay, D., & Maibaum, T. S. (eds.), *Handbook of logic in computer science* (Vol. 5: Logic and Algebraic Methods, pp. 1–37). Oxford: Oxford University Press.

Osman, A. (2014). *The Zāhirī madhhab (3rd/9th–10th/16th century): A Textualist theory of Islamic law.* Leiden: Brill.

Parsons, T. (2014). *Articulating medieval logic.* Oxford: Oxford University Press.

Peacock, A. C. S. (2015). *Great Seljuk Empire.* Edinburgh: Edinburgh University Press.

Peregrin, J. (2014). *Inferentialism. Why rules matter.* New York: Plagrave MacMillan.

Plato. (1997). *Plato. Complete works.* (J. M. Cooper, Ed. & Trans.) Indianapolis: Hackett.

Popek, A. (2012). Logical dialogues from middle ages. In C. B. Gómez, S. Magnier, & F. J. Salguero (Eds.), *Logic of knowledge. Theory and applications* (pp. 223–244). London: College Publications.

Prawitz, D. (1965). *Natural deduction*. Stockholm: Almqvist & Wiksell.
Primiero, G. (2008). *Information and knowledge*. Dordrecht: Springer.
Prior, A. (1960). The runabout inference-ticket. *Analysis, 21*, 38–39.
Quine, W. V. (1969). *Ontological relativity and other essays*. New York: Columbia University Press.
Rahman, S. (2001). On Frege's nightmare: A combination of intuitionistic, free and paraconsistent logics. In H. Wansing (Ed.), *Essays on non-classical logics* (pp. 61–90). New Jersey/London/ Singapore/Hong Kong: World Scientific.
Rahman, S. (2002, October). Un Desafío para las Teorías Cognitivas de la Competencia Lógica: Los Fundamentos Pragmáticos de la Semántica de la Lógica Linear. Man 25(2): 381–432.
Rahman, S. (2012). "Negation in the logic of first degree entailment and Tonk. A dialogical study". In S. Rahman, G. Primiero, & Mathieu Marion, *The* Realism-antirealism debate in the age of alternative logics (pp. 213–250), Dordrecht: Springer.
Rahman, S. (2019). The logic of reasons and endorsement. In C. Weiss (ed.). *Constructive semantics*, Springer. Chapter I. In print.
Rahman, S., & Carnielli, W. (2000). The dialogical approach to Paraconsistency. *Synthese, 125*(1–2), 201–232.
Rahman, S., & Iqbal, M. (2018). Unfolding parallel reasoning in Islamic jurisprudence. Epistemic and dialectical meaning within Abū Isḥāq al-Shīrāzī's system of co-relational inferences of the occasioning factor. *Cambridge Journal for Arabic Sciences and Philosophy, 28*, 67–132.
Rahman, S., & Keiff, L. (2005). On how to be a Dialogician. In D. Vanderveken (Ed.), *Logic, thought and action* (pp. 359–408). Dordrecht: Kluwer.
Rahman, S., & Rückert, H. (2001). Dialogical Connexive Logic. *Synthese, 125*(1–2), 105–139.
Rahman, S., & Tulenheimo, T. (2009). From games to dialogues and Back: Towards a general frame for validity. In O. Majer, A. Pietarinen, & T. Tulenheimo (Eds.), *Games: Unifying logic, language and philosophy* (pp. 153–208). Dordrecht: Springer.
Rahman, S., Clerbout, N., & Keiff, L. (2009). On dialogues and natural deduction. In G. Primiero & S. Rahman (Eds.), *Acts of knowledge: History, philosophy and logic: Essays dedicated to Göran Sundholm* (pp. 301–336). London: College Publications.
Rahman, S., Clerbout, N., & Redmond, J. (2017). Interaction and equality. The dialogical interprepretation of CTT (in Spanish). Critica, vol. 49, N° 145, pp. 51–91.
Rahman, S., Fiutek, V., & Rückert, H. (2010). A dialogical semantics for Bonanno's system of belief revision. In P. E. Bour, M. Rebuschi, & L. Rollet (Eds.), *Construction* (pp. 315–334). London: College Publications.
Rahman, S., Granström, J. G., & Farjami, A. (2019.) Legal reasoning and some logic after all. The lessons of the elders. In Gabbay, D, Magnani, L, Park, W, & Pietarinen, A-V (eds.), *Natural arguments. A tribute to john woods*. In print.
Rahman, S., McConaughey, Z., Klev, A., & Clerbout, N. (2018). *Immanent reasoning or equality in action. A Plaidoyer for the play level*. Dordrecth: Springer.
Rahman, S., Zidani, F., & Young, W. E. (2019). Ibn Hazm on heteronomous imperative. Landmark in the history of the logical analysis of legal norms. In Armgardt, M. et al (eds). *Legal Reasoning Contemporary and Ancient Perspectives*. Springer. Forthcoming.
Ranta, A. (1988). Propositions as games as types. *Syntese, 76*, 377–395.
Ranta, A. (1994). *Type-theoretical grammar*. Oxford: Clarendon Press.
Read, S. (2008). Harmony and modality. In C. Dégremont, L. Kieff, & H. Rückert (Eds.), *Dialogues, logics and other strange things: Essays in honour of Shahid Rahman* (pp. 285–303). London: College Publications.
Read, S. (2010). General elimination harmony and the meaning of the logical constants. *Journal of Philosophical Logic, 39*, 557–576.
Redmond, J., & Rahman, S. (2016). Armonía Dialógica: tonk Teoría Constructiva de Tipos y Reglas para Jugadores Anónimos. *Theoria, 31*(1), 27–53.
Rückert, H. (2011). *Dialogues as a dynamic framework for logic*. London: College Publications.
Schacht, J. (1959). *The origins of Muhammadan jurisprudence*. Oxford: Clarendon Press.

Schröder-Heister, P. (1984). A natural extension of natural deduction. *Journal of Symbolic Logic, 49*, 1284–1300.
Sellars, W. (1991). *Science, Perception and Reality*. Atascadero-California: Ridgeview Publishing Company.
Shafiei, M. (2017). *Intentionnalité et signification: Une approche dialogique*.Paris: PHD-thesis, Sorbonne.
Smullyan, R. (1968). *First-Order Logic*. New York: Springer.
Soufi, Y. (2017). *Pious critique: Abū Isḥāq al-Shīrāzī and the 11th century practice of juristic disputation (Munāẓara)*. Toronto: University of Toronto. (Unpublished dissertation).
Soufi, Y. (2018). The historiography of Uṣūl al-Fiqh. In A. Emon & R. Ahmed (Eds.), *The Oxford handbook of Islamic law* (pp. 249–267). Oxford: Oxford University Press.
Spectorsky, S. A. (1982). Aḥmad Ibn Ḥanbal's Fiqh. *Journal of the American Oriental Society, 102*(3), 461–465.
Stewart, D. (2016). Muḥammad B. Dā'ūd al-Zāhirī's manual of jurisprudence, al-Wuṣūl ilā Ma'rifat al-Uṣūl. In W. B. Hallaq (Ed.), *The formation of Islamic law* (pp. 277–315). New York/London: Routledge.
Sundholm, G. (1997). Implicit epistemic aspects of constructive logic. *Journal of Logic, Language and Information, 6*(2), 191–212.
Sundholm, G. (2001). A Plea for logical atavism. In O. Majer (Ed.), *The Logica yearbook 2000* (pp. 151–162). Prague: Filosofía.
Sundholm, G. (2006). Semantic values for natural deduction derivations. *Synthese, 148*, 623–638.
Sundholm, G. (2009). A century of judgement and inference, 1837-1936: Some strands in the development of logic. In L. Haaparanta (Ed.), *The development of modern logic* (pp. 264–317). Oxford: Oxford University Press.
Sundholm, G. (2012). Inference versus consequence revisited: Inference, conditional, implication. *Synthese, 187*, 943–956.
Sundholm, G. (2013). Inference and Consequence in an Interpeted Language. Talk at the Workshop PROOF THEORY AND PHILOSOPHY, Groningen, December 3–5, 2013.
Tahiri, H. (2008). The birth of scientific controversies: The dynamic of the Arabic tradition and its impact on the development of science: Ibn al-Haytham's challenge of Ptolemy's *Almagest*. In S. Rahman, T. Street, & H. Tahiri (Eds.), *The Unity of science in the Arabic tradition* (pp. 183–225). Dordrecht: Springer.
Tahiri, H. (2014). Al Kindi and the universalization of knowledge through mathematics. *Revista de Humanidades de Valparaíso, 4*, 81–90.
Tahiri, H. (2015). *Mathematics and the mind. An introduction to Ibn Sīnā's theory of knowledge*. Dordrecht: Springer.
Tahiri, H. (2018). When the present misunderstands the past. How a modern Arab intellectual reclaimed his own heritage. *Cambridge Journal for Arabic Sciences and Philosophy, 28*(1), 133–158.
Talas, A. (1939). *L'enseignement chez les Arabes: La madrasa Niẓāmiyya et son histoire*. Paris: P. Geuthner.
Tasistro, A. (1993). *Formulation of Martin-Löf's theory of types with explicit substitutions*. Gothenburg: Master's thesis, Chalmers University of Technology.
The Univalent Foundations Program. (2013). *Homotopy Type Theory: Univalent Foundations of Mathematics*. Retrieved from http://homotopytypetheory.org/book.
Trafford, J. (2017). *Meaning in dialogue. An interactive approach to logic and reasoning*. Dordrecht: Springer.
Troelstra, A., & van Dalen, D. (1988). *Constructivism in mathematics*. Amsterdam: North-Holland.
van Heijenoort, J. (1967). Logic as Calculus and logic as language. *Synthese, 17*, 324–330.
Weiss, B. (2010). *The search for God's law: Islamic jurisprudence in the writings of Sayf al-Dīn al-Āmidī* (Revised ed.). Salt Lake City: University of Utah Press.
Weiss, B. G. (1992). *Search for God's law, Islamic jurisprudence in the writings of Sayf al-din al-Amidi*. Salt Lake City: University of Utah Press.

Weiss, B. G. (1998). *The Spirit of Islamic law*. Athens/London: The University of Georgia Press.
Wittgenstein, L. (1922). *Tractatus Logico-Philosophicus*. Lille: Kegan Paul.
Woods, J. (2015). *Is legal reasoning irrational? An introduction to the epistemology of law*. London: College Publications.
Young, W. E. (2017). *The dialectical forge. Juridical disputation and the evolution of Islamic law*. Dordrecht: Springer.
Zermelo, E. (1930). Über Grenzzahlen und Mengenbereiche. *Fundamenta Mathematicae, 16*, 29–47.
Zysow, A. (2013). *The economy of certainty. An introduction to the typology of Islamic legal theory*. Atlanta: Lockwood Press.

Name Index

A

Aczel, P., 219
Ahmed, R., 16
Al-Baghdādī, al-Khaṭīb, 4, 101
Al-Bājī, Abū al-Walīd, 5, 9
Al-Banjarī, Muhammad Arsyad, ix
Al-Bāqillānī, Abū Bakr, 7, 10, 11
Al-Baṣrī, Abū al-Ḥusayn, 9, 24, 26, 43, 49, 51
Alchourrón, C.E., 238, 239
Al-Ghazālī, Abū Hāmid, xii, xiii, 1, 11
Al-Jaṣṣāṣ, Abū Bakr, 7, 9
Al-Juwaynī, Abū al-Ma'ālī, 3, 4, 7, 10–13, 15
Al-Marghīnānī, 'Alī ibn Abī Bakr, 14
Almog, J., 217
Al-Shīrāzī, A.I., 1–16, 19–90, 95–143, 241, 243–245
Al-Subkī, Tāj al-Dīn, 2–6, 10, 14, 15
Al-Zarkashī, Badr al-Dīn, 12, 13
Aristotle, 25, 32, 34, 41, 43, 60, 114, 156, 217
Austin, J.L., 147

B

Barnes, j., 216
Barrio, E., 195
Bartha, P.F.A., 24, 26, 36, 60, 115, 143, 246–248
Beirlaen, M., 195
Bou Akl, Ziad, 104
Brandom, R., xiii, 145, 147, 148
Brewer, S., xi, 238, 240

C

Carnap, R., 217
Carnielli, W., 195
Castelnérac, B., x, 22
Cellucci, C., 26
Chaumont, E., 11, 12
Clerbout, N., x, 30, 32, 66, 80, 128, 134, 148, 172, 181, 195, 197, 198, 215, 248
Cooper, J.M., 41
Crubellier, M., x, 43, 156, 217

D

David, J., 25
Diller, J., 221
Dummett, M., 216
Duthil-Novaes, C., 90, 194, 196
Dybjer, P., 200

E

El Shamsy, A., 6, 7
Ephrat, D., 2

F

Farjami, A., 107
Felscher, W., 66, 128
Fiutek, V., 195
Fontaine, M., 195
Frege, G., xiii, 172, 174, 215, 228
French, R., 196
Fyzee, A.A.A., 110

S. Rahman et al., *Inferences by Parallel Reasoning in Islamic Jurisprudence*, Logic, Argumentation & Reasoning 19, https://doi.org/10.1007/978-3-030-22382-3

G
Garner, R., 233
Gentzen, G., 227
Gili, L., 34
Ginzburg, J., 29
Girard, J.-Y., 195
Golding, M., 240
Goodman, N., xi
Granström, J.G., 25, 29, 219

H
Hale, B., 216
Hallaq, W., viii, xiii, 9, 10, 13, 20, 21, 23, 26, 34, 37, 44, 58, 62, 90, 238, 239
Hallaq, W.B., 20
Herder, J.G., 211
Hintikka, J., 148, 149, 191, 203
Hītū, Muḥammad Ḥasan, 2
Hodges, W., 208
Howard, W.A., 173, 220

I
Ibn al-Farrā', Abū Ya'la, 9
Ibn al-Jawzī, Abū al-Faraj, 5
Ibn al-Qāṣṣ, 3
Ibn al-⍰alāḥ, al-Nawawī, 2
Ibn Fūrak, Abū Bakr, 10
Ibn Ḥazm, 9
Ibn Kathīr, Ismaīl ibn 'Umar, 2
Ibn Khallikān, Abū al-'Abbas, 2
Ibn Qāḍī Shuhba, 3
Ibn Qudāma, 13
Iqbal, M., ix, 1, 2, 10, 13, 16, 19

K
Keiff, L., 42, 66, 128, 145, 152, 195, 197
Klev, A., x, xiv, 30, 32, 41, 66, 128, 146, 148, 172, 181, 200, 215, 219, 248
Krabbe, E.C., 42, 66, 128, 171

L
Leibniz, 116, 156, 238
Lorenz, K., x, 44, 46, 66, 128, 149, 150, 171, 191–195, 197, 203, 205, 208–211
Lorenzen, P., x, 44, 66, 128, 171, 193, 195, 197, 204, 205
Lowry, J.E., 6, 10–12
Lucas, S., 6

M
Makdisi, G., 11, 14
Marion, M., x, 22, 30, 41, 43, 145, 146, 156, 191
Martin-Löf, P., x, xiv, 22, 23, 29–31, 41, 145–147, 161, 171, 174, 178, 200, 202, 203, 205–208, 211, 215, 218, 219, 222, 223, 226
McConaughey, Z., x, 30, 32, 43, 66, 128, 172, 181, 215, 248
McDowell, J., 181
Messick, B., 2
Miller, L.B., x, 21, 44–46, 60, 62, 245
Mittelstrass, J., 209
Mittermaier, A., 1

N
Nordström, B., 29, 218, 225, 233

O
Osman, A., 8

P
Peacock, A.C.S., 2
Peregrin, J., 47, 171, 181, 202
Petersson, K., 29
Plato, 41, 156, 209
Popek, A., 22
Prawitz, D., 227, 230, 231
Primiero, G., 29
Prior, A., 26, 41, 197, 199

Q
Quine, W.V., 216

R
Rahman, S., ix, x, 1, 2, 10, 13, 16, 19, 20, 24, 30, 32, 43, 66, 75, 128, 132, 148, 149, 172, 181, 195, 197, 199, 201, 215, 248
Ranta, A., 29, 30, 32, 116, 149, 150, 204
Read, S., 200
Redmond, J., 66, 128, 197
Rückert, H., x, 22, 30, 41, 66, 75, 128, 132, 156

S
Schacht, J., 6, 13
Schröder-Heister, P., 233
Sellars, W., 181
Shafiei, M., 148
Smith, J.M., 29
Smullyan, R., 199
Soufi, Youcef, x, xiii, 1–16
Spectorsky, S.A., 6
Stewart, D., 10
Sundholm, G., 29, 41, 147, 149, 172, 186, 194, 195, 205, 215, 224

T
Tahiri, H., 21
Talas, A., 2
Tasistro, A., 223
Trafford, J., 193–197, 200, 205, 208
Troelstra, A., 221, 229
Tulenheimo, T., 66, 128

V
van Dalen, D., 229
van Heijenoort, Jan, 172

W
Weiss, B., 15
Weiss, B.G., 24
Wittgenstein, 1, 148, 191, 209
Woods, J., x, xi, xiii, 240, 244
Wright, C., 216

Y
Young, W.E., viii, 1, 9, 10, 12, 20–24, 26, 34, 44–46, 49, 50, 54–58, 60, 62, 64, 89, 96, 97, 105, 106, 112, 116, 237, 239, 249

Z
Zermelo, E., 219
Zysow, A., vii, x, xii, 15, 143

Subject Index

A

Absurdum, 46
ʿAdam al-taʾthīr, 51, 56, 58
a fortiori, 11, 239
ʿaks, xii, xiii, 31, 35–40, 50, 54, 65, 68, 77, 113, 244
Analogy, ix, x, xiv, 7, 9, 11–14, 21, 28, 95, 98, 115, 116, 120, 141, 202, 238, 239, 241, 246, 247
a pari, ix, 95, 238, 239
Application, viii, ix, xi, xii, 22, 24, 27, 30, 36, 40, 46, 59, 90, 95, 96, 98, 99, 101–104, 115, 119, 120, 137, 139, 141–143, 155, 158–160, 162, 169, 183, 216–219, 221, 226–228, 230, 237
aṣl, 24, 49, 53, 56, 59, 61–65, 67, 68, 74, 77–79, 95, 97, 106, 112, 114, 117, 118, 119, 121, 124, 126, 127, 139
Assertions, xi, 23, 28, 29, 32–34, 38–40, 43, 48, 50–52, 54, 56, 59–61, 63, 67, 76–79, 87–89, 118, 124, 137, 138, 146, 147, 149, 156, 173–175, 185, 186, 194, 203, 204, 207, 209, 222, 224, 246
Assumptions, 1, 8, 24, 41, 46, 51, 105, 109, 114, 125, 147, 208, 222, 224–228, 231, 233, 241–243, 246

B

Bool, 171–176
Boolean, 172, 174–181

C

Choices, viii, 22, 25, 36, 37, 39, 40, 44–47, 50, 53, 54, 78, 80, 82, 87, 88, 133, 135, 148, 153, 155, 159, 160, 165, 166, 177, 182, 184–186, 194, 198, 204–207, 218
Conjunction, 21, 39, 58, 60, 73, 87, 117, 127, 131, 132, 136, 153–155, 158, 159, 183, 184, 198, 199, 205, 206, 221, 233, 242
Constructive, 38, 50, 53, 54, 79, 137, 196, 204, 206
Contents, 34, 42, 149, 150, 156, 160, 181, 195, 196, 227, 231, 234, 239, 243
Context, x, xiii, 1, 4, 13, 14, 16, 23–25, 30, 33, 36–40, 42, 44, 46, 49, 53, 66, 80, 81, 90, 95, 99, 101, 116, 120, 134, 135, 147–149, 151, 156, 167, 178, 195, 198, 205, 211, 226, 227, 231, 237, 238, 240, 245–248
Cooperative, 21, 42, 46–48, 54, 55, 62, 77, 79, 82, 142, 182, 195, 196
Copy-cat, 81, 155, 156, 179, 192
Core, 29, 47, 87, 148, 156, 183, 198, 203, 205
Core of the strategy, 87, 183, 198
Correct naming, 9
Curry–Howard isomorphism, 173, 175

D

dalāla, 96, 98, 115, 118, 123, 126, 138, 139, 142
Decision, vii, viii, 8, 13, 19, 20, 30, 33, 34, 44, 50, 58, 185

S. Rahman et al., *Inferences by Parallel Reasoning in Islamic Jurisprudence*, Logic, Argumentation & Reasoning 19, https://doi.org/10.1007/978-3-030-22382-3

Definitional, 116, 157, 159, 167–169
Definitional equality, 159, 167–169
Demonstration, 88, 105, 147, 182, 184, 191, 196, 197, 224
Dependent, x, 38, 89, 98, 103, 145, 161, 172, 176, 181, 186, 194, 200, 222, 239, 242
Destructive, 50, 51, 54–56, 60, 62, 79, 196, 245
Dialectical, viii–x, xiii, 1, 5, 19–21, 23, 24, 26, 28–30, 37–44, 46, 47, 53, 59, 76, 89, 90, 99, 114, 115, 117–120, 136, 143, 237, 245, 246
Dialogical, ix, x, xiv, 1, 14, 16, 21–23, 29, 30, 37, 39–41, 43, 66, 81, 90, 117, 128–142, 145, 156, 182, 191, 194, 195, 203, 205, 237, 245
Dialogical roots of equality, 160–171
Dialogue, x, 16, 30, 41–44, 47–51, 54, 69, 74, 80–82, 117–121, 123–129, 131–135, 137, 138, 148, 150–160, 165–169, 171, 190, 194, 195, 197, 199–203, 207, 208, 210, 211
Disjoint union, 231, 233, 234
Disjunction, 37, 38, 40, 87, 103, 153, 175, 198, 199, 204–206, 234
Double negation, 25

E
Efficiency, xii, 21, 31, 35, 37, 39, 40, 42, 46, 48–52, 56, 58, 60, 61, 63, 80, 82, 89, 96, 98 99, 104, 113, 114, 142, 211, 240, 244
Elimination, 186, 194, 199, 206, 207, 227, 228, 230, 233, 240
Epistemic, ix, 19, 21, 22, 26, 41, 43, 44, 47, 95, 99, 106, 116, 146–148, 172, 203, 207–209, 246, 248
Epistemological, vii, x, xi, xiii, 8–11, 19, 22, 23, 25, 42–44, 46, 49, 90, 96, 97, 114, 147, 181, 237
Equality, 89, 112, 116, 155–160, 168–169, 176, 211, 220, 227, 230
Evident, 10, 25, 96, 102, 147
Extensive form of a dialogical game, 80, 134, 210
Extensive form of a strategy, 82, 141, 184, 186

F
farq/al-farq, 119, 120, 137, 139, 141
fasād al-waḍʿ, 51, 56, 58, 60
fiqh, vii, viii, x, 20, 22, 23, 27
Function, x–xii, 30, 31, 33, 34, 36, 38–40, 82, 87, 89, 99, 110, 141, 167, 168, 171, 172, 180, 194, 216, 219, 222, 223, 225–231, 233, 234, 241, 243

G
Game, 23, 30, 42, 43, 46, 69, 70, 80, 81, 90, 129, 134, 143, 145–150, 156, 165, 166, 179–182, 191–194, 196, 202, 210, 245
Geltung, 46
Global meaning, 133–142, 160, 165–169, 190, 197, 199, 206

H
Heuristic, viii, x, 21, 22, 28, 44, 47, 90, 99, 115, 182, 184, 237
Hypothesis, 26, 98, 105, 224

I
Identity, 46, 70, 114, 116, 129, 136, 142, 216–221, 223, 226, 227, 238, 241
ifḥām, 44–47, 64
ijtihād, 4, 7, 11, 20–22, 89
ilzām, 44–47, 62, 66, 69, 124, 126, 128
Indication, ix, xiv, 12, 25, 26, 29, 38, 58, 95–143, 168, 169, 239, 248
Indicator, 98, 99
Inqiṭāʿ, 44–47
Instructions, 131, 134, 135, 154, 155, 157–160, 163–169, 182
ithbāt, 29

J
jadal, vii, 2, 5, 9, 10, 15, 20, 23, 24, 37, 44, 46, 49, 90, 237
jalī, 96
jalī and al-jalī, 26
Judgement, xi, 9, 29, 31, 32, 35, 147, 161, 173, 207, 215–226, 229, 233

K
kasr, 51, 55, 57
kasr, 51, 55, 57
khafī, 96
khaṣīṣa, 99–109, 111, 114, 118, 119–121, 123, 124, 136–140, 142, 247, 250

Knowledge, vii, ix, x, 1, 3, 4, 19, 21, 23, 25, 30, 44, 46, 47, 49, 87, 90, 95, 97, 98, 118, 138, 142, 145, 147, 182, 185, 203, 204, 211, 237

L

Latent, 26, 96
Local meaning, 87, 129–133, 150–166, 183, 190, 197, 198, 201, 205, 206
Local reasons, 23, 150–160, 162–169, 171, 182, 183, 185, 195, 197, 207, 211, 245

M

Material, 20, 42, 43, 46, 47, 53, 87, 149, 151, 171–181, 190, 195, 196, 202, 203, 210, 245
Metalanguage, 149, 217, 223
Metalogic, 46, 148, 149, 156, 181
Muʿāraḍa, 47, 50, 54, 62, 77–79, 137
mujtahid, 20, 21, 112
muṭālaba, 50, 52, 53, 65, 67, 77, 119, 122, 124, 125, 127, 137, 139

N

naqḍ, 51, 55, 56
naṣṣ, 26
Natural deduction, 40, 175, 194, 224, 225, 230, 233
Natural number, x, 33, 59, 172, 178, 217, 218, 229
naẓīr, 99, 108–114, 118–120, 124, 126, 136, 137, 139, 140, 142, 247
Negation, 75, 133, 173, 194, 201
Nominal, 166

O

Object, 1, 29, 105, 148, 216
Object language, 29, 32, 148, 155, 156, 160, 171, 182, 183, 191, 210
Occasioning factor, viii, ix, xi–xiii, 19–90, 95–99, 101, 104, 105, 108, 114–116, 118, 119, 123, 126, 139, 140, 142, 237, 240, 241, 248
Ontological, xiii, 116, 209

P

Parallel, x, xiii, xiv, 1, 6–9, 12, 19, 23–25, 27, 90, 109, 112, 114, 119, 124, 137, 139, 238, 240, 246, 248
Pensée aveugle, 156
Posit, 12, 13
Predicate, 34, 41, 175, 193, 204, 209, 216, 217, 226, 229, 238, 239, 241
Predication, 203
Predicator, 34, 41, 175, 193, 203, 209, 216, 226, 229, 238, 241, 248, 249
Premiss, 41, 147, 200, 231–233
Presupposition, 168
Prop, 34, 71, 103, 105, 106, 109, 110, 112, 116, 120, 122, 130, 151, 161, 169, 220, 221
Propositional equality, 116

Q

qalb, 51, 55, 56, 60, 62
qiyās al-dalāla, 12–15, 25, 27, 42, 95–143, 246, 247
qiyās al-ʿilla, 19–90, 241, 243
qiyās al-shabah, 11–13, 25, 27, 95–143, 241, 246, 247
Quantifiers, 37, 39, 41, 113, 151, 164, 172, 176, 207, 241

R

Range-course, 22, 24
Resemblances, 11, 12, 25, 26, 28, 42, 95–143, 239, 247
Resolution, 135, 155, 157–160, 166, 168, 169
Resolution of functions, 168
Resolution of instructions, 82, 135, 155, 157, 160, 166

S

Sabab, 25
Selection, 42, 249
Sequence of moves, 43, 48, 80, 89, 134, 192
shabah, pl. *ashbāh*, 11, 12, 25, 28, 95–143
Sharʿ/Sharīʿa, 24
Socratic rule, 41–44, 75, 81, 133, 134, 146, 151, 155, 159, 160, 167–169, 176, 179, 190
Starting rule, 80, 134

Strategic reasons, 39, 40, 48, 60, 87–89, 150, 160, 181–186, 207, 245
Strategy level, 47, 74, 150, 182, 186, 190, 192–197, 199–202, 245
Structural rules, 48, 69, 80–81, 117, 129, 133–135, 141, 160, 165, 166, 176, 190, 194, 196, 197, 201, 207
Subset-separation, 34
Substitution, 29, 31, 36, 104, 114, 116, 136, 155, 161, 162, 164, 165, 168, 169, 223, 227, 231, 238, 239, 241
Substitution of instructions, 155, 160, 167–169
Syntactic, 149, 156, 157, 171, 181, 216

T
ta'līl, 29
ta'thīr, 96
tanāquḍ, 64, 68, 75
tard, 31, 35–40, 50, 54, 65, 68, 77, 99, 102, 104, 109, 113, 244
Terminal, 82, 141
Tree, 20, 54, 58, 62, 79, 87, 137, 183, 185, 221

U
Universal, 36–41, 43, 49, 51, 59, 77, 87, 88, 104, 109, 143, 164, 165, 172, 176, 186, 207, 210, 217, 240, 241, 244
uṣūl al-fiqh, 2, 9–11, 13, 15, 19, 23, 24, 27, 36, 89, 237, 247

V
Validity, 11, 26, 46, 80, 81, 97, 110, 114, 126, 133, 171, 199, 242, 245, 246

W
waḍ', 51, 56, 58, 60
wāḍiḥ, 96
waṣf, pl. *awṣāf*, 24, 31–37
Winning strategies, 40, 46, 62, 80, 82, 87–89, 133, 137, 142, 149, 160, 183, 184, 186, 190, 192, 193, 196, 198, 202, 206, 207, 210, 245

Printed in the United States
by Baker & Taylor Publisher Services